SOILS AND MICROMORPHOLOGY
IN ARCHAEOLOGY

CAMBRIDGE MANUALS IN ARCHAEOLOGY

Series editors

SOILS AND MICROMORPHOLOGY IN ARCHAEOLOGY

Marie Agnes Courty
CNRS Institut National Agronomique
Paris Grignon

Paul Goldberg
Institute of Archaeology
Hebrew University of Jerusalem

Richard Macphail
Institute of Archaeology
University of London

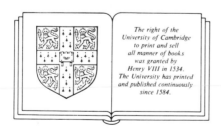

The right of the
University of Cambridge
to print and sell
all manner of books
was granted by
Henry VIII in 1534.
The University has printed
and published continuously
since 1584.

Cambridge University Press

Cambridge
New York   New Rochelle   Melbourne   Sydney

Published by the Press Syndicate of the University of Cambridge
The Pitt Building, Trumpington Street, Cambridge CB2 1RP
40 West 20th Street, New York, NY 10011, USA
10 Stamford Road, Oakleigh, Melbourne 3166, Australia

First published 1989

Printed in Great Britain at Cambridge University Press, Cambridge.

British Library cataloguing in publication data

Courty, Marie Agnes
Soils and micromorphology in archaeology.
1. Soils. Micromorphology
I. Title   II. Goldberg, Paul
III. Macphail, Richard
631.4'3

Library of Congress cataloguing in publication data

Courty, Marie Agnes.
Soils and micromorphology in archaeology / Marie Agnes Courty,
Paul Goldberg, Richard Macphail.
     p.   cm. – (Cambridge manuals in archaeology)
Includes index.
ISBN 0 521 32419 X
1. Soil science in archaeology.   2. Soil micromorphology.
I. Goldberg, Paul.   II. Macphail, Richard.   III. Title.   IV. Series.
CC79.S6C68 1989
930.1'028--dc19   88-30763
                              CIP

ISBN 0 521 32419 X

SE

Practice is the best of all instructors.

Publius Syrus

The three friends looked at each other
And burst out laughing.
They had no explanation.
Thus they were better friends than before.

Three friends in *The Way of Chung Tzu* by Thomas Merton

CONTENTS

Contents

II PROCESSES AND FEATURES

III CASE STUDIES

Contents

PLATES

FIGURES

xi

Figures

Figures

TABLES

PREFACE

Micromorphology is concerned with the study of undisturbed soils and loose sediments and other materials (e.g., bricks, mortars, ceramics) at a microscopic scale. The most practical and most commonly used technique – and that which is emphasized in this book – involves the use of the thin section, which is a 25 to 30 micron-thick slice of soil or sediment, mounted on a glass slide. Our experience over the past several years with geological and pedological problems in archaeology has convinced us that micromorphology is the most suitable technique for tackling a broad spectrum of geoarchaeological problems that other methods by themselves are not capable of doing.

The principal aims of this book are essentially twofold and complementary. The first is to explain the basic micromorphological techniques and to provide the basic information necessary for the study and interpretation of thin sections from archaeologically related soils and sedimentary materials. The second, and no less important, is to demonstrate to the reader the value and usefulness of the method by presenting cogent examples of its application in a variety of archaeological situations and phenomena. Micromorphology is a technique and not an end in itself, and consequently should not be a substitute for field work nor make other analytical techniques redundant. We hope to show that it should constitute one of the first investigative steps or procedures used to study soils, sediments and materials associated with archaeological sites.

We begin with a brief introduction to basic soil science, its role in archaeological studies and a discussion of standard soil analytical techniques and their limitations. The first major part of the book shows that a complete micromorphological study must begin with a serious field investigation which comprises a detailed study of the archaeological site and its surroundings, including complete field descriptions. These procedures are accompanied by the development of appropriate sampling strategies, coupled with the collection of the necessary samples. Chapter 3 presents a guide to the technical aspects of sample treatment and thin-section preparation. This is followed by a discussion of microscopic techniques, which have been applied to specific problems during the past decade. The principles of these methods will be explained, although most of the discussion will concern the optical polarising microscope, since, although it is a simple tool, it remains capable of solving most of the problems encountered in archaeological deposits. The first part closes with a presentation of a system of description of archaeological deposits based on the recently published *Handbook for Soil Thin Section Description* but mofidied to include those aspects specific to the archaeological context. We have taken care to avoid using too much jargon and have attempted to choose the most self-explanatory terms.

Part II is composed of three sections that illustrate the most common types of fabrics and constituents observed in archaeological contexts. These are grouped under three headings: (a) sediments, including a discussion of the origin and environment of deposition of geological sediments; (b) anthropogenic features, which are naturally of principal interest, including, for example, discussions of soils strongly influenced by man, ashes and charcoal, bricks, mortar and ceramics; and (c) post-depositional processes and related features that include changes connected to soil development and any other transformations that can alter the the original character of the material.

In the third part of the book we present various case studies based on our own research experience. We hope that these will illustrate virtually all the points made in Parts I and II. Included in Part III are regional studies, demonstrating how broad-spectrum observations from the field down to the microscopic level can be used to help reconstruct the regional, geomorphological and land-use history of an area. Another study is devoted to deposits from caves and rock shelters, since they have been intensively occupied and studied by prehistoric and modern man, respectively. We also give some examples of several open-air sites, ranging from low-density (rural) to high-density (urban) occupation.

Whilst we have endeavoured to make this handbook practical on its own terms – in both the laboratory and the field – we are aware of the varied background of our readers and of the fact that some will require additional material in order to follow the arguments. Most of this information should be found in the list of references at the end.

Finally, we would like to emphasise that this book is intended to be used as a manual and not a treatise on geo-archaeology/archaeo-geology, archaeostratigraphy or site-formation processes. Rather, we hope that whatever guidance we can offer from our own experience will excite the imagination of others to try the technique.

ACKNOWLEDGEMENTS

Though this book represents a communal effort, it would not have been possible without the support of numerous institutions, colleagues and friends. A considerable part of the information presented comes from samples collected from archaeological sites, and we are grateful to many archaeologists for their assistance and support: Ofer Bar-Yosef (Netiv Hagdud); Na'ama Goren (Berekhat Ram); the members of the Franco-Israeli team at Kebara, especially Henri Laville; the Indo-French Archaeological team (India); Jill Macphail (Prato Mollo, Lago Nero); Roberto Maggi (Uscio, Arene Candide), Jean-Pierre Mohen (Fort Harrouard); Renato Nisbet (Val Chisone, Vislario); Jean-Paul Raynal (Taforalt); Jean-Philippe Rigaud and the staff from the Institut du Quaternaire in Bordeaux (Abri Vaufrey); and Harvey Sheldon.

A number of organisations contributed financial assistance either directly to one of us or to some of the projects we have had the pleasure to be associated with. These organisations include the English Historic Buildings and Monument Commission; the Historic Buildings and Monuments section of the Scottish Development Department; the Soprintendenza Archeologica della Liguria; Pinerolo Museum; the Soil Survey of England and Wales; the Macaulay Institute for Soil Research; the French Ministry of Foreign Affairs and the L.S.B. Leakey Foundation (for the Kebara excavation); the C.N.R.S. (for Fort Harrouard); the French Ministry of Foreign Affairs (for India and Taforalt); the Archaeological Survey of India; and the Service Archéologique du Maroc. We warmly acknowledge this aid. Additional finance was provided by the British Academy and Carl Zeiss (Jena) who generously subsidised the cost of the colour plates. We would also like to thank David Harris and Susan Limbrey for their help in obtaining funding for these plates.

Throughout the period of manuscript preparation we were greatly encouraged by several friends and scholars whom we would particularly like to thank. Outstanding among them are Gaston-Barnard Arnal, Ofer Bar-Yosef, Don Brothwell, Sylvia Christensen, Jean-Pierre Daugas, Tom Levy, Jean-Claude Miskovsky and Dan Yaalon. Several specialists also contributed invaluable information and advice, and we owe them a great deal. They include Mike Allen, Louis-Marie Bresson, Peter Bullock, Allan Chapman, Susan Colledge, Ian Cornwall, David Liversage, Daniel and Claude Mordant, Chris Murphy, Per Nørnberg, Fernand Page, Gilbert Pion, Hema Raghavan, John Romans, Clare de Rouffignac, Rob Scaife, Jean-Pierre Texier and Julia Wattez. The

xix

Acknowledgements

kindness of the late Professor François Bordes during the early stages of our micromorphological studies is also warmly acknowledged.

Technical assistance in the form of advice and illustrative material was graciously furnished by Janine Berrier, Jean Christophe Carle, Peter Dorrell, Pierre Guilloré, Maya Kooistra, Stuart Laidlaw, Claire Lucet, Michel Robert, John Romans and Daniel Tessier. The Laboratoire des Sols at I.N.R.A. (Versailles) provided SEM facilities and the Soil Survey Institute of Wageningen kindly supplied us with illustrations. The Département des Sols at Grignon (I.N.A.) offered invaluable logistic support as well as hospitable and convivial working conditions. Similarly the Institute of Archaeology (London), Macaulay Institute of Soil Research (Aberdeen) and Soil Survey of England and Wales are thanked for their encouragement over the years.

There are a few people to whom we owe special thanks. Henry Wright of the University of Michigan many years ago prompted Paul Goldberg to pursue micromorphology by remarking that it would be nice one day to find a technique that could analyse in detail an archaeological layer only millimetres thick. Similarly, Richard Macphail wishes to thank Mike Bridges, who showed him his first thin section, and Helen Keeley and Clifford Price, who actively supported the application of micromorphology to archaeology in England. Discussions with Peter Bullock, John Dalrymple and Chris Murphy have been both stimulating and inspiring. Peter Richards of Cambridge University Press was from the outset supportive of our efforts and we are glad to have been able to work with him. The most helpful of all was Nick Fedoroff, who, day and night, came up with crucial information at short notice and provided much-needed balance and breadth to our presentation; to answer a barrage of questions at 1:00 am requires a very special character!

Finally, we owe a great deal of gratitude to our opposite numbers (Sara, Jill and Nick) for their patience, especially Nick who, as our senior resident consultant micromorphologist, came in for more than his share of problems.

I

BASIC PRINCIPLES

1

INTRODUCTION

The scale of archaeological units varies from the region, through the individual site, to the stratigraphic layer. The choice of scale depends upon the researcher's goals or specific interests. The implementation of such goals, at whatever scale, however, falls into the realms of archaeostratigraphy (Gasche and Tunca, 1983), geoarchaeology or archaeological geology (Gifford and Rapp, 1985). The philosophical distinctions between these two so-called subdisciplines are addressed in Butzer's (1982) excellent discussion of the issue; the aim of this book is a more practical one, that of introducing the techniques and application of micromorphology in a general sense. The application of micromorphology to particular situations requires an individual approach.

Thus, a focus on regional problems might consider a series of sites within a sequence of stream terraces that occur over distances of many tens of kilometres, as a means of reconstructing regional palaeoenvironments (including palaeoclimates). This allows the possibility of establishing how such former environments would have influenced the activities of the site inhabitants, such as hunting and gathering and herding practices, and cultivation. A tacit assumption, however, commonly made by some Old World archaeologists working with Holocene sites is that the present-day landscape is essentially the same as that during the occupation of a given site. The occurrence of wide-spread Holocene alluviation in the circum-Mediterranean zone (e.g., Vita–Finzi, 1969) and massive soil erosion and soil degradation in Europe through continued intensive land use since the Bronze Age shows that this is not necessarily the case (Macphail, 1986).

The more local scale of a few square kilometres overlaps with the regional, though one might wish to consider at this scale problems relating to sources of raw materials, such as flint, stones, fine sediments for mud-bricks, water and vegetation. Other issues might centre around explanations for certain types of construction, such as the famous Neolithic wall at Jericho (Bar–Yosef, 1985), or the technologies used to build the rampart at the Neolithic/Bronze Age site of Fort Harrouard, near Paris: was burned lime used there in the preparation of the chalky core (see Chapter 14)?

At the level of the site itself, we enter into problems of stratigraphy, which undoubtedly occur at larger scales as well. Many of these problems are sub-sumed under the title of 'site-formation processes'. In fact, much of the material in this book could be viewed in this context, which takes into account humans

3

and other animals as geomorphic and sedimentary agents, and many other site-modifying factors. Related phenomena include archaeological dumps and fills, the effects of soil formation, trampling and burrowing, and the remains of specific site-settlement activities associated with lithic, metallurgic and ceramic technology, and cooking – resulting in ashes, charcoal and cinders, for example.

For purposes of illustration, let us consider a hypothetical archaeological site, which is situated along the banks of a small stream, at the foot of low-lying hills. In addition, let us suppose that our site has a long sequence, with prehistoric material (say, Palaeolithic) at the base, ranging up to historical, tell-like occupations at the top. Depending upon the investigator's field of expertise (archaeologist, geologist, pedologist, other environmentalist – seeds, pollen, snails), it is possible to ask several different types of question of this site. Some suitable questions to pose might be: What kinds of human activities took place here and how have these changed through time? How is the site stratigraphically and palaeoenvironmentally connected to its surroundings, which include fluvial and colluvial depositional environments? To what extent is man and human activity responsible for the accumulation of the site sediments or, more generally, how was the site built?

Whereas it is generally not so difficult to pose questions such as these, it is much more problematical to conjure up methods of answering them satisfactorily. Until recently, a common strategy (in addition to archaeological excavation of the site) would consist of a systematic geological sampling of as complete a profile as possible. Bulk samples would be taken back to the laboratory and subjected to a variety of analytical procedures that might include grain-size analysis, clay- and heavy-mineral determination, and perhaps a few chemical evaluations of phosphate, organic matter and acidity (pH). Such a methodology might suffice for the predominantly geological layers (such as fluviatile silts) and could provide valuable information concerning their origin, their environment and conditions of deposition (e.g., high vs low energy).

However, a more serious problem arises with the analysis of the so-called 'cultural' or 'occupation' levels or those stratigraphic units which have enregistered a combination of sedimentary and pedogenic events. What, for example, is the significance of a particle-size analysis of a sample consisting of mineral components, such as silt and clay, intimately mixed with bone, ash, vegetable matter and various types of coprolites? (As we will attempt to show, this combination of elements occurs repeatedly in many types of sites across the world.) Also, it is not difficult to show that bulk analysis of calcium carbonate cannot distinguish primary calcium carbonate from that which was precipitated at a later date, perhaps during a soil-forming episode. Similarly, other common analytical techniques (e.g., pH, organic matter) would have difficulties in pinning down the composition and origin of a 'black layer' which could represent a humic horizon of a fossil soil, an archaeological 'dump' deposit or both. In other words, a single analytical technique, even used in conjunction with a battery of others, fails to unravel the compound effects of two successive events (be they geological, archaeological or pedological) superimposed on the same material. A more discerning technique is evidently needed to resolve such complicating effects.

Based on our experience with such 'geoarchaeological' problems, it is clear to us that micromorphology is the most suitable technique to unravel these sorts of complex problems. Micromorphological data not only can be used to make inferences concerning the origin of a given material, its mode of formation and any processes that might have modified it subsequent to its emplacement, but also can provide interpretative material for the archaeologist who might not have any notion of the significance of a certain archaeological 'feature' or sedimentary unit, thereby adding a new breadth to the archaeological interpretation of the site.

Micromorphology is not a new technique in the field of earth science, which includes disciplines such as geology, geomorphology and pedology. While the use of thin sections in geology by Sorby in England is well over a hundred years old, it was only about 50 years ago that Kubiena (1938) first began to look at undisturbed soils in thin section. In the 1950s it was applied for the first time to the archaeological context by Cornwall (1958), who used it as a means of reconstructing past environments as well as of understanding certain anthropogenic features such as ashes, cremations and floors. Somewhat later, Dalrymple (1958), a student of Cornwall, illustrated the use of micromorphology by showing how humic horizons could be distinguished from occupation layers.

Although in the 1960s and 1970s the use of micromorphology in soil science developed relatively rapidly, its application to archaeological problems declined and was confined essentially to provenance studies of pottery (Peacock, 1969). This decline was probably due to several factors. First of all, there were technical problems both of impregnating large masses of loose sediment and of making thin sections larger than the small (22 × 40 mm) format used in geology. However, these restrictions have largely disappeared with improvements in impregnation techniques. A second problem centred around the use of an appropriate terminological framework with which to describe the thin sections and the lack of a methodology to interpret them. In contrast to petrography, which has been in existence for a century and is well studied, with its own vocabulary, micromorphological investigations in archaeology had to make do with Brewer's (1964) pioneering descriptive classification that was largely based on his experience with Australian soils. In addition to the fact that his terminology made soil micromorphology somewhat incomprehensible to the soil scientist and layman alike, it was also not very applicable to archaeological contexts and materials. Although this situation has improved to some extent by the recent appearance of the handbook for soil thin-section description (Bullock *et al.*, 1985), the gap between soils and archaeological sediments and materials still remains.

With the above considerations in mind, we believe that a book describing the workings and applications of soil micromorphology in archaeology would be of benefit to archaeologists, geologists and pedologists alike. For archaeologists, for example, we hope to show that our exposition will offer a new approach that will promote the solution of certain archaeological problems and that certain micromorphological observations might lead them to evaluate and reconsider certain interpretations both during and after the excavation. To the 'archaeogeologist', used to employing an array of traditional methods (e.g., grain-size and chemical analyses), this manual might be useful in demonstrating that these techniques are often quite limited in their ability to solve many archaeologically related problems – such as the nature of *dark earth* found in historical deposits – whereas micromorphology is well suited to solving just these types of problems. Finally, both the geologist and the pedologist may gain an appreciation of the role of human groups and other animals in sedimentary and soil-forming processes, for sometimes pedologists have a tendency to regard the 'soil profile' as a quasi-static body that forms in place from the top down and they sometimes fail to place it in its more dynamic, regional geomorphic setting, often neglecting our species as a pedomorphic agent.

In sum, we should remind ourselves that geology and archaeology are both historical sciences and that practitioners in both fields are really detectives, attempting to unravel complicated, interactive bits of the earth's most recent history. In this light, we consider a thin section to be a 'page' of a chronicle whose micromorphological characteristics provide the keys for deciphering that page and for reconstructing at least part of that history.

BASIC CONCEPTS IN SOIL SCIENCE AND CURRENT METHODS

2.1 Basic concepts in soil science

2.1.1 Introduction

As we previously mentioned, soil micromorphology has its roots in the soil profile and much of its terminology and concepts have been developed from works in pedology. As a consequence of this historical reality, the reader should have some knowledge concerning the basic notions of soil science and the methodologies involved in order to appreciate more fully the micromorphological approach. Thus in this chapter we provide a brief description of some of these concepts and follow this in the second part with an account of a few of the most important and modern methods employed in the study of soils.

Human recognition of the *soil* as constituting an essential life-support system had already occurred during the first stages of early agriculture, when soils were intuitively classified according to their suitability for cultivation (e.g., the so-called loam terrains of Wooldridge and Linton, 1933; see also Davidson, 1982). Early on it was realised that some basic soil properties could be easily modified in order to improve the quality of the soil. The addition of manure, for example, to ameliorate soil fertility is known to have been practised for a few thousand years (at least since the European Bronze Age) but the admixture of lime to acid soils is a more recent, historic practice (Goudie, 1981).

In the last century an empirical approach to the study of soils has been replaced by more scientific ones. This has been stimulated on the one hand by the introduction of modern scientific techniques and on the other by the increase of population, which has made intense demands on the soil, commonly resulting in soil loss by erosion and salinisation.

During its evolution, soil science has rapidly split itself into various specialised fields, which include soil chemistry, soil mineralogy, soil physics and soil fertility. In addition, researchers from other disciplines have interests that overlap with those of soil scientists: geomorphologists, for example, regard soils as being part of the landscape, whereas zoologists view soils as representing part of a specific ecosystem. Therefore, because of the diversity of these different approaches, only a general definition of soil can be proposed. Soil is here defined as a natural body of mineral and organic constituents that results from the combined action of climate, organisms and man on a mineral or organic material.

2.1.2 *Soil-forming processes*

Soil development can affect both indurated rocks and unconsolidated sediments and induce chemical, physical and physico-chemical transformations of the original properties of the parent materials: soil consituents can move up or down, either mechanically or chemically, or they may be affected by animal activity, or may suffer *in situ* chemical changes. These transformations that are basic to a soil represent the **elementary soil-forming processes** and these are described in detail in Chapter 8. They are rather broadly defined and may comprise pedoturbation, especially bioturbation, humification, translocation of solid particles, movement of solutes (liquids), and mineral weathering and neoformation (the formation of new minerals in the soil).

The above concept of elementary pedogenic processes differs somewhat from that of soil scientists, who consider them to be a complex succession of reactions or processes. Some examples of these higher-order processes include (Buol *et al.*, 1973):

> *Pedoturbation* – Mixing and homegenisation of soils or sediments by plant and faunal activity.
>
> *Soil ripening* – Physical, chemical and biological changes in organic soils that enhance microbial activity.
>
> *Leaching and decalcification* – Leaching involves the downward percolation of soil solution of cations such as Na^+, K^+ and Mg^+. Related to this is decalcification, the loss of calcium carbonate from the parent material by the action of weak acids.
>
> *Alkalisation and salinisation* – In areas of low rainfall and high evapo-transpiration there is no leaching. As a consequence there is a marked accumulation near or on the surface of sodium ions, and soluble sulphates and chlorides of calcium, magnesium, sodium and potassium.
>
> *Humification* – The transformation of raw organic material into humus.
>
> *Illuviation and eluviation* – The movement or translocation of material from one locality in the soil (eluviation) to another locality in the soil, where it accumulates (illuviation).
>
> *Gleying* – Under conditions of waterlogging there is a lack of available oxygen, and various elements, such as iron, are found in reduced states. The result is the formation of grey and brown red mottles, commonly associated with dark, bluish-black ferro-manganese nodules that are sometimes mistaken for charcoal.

Thus, for soil scientists podzolisation is a pedogenic process that results from microbial activity, release of soluble organic matter and downward leaching of organic matter from the surface, and an accumulation with depth of aluminium and iron-organic complexes. We, in contrast, tend to view each of these individual processes (leaching of organic matter, accumulation of iron) as representing an elementary soil-forming process. In any case, the net result of these individual processes is to produce vertical differentiation of the substrate, resulting in the formation of **soil horizons** (see Table 2.1).

Soil horizons are generally evident in the field and may be clearly distin-

Table 2.1. *Soil horizons: designation and general characters (Modified from* Soil Taxonomy, *Soil Survey Staff, 1975)*

Organic horizons

O   organic litter from plants and animals deposited on the mineral surface (fresh or partly decomposed organic materials)

    O1   distinct plant remains (fresh fallen leaves, leaf fragments, needles)

    O2   mostly indistinct plant remains (decomposed plant remains and faunal excrement)

Mineral horizons

A   organo-mineral horizons that have lost fine particles (fine silt and clay) and soluble components (iron, aluminium, alkaline earth)

    A1   biological incorporation of organic matter into the mineral fraction

    A2   loss of fine particles or soluble components with resultant concentration of quartz or other resistant minerals in sand and silt sizes

Transitional horizons

    A3   properties of an overlying A plus subordinate properties of an underlying B

    AB   upper part dominated by properties of A, lower part dominated by properties of B.

    AC   subordinate properties of both A and C (B is absent)

Variant

    Ap   Disturbance by cultivation or pasturing

B   Enriched in fine particles, soluble components or humus or altered mineral horizon without sedimentary structures

    B1   transitional A1/B or A2/B properties of an underlying B2 plus subordinate properties of an overlying A2 or A1

    B2   The most strongly expressed part of the B horizon

    B3   transitional B/C or B/R association of clearly expressed properties of both B and C (or R)

Specific suffixes

    h   accumulation of decomposed illuvial organic matter

    ir   accumulation of illuvial iron

    t   accumulation of illuvial clay

C   Unconsolidated or weakly consolidated materials weakly affected by pedogenic processes (sedimentary structures are partly or totally preserved)

R   Underlying consolidated bedrock

General suffixes

    b   buried soil horizon

    ca   accumulation of alkaline earth, commonly calcium

    cs   accumulation of calcium sulphate

    f   permanently frozen soil

    g   strong gleying

    m   strong cementation, induration

    sa   accumulation of salts more soluble than calcium sulfate

    si   cementation by siliceous material soluble in alkali

    x   Fragipan characters

I, II, III . . . Lithological discontinuities

guished on a recently exposed section. They are roughly parallel to the soil surface and may differ from overlying and underlying horizons by their composition, colour, structure, texture or consistence. A *soil profile* is a two-dimensional representation of a soil – which is naturally a three-dimensional feature – and consists of a vertical succession of horizons which, in a simple situation, are genetically related. The basic succession of a soil profile comprises three main parts (Table 2.1):

> The surface horizon can be divided into two parts, consisting of a mineral (*A horizon* and the uppermost part called the *humic layer* or *O horizon*.
>
> The *B horizon* underlies the organic-rich surface horizon and shows some of the initial characteristics of the parent material that have been altered by various soil-forming processes; it is usually called a mineral or subsoil horizon and contains accumulations of materials leached or translocated from the A horizon.
>
> The *C horizon* is the lower part of the soil that is little affected by pedological processes and is composed of essentially the original rock or sediment, commonly called the parent material.

As also noted in Table 2.1 the horizons themselves can be further subdivided or described with the addition of suffixes or prefixes which point out certain characteristic features. An 'Ap' horizon, therefore, is an A horizon which shows signs of ploughing or other disturbance due to cultivation. Similarly, a 'Bg' horizon is one that shows signs of gleying (iron mottling), resulting from waterlogging.

2.1.3 *Factors of soil formation*

Soil-forming processes are controlled by a variety of factors, among which five can be considered as essential: climate, biota, parent material, topography and time (Jenny, 1941). Understandably, these factors are strongly interrelated and, as a consequence, it is usually quite difficult to estimate the individual role of each factor in the formation of a given soil. Although climate, for example, exerts a direct control on soil-formation processes through temperature and precipitation, it also affects the kind of vegetation present, which in turn influences the type of fauna found within the soil.

Parent materials also greatly influence the resulting soil type, other things being equal. For example, on unconsolidated, fine-grained and easily weatherable sedimentary parent materials, such as loess, horizon differentiation occurs relatively rapidly. In contrast, in soils developed on massive granite, the first stages of transformation of rock into fine earth require some time and thus soil development will take longer and horizon differentiation will occur at a much slower pace. Within the same area of a few hectares under the same climatic and topographic conditions, we can find base-rich rendzinas and calcareous soils on chalk and, adjacent to them, highly acid podzols on sands – a typical situation in southern England and northern France. Thus, the type of parent material can influence both the rate of soil development and ultimately the type of soil that will be produced.

Time also plays a role. Where there is a mosaic of moderately differing parent materials, long-term weathering will produce a uniform mantle of similarly leached topsoil. Only if this cover is removed by erosion will the different parent materials become apparent and reassert themselves.

Topography can strongly influence the types of soil developed in an area where other factors such as climate and parent materials remain constant. For example, along a slope we may find well-drained soils at the top, shallow and eroded soils along the midslope and cumulative, poorly drained soils at the base of the slope. Thus pedologists recognise a *soil catena* which 'is a range of soils in a section of landscape covering hill top, slope and valley bottom in which profiles have developed differentially according to drainage conditions, percolation of soil solution downslope through the soils and the effects of soil movement' (Limbrey, 1975: 83) (Figure 2.1).

Classically, soils which are distributed along climatic belts or zones and in which climate is the most important soil-forming factor are generally known as **zonal soils**. Other soils, where climatic factors are less dominant than local factors such as parent material or drainage conditions, are known as **intrazonal soils**. **Azonal soils** are incipient, weakly developed soils.

2.1.4 *Soil behaviour and soil genesis*

Methods and techniques commonly used in soil science have been developed either to characterise *soil behaviour* – the instantaneous evolution of the physical, physico-chemical and chemical properties of soil constituents – or to study *soil genesis* or the history of soil development, which is of more interest to archaeologists.

Soil physicists focus on the relationships between 'external parameters', including water content, temperature, pressure, and the physical characteristics of soils. For these reasons they carefully analyse the conditions at the solid–void interface (the void size varying between mm and nm) and concentrate mostly on the soil structure.

Agronomists attempt to characterise the interactions between plants and soils. The methods of nutrient uptake by plants can be characterised by detailed investigations at the root–soil interface; similar concerns may centre around soil properties that inhibit plant growth as, for example, where the formation of surface crusts under heavy rains limits seedling emergence, or plant toxicity is related to the excess of trace elements.

Studies of soil genesis relate to the construction of the history and evolution of a soil, including the nature and relations between horizons in soil profiles. This is usually accomplished by inferring from both the features observed in the field and analytical data, the kind of soil-forming processes that have induced these properties, including the nature and origin of the parent materials, and the recognition of different stages of pedological development. The final reconstruction takes into account the physical, chemical, physico-chemical and

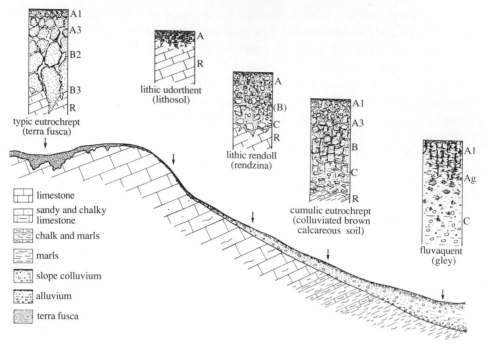

Figure 2.1   Soil *catena* showing schematic toposequence of soils along a chalky limestone slope.

mineralogical properties of a soil and should represent an essential, preliminary stage to any further investigations.

2.1.5 *Soil types, classification and mapping*

Much has been written about the classification of soils, which in itself testifies to the difficulty in categorising them. Early attempts at classification in the last century used particle-size distribution combined with agricultural considerations, such as productivity (Buol *et al.*, 1973). This was followed in Russia by Dokuchaev's work which emphasised the role of climate in classifying soils. The American Marbut developed these ideas in the 1930s and stressed the roles of climate and vegetation as major soil-forming factors. The most recent scheme adopted in the United States involves an objective, hierarchical system of classification which is arranged from high to successively lower levels of generalisation and supposedly avoids imparting any genetic connotations to the defined soil classes.

Needless to say, most natural systems do not lend themselves to 'clean' classification schemes and soils are no exception. One of the principal problems arises from the fact that the operational class limits between groups are rather arbitrary, since variations in soil properties are essentially continuous. Moreover, unlike biological systems in which individual species or genera can be shown to evolve within a temporal framework, soil systems are multifaceted and a given soil can be a result of global (i.e., climatic) factors as well as very localised ones which are independent of temporal considerations.

A large variety of classificatory systems have been adopted because various kinds of approaches have been used and different basic principles have been stressed. One scheme might favour climate or topography, another one soil profile development, while a third scheme may emphasise one or a set of soil properties – for example, hydromorphism, where the degree of drainage is considered to play an important role. Each system was primarily adapted to the characteristics of soils occurring in the country where the system was applied, and workers were encouraged to assign their soils to their local classification prior to using an international equivalent.

Undaunted, soil taxonomists and pedologists (FitzPatrick, 1971) continue to produce soil-classification systems. At present, the two systems most widely used all over the world are the FAO/UNESCO and American Soil Classification. The former has been applied to produce the Soil Map of the World in which 26 major divisions have been introduced. The American classification distinguishes ten major orders (Table 2.2).

A main usage of soil classification is for soil mapping, where relationships between different soil profiles and their distributions over the landscape are recorded on a map. The purposes of preparing such maps are variable and could concern issues of land capability, agriculture and erosion potential.

2.1.6 *Basic concepts in the study of ancient soils or soil history*

Soils themselves can be modified during their development. We can illustrate this with a hypothetical soil developed on a loessic, grassy steppe under a continental climate. This soil is characterised by a dark brownish-black A horizon up to 1 m thick, in which there is considerable biological activity on the part of earthworms, burrowing rodents and grass roots that aid in the downward mixing of the humic horizon. This A horizon rests relatively abruptly on pale brown, generally calcareous loess of the C horizon. During the formation of this soil there is an overall equilibrium between the various chemical, physical and biological processes and it may thus be considered as a **monophased** soil (Fig. 2.2). If, however, it is simply buried by a later accumulation of loess, it could be considered as a **buried monophased** paleosol or **truncated** paleosol if the upper part of the soil were to be removed by erosion.

If the climate were to become more humid, a forest cover could develop and a different set of equilibria would be established. This in turn would result in the superimposition of a different type of soil that displays a different collection of pedological processes and features. Organic matter, for example, will be more completely broken down by bioturbation and humification, and a B horizon will begin to develop, in which there are clear signs of translocation of clay (the argillic horizon). This 'telescoping' or superimposition of two distinct, major pedological events on the same profile results in what can be called a **polyphased**

Table 2.2. *Basic principles of the soil taxonomy*

Orders

Aridisols:	water unavailable to mesophytic plants for long periods
Alfisols:	with an argillic horizon and high base status
Entisols:	little or no evidence for development of pedogenic horizon
Histosols:	dominantly organic (bogs, moors, peats, mucks)
Inceptisols:	soils of humid regions with altered horizon that have lost bases, or iron, or aluminium but retain some weatherable minerals
Mollisols:	very dark-coloured, base-rich soils of the steppes
Oxisols:	reddish, yellowish or greyish soils of tropical and subtropical regions that have mostly gentle slopes on surface of great age
Spodosols:	characterised by a spodic horizon (subsoil accumulation of iron, aluminium and organic matter)
Ultisols:	low base status soils of mid to low latitudes with an argillic horizon

Diagnostic surface horizons: epipedon

Histic:	peat or derived from peat
Mollic:	underground decomposition of organic residues in the present of bivalent cations, particularly calcium
Umbric:	rich in organic matter less than 50% base-saturated
Ochric:	light-coloured
Anthropic:	long continued used of the soil by humans
Plaggen:	man-made surface layer, 50 cm thick, produced by long, continued manuring

Master subsurface diagnostic horizons

Argillic:	significant accumulation of silicate clays by illuviation
Natric:	specific kind of argillic horizon in which clays are dispersed due to the presence of exchangeable sodium
Spodic:	accumulation of iron, aluminium and organic matter
Agric:	significant accumulation of illuvial clay, silt and humus under the plough layer
Cambic:	weakly altered horizon because of either pedoturbation, slight silicate weathering, leaching of soluble components
Oxic:	highly weathered horizon mostly consisting of insoluble minerals, 1/1 silicate clay, aluminium and iron oxides

Other diagnostic criteria

Fragipan:	high bulk density, cemented when dry, brittle when moist
Albic:	light-coloured horizon due to removal of clay and oxides
Calcic:	horizon of accumulation of calcium carbonate or of calcium and magnesium carbonate. When strongly cemented is called *petrocalcic*
Gypsic:	horizon enriched with secondary sulfate. When strongly cemented is called *petrogypsic*
Salic:	horizon enriched in secondary soluble salts
Sulfuric:	horizon with pH 3.5 and jarosite mottles
Plinthite:	iron-rich, humus-poor mixture of clay with quartz and other dilutents
Duripan:	sub-surface horizon cemented mostly by silica
Permafrost:	layer in which the temperature is perennially at or below 0°C

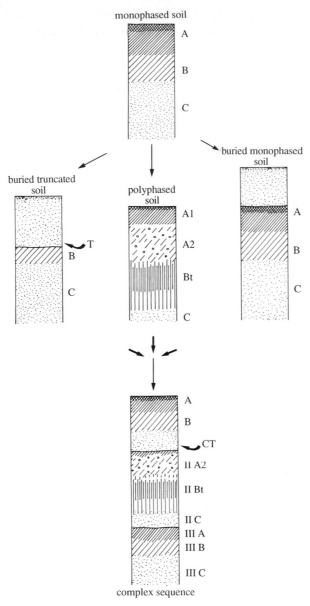

Figure 2.2   Hypothetical development of soil profiles through time. (T: truncation)

soil; if climatic and pedological conditions were to vacillate cyclically between these two states a **polycyclic** soil would be produced. Finally, if these pedogenic events were shuffled with periods of loess deposition, a series of buried paleosols would be obtained. Intuitively, we see that the number of preserved buried paleosols and the extent to which each is poly- or monophased depends upon the respective rates of sedimentation and the soil-forming processes. Thus the horizons developed during each soil-forming phase can be superimposed upon each other or separated and 'diluted' by an intervening period of deposition.

In summary, the soil is an open system, reacting to environmental changes of climate, vegetation, and biological and human factors. Soil properties are thus gradually modified but the intensity and the rate of the induced changes vary according to the specific kind of soil-forming process considered. Daily, seasonal, yearly or longer-term changes may occur and analytical data must be interpreted in the light of the variability in these rates of change.

In the following part we present a critical review of the most common traditional techniques used in modern-day soil science. Although the details of various methods are available in several textbooks (cf. References), we focus our attention here on the aims and principal applications involved in a given analysis.

2.2 **Analytical methods in soil science**
Having presented some of the fundamental concepts of soil science, we now turn to a discussion of some of the most common analytical techniques that are used to infer the development of a given soil profile. Figure 2.3 presents a flow chart of techniques followed in the routine analysis of soil samples. Details pertaining to the specific laboratory methods themselves can be found in Avery and Bascomb (1974) or Soil Survey Staff (1975).

2.2.1 *Particle-size analysis*
Particle-size analysis was introduced early in the history of soil science, because soil scientists noted a relation between the size of elementary constituents and the hydraulic characteristics of soils. 'Light', sandy soils, for example, were well drained whereas 'heavy' clay soils were susceptible to waterlogging.

Texture can be appraised in the field by rubbing the soil between the fingers (sands are 'gritty', silts are 'soapy' and clays are 'sticky'; see Chapter 3), but for exact measurement laboratory separation is required. After any organic matter is removed and the soil chemically and physically broken up into its mineral constituents, size analysis is usually accomplished by sieving of the coarse fraction and by sedimentation from suspension of the finer silt and clay fractions, which are measured by pipette or hydrometer analysis. Three main size classes are generally recognised as well as numerous subdivisions: sand (2 mm to 63 or 50 μm), silt (63 or 50 μm to 2 μm) and clay (finer than 2 μm), though limits between classes can vary among disciplines and countries.

Particle-size or granulometric analysis is now a widespread practice in soil science, since the high surface/volume ratio of clays, for example, has an important influence on certain chemical attributes of the soil. In addition, these results are commonly extrapolated in order to estimate certain physical properties of soil, as, for example, the prediction of the physical behaviour of soils

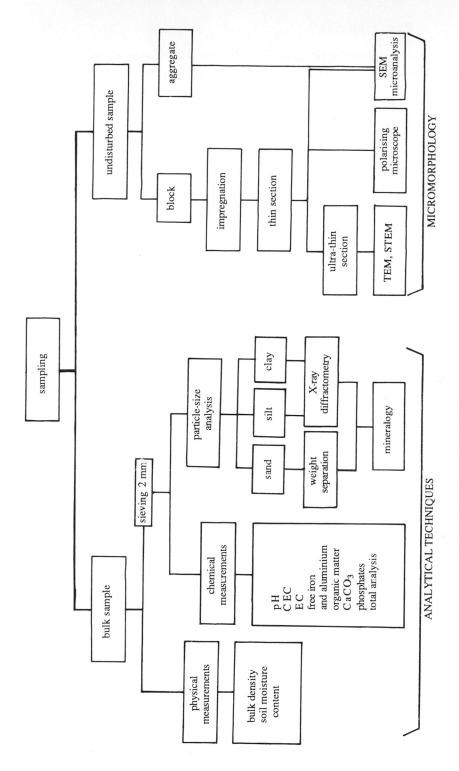

Figure 2.3   Flow chart for the laboratory study of a soil sample.

under cultivation or the detection of signs of pedological development. With regard to the latter, a net increase in the clay content between the A and the B horizons is used to confirm the presence of an argillic horizon, or to demonstrate lithological discontinuities. In many cases, however, the results are less than satisfactory since the size-distribution and morphology of *undisturbed* soil aggregates – essential data in the characterisation of soil behaviour – cannot be investigated by the above methods involving bulk samples.

Whereas in soil science particle-size analysis is usually carried out to characterise soil properties, in Quaternary geology (especially in the study of archaeological sediments) particle-size analysis has been widely used to identify the nature, dynamics and environments of sediment deposition. Results are generally plotted on different types of graphs referring to respective statistical distributions, including log-normal and hyperbolic (Figure 2.4). Various kinds of supposed diagnostic particle-size distributions have been distinguished, such as those typical for aeolian sand or for loess (Figure 2.4). The interpretation of such results is made difficult, however, if a deposit is the outcome of more than one agent of sedimentation, e.g., aeolian sediments which have been reworked by water, or original parent materials which have been strongly altered by post-depositional processes (e.g., an originally calcareous deposit that has been later decalcified).

Furthermore, size analyses are plagued by a number of theoretical and operational problems that concern grain shape and density. In the case of a heterogeneous sediment, for instance, well-rounded quartz sand grains and flaky mica particles have notably different densities, as well as shapes, and grains of the same size will not settle out at the same rate. Consequently, the particle-size distribution obtained does not reflect the true textural composition or hydraulic characteristics of the original sediment. In addition, how should a sediment that is cemented (either by iron or by calcium carbonate) be characterised? In such cases, particle-size analysis requires a preliminary chemical destruction of the cement which may partly alter the iron or calcareous components which were present in the original sediments. Or in a Quaternary sediment containing eroded soil fragments, the particle-size distribution of the aggregates themselves will not be recognized and may lead to misguided inferences concerning the energy of deposition. Clearly, some other technique is needed to observe the distribution of sizes (and shapes) of sediments.

When applied to archaeological soils, size analyses are of more limited value because natural sediments may have suffered from anthropogenic disturbance or have been mixed with various components, such as ash and charcoal; size distributions of the latter are difficult to measure, especially after sample pre-treatment. Thus, results obtained from such anthropogenic mixtures can be questionable, to say the least. In spite of these problems, particle-size analysis represents an initial step in the characterisation of soils but results have to be interpreted cautiously and with the help of other analyses.

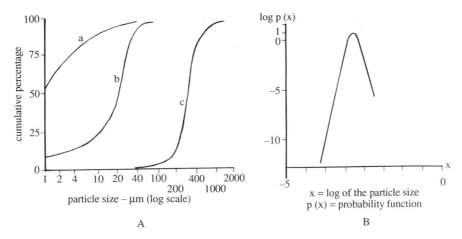

Figure 2.4 Examples of particle-size distributions: A. Log-normal distributions of (a) aerosolic dust from the ocean, (b) loess and (c) dune sand (modified from Jackson *et al.*, 1971); B. Hyperbolic distribution of dune sand. (Modified from Bagnold and Baindorff-Nielsen, 1980)

2.2.2 *Physical measurements*

The main purpose of carrying out physical measurements is to predict the behaviour of soils under various kinds of land use, especially under cultivation.

Bulk density represents the weight per unit volume of soil and therefore gives an indication of the amount of pore space in the sample. In general, it is used to depict the physical behaviour of the soil, such as its shrink–swell capacity, which is an important factor in soil management. The presence of roots, for example, decreases the bulk density. Unfortunately this measurement tells us nothing about the nature of the porosity, which may have palaeoenvironmental significance, viz., whether the pores were formed by roots, fauna, or by air bubbles after irrigation.

Soil moisture content and soil temperature are important for understanding soil–plant relationships. **Hydraulic conductivity** measures and describes the flow of water in the soil and thus permits an estimate of soil permeability. Specific laboratory measurements can be carried out to study the type of flow associated with the different types of pores, coarse fissures or fine channels. An assessment of soil water flow with time is critical in providing essential background information for thermoluminescence dating of sediments and burnt flints.

Many physical properties vary considerably within the profile. Consequently they represent valuable data in the characterisation of present-day soils. In buried soils, however, their value is limited, for the same reasons as those stated for bulk density analysis.

2.2.3 *Chemical measurements*

In addition to total elemental analyses discussed below, many other chemical analyses are routinely used in the depiction and interpretation of soil profiles, and most published papers in the field of soil science contain these data.

Total analysis of the major elements from bulk samples – This type of analysis, adopted from geology, was early introduced in soil science, before the introduction of other techniques. Although originally performed with wet chemical techniques, it is now commonly carried out using sophisticated laboratory equipment, such as atomic absorption. Relative proportions of various elements from one horizon to the next are then compared and the effects of different soil-forming processes inferred.

Whereas this type of analysis was worthwhile and feasible in the past, when no other analytical techniques were available, it is no longer carried out – or only for some specific purpose, such as a study of weathering – because the results obtained are crude: elements from the mineral constituents and those present in the soil solution cannot be separated. Analyses at a particular point on the sample can now be performed, thanks to the introduction of electron microprobes which permit elemental analysis of a known volume of sample (see Chapter 4).

Other general analyses include:

pH, cation-exchange capacity and electrical conductivity – These are very common methods used in soil science to characterise the equilibrium between the soil and the soil water solution.

pH is a measurement of soil alkalinity and acidity and ranges between 2 and 10 for most soils, commonly between 4 and 8 (pH 7 is neutral). pH values can vary within a soil profile, or even the same horizon, and can reflect very localised conditions. For example, pH can be lowered adjacent to leguminous roots in a calcareous soil because of a preferential leaching of calcium carbonate along the roots. Consequently, in present-day soils valuable inferences can be made about continuing soil-forming processes on the basis of pH fluctuations within and between horizons. In soils that have developed over a long period of time, pH reflects upon the present-day aqueous phase. In buried soils not well protected from water percolation, the measured pH can be wholly different from the original value before burial.

Nevertheless, in spite of these limitations, pH can be a valuable measurement. Low pH increases the potential for preservation of pollen in the soil, although acid conditions are not favourable for mollusc or bone preservation, which is encouraged in slightly alkaline conditions. An extremely low pH may be associated with ripening of marine sediments involving the breakdown of sulphides to sulphuric acids; in desert environments, highly alkaline soils may be associated with concentrations of sodium.

Cation-exchange capacity is a measure of the amount of exchangeable cations, hydrogen and the percentage base saturation in the soil solution, i.e., how many cations a soil may retain. Clays can absorb ions with a positive charge (hydrogen and cations) and exchange them with those present in the solution. The upper limit for this exchange is the exchangeable capacity or saturation capacity of the clay. The relative proportions of the saturating ions allow characterisation of the physical and agronomical properties of the soil and are especially important in the control of plant nutrition. The exchange capacity varies with the pH and the type of clay minerals: at the same pH it is higher in chlorite than in kaolinite. The same limitations as those discussed for pH are applicable to measurements of exchange capacity, especially since it is linked to organic matter content, which is greatly diminished in buried soils.

Electrical conductivity of a soil solution or saturated extract is determined in order to identify the presence of soluble salts, and the measured result is proportional to the soluble salt content. Both anions (bicarbonate, carbonate, sulphate and chloride) and cations (sodium, calcium, magnesium and potassium) are measured in a saturated extract. Electrical conductivity data are particularly useful in arid and semi-arid soils as well as in some specific saline environments in more humid climates, such as saline marshes, and provide a rapid and easily measured indication of the degree of salt accumulation in the soil. These properties, which again can vary through time, may also affect the preservation or corrosion of metal artifacts or the disintegration of poorly made ceramics.

'Free' iron and aluminium content refers to aluminium and iron in the sample that is soluble in sodium dithionite and as such is a reflection of the amount of iron mobility in the soil. Unfortunately, such measurements do not indicate where the iron is localised in the horizon. They are also used to determine 'weathering indexes', whereby the ratios of free Al/total, Al and free Fe/total Fe both increase with increasing alteration. Changes in the state of iron also influence such properties as magnetic-susceptibility enhancement as in aerobic, biologically active topsoils. These measurements provide useful data to help portray some soil-forming processes, such as podzolisation, hydromorphism, and the degree of leaching and illuviation. A variety of other chemical extracts have been used to give greater precision in such studies.

Organic matter – Because soil development is predominantly concerned with the transformations occurring at the interface between plant cover and mineral constituents, a great deal of attention in soil science has been devoted to the biological or physico-chemical transformations of fresh organic matter into humic substances, a complex series of processes which is termed **humification**. Carbon and nitrogen are the two major elements that can be used to trace the evolution of organic matter through the humification process. 'Organic' carbon refers to the carbon from atmospheric CO_2 which is fixed by the micro-organisms and the plants through the process of photosynthesis whereas 'organic' nitrogen refers to atmospheric N_2 which is fixed by plants and organisms such as legumes, algae and bacteria.

An overall characterisation of organic matter content is provided by the amount of material lost on ignition at 550°C, which excludes the carbon derived from calcium carbonate that is liberated at much higher temperatures (1000°C). Other methods involve 'wet' oxidation of the organic carbon. Organic nitrogen content is determined by the macro-Kjedhal method. When combined, both these measurements can be used in the calculation of the C/N ratio, which serves as an estimate of the degree of decomposition of organic matter.

The above measurements, however, can only help to identify the production potential of cultivated soils and to estimate the rate of mineralisation of the organic matter. For a better characterisation of the humification process, more detailed investigations are necessary that employ chemical fractionation of various types of organic matter. Organic substances are fractionated into their various constituents: these may be grouped into fulvic acids, which cannot precipitate under acid conditions, humic acids, which can precipitate under acid conditions, and a 'humin' residue which cannot be extracted. Overall, young soils possess a large number of hydrolysable components whereas ancient soils do not.

The study of organic matter is generally a complex subject because of the complicated interrelationships between the organic and inorganic (mineral) components and biological activity. Moreover, the nature of the analytical results obtained is strongly dependent on the way the organic substances are bound to the mineral components; different extraction procedures can yield different results. Nevertheless, carbon from organic matter in both topsoils and subsoils can be extracted and radiocarbon dated, although the results must be accepted and interpreted with caution.

Plant nutrients – In addition to nitrogen and potassium, phosphorus is important in soils because of its role as a fertiliser. Although both organic and inorganic forms of phosphorus are present in the soil, soil scientists are principally interested in the soluble forms that are available to plants. Generally, total phosphorus content is measured by attacking the sample with a strong acid. This is then followed by successive fractionations of lesser chemical intensity which are used to determine the organic phosphorus content. The resulting data are primarily used in studies of soil fertility to determine whether a lack of available phosphorus would require the addition of fertilisers to the soil.

In contrast to potassium, which is a highly mobile element, phosphorus seems to remain moderately stable in the soil over long periods and because background amounts of phosphorus from natural sources are generally low (except near phosphorus mines or pegmatites), phosphate analysis is commonly performed in the surroundings of archaeological sites, in areas which may have been affected by various kinds of human activities. Thus it can be an effective means of identifying the presence of former sites which might otherwise escape detection. In these cases measurement of phosphorus is an easy and inexpensive method of detection, which may even be done in the field and is often used as a survey technique in conjunction with those of geophysical prospecting.

Because of the high amount of phosphorus in animal excrements and human refuse, phosphate analysis has been used to trace areas of past farming activity (Eidt, 1984). Over the past decade Eidt (1984) has developed sophisticated fractionation techniques for separating the different types of organic phosphorus and has established a correlation between the amount of total phosphorus and different human activities (low in cultivated areas to high in occupation zones).

In spite of the advances made by Eidt's work, several methodological uncertainties and limitations still remain. Foremost among them is that the significance of the different forms of phosphorus that are extracted during fractionation is not readily apparent or convincing. Moreover, it is difficult to identify the origin of phosphorus from these chemical data, since, for example, organic manure and mineral anthropogenic products such as ash both have comparatively high phosphorus contents. In addition, as will be shown below, under certain conditions phosphorus can be mobile and recrystallise as various minerals (see Chapter 8).

CaCO$_3$ content – The calcium carbonate content may be evaluated in the field by applying dilute hydrochloric acid and noting the resulting effervescence. In the laboratory, the total amount of CaCO$_3$ is more precisely determined by measuring the amount of CO$_2$ produced after attack by hydrochloric acid. The results are important in characterising the type and amount of dissolution/reprecipitation processes in soils originally rich in calcium carbonate. In alkaline soils and sediments this measurement can furnish more precise information than pH.

2.2.4 *Mineralogical analysis*

A variety of mineralogical analyses can be performed on both the coarser and finer fractions, yielding information on the origin of parent materials and post-depositional (including pedogenic) changes.

Mineralogical analysis of the coarse fraction usually involves separation of the 'lighter' minerals – those with specific gravities, *c.* 2.65, such as quartz and feldspar – from the 'heavy minerals' which have specific gravities > 2.85. The latter include opaque minerals such as haematite, goethite and magnetite, and translucent minerals, comprising such varieties as hornblende, augite, tourmaline and rutile. Whilst heavy minerals are visible in thin sections, they usually occur in low proportions and are dispersed throughout the slide. Thus, study of heavy minerals is made more efficient if they are concentrated and separated from the other elements of the coarse fraction. This separation is usually accomplished by centrifugation of the sample in a heavy liquid (S. G. 2.8), such as bromoform, and the concentrate is mounted on a slide and observed with the petrographic microscope.

The mineralogy of the coarse fraction, particularly the heavy minerals, has been most commonly used to characterise parent materials and to infer the provenance of glacial and loessic deposits. It can also serve as an indicator of weathering by noting the ratio of easily weatherable minerals (e.g., feldspar, hornblende, epidote) to those resistant to weathering (e.g., zircon, tourmaline and rutile).

Mineralogy of the clays – Because very fine particles play an important role in soil-forming processes (especially with regard to properties of fertility and soil behaviour), the determination of the clay mineralogy is a classical analysis in soil science. It readily permits the identification of the types of parent materials and the recognition of some of the weathering products and processes. Thus large-scale environmental events may be reflected by the clay mineralogy.

Clay mineral analysis is normally carried out on the <2 micron fraction which is mechanically separated from the bulk of the sample, and most commonly studied by X-ray diffraction techniques in which the relative proportions and types of the different clay minerals are estimated according to their position and amplitude on the diffractogram (Figure 2.5). Alternatively, the types of clays can be identified by thermal analysis, whereby clays are heated at successively higher and specified temperatures, the different clays being recognised according to the manner in which they absorb or emit heat.

2.2.5 *Concluding remarks*

Most of the techniques described above constitute more or less routine procedures used by soil scientists and represent basic data in various publications in the discipline. In many instances they supply much information that can be used to describe a soil and to make inferences about its genesis and history. In many cases, however, they provide data whose relevance to the problem is doubtful or misleading and can lead to erroneous or misguided interpretations. This is commonly the case in the investigation of paleosols (particularly polyphased ones) or materials and soils associated with archaeological sites.

In the case of paleosols, for instance, it is possible to question the relevance of pH measurements, which may have nothing to do with the conditions of the former soil when it developed. Similarly, organic matter may be considerably diminished and perhaps preferentially replaced by iron minerals; thus, chemical measurements can underestimate the organic matter and overestimate the iron of the original soil. Likewise, determination of the percentage of clay or silt in a profile does not indicate how these components are geometrically distributed within the bulk sample. In other words, granulometric analysis of 'total clay content' does not distinguish clay originally present in the sample from clay which has been translocated through the profile with depth; it is also incapable of recognising or isolating separate and distinct events of clay translocation, a relatively common phenomenon in mid-latitude paleosols. Finally, results from a clay mineralogical analysis performed on a bulk sample do not reveal the locations of these clays within the sample: the matrix of the sample may be

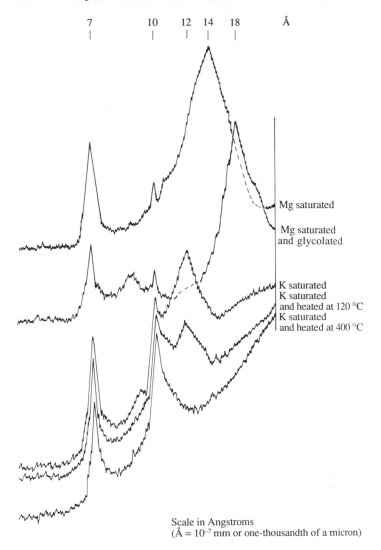

7   10   12   14   18   Å

Mg saturated

Mg saturated
and glycolated

K saturated
K saturated
and heated at 120 °C
K saturated
and heated at 400 °C

Scale in Angstroms
(Å = 10^{-7} mm or one-thousandth of a micron)

Figure 2.5   Diffractogram produced by X-ray diffraction analysis. The peak of 14Å (Mg saturated) that shifts to 18Å (Mg saturated and [ethylene] glycolated) indicates the presence of swelling clay minerals of the smectite type. This diagnosis is confirmed when clay minerals are saturated with K and then heated: the peak gradually shifts from 12–14Å to 10Å. Smectite is here associated with kaolinite, as indicated by the peak at 7Å, stable under the different treatments.

composed predominantly of one type of clay, whereas voids may be filled or coated with a different type of clay. A technique sensitive to these problems is needed to place such results in proper perspective.

In the case of soils, sediments and materials associated with archaeological sites, such issues and problems are even more acute. Determination of gypsum or calcite content of a whole or decayed mud brick, for example, does not differentiate primary from secondarily precipitated minerals, nor can it show how much solution/reprecipitation has taken place. Similarly, a chemical analysis of this or any other material does not indicate the selective contributions of various archaeological components – such as bone, mortar, organic matter, rock fragments or soil aggregates – which are widespread in many archaeological sites and deposits.

A technique which we believe can eradicate some of these problems in soil science and in archaeology is micromorphology. Detailed observation of a thin section can not only permit a better understanding and interpretation of a 'traditional' analysis but is capable of unravelling a complex history of a soil or sediment on its own. The effects and results of particle translocation, leaching or secondary precipitation are clearly evident and successive pedological 'events' or processes can generally be distinguished, e.g., translocated clay coating a void is in turn coated or overlain by precipitated calcite crystals. Such 'microstratigraphic events' are difficult or impossible to recognise with traditional methods.

Many of the following chapters attempt to illustrate how the technique of micromorphology can be used – not to the exclusion of other techniques – to interpret the history of soils, sediments and archaeologically related materials.

3

FIELD STRATEGIES

3.1 Introduction

Having presented some general concepts in soil science, we may turn to a consideration of how a micromorphological study is begun. Since this originates in the field, we begin with a discussion of field methodologies, such as profile description and sampling.

A survey of the literature or attendance at recent international geology or archaeology meetings will reveal that geological (a term used in a broad sense) contributions to archaeologically related projects fall into two main categories: (a) those that deal with the archaeological site proper as the main focus of investigation (a 'geo-archaeological' emphasis) and are usually written by geologists or other environmentalists working in close cooperation with the archaeologist, usually during the excavation of the site; and (b) those which concentrate more on the Quaternary evolution of the landscape and palaeoenvironments, and use sites chiefly as chronological and spatial markers ('archaeological geology'). The latter group may also include a high proportion of Quaternary stratigraphers, composed of geologists (*sensu stricto*), geographers and a few impassioned archaeologists. Generally, there are very few researchers who work at both scales. To illustrate the above let us consider two different cases.

Case 1 – A team is excavating a prehistoric cave developed in sandy limestone, set a few metres above a small valley and filled with several metres (> 10) of deposits (Figure 3.1). The most pressing questions that face the excavators are: (1) what is the source of the cave filling and (2) how did it get into the cave (i.e., mode of transport)? These questions have several ramifications that relate to regional and site-specific problems encompassing those of climatic change, past human activities and general excavation strategies. A few possibilities are:

(a) – Greater or lesser contributions of stream-derived sediments in the cave may be related to higher stream discharges, which in turn may be tied to changes in climate.

(b) – Alternatively, changes in the amount of aeolian sediment in the cave, in the form of sand or silt (loess), may be conditioned by changes in aridity and/or vegetation, again a palaeoclimatic consideration.

(c) – The same holds true for the amount of karstic activity, measured by the amount of solution and collapse of the roof and walls; the latter may also be controlled by freeze–thaw activity (cryoclastism).

(d) – A shift of emphasis to the site-specific level would be represented by sediments deposited by water, either flowing in channels or on the surface (runoff). This might not only tell something about the external geometry of the mouth of the cave but would bring up the possibility that the archaeological material might not be strictly

27

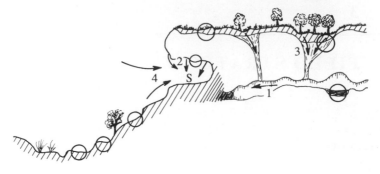

Figure 3.1   Sediment sources and possible sampling localities in the study of a hypothetical prehistoric cave. Arrows show sources [(1) karstic deposits, (2) wall disintegration, (3) runoff and (4) aeolian sediments] and paths of sediment transport; circles indicate positions of samples. S: location of the studied sequence.

in situ and that certain excavation strategies, such as **décapage** or three-coordinate recording of artifacts, may be over-exacting.

(e)   – Finally, examination of the contents of hearths might reveal the types of materials that were burned. This has implications for the archaeologist and also serves to indicate the types of vegetation close to the site.

In order to attempt to resolve some of these issues, an excavator would be obliged to examine and sample materials in the neighbourhood of the site, including the stream flood-plain, the bedrock for insoluble residues, various soil types both beneath the cave entrance and on the plateau overlying it. In addition, it would be desirable to collect sediments from any nearby karstic cavity fillings.

Case 2 – In this instance, let us hypothesise a multi-component, stratified site located astride the banks of a large stream that drains an area of several thousands of square kilometres. Thus we are here dealing with macroenvironmental problems that range in space between tens to thousands of square kilometres, and in time from hundreds to thousands of years.

Typical directions of enquiry that may be investigated include:

(a)   – The regional stratigraphy that comprises periods of alluviation and incision and the formation of stream terraces. The occurrence of archaeological sites within any of these units would naturally be of use in dating such sequences. Similar strategies would be valid for other environments, such as aeolian (sand dunes), lacustrine or, less commonly, marine. Paleosols not only serve as palaeoenvironmental indicators but are often considered to be among the best time-stratigraphic markers. When the resulting stratigraphic sequences are coupled with additional pollen, faunal data and miscellaneous features such as travertines and mottles produced by *gleying*, they permit us to make reasonable palaeoenvironmental and palaeoclimatic interpretations, depending on the quality of the data, of course.

(b)   – Closer in scale to the archaeological site is the attempt to reconstruct or identify former patterns of land-use, such as irrigation systems, cultivation and quarrying of certain raw materials. The study of individually cultivated fields would return the focus of the investigation to the archaeological site, as in the first case.

(c)   – Overlapping the two types of cases is a consideration of the location of sites within a regional context, as, for example, in the accretionary landscape of the Po Plain in Italy. Here, prehistoric and archaeological sites may be deeply buried beneath several metres of alluvium. In contrast, on an eroded landscape, such as in parts of the Mediterranean Basin or the Chalklands of Europe, soils and archaeological materials have been stripped from the plateaux and redeposited either locally as colluvial valley fills, or more distantly, as alluvium.

Where possible, one starts with previously published background material consisting of satellite imagery, aerial photographs, and with geological, vegetation, soil and topographic maps, and then proceeds to search for significant profiles in natural exposures or road cuts, quarries, wells or building foundations, as archaeological sections may often be insufficient or too shallow. Where necessary, some additional man-made pits may have to be dug.

With these guidelines in mind, and taking into account the amounts of time, manpower and money available, some of these localities would be selected for eventual study and sampling. In the remainder of this chapter we discuss various procedures for describing and sampling these localities.

3.2 Field description

Almost any micromorphological study begins in the field. Thus it is imperative that field observations be as complete and systematic as possible, since it is upon this background that later micromorphological observations and interpretations are built.

There are many ways of describing a profile and its surroundings, and geological descriptions differ from pedological ones, for example. The descriptive criteria presented below are quite similar to those used by many field pedologists (e.g., Soil Survey of England and Wales: Hodgson, 1974) but we have modified them to include those features pertinent to the archaeological context. These criteria are summarised on the field-description sheet (Figure 3.2), which includes the main characteristics of the general environment of the site and presents the basic archaeological data. For each unit distinguished in the field, we have selected a set of characteristics that are not only the most representative but also the most applicable to the interpretation of a thin section. Consequently, the descriptive criteria set out here pertain especially to fine-grained materials which can be studied micromorphologically and not to coarser materials, such as gravels.

3.2.1 *Site characteristics*

Site: The conventionally accepted name of the site.

Locality: This includes the local name, the name of the area or of the closest village. The distance and direction to main town or roads may also be given.

Type of site: Archaeological nature of the site, such as barrow, cave, shelter, soil buried beneath barrow, succession of occupation deposits, colluvially buried artifact scatter, ancient cultivated area. Some local characteristics, including drainage, may be specified.

Site

Site **Geology** **Archaeological context**

Locality **Other data**

Type of site **Climate** **Date of sampling**

Grid ref., lat./long.

Physiography
Altitude
Position
Slope

Section/Profile Nº **Land use and vegetation** **Described by**

Unit depth thickness	Continuity and boundary	Moisture	Colour and variations	Texture, stoniness	Structure, porosity	Other characteristics	Anthropogenic evidence	Archaeological questions
1 0 * 0–5 cm								
2 * 0–13 cm 11 cm								

* = bulk sample

⊥ vertical extent of the undisturbed sample

Figure 3.2   Field description sheet.

Section/profile: Section code or trench number with orientation noted (e.g., south-east facing).

Grid reference: Latitude and longitude or any other type of coordinates are indicated.

Physiography:

> *altitude* – The value taken from map or 'measured in' from a point above Ordnance Datum (OD), in metres above sea level (also, but less desirable, in feet).
>
> *position* – Indicates the kind of physiographic unit in which the site occurs (e.g. plateau, slope, valley bottom, near to river, beach, etc.). In the case of a slope, the orientation and inclination is specified (e.g., N25E, 10SE; cliff). Some space is left in the box for a field sketch (cross section or map).

Geology: This denotes not only the rocks on which the site occurs but also the types of available parent materials around the site, including rocks, stones and superficial deposits (e.g., paleosols, colluvium, alluvium, loess, and recent flood deposits). When known, their ages are specified.

Climate: Annual rainfall and mean annual temperature are most commonly recorded. Other details of weather and climate (e.g., recent heavy rain, dust storms or tornadoes) may also be noted.

Land use and vegetation: When known, it can be very important to record the recent types of past land use, since in certain cases (e.g., fallow, cultivated, recently cultivated, irrigated, fertilised, slashed and burnt fields, abandoned villages and urban settings), subsequent micromorphological interpretations may be dependent upon it. Natural vegetation (tree cover, grass) of the area should be described.

Archaeological context: This comprises 'cultural' period(s) and, where possible, absolute dates, and the method used to obtain them. Examples: Lower Palaeolithic, 200,000 BP, U–Th; Middle Palaeolithic, 50,000 BP, TL on burnt flint; Epi-Gravettian, 18,000 BP, radiocarbon; Middle Neolithic, 5,800 BP, tree rings; upper Bronze Age, pottery. If known, the nature of the inferred site activities should also be specified (e.g., flint chipping, industrial, 'living floor', midden, hearths, structures, ard marks, abundance and distribution of artifacts).

Other data: Here, current or past analyses that have been performed on the archaeological deposits are indicated. These can be environmental analyses, such as molluscs, macro-plant remains (charcoal, seeds, cereal grains), pollen, phytoliths, diatoms, as well as physical, chemical or mineralogical analyses.

3.2.2. *Column headings*

Unit. A unit is defined as a three-dimensional body of homogeneous character, recognised during excavation by its colour, texture, inclusions, structure and other features. Units can have three origins: geological, pedological and anthropogenic.

A *geological unit* comprises mineral or organic materials whose deposition or genesis is related to geological processes (see Chapter 4). Most geological units observed in archaeological sites are the result of sedimentary processes and in this book we will deal predominantly with sedimentary units. However, volcanic deposits (e.g., lava or tuffs) can also occur. Sedimentary units are separated from each other by discontinuities that indicate a new depositional event.

Pedological units consist of mineral and organic materials that have undergone soil-forming (pedological) processes under the combined action of climate and living organisms which have altered the characteristics of the original parent material. Under a cover of vegetation, deposits are gradually modified, generally from the soil surface downward, and transformed into a vertical succession of horizons, which together form a soil profile. In some specific circumstances archaeological deposits have been affected over a period of time by pedological processes and soil profiles can be developed on them. In this case pedological units can be described as horizons and the nature of the horizon can be recognised on the basis of the field characteristics (Figure 3.2). In cases where archaeological deposits have been protected from the action of vegetation and only slightly affected by the action of climate (e.g., because of quick burial, or when they are located in caves and rock shelters), soil development is weak and classical horizons cannot be identified with any certainty.

Anthropogenic units consist of material deposited or formed through human activity, e.g., ashes, decayed mud bricks, dumps, middens, foundations, mortars and walls. We also employ the term *anthropic* (Table 2.2) to cover soils produced by human activity, or soils which include reworked anthropogenic materials.

An *archaeological layer* is usually delineated during the excavation by the distribution of the archaeological materials and by the characteristics of the sediments. Consequently, it can be a combination of the different units. It may: (1) comprise one or several anthropogenic units, e.g., an occupation deposit containing several ash beds; (2) represent a combination of anthropogenic units and pedological units, e.g., a cultivated horizon on a buried soil; or (3) be a combination of anthropogenic and geological units, for example, a colluvium containing pottery sherds or flints.

Each section studied can be divided into either a succession of geological units, pedological units or anthropogenic units according to the descriptive criteria used (Figure 3.3). The purpose of an archaeological stratigraphy is to integrate all these different units, which unfortunately often overlap. Understandably, this can result in complex stratigraphy, in which the respective roles of geological, pedological and anthropogenic processes are confounded and not clearly distinguishable. Field researchers, then, must realise that stratigraphic boundaries made in the field are only tentative and subject to confirmation in the laboratory. Thus they should not cling too rigorously to what has been defined in the field.

Depth and thickness. Give the modal and extreme variations of the depth and thickness of the unit.

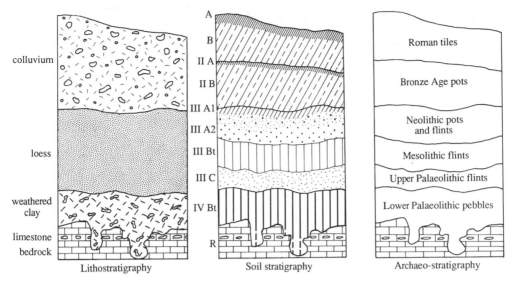

Figure 3.3   Three views of the same stratigraphic profile as seen from the standpoints of lithostratigraphy, soil stratigraphy and archaeo-stratigraphy, respectively.

Continuity and boundary. State whether a unit is continuous or discontinuous across the section studied, noting the degree of continuity, since archaeological sections may often contain several discontinuous lenses, whose extent should be noted.

Boundary distinctness. The transition between one unit and another is recognised by the variation in one or more characteristics. Seen in the field there may be a zone of uncertainty which should be defined. These boundaries may be selected from a number of criteria, geological, pedological or anthropogenic, and it is important that the criteria defining the boundaries are clearly stated, because these boundaries may differ for each type of unit. The type of boundary between two units is also characterised according to the thickness of the zone of transition between them. These are: sharp (0–0.5 cm), abrupt (0.5–2.5 cm), clear (2.5–6 cm), gradual (6–13 cm), and diffuse (more than 13 cm).

Boundary form. A boundary may be smooth (a surface with few irregularities), wavy (a surface with regular, shallow variations in depth) or irregular (a surface with irregular variations in depth). It may also be useful to note whether a boundary is flat or inclined. From the field characteristics of the boundary, some preliminary interpretations can be attempted at this stage and later checked against the micromorphological data. For example, a smooth boundary between two geological units can be a reflection of the original depositional events. Similarly a sharp, smooth boundary between two anthropogenic units can indicate a marked change in human activity (see Figure 3.4 for other examples).

Moisture. The degree of moisture can relate to current climatic conditions and to the movement of soil water within the section. Moisture is important

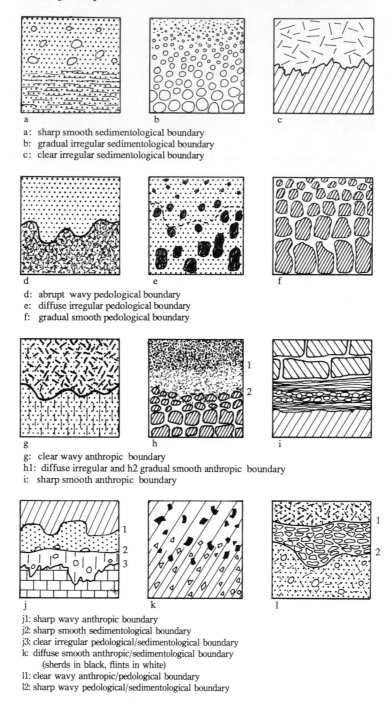

a: sharp smooth sedimentological boundary
b: gradual irregular sedimentological boundary
c: clear irregular sedimentological boundary

d: abrupt wavy pedological boundary
e: diffuse irregular pedological boundary
f: gradual smooth pedological boundary

g: clear wavy anthropic boundary
h1: diffuse irregular and h2 gradual smooth anthropic boundary
i: sharp smooth anthropic boundary

j1: sharp wavy anthropic boundary
j2: sharp smooth sedimentological boundary
j3: clear irregular pedological/sedimentological boundary
k: diffuse smooth anthropic/sedimentological boundary
       (sherds in black, flints in white)
l1: clear wavy anthropic/pedological boundary
l2: sharp wavy pedological/sedimentological boundary

Figure 3.4   Types of boundaries between units.

because many horizons will appear both darker and less firm when moist than when dry, thus affecting the descriptions of colour and consistence. The material in thin section is of course seen in its dry state.

Colour and colour variations. As colour may relate to a large number of phenomena it is often utilised as a diagnostic criterion to recognise units. Many questions posed by archaeologists often refer to the significance of a particular colour of material. Ironically, many colour variations occur naturally and often have no specific archaeological significance, although in several cases colour can reflect pedological processes that allow soil scientists to interpret soils. Moreover, one must be aware that particular parent materials – because of their geologically inherited red colour (such as the Devonian red-beds of England) – can produce reddish materials which look similar to both paleosols and burned deposits. Furthermore, since this inherited red colour dominates, the effects of pedological processes show up poorly, and horizon boundaries are difficult to distinguish. They can only be seen in thin section.

Within a unit, the dominant colour is described first. Colour variations relating to geological inclusions, soil phenomena, e.g., gleying (mottles), biological reworking, anthropogenic materials and mixing are noted and their abundance stated.

For standardisation, the moist colour of the material – i.e., that after being wetted from a wash bottle – should be given. In addition, the air-dry colour can be noted if this shows up variations more clearly. Colours are recorded by comparison with a *Munsell Soil Colour Chart* (Munsell Color Company Inc., Baltimore, Md., USA; 10YR7/3 = 'dull yellow orange'). In the field we see colours by reflection, and lighting conditions affect how we see contrasts. Thus, colours should be determined under standard lighting conditions, such as shaded daylight. Finally, colour differences seen in the field are often different from those viewed in thin section. There is an additional problem in interpretation arising from the fact that colour perceptions vary from person to person.

Texture and stoniness. Geologists and soil scientists use different criteria to define texture. **Soil texture** refers to the relative proportion of the various size groups of individual soil grains and specifically refers to the proportion of material (sand, silt and clay) smaller than 2 millimetres in diameter. Geologists, on the other hand, take a broader view and include within the definition the concepts of roundness, shape, grain and size and fabric (Pettijohn *et al.*, 1972). We will consider here only grain size, since the other factors are discussed in Chapter 4.

In order to classify the continuum of grain sizes from large boulders down to individual particles of clay, geologists and pedologists have devised a number of grade scales. Although the names of these classes of grades vary from one country to another and between disciplines (geology vs. pedology), each class interval bears a constant relationship to its neighbour, generally a logarithmic one, as in the commonly used phi (Φ) scale. Examples of some of these grade scales are given in Figure 3.5.

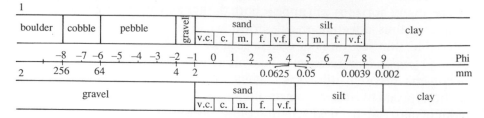

Figure 3.5   Grade scales of soils and sediments using the (1) Wentworth (1922) and (2) Soil Survey Staff (1975) terminologies. v.c.: very coarse   c: coarse   m: medium   f: fine   v.f.: very fine.

Mixtures of particle sizes can also be classified and are usually illustrated with triangular diagrams in which percentages of sand, silt and clay occupy each corner of the diagram (Figure 3.6). As with grade scales, the boundaries and names for the different particle-size classes are quite variable and one should state the scheme being followed. We generally use the particle-size grades of the British standards: sand/silt boundary = 62 microns; silt/clay = 2 microns.

In the field, the percentages of sand and silt and clay can sometimes be estimated with the fingers. Similarly, plasticity, which serves as an estimate of the clay content, is determined by rolling a moist sample between the fingers (for full details, consult Soil Survey Field Guide: Hodgson, 1974). Although the precise estimation of particle size is often made difficult by the presence of organic matter and by cementation, a general appreciation of textural variations is useful in distinguishing different units. In any case, the name given in the field can only be approximate.

Stoniness can often be readily appreciated in the field, where approximate percentage, size range, shape and some petrological characteristics can be noted. In the case of extremely stony units, shape and distribution of stones is best seen in the field. In some sites the presence of stones may be the sole result of human intent and, if so, the archaeologist should be made aware of this.

Bedding and sedimentary structures. For sedimentary units, recognition and description of the types of bedding and *sedimentary structures* – i.e., the organisation of bedding – are particularly important. In conjunction with the study of the geometrical relationships between individual clasts – *sedimentary fabric* – these are useful indicators of agents of deposition, sedimentary environments and conditions of flow and also aid in the assessment of palaeocurrent directions (Pettijohn *et al.*, 1972).

Beds can be of equal or unequal thickness, and laterally continuous or discontinuous. Moreover, they commonly display one or more of the following characteristics (Figure 3.7):

> **Massive bedding** – In this case bedding is apparently lacking, (though X-ray radiographs reveal that, in fact, some form of bedding is present). Loess is a good example of this type of bedding.

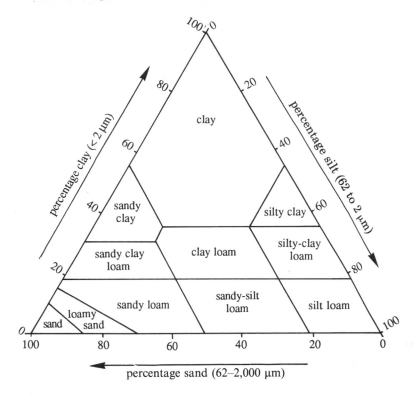

Figure 3.6 Typical triangular diagram showing names and boundaries of particle size classes used in soil science, (Modified from Hodgson, 1974)

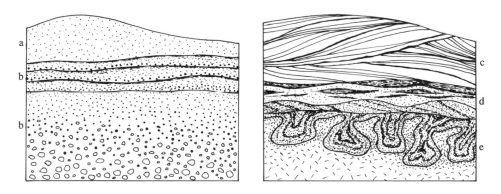

Figure 3.7 Some representative types of bedding and sedimentary structures: (a) massive bedding, (b) grading-bedding, (c) crossbedding, (d) lenticular structures, (e) deformation structures.

Laminated bedding – This type of bedding is quite common and can result from a variety of flow conditions.

Crossbedding – Crossbedding is one of the most prominent types of bedding and is actually composed of sets of laminated units. Many different subtypes have been recognised, depending on the geometry of the sets of laminations. The shape and degree of convergence of the bedding are noted, although these vary within a set of crossbeds depending upon the orientation of the section with regard to the structure; the best sections are those parallel to the inferred flow direction. *Ripple marks* are a small-scale crossbedding feature and likewise take on a variety of forms.

Graded bedding – This phenomenon is shown by the upward decrease in grain size within a bed and forms in response to a decrease in current velocity.

Bedding deformation structures – These structures are generally produced shortly after sedimentation, when a layer of sand is deposited upon a finer-grained, water-saturated sediment, such as in overbank deposits in streams. They are represented by various types.

Soil structure, character. Soil structure deals with the shape, size, degree of development of the aggregation of particles. Usually five main types of soil structure are distinguished, according to shape. These are further described according to size and degree of development. **Granular** or **crumb** structure constitutes spheroids or polyhedrons with poor accommodation, i.e., they do not fit together well. Granules have curved faces and are generally regular in size whereas crumbs have irregular surfaces and may vary in their size distribution. **Blocky** structures, which are polyhedral in shape and have three dimensions of the same order of magnitude arranged around a point, are divided into two classes, subangular and angular, depending upon the shape of their faces (Figure 3.8). With **prismatic** structures the vertical dimension is longer than that of the horizontal, and hence they are readily distinguished from blocky structure. **Platy** structure is governed by its horizontal dimension, and when plates are irregular in shape they may be described as lenticular.

When material has little or no aggregation, it is structureless and two types can be distinguished. With single grains, primary particles separate individually when dry, but may be held together by surface tension when moist or wet. Massive material can be held together as a result of a variety of processes, e.g., cementation and compaction, and has a homogeneous appearance and does not break apart in any preferred direction.

The degree of wetness can affect the type of structures expressed. For example, clay which has a massive structure under normal drainage conditions can develop in a dried-out section, a strong prismatic structure, which has no relation to previous pedological processes. Structural fissures disposed horizontally and not vertically may indicate recent structural formation.

In the field, units are described as either loose, weak, firm, strong or rigid. However, care should be taken as these classes vary according to the degree of soil moisture. Such descriptions can thus be both meaningless and misleading and relate little to the inherent soil character as seen in thin section. In the case

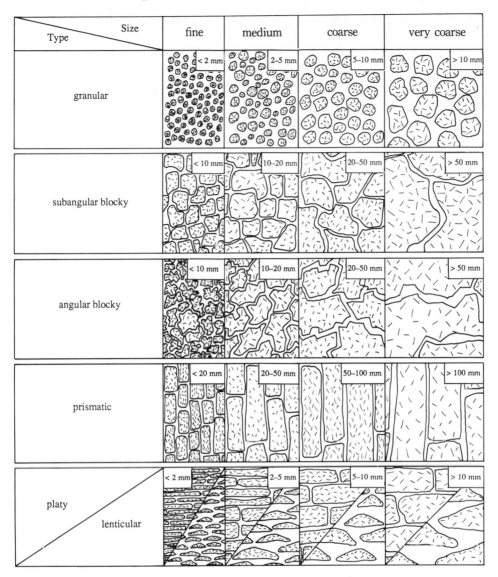

Figure 3.8   Types of soil structure and their variations at different scales.

of materials cemented by mineral components, e.g., calcium carbonate, silica and sesquioxides, an assessment of material strength can provide an estimation of the degree of cementation.

Porosity. This refers to the size, shape and quantity of voids that can be distinguished in the field. This macroscopic porosity is also observable in thin section along with smaller-scale voids, as described in Chapter 4. The porosity is closely related to the soil structure by way of the abundance of fissures and biological activity, such as rooting and burrows. Fissures or cracks can be distinguished from pores by their preferentially vertical or horizontal orientation. Porosity sizes vary from very fine (0.5–1 mm), fine (1–2 mm), medium (2–5 mm), coarse (5–10 mm) to very coarse (>10 mm).

Other characteristics. Within units it is possible to distinguish specific characteristics based on two or more of the phenomena previously described. These comprise pedogenic features, which may be interpreted or suspected in the field, but are later confirmed by thin-section observation or by chemical and physical analyses. For example, the presence and amount of organic matter may be assessed on the basis of colour, texture and the experience of the soil scientist. In the case of biological activity, it is important to differentiate between active and fossil evidence of faunal activity. Thus the present activity of worms and fresh roots has to be noted but previous activity may be assessed from variations in structure, porosity and colour. Nodules, for example, may be readily seen in the field and their contents determined by simple tests (e.g., 10% HCl for calcium carbonate). Where present, the variations in nodule morphology should be described and their quantity estimated. Manganese impregnations may be differentiated from charcoal by their lustre and disposition in the field.

Archaeological evidence. This refers to the presence, distribution and abundance of archaeological materials and features interpreted by the archaeologist and includes the presence of such materials as pottery, flints, charcoal, slag, ashes, etc. and features such as ard marks, ditches, floors, middens and hearths.

Archaeological questions. During excavation a number of phenomena are encountered which do not have an obvious archaeological significance. They may relate to one specific characteristic, such as colour, which may have a geological, pedological or anthropogenic origin. For example, one of the most common problematic issues is whether the occurrence of 'black layers' represents an ancient, humic-rich layer of an old ground surface, or whether they are of anthropogenic origin caused by finely dispersed charcoal. An additional problem centres around white units: are they ash layers or are they 'natural' phenomena such as the pedogenic accumulation of calcium carbonate? Finally, field workers are commonly perplexed by the dispersal of archaeological material throughout the vertical extent of a given unit. Could these materials have been integrated into the unit by sedimentary phenomena, by biological mixing of discrete occupation layers after deposition, or by human activities, such as dumping (cf., Wood and Johnson, 1978)?

3.3 Sampling
3.3.1 *Tactics*
The location and number of samples collected during the course of a human research project is closely dependent on the type of archaeological project and the kinds of questions being posed. Where a whole stratigraphic sequence needs to be examined, a sequence of systematic samples will be necessary. On the other hand, for a specific problem – such as the composition or colour of a certain layer or the identification and estimation of the amount of anthropoge-

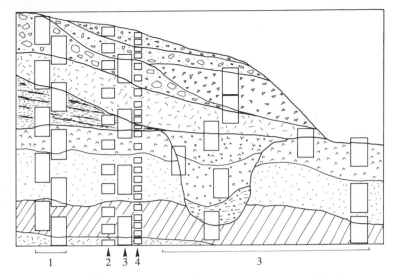

Figure 3.9   Different strategies employed to sample a profile: (1) systematic, continuous sampling of undisturbed material for micromorphological study, (2) bulk sampling for chemical and physical analyses, (3) selective sampling for micromorphology, (4) sampling for pollen analysis.

nic components within sediments or soils – selective sampling is recommended.

Systematic sampling – Continuous systematic sampling is used to detect small variations within a section and is used to reconstruct the geological, pedological and archaeological history of the sequence, assuming that all three exist. This type of sampling procedure requires samples to be taken from a column, one above the other, without any gaps between them. Shifts of a few centimetres to the right or left to avoid stones, bones or other archaeological material yet to be excavated, are not significant. A slight overlap at the boundaries between two samples is even recommended (overlapping sampling).

If a given unit appears to be homogeneous in the field, it may be necessary to take only a representative sample, leaving 5–10 cm between samples. This 'discontinuous systematic sampling' is most often sufficient to study the pedological development of soil profiles.

Selective sampling – This strategy is employed when a specific question is being asked. It is also commonly used to fill in a profile which has been sampled systematically and in which marked lateral variations occur, a feature commonly found in archaeological sites (Figure 3.9).

So far, we have been concerned with sampling from a vertical profile, as is usually done in geological and pedological studies. In archaeological sites, however, samples may need to be collected at different locations within the same unit. This type of sampling serves the dual purpose of monitoring lateral variations on the same 'living floor' and also of collecting and storing information from parts of the site that may disappear in the course of excavation. In the case of a hearth, for example, a sample could be taken from inside and at certain locations radially away from it in order to observe the lateral distribution of ashes and charcoal. A similar strategy could be used in the case of a large excavated room where the localisation of different activity areas is sought. In this case, however, a systematic sampling approach may be taken if samples are collected at regular intervals over a gridded area.

We wish to stress that, regardless of the type of strategy employed, sampling can be carried out during the excavation by the archaeologists themselves and it does not require the expertise of a 'specialist' who has not yet arrived at the site.

Bulk sampling – In conjunction with sampling for micromorphological studies, it is good practice to collect a series of bulk samples that can be used for chemical and mineralogical analyses. These could be taken at the same time and place as the micromorphological samples, but unit boundaries should be avoided (Figure 3.9). Samples for palynology and microfauna, for example, should also be collected from these same localities.

3.3.2 *Sampling procedures*

A working principle of micromorphology is to study undisturbed, oriented samples. Consequently, one of the main objectives of micromorphological sampling is to preserve the original organisation and integrity of the materials to be studied.

Archaeological sediments are commonly loosely to poorly cemented and there is a great risk of collapse when they are sampled. To avoid this, samples are taken with the aid of a metal box (professionally known as 'Kubiena tin' or box) which is carefully inserted into the unit (Figure 3.10). At the same time, the material surrounding the box is neatly removed with a knife. When the box has been fully inserted, a knife is introduced to detach the box and sample from the surrounding material. Both sides of the box are covered with lids and held in place with masking tape, while at the same time the orientation of the sample is indicated by means of an indelible marking pen (e.g., TOP, or arrows pointing to the top). In general, it is best to replace the front lid and label it before removing the sample. The sample should then be marked with the name of the site and the sample number. While the date of sampling and number of the profile may also be given, it is wise to avoid writing too many comments on the sample, since these may be obliterated during the course of the various labora-tory treatments. The location and depth of a single sample or series of samples should be marked on the archaeologist's profile drawing so that the relation-ships between archaeological levels and other samples (e.g., pollen) can be readily understood. Photographing labelled sample locations also provides a useful reference and reminder, as it may be many months before actual laboratory study of the thin sections takes place.

Disturbance of loose, powdery materials often cannot be avoided, either

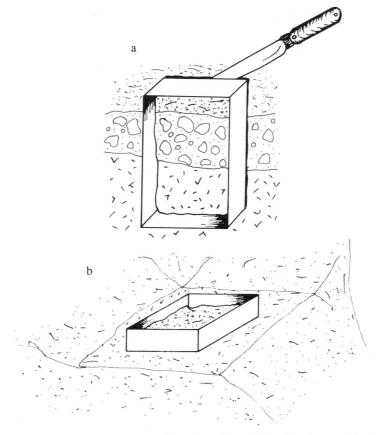

Figure 3.10   Tin boxes ('Kubiena boxes') used for collecting undisturbed samples: (a) traditional sampling of several units from a vertical profile, (b) horizontal sample normally collected from one unit in order to monitor lateral (horizontal) changes in that unit, as in a hearth, for example.

during sampling or transport. This can be minimised by placing soft padding between the sample and the metal covers or by partially case-hardening the sample in the field with water-glass (sodium silicate solution), rhodoplas (polyvinyl acetate) or some other suitable cementing agent. In spite of these precautions, however, very loose material can collapse and one may be forced to work with an artificially aggregated sample which limits the scope of micromorphological observations to those of composition and texture.

Firm sediments can be sampled without the necessity of a Kubiena box. A block is cut from the layer with a knife, or a hammer if the deposits are cemented. The block is then wrapped with tissue paper or newspaper, which is firmly taped in place. The sample number is marked as described above.

The size of the samples depends upon the sampling strategy chosen and on the size of the thin section that will eventually be made. A convenient, average size block of $10 \times 6 \times 6$ cm is normally adequate.

THE MICROSCOPIC APPROACH

4.1 **Introduction**

In the previous chapter we discussed some of the practical considerations involved in field work, the first phase in a micromorphological study. In this chapter we make the bridge between field work and micromorphological observation and consider some of the techniques of microscopy and thin-section preparation.

Although the first microscopes were designed at the beginning of the seventeenth century, it was not until the intervention of the polarising microscope in the 1850s that the microscope became a scientific instrument of immense importance to many disciplines, from medicine to geology and botany to metallurgy, and remained so until the increased use of the electron microscope in the last 30 years suggested a decline in interest in the optical microscope. However, it is clear today that submicroscopic techniques cannot ursurp the place of the light microscope.

Before the end of the last century, methods for identifying minerals and rocks were more or less known and technical advances concerning thin-section preparation of rocks had tapered off by the first half of the twentieth century. Moreover, the recent technical improvements in resolution and more powerful magnification have not advanced our basic understanding of rocks but simply improved our knowledge in some specific fields, notably the mineralogy and geometric arrangement of fine particles.

On the other hand, progress in the study of undisturbed samples of loose material with microscopic techniques has advanced recently and has continued to make progress because of the increased interest in soil micromorphology since the 1930s. Although there were initially technical problems in producing indurated samples, these have been overcome within the last 30 years by the introduction of petroleum-based products that can successfully impregnate soils and soft sediments.

It is rather surprising to note that microscopic techniques were applied to the study of archaeological sediments and soils only recently, in spite of the fact that the optical and scanning electron microscopes were already commonly used in archaeology to identify pollen, charcoal, phytoliths and the microwear patterns on flint tools, and to analyse the petrography of ceramics, stone axes and cherts.

With existing microscopic techniques it is possible to investigate the same sample in increasing detail, from the naked eye to the highest magnification. Furthermore, we may distinguish two continuous – or at least semi-continuous – spectra of microscopic observations:

> volume-based studies of three-dimensional surfaces of clods observed with the naked eye, binocular and scanning electron microscopes (SEM) and
>
> areal or planar observations involving the study of thin sections with the naked eye, standard micro-film reader, and polarising microscope (MPol), and of ultra-thin sections with the transmitted electron microscope (TEM).

In addition, there are several instruments used for microanalysis – more widely called **microprobes** – that operate in conjunction with MPol, SEM and TEM. Each of these instruments can be linked with a photographic system and the various types of resulting photomicrographs can be compared.

Below we explain and illustrate the essential principles of the most commonly used microscopic tools as well as summarise the specific treatment required for each type of observation. Since this book concentrates on the study of thin sections using the polarising microscope, major emphasis will be placed on the observation of thin sections prepared from undisturbed samples (see, e.g., Bisdom, 1981; Bisdom and Ducloux, 1983 for information on submicroscopic techniques).

We have decided not to explain the details of the fundamental principles and applications of different submicroscopic techniques because, with the exception of the SEM, most of them have not been applied to the study of archaeological sediments and soils and their potential uses in this field have still to be explored. However, some possible applications in this field are proposed at the end of this chapter.

4.2 **Techniques of optical microscopy**
4.2.1 *The optical and polarising microscope*
A beam of light can either be reflected by the object under study (reflected light) or pass through it (transmitted light). In geology and pedology, reflected light microscopy is used to study polished, impregnated blocks, thin sections, rock surfaces and sand grains. When the microscope is equipped for observation with transmitted polarised light, only thin sections can be studied. Polychromatic light sources are most commonly utilised but special wavelengths can also be selected for specific purposes, such as fluorescence miscroscopy. A useful set of equipment comprises the polarising microscope itself, a fluorescent attachment and a fibre optic light source for reflected light.

The resolution of individual objects in thin section depends upon two factors. One concerns the propagation of light by waves, so that the resolution power of the light microscope itself is limited to 2,000 nm (or 2 microns). Thus, two points cannot be seen as distinct entities below 2,000 nm, which requires an effective magnification of 1,000 × . Beyond this limit the eye will not be able to detect any new detail. A second factor is related to the thickness of the thin section (25–30 μm), below which it is difficult to discern most individual particles, although small (a few microns in diameter), highly contrasted particles such as charcoal can be recognised.

Even at the lowest microscopic magnifications (ca. × 20), only a few square millimetres of a slide can be studied. To examine larger fields a standard microfilm reader is commonly employed that facilitates the correlation between observations made at macroscopic and microscopic scales.

4.2.1.1 Observation under transmitted light

Polarising microscopes are equipped with two nicols or polarising filters, which aid in the study and measurement of optical properties of crystalline and amorphous substances. When the nicols are parallel, crystals or substances are said to be observed under **plane polarised light** (PPL) or plane light. On the other hand, when the nicols are crossed, crystals are said to be observed under **crossed polarised light** or crossed nicols (XPL).

A standard microscope has four or five objectives (Plate I), which furnish total magnifications ranging from 10 up to 1,000 times. The eyepiece, normally with magnifications of 8 × to 12 × , is commonly equipped with a micrometer, which permits the observer to measure the size and abundance of various objects at each magnification. Observations with the polarising microscope, even at the lowest magnifications, permit the study of only a few square millimetres. The polarising microscope is especially designed to investigate specific properties of minerals (see Moorhouse, 1959; Kerr, 1959; Carozzi, 1960; Wahlstrom, 1979; Scholle, 1978, 1979; Tucker, 1981 for details).

Under plane light there are several properties of minerals which aid in their description and identification. These are described briefly below.

Colour and pleochroism. Minerals are generally classed as opaque or non-opaque:

Opaque minerals are normally studied in reflected light and the colour, lustre and cleavage are noted (see below). In reflected light pieces of charcoal, for example, can sometimes be distinguished from grains of oxide by their internal structure.

Non-opaque minerals are by and large the most commonly studied and they may be colourless or noticeably coloured. Some exhibit **pleochroism**, or changes in colour with rotation of the microscope stage.

Crystal form is a useful characteristic for identifying minerals that have well-developed crystal faces. Common crystal forms are cubic, quadratic, orthorhombic, monoclinic, triclinic, rhombohedric and hexagonal.

We can also consider the degree of development of the crystal face: **euhedral** crystals or grains are those which are well formed and have grown in an unrestricted environment; **subhedral** crystals show only part of their crystal form because of some constraints during their growth; when the crystal form is absent, grains or crystals are said to be **anhedral**.

Analysis of form can thus help in the reconstruction of the environmental conditions of crystal growth, although the original form of crystals within sediments and soils is not easily identifiable because grains are commonly broken or rounded. Nevertheless, form is a valuable criterion for studying secondary crystals and for some strongly resistant crystals such as pyrite, garnet, olivine, hornblende, sphene and tourmaline.

Cleavage defines the way in which minerals break apart and aids greatly in their identification. Certain minerals such as mica and talc exhibit one direction of cleavage, whereas others – hornblende, orthoclase and pyroxene – exhibit two. Commonly, the angle between two cleavage directions is diagnostic as for example the mineral hornblende where the two cleavage planes meet at an angle of 56°; for plagioclase this angle is close to 90°.

Shape is another property that characterises certain minerals. For example, a flaky shape is the most common one for mica.

Refractive index and relief are criteria used for identifying transparent minerals and are determined with plane light through careful observation of the grain boundary of the mineral. The relief is the distinctness a mineral displays with reference to the medium it is mounted in and is dependent on the difference in refractive index between the two. In impregnated samples the refractive index of mineral grains and crystals is compared to that of the resin (polyester refractive index is about 1.54). Minerals display a high relief if their refractive index is greatly different from that of the impregnative resins; this becomes lower as it approaches the refractive index of the medium. Thus in a polyester mounting medium, zircon (refractive index of *c*.1.67) has a high relief whereas feldspar (index of *c*. 1.53) has low relief.

4.2.1.2 Properties under crossed nicols

Additional and often diagnostic properties are observable under crossed polarised light. **Isotropic minerals** are transparent or coloured under plane polarised light but become and remain dark when the nicols are crossed and the stage rotated. All minerals crystallising in the isometric crystallographic system and amorphous substances such as glass, opal and most impregnative resins show this property. The isotropism of the latter readily allows us to recognise void spaces.

Anisotropic minerals transmit coloured light under crossed nicols but become dark four times when the stage of the microscope is rotated 360°. Light refracted by anisotropic minerals is divided into two paths of different refractive index. The numerical difference between these two is easily appreciated under crossed nicols and its value is called the **birefringence**. We usually speak of *low* (e.g., quartz: 0.009), *medium* (hornblende: 0.016 to 0.025) and *high* birefringence (calcite: 0.172). Under crossed nicols, the light transmitted by anisotropic minerals exhibits a specific range of wavelengths depending essentially upon the type of crystal. These are called **interference colours** and vary according to the orientation and the thickness of the minerals.

When the thickness of the thin section is known, the birefringence of a mineral can be estimated from a chart (Figure 4.1) by noting the maximum interference colour. At the standard thickness of thin sections ($25\,\mu$m to $30\,\mu$m), the interference colour of quartz varies from light grey to white, which is in the first order, whereas calcite has a bright white interference colour in the higher orders.

Under **circularly polarised light** anisotropic minerals are never extinct. This is very useful in the study of the distribution of some specific constituents, such as clay coatings, quartz or calcium carbonate.

Other optical properties, such as axial figures, sign elongation and dispersion, are also useful criteria for identifying minerals and each can be measured under the polarising microscope using additional equipment (condenser, Bertrand lenses, accessory plates).

Interference differential contrast microscopy utilises a substage condenser in order to increase the definition of fine constituents. This is especially useful with transparent minerals of weak birefringence (Plate Ie).

4.2.1.3 Dark field
With this technique a special shutter is placed below the stage of the petrographic microscope in the path of the transmitted light. This produces a dark background around the image, roughly similar to the effect of using semi-reflected/transmitted light. It is useful in the recognition of iron, charcoal and carbonates.

4.2.2 *Reflected light*
Reflected microscopy is based on the principle that absorption or reflection of emitted light varies according to the type of object illuminated. Objects can be differentiated under reflected light by their reflective power, which can be defined as the ratio of reflective intensity to emitted intensity. Reflective intensity can be appreciated by the eye or measured more precisely when the light microscope is equipped with a photo-electric cell. In the normal reflected-light microscope the light beam is perpendicular to the object. Another practical method is to light the object from the side (**oblique incident light**), preferably with a strong light source (e.g., fibre optics). Reflected light is commonly used to identify opaque and quasi-opaque minerals. Thus, ferruginous oxides and hydroxides can be differentiated from humic features. However, as they are commonly intermixed in soils, impregnation by one component can completely mask the optical characteristics of the other. Nevertheless, burning of iron-rich mineral matter shows up red in oxidising conditions and black under reducing conditions.

4.2.3 *Fluorescence microscopy*
Fluorescence microscopy is based on the property of a number of substances to emit secondary luminous energy of higher wavelength when they are excited by

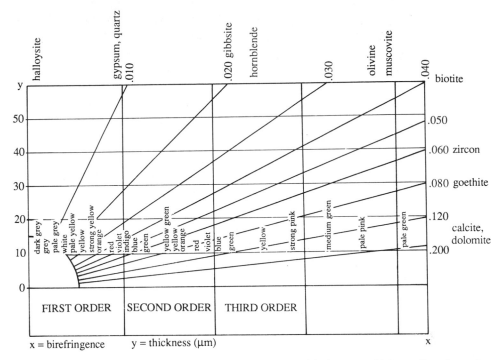

Figure 4.1   Diagram illustrating the relationship between thickness (in microns), birefringence and interference colour of commonly occurring minerals. (The interference colours are given for *c*. 30 μm thick thin section.)

primary energy of short wavelength such as green light, blue light, ultra-violet light and infra-red light. The wavelength of this secondary luminous energy is specific to the nature of the substance excited.

Specific filters are placed between the exciting source and the object (exciting filters) and between the object and the eye (stopping filters). These filters can be adapted for both reflected light and transmitted light. In transmitted light the image has to be observed using a dark field condenser and much of the excited emitted beam is absorbed. Consequently, observation in reflected light gives a more precise image and is recommended. The intensity of the fluorescence observed for a given constituent is related to the characteristics of the filters and the types of objectives used. Thus observations of fluorescence colours should indicate the types of filters and lighting conditions (reflected vs. transmitted).

Fluorescence microscopy detects with great sensitivity substances which cannot be observed under usual types of lighting conditions, as, for example, phosphate minerals or impurities within minerals. Thus, the accumulation of phosphate, which is quite common in archaeological materials (bones, coprolites), can be more easily detected. Fluorescence is also valuable in the study of organic matter. Fresh and slightly decomposed organic components have very bright fluorescence colours, which decrease in intensity upon decomposition. A large number of organic components can be identified, such as cellulose, lignified tissues, spores, exines, pollen (Plate Id) and chlorophyll. However, the latter, like many highly soluble organic components, is often dissolved by the resins. Intensity and colour of fluorescence also vary when the substance is excited for a long time. Known as 'fading', this property is used to study the evolution of fossil organic substances.

The use of highly fluorescent resins should be avoided if the natural fluorescence of constituents is eventually to be studied. This is mentioned because many workers make it standard practice to add fluorescent dye to the impregnating medium. Fluorescent components can be added to the resin, however, in order to study the void pattern or to monitor the distribution of some specific components, such as organic substances.

4.3 **Scanning electron microscopy (SEM)**

Scanning electron microscopes offer the opportunity to study the three-dimensional aspects of objects at a continuous range of magnifications that varies typically from $\times 100$ to $\times 60,000$. The surface of a specimen is scanned by a focused beam of high-energy electrons. When bombarded with electrons, substances emit a large number of signals, the most common of which are: secondary and back-scattered electrons, X-ray, photonic radiation and transmitted electrons. Each of these signals can be analysed by specific detectors.

Detection and imaging of *secondary electrons* is one of the basic functions of the standard scanning electron microscope (SEM). Secondary electrons are captured and their energies are transformed into an electric current that produces an electronic image of the surface of the sample, thus permitting the study of the surface structure. As there are no lenses between the sample and the display screen, the SEM produces images with great depth of field at all magnifications (100 to 500 times greater than the light microscope), and the images obtained are in a sense three-dimensional electron optical data. The useful resolution obtained by the SEM is about 7 to 3 nm.

The scanning electron microscope is commonly used to study clods (aggregates, grains) a few centimetres in size, although similar sized domains cut out from thin sections can also be observed after impregnative resins have been removed. As SEM images are colourless and exhibit only slight differences in grey colour, samples have to be oriented and described carefully so that colour variations not visible under the SEM can be precisely located. For clods this is done under a binocular microscope and for thin sections under a polarising microscope. A sketch of the sample will also help to correlate the macroscopic and microscopic observations with the submicroscopic ones. In order to make the samples electrically conductive, they are coated with a thin, continuous film of metal (gold, platinum) or carbon.

Scanning electron microscopes have been used for many years to study unconsolidated sediments, since no specific treatment is required. The most

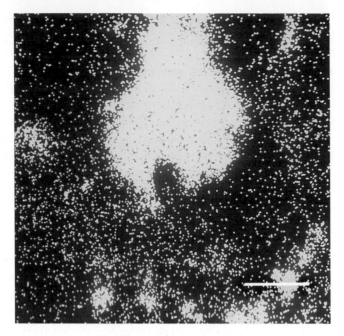

Figure 4.2   Surface X-ray detection of calcium in a burnt organic layer. The
concentrations of white in the X-ray image display the distribution of calcium
derived from the ashes of a burnt root fragment. (Bar = 94 μm)

common applications relate to morphological investigations of the constituents, such as clay minerals, calcium carbonate crystals, humic acids or plant
phytoliths. The study of surface features of individual detrital grains
(exoscopy), notably quartz, has been used to reconstruct the detailed history of
each grain (Le Ribault, 1977). Rock weathering and structural behaviour of
soils can also be characterised.

4.4 The microprobe – Energy dispersive X-ray analyser (EDXRA)

Elemental analysis can be performed by the microprobe. A sample bombarded
with electrons emits X-rays of specific wavelengths which can be analysed by an
energy dispersive detector system. Elements with atomic weights ranging from
those of beryllium (= 9) to uranium (= 238) can be detected. In addition to
elemental analysis of a micro-area, it is possible to obtain both a line profile –
which displays the density distribution of elements throughout the scanned
surface – and a two-dimensional analysis of this surface (Figure 4.2). The
distribution of elements that are difficult to detect in thin section (e.g., iron [Fe],
phosphorous [P] or manganese [Mn]) are clearly visible with the microprobe.
However, elements that are present only in small amounts ($<0.1\%$) are
difficult to detect.

With the recent advent of equipment combining SEM and microprobe
analysis, both elemental and structural analyses can be carried out simulta-

neously. In the most modern electron microscopes, resolution down to the atomic level is possible.

4.5 Additional ultra-microscopic techniques

4.5.1 *Transmitted scanning electron microscopes (STEM)* are equipped with a detector for *transmitted electrons*, thus permitting observation of internal structure. In addition to the morphology seen in transmission, electron beam and convergent beam micro-diffraction patterns can be obtained. This system needs further development before it can be employed more routinely.

4.5.2 *Back-scattered electrons* are produced when a beam of high-energy electrons strikes a sample and the electrons are elastically back-scattered. Elements can be differentiated on the electronic image by their brightness and thus atoms of the heavier elements which possess higher back-scattering properties, appear brighter. Back-scattered electrons are detected and visually displayed by the same system as that used with secondary electrons but they provide better three-dimensional definition of morphology. Because of their high quality at high magnifications, images given by back-scattered electrons are the most suitable for measurement studies, especially of micro-void patterns (Figure 4.3). Back-scattered electrons are used to investigate *atomic number contrast* and *topographical contrast*.

4.5.3 *Transmission electron microscopes (TEM)*

The transmission electron microscope (TEM) is built on the same principle as that of the optical microscope but light is replaced by an electron beam, and optical lenses by electromagnetic ones; electrons are transmitted onto a fluorescent screen. The resolving power is up to 1,000 times better than the light microscope and objects of only a few nanometres can be recognised.

The transmission electron microscope can be used to study suspensions or thin sections that are very thin (not exceeding a few hundred to a few thousand nm) and essentially transparent to electrons. Such 'ultra-thin sections' cannot be obtained by normal mechanical grinding or polishing, and other thinning techniques are needed. Ultra-microtomy can be used for homogeneous, soft materials such as pure mineralogical clays, whereas thinning by ion bombardment is better suited to heterogeneous materials, although in most cases the final thickness is irregular.

Selection of samples for studying under TEM is carried out with the polarising microscope on standard thin sections. The selected area is cut out and an ultra-thin section prepared. As with the SEM, the TEM can also be equipped with wavelength dispersive X-ray spectrometers or energy X-ray analyser.

High-resolution transmission microscopes are used to study the crystallographic spacing of clays at the nanometric level and individual clay minerals

Figure 4.3   Back-scattered electron image. Microporosity in the massive wall of a termite channel flanked by loosely packed pseudo-excrements. From a thin section of an oxisol in Kenya. (Photo by Dr E.B.A. Bisdom). (Bar = 280 μm)

can thus be identified. The TEM is also a suitable tool for investigating organic matter and processes of humification.

4.5.4 Several methods have recently appeared – e.g., *Auger electron spectroscopy* (AES) and *Particle induced X-ray emission* (PIXE) – which offer great potential for performing microanalyses on samples with low atomic number. Most of these, however, require further development before they can be routinely applied to soils and archaeological samples.

4.6 Non-electronic microchemical analyses
In addition to an electronic beam, other types of energy can be used to bombard or excite a specimen. Some of the more common methods include:

4.6.1 *Electron spectroscopy for chemical analyses (ESCA)*
With this technique a sample is irradiated with X-rays or ultra-violet photons and the ejected photo-electrons are collected. From the energy of the ejected electron, it is possible to detect all elements except hydrogen and to make inferences about the types of bonding present in compounds.

The size dimensions of the analysed portion of the sample are limited to a surface of about 3 nm and a depth of between 2 to 10 nm, a limiting factor in analysing heterogeneous samples. The minimum detectable concentration is 0.1%.

4.6.2 *Ion microprobe mass analyser (IMMA) and secondary ion mass spectrometry (SIMS)*

A sample observed through a binocular microscope is bombarded with a beam of energised ions which causes ejection of atoms at the surface of the sample. A fraction of the ejected particles will be charged and their secondary ions will be collected in a mass spectrometer according to their mass-to-charge ratio. With *ion microscopy* there is no limitation as to atomic number and it is possible to measure even trace concentrations. The second generation of instrumentation (SIMS) allows quantification analysis with an uncertainty of only a few per cent. Ion microscopy will usually constitute the final stage of *in situ* soil research.

4.6.3 *Laser microprobe mass analyser (LAMMA)*

In this case a laser is used to bombard the sample and the generated ions are analysed by a mass spectrometer at the same time as a high-quality optical microscope views the sample. Elements with atomic numbers between 3 and 92 can be analysed over a surface of a few square microns. However, only very thin sections can be used. The LAMMA has the advantages of not requiring special sample treatment and of being relatively inexpensive. The technique is limited, however, by the fact that the surface analysed is destroyed by the laser beam, so that no image of the distribution of the elements can be obtained.

4.6.4 *Raman molecular optical laser examiner (Raman MOLE) or laser microspectral analyser (LMA)*

These techniques study the spectral distribution of inelastically scattered light by the irradiation of the sample with a monogenetic beam of light (laser beam). Constituents present on a surface of only a few square microns are analysed. It is a non-destructive method that has become routinely practicable. It can be focused at a point or used to produce an image of the distribution of elements.

4.7 Microradiography of thin sections

Microradiography provides the opportunity to examine large-scale attributes of a sample, such as bedding, structure and porosity. A thin section or a slice of the block from which it has been prepared is placed on a piece of X-ray film and irradiated with 'soft' X-rays such as those used in hospitals. Exposure times and doses vary according to composition of the sample and thickness of the block (Carver, 1971). In comparison to the quantitative analysis of microprobe techniques, this is a qualitative, inexpensive method that is easily applied.

4.8 Staining techniques of thin sections or polished blocks

Qualitative microchemical determination can be obtained by staining or bleaching a thin section or polished block with specific solutions (Carver, 1971). The distribution of an element, mineral or chemical substance can be observed under the polarising microscope, using fluorescent light if it is needed. Staining is commonly used in rock petrography to discriminate orthoclase from plagioclase and calcite from dolomite. In soil materials staining can be applied to differentiate various organic constituents or to emphasise the void pattern (Figure 4.4a). After staining, humic compounds, for example, are more easily distinguishable from brown iron oxides.

4.9 Quantification

Quantitative characterisation of different components can be obtained using image analysing systems such as the Quantimet 720. The image formed by an electronic or an optical microscope is scanned with a video-camera and transformed into picture points. These are then converted into electrical pulses that are classified by their levels of grey. These differences in greyness permit the distinction between grains and voids, for example (Figure 4.4). Because of the small field of view of the microscopes, only a few square millimetres can be scanned at a time. Scanning of larger fields can be done, however, from photographs obtained by placing the thin section in a photographic enlarger. Different patterns can then be classified according to the problems selected: sizes and shapes of both grains and voids (Figure 4.4a and b). Area, perimeter, orientation and irregularity can also be sketched and determined. Shape characterisation, for example, can be used to differentiate alluvial sands from aeolian ones.

When a Quantimet or similar system is not available, semi-quantitative analysis using *point-counting techniques* is useful. Point counting can be carried out by hand or automatically and the abundance, distribution and morphology of voids and coarse components can thus be estimated. However, a detailed study of the morphology of the void pattern would require a three-dimensional analysis. This can be effected by using a group of serial thin sections cut from the same block or from the study of the block itself under reflected light. The latter is by far the cheaper solution.

In summary, with the development of new techniques, *in situ* microchemical analyses of soil materials can be obtained from thin sections, polished blocks or unconsolidated materials. All the elements in the periodic table can be detected and quantified, and the chemical bonding of atoms can be characterised. However, problems of correlation between observations at low magnification using the optical microscope and submicroscopic ones using sophisticated electronic techniques are far from being solved and compatibility between the different techniques needs to be improved.

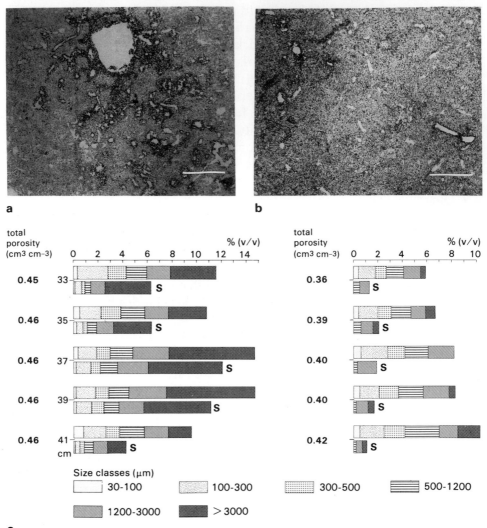

Figure 4.4   Two photographs of horizontal thin sections made of stained soil samples: (a) grassland with large faunal channels and smaller root channels and (b) arable land with a compacted layer in which only root channels occur. The stained voids have dark-coloured walls. Depth of the sections 37 cm. (Bars = 10 mm) In (c) is shown the pore-size distribution of voids > 30 microns ∅ of these thin sections measured by image analysis with a Quantimet 720. A is for grassland and B is for arable lands. The upper histogram for each pair gives the total porosity whereas the lower is only those of the voids with stained walls. (Courtesy of the Soil Survey Institute, Wageningen, the Netherlands)

In a similar vein, the researcher should also be aware of the non-continuity of the levels of observation with the optical microscope. Thus, depending upon the available configuration of objectives and eyepieces, the observer jumps from one magnification to another without being able to monitor a feature over a continuous range of magnifications. Such a technical limitation, which induces artificial gaps in our observations, does not exist for the SEM, for example, where a continuous range of magnifications is available at the turn of a dial.

4.10 **Thin-section preparation**

Having considered several of the techniques used to study thin sections, we now discuss the methods used to prepare them. We stress here that the key to a successful micromorphological study is obviously a high-quality thin section which encompasses proper treatment of the sample from the field through successive steps of drying, impregnation and grinding (Jongerius and Heintzberger, 1963; Brewer, 1964; FitzPatrick, 1984; Murphy, 1986).

4.10.1 *Drying and Impregnation*

As noted in the section on sampling, samples must be protected from physical disturbances during both transportation and preparation in order to preserve their original field morphology. Once in the laboratory, they should be moved as little as possible prior to impregnation, particularly in the case of loose materials.

Since many of the standard media used to impregnate the samples are non-miscible with water, it is imperative that any traces of moisture be completely removed from the samples before impregnation. In most cases this can be effected in a drying-oven at 40–60°C. Increasing the temperature in steps will avoid severe disturbances and prevent the appearance of artifactual defects, such as cracking. However, for materials very rich in clay or organic matter and those containing abundant water (e.g., peat, mud, lake deposits) or salt, drying at room temperature, even if gradual, will create drastic changes in the original morphology of the sample (e.g., development of large cracks, decomposition of fresh organic matter and the crystallisation of salts around the outside of the samples). In order to prevent or minimise such phenomena, materials can be freeze-dried or the water can be slowly replaced by acetone before impregnation. In the case of the latter, the samples are immersed in liquid acetone, although with this procedure clayey materials risk collapse. To avoid this, acetone vapour is commonly used, and replacement by acetone is usually complete after a few months. Results from various experiments designed to evaluate these problems suggest that thin sections prepared by the replacement method are of better quality than those made by freeze-drying techniques. There is the possibility, however, that acetone can remove soluble humic substances.

In order to ensure optimal impregnation, penetrating resins should possess the following characteristics:

> low viscosity that enhances impregnation by capillary action;
> good transparency, stable refractive index, and be isotropic and non auto-fluorescent;
> non-reactivity with soil substances (although reactions with very soluble substances are difficult to avoid);
> stable composition to ensure regular polymerisation and hardening;
> only weakly exothermic reaction;
> hardness when cured;
> low toxicity and low cost.

Viscosity is usually decreased by the addition of an organic agent, either acetone, monostyrene, acrylic monomer or propylene oxide. Lowering of the viscosity by heating the resin should be avoided because some substances (e.g., gypsum) can react with hot resin.

Besides the addition of an organic dilutant, a small quantity of catalyst is necessary to start the polymerisation. Since this is an exothermic reaction, slow polymerisation is desirable in order to avoid unwanted heating of the sample. For this reason the addition of an accelerator to speed up the rate of polymerisation is cautiously recommended. Other substances can be added for specific purposes, such as colouring or fluorescent dyes, provided that they do not modify the properties of the resins.

Three classes of resins can be distinguished on the basis of chemical composition.

> The **unsaturated polyesters** are the most commonly used since they satisfy most of the above conditions.
>
> The **epoxy resins** – the best-known being Araldite – are of very good quality but are less commonly used for soil materials because of their higher viscosity in comparison with that of the unsaturated polyester resins. Furthermore, they are more expensive than the polyester resins and can react with weathered materials and produce swelling.
>
> Other resins are sometimes employed for specific reasons. **Metacrylate**, for example, is used because of its very low viscosity, although it is highly toxic. **Carbowax** has the advantage of being soluble in water and suitable for studying water-saturated samples, such as peats. However, it is anisotropic, which makes observation difficult and tiring, and the impregnated blocks are rather soft.

The common procedure for impregnation can be outlined as follows (Figure 4.5):

1   The sample or samples are placed on a leak-proof tray or container (e.g., aluminium foil tray), which is put into a vacuum chamber; a vacuum is required to encourage capillary rise.
2   The impregnating mixture is added to the sample container in small quantities by dripping it from a large vessel outside the chamber; the resin is allowed to rise up into the samples by capillary action (Figure 4.5b). When the resin has reached the upper part of the sample, the sample container can be completely topped up. Because the

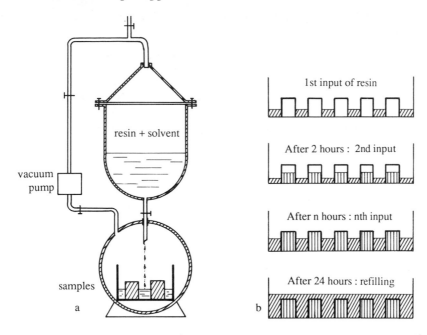

Figure 4.5 (a) Diagram of apparatus used in impregnating samples under vacuum. (b) Diagram illustrating the gradual capillary rise of the resin in the samples with time.

vapours are toxic, sample impregnation (and later polymerisation) should be allowed to take place in a ventilated room, preferably under a hood, in which the temperature is stabilised at about 20°C. Polymerisation will take one to three months, depending upon the amount of hardener used, the freshness of the resin, temperature, etc. When the impregnated block is moderately hard, complete hardening is achieved by placing it for a few days in an oven at a temperature of 40–50°C. Exposure to ultra-violet light also accelerates the polymerisation process.

Even when these procedures have been followed carefully, impregnation is sometimes incomplete and this will naturally affect the quality of the finished thin section. Samples with closed pores, for example, are difficult to impregnate. In addition, resins or solvents sometimes react with certain substances and create artifacts which can limit subsequent observations and interpretations.

4.10.2 *Grinding*
Once cool, samples are removed from the container and are ready for sawing with a diamond saw. Generally, 5-mm-thick slices are cut from the impregnated blocks and ground to the required thickness. Grinding by hand on a flat surface with powders (carborundum or corindon) or on turning abrasive discs is no longer commonly used for soil materials as it does not produce large, well-planed surfaces. Industrial semi-automatic and automatic machines have been available for more than 20 years and are of the same basic type as those used for

Figure 4.6   Automatic thin-section machine (type SNPA). Samples mounted on glass slides and placed on a rotating disc at the right are ground down by lap wheel (left), which successively thins the sample. (Courtesy of G. Brot Ltd.)

the preparation of thin sections from rocks, although for soils they have to be modified for the larger size of the sections. In contrast with the preparation of rock thin sections, the cooling liquid used with soils is not water but kerosene (paraffin) or another non-polar liquid which prevents clays from swelling and being washed out. The polishing machine can be equipped with a grinding cylinder – embedded with carborundum or diamond dust – that rotates above a plate on which the slices are fixed. A more economical model is equipped with a grinding disc consisting of a diamond rim that moves parallel to another disc on which the samples are fixed (Figure 4.6). Both systems can be geared to a precision of about 1 μm, which permits automatic thin-section preparation to a thickness of 25–30 μm. Sometimes final polishing by hand is required because unconsolidated materials are heterogeneous and very hard parts do not respond to grinding and polishing in the same way as soft areas. The use of loose corindon powder for the final polishing is not recommended as some fine corindon grains penetrate the resin and produce a dusty aspect which can alter the character of the original material; fine-grained emery paper (600 or 800 grade) gives better results.

The above sequence of operations can vary according to the type of machine used and the skill of the operator. The method employed by Guilloré (1985) gives very satisfactory results and 12 very large (14.5 cm × 6.5 cm) thin sections can be prepared within one day (Figure 4.7). This sequence can be outlined as follows:

1   Using a non-permanent pressure adhesive such as contact cement, glue a slice of impregnated material to a glass slide.
2   Grind the slice using a coarse disc (360 μm) to remove all irregularities, and then a very fine grinding disc (600 μm) to polish the face.

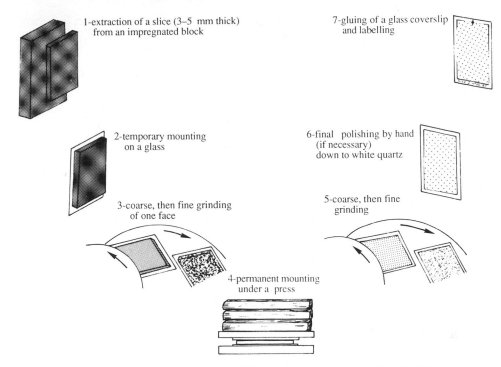

1-extraction of a slice (3–5 mm thick) from an impregnated block

7-gluing of a glass coverslip and labelling

2-temporary mounting on a glass

6-final polishing by hand (if necessary) down to white quartz

3-coarse, then fine grinding of one face

5-coarse, then fine grinding

4-permanent mounting under a press

Figure 4.7 The main stages of thin section manufacture. (Modified from Guilloré, 1985)

3 Grind one face of another glass slide so it will be of uniform and regular thickness.
4 Permanently glue the polished face of the slice to the polished side of the glass, using the same resin as that used for impregnation but with a greater amount of catalyst in order to achieve rapid hardening (1 to 2 hours). A press is required to produce both a very regular and thin layer of glue.
5 Remove the first, non-permanent glass slide.
6 Grind the slice to 25 μm using the coarse and then the very fine grinding discs.
7 If the thin sections have to be studied only under an optical microscope, glue a glass coverslip, using the same glue as in (4). If microchemical analyses have to be performed, leave them uncovered or if necessary polish them more finely using diamond paste 0.1 μm in size.

4.10.3 *Hints for making good thin sections*
In conclusion we present here an inventory of the most critical steps in making good thin sections.

Transportation and drying: During transportation the sample should be handled carefully in order to ensure its integrity. This and slow drying prevent the development of an induced porosity which could totally mask the original one. Complete drying of the sample is a requisite for effective impregnation.

Impregnation: Critical here is the ability of the sample to take up the resin, which itself is controlled by the physical characteristics of the material (e.g., amount and type of clay), as well as by the viscosity of the impregnating medium. Our experience has shown that slow rates of impregnation (of about one month) and dilute mixtures of resin will produce satisfactory results in most cases.

Grinding: It should always be kept in mind that, in comparison to rocks, the polyester resins are relatively soft materials. Consequently, heating, which can induce anisotropism, and the use of grinding powders should be avoided. During the final stages, care should be taken to avoid fracturing the mineral grains.

5

THIN-SECTION DESCRIPTION

5.1 **Introduction**

A sample consists of the solid fraction and voids, which are described differently in different disciplines. Geologists, for example, focusing on dynamic sedimentary processes, tend to emphasize the solid phases and concentrate on composition and texture and less on porosity. Soil scientists, on the other hand, are more concerned with *in situ* physico-chemical processes – commonly referred to as pedogenesis – that act on a given parent material; crucial to the pedologist's understanding of these processes and of the historical development of the soil profile is the organisation of the material and the void pattern. Lastly, a person studying archaeological soils and sediments must not only deal with the above properties but also with those that relate to human impacts on soils and sediments (anthropic/anthropogenic effects).

The scheme of thin-section observation and description proposed in this chapter represents a certain compromise between those used in geology and those used in pedology and has been modified to include archae-ological/anthropic materials. Each 'layer' (or field unit – see Chapter 4) represents the combined effects of sedimentary, pedological and anthropogenic processes whose physical result are what we call *features* which are identifiable at various scales, from field to microscopic. Thus, the basic aim of a micromorphological study is to amass a catalogue-like inventory of sedimentary, anthropogenic and pedological and other post-depositional features that provide the key for the interpretation.

While most sedimentary and pedological features are reasonably well understood and their identification made by comparison with available reference texts, only a few records and descriptions of archaeological materials and anthropic features have so far entered the literature; many have either never been discussed or have yet to be interpreted. As a result, the following chapter cannot provide a universal key for describing and interpreting archaeological sediments and soils in thin section, and instead should be regarded only as a working guide that is based upon the combined experience of the three authors; in the years to come, knowledge of these materials will improve as they are increasingly studied. For this reason it is difficult to give precise 'rules' concerning archaeological thin-section description, and the worker needs to be guided by his/her own interests or by the questions posed by the archaeologist or the site itself. We suggest, therefore, that the proposed descriptive scheme (Figure 5.1) should be viewed as a flexible document that should be adapted to the requirements of each study.

The problem still remains of what exactly to put down onto paper: how much of what is observed in the section merits being described? The answer to this question is not simple, for at one extreme we risk spending hours describing endless details which ultimately may have no significance while on the other we may skip over something which at the time seemed to lack interpretative value (based on our extant experience) but later, in the light of increased experience and knowledge, is perceived as being much more important. After all, a good description is something permanent, whereas interpretations may be ephemeral. Thus once again, we attempt to strike a balance between these two extremes and below we present a scheme for observing and describing thin sections which we believe is comprehensive enough to portray the essential characteristics of the slide and serve as a basis for future interpretation but does not burden the describer or the reader with too many details.

A number of generalised attributes, such as size, composition, shape, abundance can be recognised and measured at different magnifications throughout the course of the descriptive process, being applicable to solids as well as voids. We choose to present them here in order to obviate the need to present them a number of times.

5.2 General descriptive attributes
5.2.1 *Fabric*
The term fabric is used by both geologists and soil scientists in somewhat different ways. We have opted for a rather broad definition, similar to that of the 'soil fabric' concept of Bullock *et al.* (1985: 17). Thus, fabric concerns the total organisation of the material, including the spatial arrangement, shape, size and frequency of the constituents.

5.2.2 *Colour*
The colour of any constituent can vary greatly, depending upon the thickness of the slide, the type of light employed and the magnification used. Colours are first estimated by simply looking at the slide at × 1 in plain daylight, and later described at successfully higher magnifications in PPL, XPL and OIL. This permits identification of the elements that are responsible for imparting the macroscopic colour. For example, a light grey colour observed in the field can often be related to the presence of dark micro-contrasted particles, a few microns in diameter.

5.2.3 *Grain size*
In thin section, size measurements are performed using a micrometer mounted in the eyepiece and, if desired, these results can be compared to those obtained

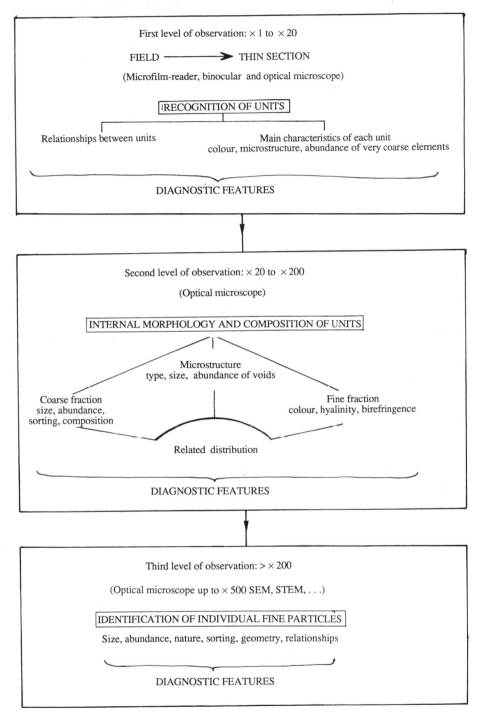

Figure 5.1   Guide to the approach to observation of thin sections.

from sieving (Friedman, 1958). More sophisticated and efficient techniques, such as computerised image analysis (see Chapter 4) produce accurate results. In any case, it should be noted that the size of grains in thin section is generally less than their maximum diameter, since the thin section cuts across the grains randomly, not necessarily in the plane of their maximum diameter.

As has previously been explained, because of the limited resolution power of the light microscope, components can be divided into two groups, the coarse and the fine fraction. The size limit between the coarse and fine fractions is not fixed but varies (commonly between 2 and 10 μm) according to the type of material studied. Once the coarse:fine (C:F) size limit has been set, it is best to keep the same limit throughout a series of slides in order to maintain compatibility. An estimate of the surface area occupied in the field of view by both the coarse and fine fraction is carried out with the help of charts, the ratio of the two areas being called the *C:F ratio*. As an example, with a C:F limit of 10 μm, a C:F ratio of 35:65 means that the materials consist of 35% coarse fraction (coarser than 10μm) and 65% fine fraction (finer than 10μm). It should be remembered that abundance estimates in thin section are areal measurements, whereas granulometric analyses using sieving are based on volumes and the results are therefore not strictly comparable.

5.2.4 *Composition*

The coarse and fine fraction may include both mineral and organic components, which should be considered separately. The **mineral fraction** may be represented by (Table 5.1):

1   **Single mineral grains** – These are individual grains that have been derived from soils, sediments or rocks. Examples: quartz, calcite, glauconite, the micas (biotite or muscovite) and opaque iron minerals.

2   **Compound mineral grains** – These include reworked fragments of soil, rock and nodules. Examples: granite, limestone, schist, humic soil fragments, clayey soil fragments.

3   **Inorganic residues of biological origin** – Such residues refer to bones, phytoliths, diatoms, fossils.

4   **Coarse fragments of human artifacts and organic materials** – Included in this category are mortar, pottery, brick and slag, organic materials (varying from roots to coprolites) and charcoal. The cellular structure of coarse fragments can be recognised and related to a specific plant tissue or organ for organic materials or to a specific plant type or charcoal.

5.2.5 *Sorting*

Related to the concepts of grain size and abundance is that of sorting, which expresses the degree of uniformity (or variability) of the different size components. Although various coefficients of sorting can be calculated, using sieve and settling-tube data (see above for problems with these techniques), rapid and very satisfactory estimates can be made from thin section with the aid of charts

Table 5.1. *The most commonly occurring single and compound mineral grains*

Single mineral grains

1 Transluscent minerals

Quartz	Plagioclase	Pyroxene
K Feldspar	Muscovite	Garnet
Biotite	Calcite	Glauconite
Hornblende	Dolomite	
Tourmaline	Gypsum	
Zircon Olivine		

2 Opaque minerals

Goethite	Magnetite	Pyrite
Haematite		

Compound mineral grains

1 Igneous rocks
Volcanic glass
Basalt/Gabbro
Granite/Rhyolite
Diorite/Andesite

2 Metamorphic rocks
Quartzite
Marble
Gneiss
Schist

3 Sedimentary rocks
Limestone
Dolomite
Various sandstones (quartzose, arkose, greywacke . . .)
Conglomerate

such as those shown in Figure 5.2. A well-sorted sediment contains an overwhelming abundance (*c.* 90%) of material of a given size whereas a poorly sorted one consists of a mixture of different sizes. Unsorted deposits contain roughly equal proportions of all grain sizes.

5.2.6 *Shape and roundness*
These have long been used to infer both the *environment of deposition* and related processes of sedimentary transport.

1 **Shape** – This refers generally to the sphericity of a particle, although in thin section only two dimensions are visible and one is confined to thinking in terms of the circularity of the grain. During the past 50 years sedimentologists have proposed many methods to measure sphericity, such as the one of Wadell (1935). Such measurements, however, are generally quite tedious to perform and simpler measures of shape have been developed. For example, the ratio of these three axes can

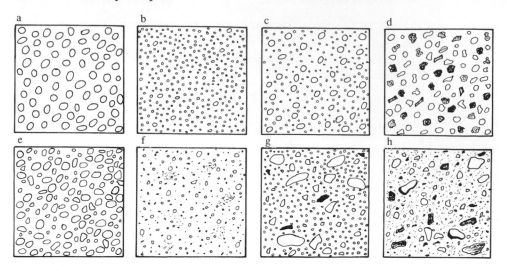

Figure 5.2   Charts used to estimate the degree of sorting of sediments viewed through the microscope:
  (a) Perfectly sorted coarse monomineralic sand
  (b) Well-sorted silt
  (c) Bimodal: well-sorted sand in well-sorted silt
  (d) Well-sorted sand of different compositions
  (e) Moderately sorted sand
  (f) Poorly sorted silt
  (g) Bimodal: poorly-sorted sand in well-sorted silt
  (h) Unsorted

also be used to characterise the general form of grains, as shown in the familiar Zingg (1935) diagram (Pettijohn, 1975).

Under the microscope, however, these three-dimensional shapes can vary from equidimensional to lozenge forms, depending upon the direction in which the grain is cut. Additional, non-quantitative terms for describing shape are platy, tabular, columnar, blocky, cylindrical, lenticular, vermiform, rod-like, fibrous, acicular, globular. Although within the last two decades much work has been done to characterise grain shapes using sophisticated techniques, such as Fourier and harmonic analysis, most micromorphological estimates of shape make use of comparative charts (Figure 5.3), which are entirely adequate for most purposes.

2 **Roundness** – Roundness concerns the sharpness of the edges and corners of the grain, and is irrespective of the grain shape. As with characterisation of shape, methods to quantify the roundness of grains exist but these are not very practicable and most researchers use two-dimensional silhouettes as above (Figure 5.3). Four rounding classes are thus represented: angular, subangular, subrounded and rounded.

5.2.7 *Abundance*

Estimation of the abundance of a particular component or any group of components can be carried out relatively quickly and with reliable results by comparing the objects in the microscopic field with patterns in abundance charts (Figure 5.4).

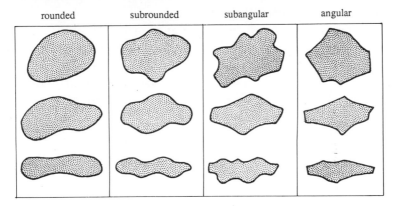

Figure 5.3   Charts used to estimate the shape and rounding of grains. (Adapted from Bullock *et al.*, 1985)

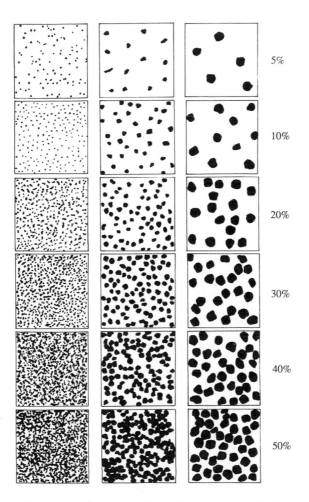

Figure 5.4   Charts to estimate the abundance of objects seen in the microscopic field. (Adapted from Bullock *et al.*, 1985)

5.3 **Approach to observation (Figure 5.1)**

A thin section must be carefully observed at a variety of scales and its features generally understood before any description is attempted, otherwise the result is a long laundry list of items of seemingly equal importance that provide no clues as to interpretation. In addition and more importantly, the researcher may fail to connect a feature observable at a low magnification (e.g., bedded layer) with its internal composition that is observable at a higher magnification (e.g., alternations of areas rich in clay, organic matter or charcoal). The degree to which the thin section is understood depends essentially upon the complexity of the material and also upon the experience of the observer. Thus, an experienced micromorphologist might require only a brief (*c.* 5 minutes) perusal of the slide at various magnifications before describing it, whereas a beginner might need to spend up to a few hours systematically looking at each feature and constituent, from low to high magnification. In any case, the final result should be a synthetic description that combines the information that has been systematically gathered, feature by feature, at each of the successive levels of observation.

5.3.1 *Mesoscopic level of observation (× 1– × 20): recognition of units*

This level of observation, commonly neglected in most micromorphological and petrographic studies, is an extremely important one for it is at this level that one links field observations with micromorphological ones. It is also here that one makes the transition from looking 'at' the various features (in the field and on polished blocks) and looking 'through' them with the microscope. Thus, a 'white layer' in the field may appear 'grey' in thin section.

At this level several different types of apparatus are employed. The binocular microscope can be used to examine not only the thin section but also the polished block from which it was prepared. This technique is particularly efficient since it affords the opportunity to make direct comparisons between the solid sample and the thin section. The microfilm reader with magnifications of about × 5 to × 20 fills in the gap between the field and the optical microscope, the minimum magnification of which is commonly × 20.

At the outset, the thin section is located in relation to its original field context (Figure 5.5), and an attempt is made to recognise the field units (as defined in Chapter 1) that were distinguished on the basis of colour, morphology and overall character. If there are no strong variations in the thin section besides the presence of millimetre-sized coarse elements (e.g., rock fragments) or of a void pattern, the thin section appears homogeneous and is seen to consist of only one unit. On the other hand, there can be large variations and the whole thin section appears more heterogeneous; for example, it can be either a vertical succession of homogeneous units with various types of boundaries (like the one in Chapter 1) or an assemblage of randomly distributed, homogeneous units. In some extreme cases, rather frequent in archaeological materials, heterogeneity can reach such a degree that it is impossible to individualise well-defined units (with

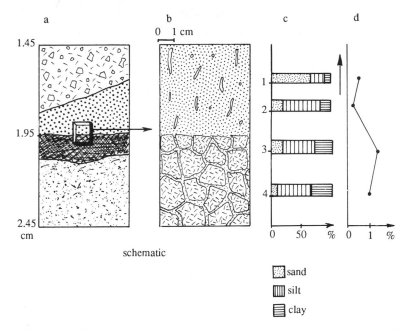

a   b   c   d

0   1 cm

1.45

1.95

2.45
cm

schematic

▨ sand

▥ silt

▤ clay

Figure 5.5   Correlations between field (a) and thin-section (b) data, particle-size analysis (c), and organic carbon content (d).

sharp boundaries) at this level of magnification; further, detailed observations must be carefully made. Such heterogeneity has high interpretative value and should be carefully noted and described.

Best observed at this low level of magnification but overlapping with higher ones are the larger elements of the coarse fraction (down to *c*. 500 μm), structure and large-scale porosity patterns.

Microstructure refers to the size, shape and arrangement of grains, aggregates and voids or in other words, the internal geometry of the soil components. It does not, however, deal with the internal fabric of the solids themselves.

For **aggregated** materials, we may use the same classification of structural types as those described in the field: crumbs, granules, subangular blocky peds, angular blocky peds and plates. For the peds themselves it is possible to assess their degree of *accommodation* – how well the peds fit together – and their degree of structural development (weak, moderate and strong) and to compare them with their expressions in the field. It is worth stressing, however, that the apparent degree of aggregation and the type of microstructure observed is a function of the magnification used and that an apparently 'homogeneous' aggregate at low magnification may be composed of smaller sub-aggregates.

For **non-aggregated** materials the description of the microstructure is limited to the study of the pattern of voids. Thus, the viewer concentrates on the morphology of the different void types and their respective abundance, size and distribution.

Pedologists recognise several types of voids, comprising packing voids,

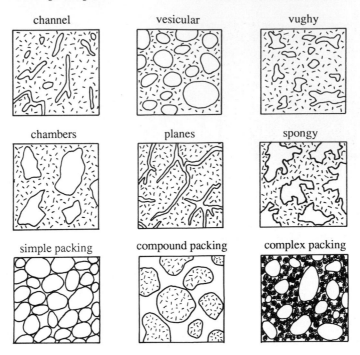

Figure 5.6   Main types of voids (vughs) following the usage of Bullock *et al.* (1985).

vughs, vesicles, channels and planes (Figure 5.6). Packing voids are further described as to sub-type, being either simple, compound or complex (Figure 5.6). Sandy, detrital sediments, being granular, are characterised mostly by the pattern of packing voids. In general, the same morphological groups are distinguished in archaeological sediments and soils although augmented with a few types specific to archaeological materials such as bricks (Figure 5.7). Finally, archaeological soils and sediments display complex microstructures of more than one type.

Also observable at this level is the manner in which the coarse and fine elements are distributed throughout the slide. A prominent example is bedding.

Once observation at this low magnification has been carried out, the researcher can begin to compare the basic microscopic components with those observed in the field and is in a position to evaluate and modify his initial field interpretations. More importantly, however, the observer now possesses some guidelines to continue effectively at the next level of magnification.

5.3.2 *Microscopic observation at low to medium magnification (× 20– × 200): description of units*

At these magnifications with the polarising microscope, we enter the first stage of true microscopic observation. The attributes of the coarse fraction (e.g., composition, size, shape) are characterised in greater detail and certain

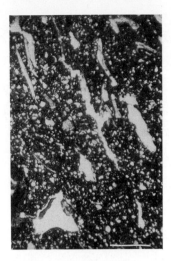

Figure 5.7   Typical narrow elongated voids and vughs associated with mud bricks (baked Harappan mud brick, Kalibangan, India). (Bar = 150 μm)

attributes of the fine matrix other than colour become more evident. Furthermore, we begin to see the geometrical relationship between these two fractions.

5.3.2.1 Fine fraction

Various properties of the fine fraction are described under transmitted and reflected light (Plate II). In **plane polarised light** (PPL), colour and limpidity are indicated, the latter being described as clear, speckled, dotted, cloudy or opaque. In **crossed polarised light** (XPL) the degree of birefringence is noted as well as the nature of the interference colours. In **oblique incident light** (OIL), the colour and character are noted.

The description of the fine fraction is generally more troublesome than that of the coarse fraction. The estimation of organic matter and charcoal within the fine fraction may be considerably more difficult than was the case for the coarse organic components. In addition, diagnostic structures are no longer recognisable and differentiation among the various types of mineral particles should be made using a combination of different lighting techniques. Finally, it is often difficult to distinguish fine charred organic components from humified ones. Recourse to additional analytical data, such as pyrophosphate extractable carbon, may be required.

5.3.2.2 The geometrical relationships between coarse and fine fractions

There are essentially five types of geometric patterns relating the coarse and fine constituents (Figure 5.8), corresponding to the concept of *related distribution* of soil micromorphologists (Stoops and Jongerius, 1975).

(a)   **Monic** ('Single population') – In this type amorphous materials or particles of uniform size occur.

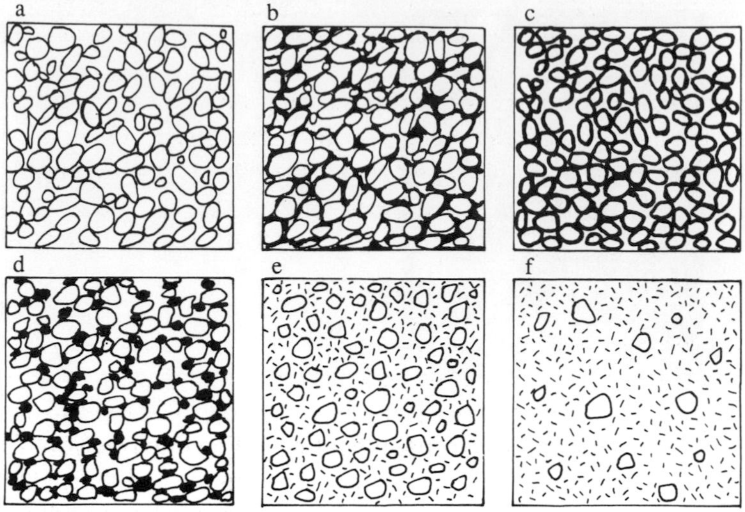

Figure 5.8   Related distribution of the coarse and fine constituents. (Modified from Bullock *et al*, 1985):
- (a) Monic
- (b) Gefuric
- (c) Chitonic
- (d) Enaulic
- (e) Close porphyric
- (f) Loose porphyric

(b)   **Gefuric** ('Linked and coated') – Finer material forms bridges or braces between the coarse particles.

(c)   **Chitonic** ('coated') – The finer material partially or entirely coats the coarser particles.

(d)   **Enaulic** ('Intergrain aggregate') – Aggregates of finer material partially fill the intergranular spaces between the coarser particles.

(e)   **Porphyric** ('Embedded') – The coarser particles occur in a matrix of finer material. Occasionally, however, the coarse material may be banded or preferentially arranged.

5.3.2.3 Birefringence fabric

Small particles cannot actually be seen observed individually under the polarising microscope. Rather, one sees the manifestations of this fabric under crossed nicols as represented by the interference colours and birefringence of the fine material and its inclusions of fine organic matter. This expression of the internal geometry is called the *b-fabric* (birefringence fabric) and is divided into two main types:

(a)   **Undifferentiated b-fabric,** when there is an absence of interference colours because the fine material is formed of isotropic or opaque minerals, or when the fine mineral material is masked by humus or sesquioxides (Plate IId).

(b)   **Crystallitic b-fabric**, when fine, birefringent materials (e.g., calcite, mica or sericite) occur in the fine mass giving it an overall birefringence (Plate IIe).

Preferred orientation of the fine matrix dominated by clay particles gives rise to a number of other different b-fabrics: **speckled b-fabric**, when particles yield a random birefringence pattern, and **striated b-fabric**, when elongated zones of birefringence show simultaneous, parallel extinction; the latter can occur in a number of patterns or be related to pores or coarse grains (see, for example, Figure 8.5a).

5.3.3 *Microscopic and ultramicroscopic observation at high magnification (> × 200): identification and geometry of elementary constituents*

At this end of the observational spectrum it is possible to resolve many issues that were not possible at lower magnifications. The fine fraction, for example, can be resolved with the optical microscope into individual particles (according to relief and contrast) and undifferentiated fine groundmass, whose respective attributes are described. The majority of micromorphological investigations using the polarising microscope terminate at magnifications of about × 500 to × 1,000, beyond which electron microscopes are more suitable. In order to resolve the individual particles of the fine mass, higher magnifications and greater resolving power are needed, such as are found with ultramicroscopic techniques (SEM, TEM).

5.4 **Concluding comments**

The recognition of the various features described above constitutes the first stage of interpreting the thin section. In order to complete the interpretation it is necessary to compare these features with existing references. In the following chapters we present the most commonly observed sedimentary, post-depositional and anthropogenic features in archaeological soils and sediments and will attempt to provide the basic keys for their recognition and understanding.

II

PROCESSES AND FEATURES

SEDIMENTS

6.1 Introduction

Researchers involved with archaeology are generally aware that many geological sediments occur in association with archaeological sites and that these sediments commonly form the basic, 'natural' material upon which subsequent pedogenic, biogenic and anthropogenic modifications operate. Moreover, in many cases an archaeological deposit has been reworked by one or more sedimentary processes. We cite as an example a distinct band of grey ashes 10 cm thick that could result from *in situ* burning or from reworking of the ashes by wind or runoff. Clearly, each of these would have different implications for both the archaeologist – the material in fact may not be *in situ* and therefore not an integral part of the 'living floor' – and for the earth-scientist, who may be able to show that the runoff event that reworked these ashes is tied to some important climatic phenomenon (e.g., flash flooding) or regime ('wetter climate'). Micromorphological data, in conjunction with others if needed, can be of great importance in solving the type of problem cited in this example. Therefore, although the title of this book includes the word 'soil', we believe that the reader should have at least a fundamental understanding of sediments and sedimentary features in order to describe and interpret those sediments found at or near a site.

Geologists tend to classify sediments on genetic criteria into four broad, somewhat overlapping groups: detrital (or clastic) sediments, chemical (or non-clastic) sediments, organic deposits and pyroclastic deposits. **Detrital sediments** are those consisting of a variety of solid materials (minerals, rock fragments, organic constituents) that have been deposited by one or more agencies of transport, such as water, wind or gravity. Examples include aeolian sand, fluviatile gravel and lacustrine clay. **Chemical and biochemical sediments** are those formed by precipitation from solution, with or without the assistance of microorganisms such as algae, and comprise such items as speleothems (e.g., stalagmites), travertine, evaporitic minerals associated with arid lakes and salt pans (nitrates, sulphates, chlorides), limestone and chert. **Organic deposits** contain a high proportion of remains of living organisms (shells, plant tissues) and are represented by shelly beach deposits and carbonaceous deposits, such as peat. **Pyroclastic deposits** are composed of fragments of various sizes resulting from explosive volcanic eruptions: volcanic bombs, lapilli and shards of ash.

Any and all of these sediments were deposited as a result of processes acting in a certain sedimentary environment. The terms 'sedimentary processes' and 'sedimentary environments' are overlapping concepts that have been much used by geologists. Precise definitions that are universally accepted are lacking, which is probably to be lauded, since this allows for a greater amount of flexibility in applying the concepts.

Nevertheless, we may conceive that, in the broadest sense, 'sedimentary processes' include generalised phenomena like weathering, erosion, transport and deposition of sediments by such agents as wind and water. The concept of sedimentary environments, on the other hand, is more comprehensive. In this book we adopt the viewpoint that 'a sedimentary environment is defined by a particular set of physical and chemical parameters that correspond to a geomorphic unit of stated size and shape' (Pettijohn *et al.*, 1972: 450). As shown in Table 6.1, delta, beach, alluvial plain and lake would all be examples of sedimentary environments, although sub-environments naturally exist for each. The alluvial environment, for example, comprises such microenvironments as the channel, the levee, the point bar and the flood plain.

One of the major goals of geologists working with sediments is to identify the sedimentary processes responsible for their deposition and to pinpoint as closely as possible the environment of sedimentation of a given deposit. To accomplish this they make use of field observations (both at the regional and local scales) and analytical data gathered from the laboratory. Field observations include: spatial distribution of units; nature of contacts; bedding and sedimentary structures; mineralogical composition and size, shape, sorting and fabric of the constituents.

In this chapter we present several examples that illustrate the use of micromorphology in recognising sedimentary processes and environments and discuss some of the criteria that permit us to interpret and reconstruct the sedimentary history of a deposit. It should be pointed out that most workers rarely base their palaeoenvironmental interpretations solely on microscopic observations, which are not always unequivocal. Rather they supplement these observations with whatever additional data are at hand, be they geological, pedological, botanical, palaeontological or archaeological.

6.2 Detrital sediments

Since the overwhelming majority of archaeological sites are associated with detrital sediments, we will place particular emphasis on this group. There are several properties that are used to study detrital sediments from the various sedimentary environments. These include rock and mineral composition, size, shape, sorting, fabric, bedding and sedimentary structures.

The typical agents of detrital sediment transport and deposition are water, wind and gravity. Yet the resulting deposit differs according to the nature of the sedimentary environment. Thus, for a meandering stream environment, chan-

Table 6.1. *Common sedimentary environments and their subdivisions (modified from Kukal, 1971)*

Marine environments	Transitional environments	Continental environments
Open shelves	Lagoons and bays	Mountain ranges
Sheltered shelves	Deltas	Intermontane
Inland seas	Beaches	troughs
Continental slopes	Mangrove swamps	Deserts
Pelagic oceans		River valleys
Deep-water trenches		Lakes
Coral reefs		Alluvial plains
		Coastal plains

nel deposits, for example, are on the whole coarser (gravels) and more poorly sorted than those accumulating as overbank deposits (silts), which themselves will differ from similar fine-grain silts washed down from neighbouring slopes; each will display different types of bedding and sedimentary structures.

6.2.1 *Aeolian environment*
6.2.1.1 Wind transport and deposition
Wind transports material by traction (creep), saltation and suspension, depending upon the size of the material and the strength of the wind. Generally, coarser particles (> 50–60 μm) are moved by traction (dragging along the surface) or by saltation (jumping). These sand particles usually end up in sand dunes (Figure 6.1). Smaller, silt-size materials are transported by suspension, commonly for vast distances, and are later deposited as aeolian dust, known as **loess**.

6.2.1.2 Sand
Aeolian sand can be derived from any type of sediment, including fluviatile, beach or glacial. In all cases, however, the finer silt fraction has been preferentially carried off, or winnowed, by suspension, leaving the coarser sediments to be transported by saltation and traction. This selectivity of the wind produces a well-sorted deposit.

The types of sedimentary structures are among the more diagnostic criteria for recognising aeolian sand deposits. In general, they tend to display high angle crossbedding, though horizontal, tabular and festoon (trough) types are also common (see Figure 3.6). Furthermore, in desertic fringe areas where rainfall is more common than in the deserts themselves, these bedding characteristics may be absent, having been obliterated by rainsplash or sheetwash.

Composition is not by itself an indicator of aeolian origin, and the mineralogy of the sand depends upon local conditions. Nevertheless, most sand

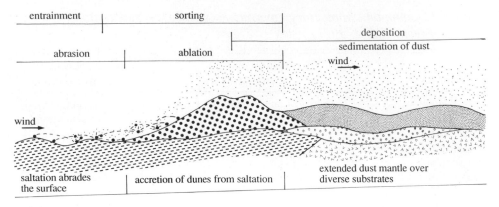

Figure 6.1   Schematic representation of aeolian processes and related sediments. (Modified from Butler and Churchward, 1983)

deposits are characterised by an abundance of quartz – because of its great resistance to weathering – and lesser amounts of feldspar and carbonates, although in basaltic terrain, aeolian sand may be composed of individual basalt grains. Micas also occur but, being rather fragile, they tend to break down rapidly and their flaky form allows them to be removed easily by suspension. Consequently an aeolian deposit rich in rounded grains of mica would reflect a relatively youthful deposit, not one extensively reworked by the wind (or water) or transported for long distances. Heavy mineral content is similarly variable but the more physically and chemically stable minerals (e.g., rutile, zircon, tourmaline, pyrite, haematite) tend to dominate.

   Another characteristic of aeolian sands, particularly of quartz grains, is their high degree of rounding produced during transit. Rounding, however, varies with grain size and finer sands are on the whole less well rounded than coarser ones. Absolute grain size is quite variable and is tied to the calibre of the source material and, to a lesser extent, to the amount of transportation (Figure 6.2a).

   When viewed under the binocular microscope, aeolian sand grains, particularly quartz, are characterised by dull and matted surfaces, long thought to be caused solely by grain impacts. Observations at higher magnifications with the SEM, however, show, in addition to traces of impact (Figure 6.3a), signs of dissolution (Figure 6.3b, c) and precipitation of silica (Le Ribault, 1977), as well as coatings of clay minerals, such as attapulgite (Figure 6.3d). Moreover, SEM has proved to be one of the most useful tools for evaluating the history of sand grains, and surface features on quartz grains can be quite diagnostic (Bull, 1981; Krinsley and Doornkamp, 1973). Typical surface features include crescentic impact marks, rounding and polishing (Figure 6.3a).

6.2.1.3 Silts
Fine material (< 40–60 μm) – commonly known as aeolian dust – is carried in suspension, and settles or is washed out of the atmosphere. Appreciable

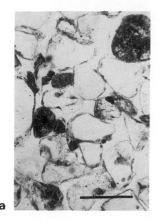
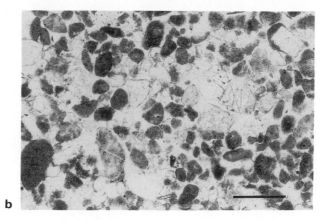

a b

Figure 6.2   (a) Moderately sorted aeolian sands consisting of subrounded quartz grains (transparent) and poorly sorted well-rounded weatherable minerals (black) derived from local metamorphic rocks. The latter indicate short-distance transport. Note the coating of fine clay around quartz grains. PPL. (Bar = 75 μm)
    (b) Sand-size grains consisting of aggregated clay blown up from semi-dry lake bottom and accumulating as a crescentic dune or lunette. From Upper Pleistocene lunette, Lake Mungo, New South Wales, Australia. PPL. (Bar = 530 μm)

accumulations on the surface are called loess. The size of an average grain of a loess deposit can vary considerably and contain different proportions of fine sand, silt and clay, depending upon the distance from the source, the type of source material and how it is deposited out of the atmosphere. Dust washed out of the atmosphere by rain, for example, is typically finer (*c.* 20 μm) than that which settles out by itself (generally between 40 and 60 μm). In either case dust and loess deposits display good sorting and are generally massive, with no traces of bedding. Both features are important identifying characteristics of these sediments. Unlike aeolian sands, silt-size grains of quartz, in particular, are usually angular and subangular, since these smaller size particles are less affected by abrasion during suspension transport.

The overall composition of loess varies over the globe, although the recipe is surprisingly uniform. The principal mineral components are quartz, calcium carbonate, feldspar, mica and clay minerals (Figure 6.4a, b). Naturally, variations arise from differences in source materials and the age of the deposit. Silt that has gone through a number of erosion–transport–deposition cycles will be impoverished in less stable and fragile minerals such as micas, carbonates, pyroxenes and amphiboles.

Aeolian silts are noted for their massiveness and ability to keep a vertical face when exposed. Commonly, however, they have been reworked by fluvial activity, which produces sedimentary structures associated with flowing water, e.g., ripple marks, fine lamination of coarse and fine beds, and graded bedding (Figure 6.4b, c, d).

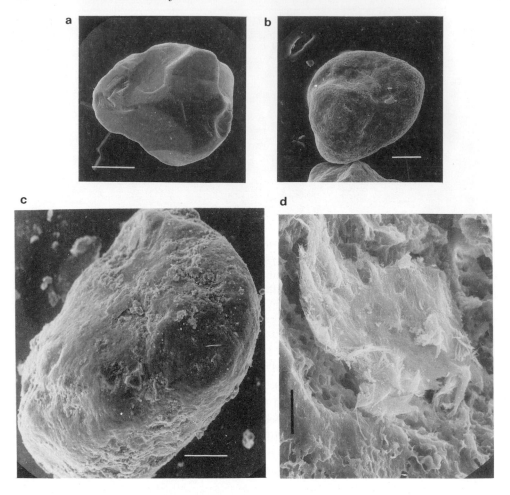

Figure 6.3   Aeolian quartz grains viewed with the SEM (Holocene sand dunes, 'edges' of the Thar Desert, north west India):

(a) Rounded polished grain with traces of impact shown by crescention marks. (Bar = 50 μm)

(b) Rounded grain exhibiting etched surface caused by silica dissolution. (Bar = 50 μm)

(c) Grain with rounded and irregular surface. (Bar = 100 μm)

(d) Detail of (c) showing pitted surface and coating of fibrous clay identified as attapulgite-type clay minerals. (Bar = 100 μm)

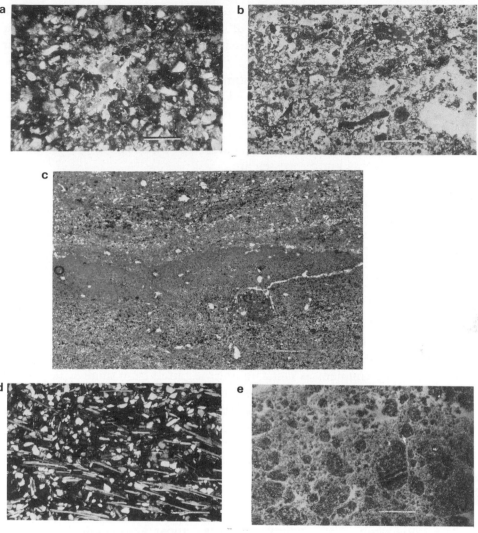

Figure 6.4   Loess and loess-like materials:

  (a) Relatively coarse loess (sandy silt) consisting mostly of angular coarse silt-like grains of quartz and calcium carbonate, and very few flakes of mica (Upper Pleistocene loess, Xifeng–Xian region, China). PPL. (Bar = 75 μm)

  (b) Photomicrograph of loess reworked by water, showing irregular bedding, fragments of superficial crusts, coarse-grained silt consisting principally of quartz and vesicular voids, Negev, Israel, PPL. (Bar = 75 μm)

  (c) Graded bedding in Late Pleistocene flood-plain sediments of the River Seine (Pincevent, France). Note sharp contact between two sedimentary units. Upon drying, these types of deposits typically form clay curls which are commonly reworked and redeposited. [cf. Figure 6.4 b]. PPL. (Bar = 5 mm)

  (d) Horizontally bedded mica flakes from Upper Pleistocene alluvial plain, northwest India. XPL. (Bar = 150 μm)

  (e) Effect of rainsplash on surface of present-day soil developed on loess under semi-arid conditions. The rainsplash has the effect of disrupting and fragmenting the soil peds (loess near Xifeng, China). PPL. (Bar = 500 μm)

Finally, aeolian dust forms a consistent component of many prehistoric caves (see Figure 10.3c). Although the ultimate origin of this dust is aeolian and is commonly blown into the cave, where it is trapped, it can also accumulate in front of the cave mouth and only later be brought into the cave by runoff, wind or man. In this regard, it is worth noting here that caves constitute a special geological environment in that they tend to accumulate and trap a vast variety of sediment sizes, shapes and compositions that are not normally found in other environments.

To summarise then, the most useful characteristics that aid in the recognition of aeolian sediments and processes are:

> shape: sand grains rounded to well rounded; silt grains more angular.
> sorting: for sands, good sorting with a unimodal (one predominant grain size) population, and only traces ($<5\%$) of finer material (silt + clay); for silts, good sorting.
> surface features (generally on quartz grains): with binocular microscope, dull grain surfaces; under SEM, angular impact marks, smoothing and rounding of grains.
> composition: for sands, general absence of fragile minerals (e.g., mica).
> bedding: sands, crossbedded; silts, massive with no fine laminations.

6.2.2 *Aquatic processes and fluvial environments*

The bulk of sediments that are likely to be encountered in archaeological problems is related to the effects of water and the variety of associated sedimentary environments is vast, running the gamut from small-scale puddles and rills to large-scale fluvial systems which are composed of many subenvironments. We will use a generalised fluviatile (river) environment to illustrate many types of processes and sedimentary characteristics (both field and microscopic) associated with running water.

6.2.2.1 Erosion, transportation and deposition

A typical stream system in a temperate climate might contain the following elements (Figure 6.5):

The active channel which flows in a wavy, meandering course carries the water for most of the year, except during periods of flooding. At these times of peak flow, the channel overflows and water is spread over the banks, resulting in the formation of a natural levee and alluvial plain and backswamp constructed of overbank deposits; associated with the alluvial plain are ox-bow lakes which constitute the remains of former meanders.

Solid material derived from slopes and river banks is transported by the channel, either by traction (bed load) or in suspension (Figure 6.6). The coarsest material in the bed load (sand and gravel) is generally confined to the floor of the channel and transported by the stream during floods. The composition of channel deposits is affected by, among other things, the velocity of flow, mixing with material carried in suspension and that scoured from the banks. Two types

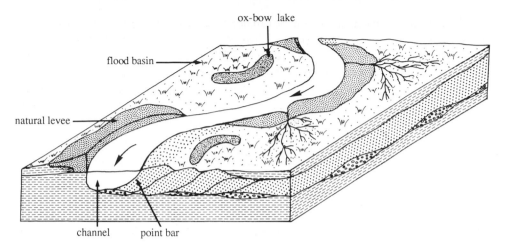

Figure 6.5   Schematic diagram showing the main elements of a typical stream system. (Modified from Reineck and Singh, 1975)

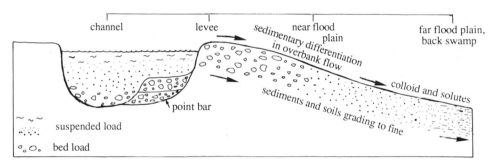

Figure 6.6   Sediments and transport in streams. (Modified from Butzer, 1976)

can be recognised: gravels and coarse sands, and finer material, generally confined to lower reaches of the stream.

In a downstream direction, the coarse channel deposits tend to become finer grained, more rounded and spherical and there is a decrease in unstable mineral components; sorting is quite poor. Major types of sedimentary structures associated with coarse channel deposits are large-scale ripple marks, trough and planar cross laminations, although unstratified, chaotically emplaced gravels are common; pebbles are commonly oriented with their long axes dipping upstream, a phenomenon known as **imbrication**.

Suspended load is also carried in the channel and, if flow subsides, it can be deposited on top of coarser gravels. This finer material is also transported further downstream or, if the volume of water is great enough, can be carried over the levee and be deposited as overbank deposits. Overbank or flood plain deposits are fine grained, consisting mostly of silt and clay and some fine sand.

As the stream overflows its banks, energy decreases laterally, resulting in the deposition of the coarsest suspended load on the levees and progressively finer sediment in the direction of the lower flood-plain and back-swamp areas. In a vertical sense, as a consequence of this decrease in velocity, coarser particles settle out first, followed by finer sediment which produces clear graded bedding (Figure 6.4c). This mixing of grain sizes, furthermore, results in an overall sediment that is only moderately to poorly sorted.

In contrast to channel deposits, overbank sediments are much richer in organic matter which results from the burial of grasses and shrubs growing on the flood-plain surface.

Sedimentary structures within flood-plain deposits are characterised by thinly bedded units, which, depending upon the magnitude and duration of a flooding event, vary in thickness from millimetres to a few centimetres. Ripple marks are quite common, as are deformational structures, the latter being related to the soft, water-saturated nature of the sediment. This saturation is also responsible for the occurrence of mottling and iron staining, commonly observed in flood-plain sediments (Plate VIIa).

Between flooding events, overbank deposits are subjected to drying, which results in the formation of mud cracks and curls of clay. The latter in particular are commonly picked up and reworked by water during the next flooding event and incorporated into the new deposit (cf. Figure 6.4b). These clay curls are readily recognised in thin section and provide an important tool for recognising this type of sedimentary environment.

Finer grains, as in the case with pebbles, also display orientation fabric and the long axes of grains tend to be oriented in the downstream direction (Figure 6.4d).

Grain sphericity in overbank and other fine-grained fluvial deposits is of little significance and observed variations could be a function of fracture during transport or introduction by a tributary of grains with different shape. Rounding, on the other hand, is somewhat more meaningful, and could represent either a greater degree of transport, chemical solution or inheritance from other deposits.

The surface textures of quartz grains as seen under the binocular microscope are generally shinier than those from aeolian deposits. Under the SEM, surface features vary according to the type of the fluvial environment (Le Ribault, 1977). High-energy environments (e.g., mountain streams) show numerous traces of impacts which are locally polished; previously formed siliceous coatings are also dissolved. In streams with lower energy flows (e.g., lower reaches of a meandering system), the traces of impact are less pronounced and small globules of silica are precipitated on flat surfaces or in depressions of the grain; diatoms are frequently found plastered onto the grain surfaces. In very low-energy environments (e.g., flood-plain, delta or mudflow), silica coatings and diatom traces are more numerous, even to the extent that they can cover formerly developed surface features.

A special case of the fluvial environment is that associated with *karstic* caves, although the same general processes can be recognised as those described for open fluvial systems. In this case, however, flow in subterranean fluvial channels is responsible for the deposition of sediments. Although the overall sediment produced by such deposition is not radically different from that in more typical fluviatile environments, it does display remnants of dense, deep-red, decalcified clay that is typical of karstic environments. These fragments, known as *papules*, are derived from accumulations of insoluble clay residues from the limestone that have been reworked by fluvial activity.

An additional sediment type, found typically at the base of sequences in prehistoric caves in France, is one consisting of poorly sorted, coarse-grained, angular sand, essentially devoid of finer material. This type of deposit results from the liberation of the quartz grains within the bedrock by solution and selective removal of finer-grained components by the winnowing action of the stream flowing at this elevation during this time. The subsequent lowering of the groundwater table effectively removed the cave from the effects of fluvial karstic activity.

To sum up, the features associated with fluvial deposits can vary greatly depending on their relationship to the channel (high energy) or the levee and flood plain (low energy). In the former case, deposits are coarser (gravels and coarse sands), show large-scale sedimentary features (crossbedding, or non-bedded massive gravels) and numerous traces of impacts on sand grains. Lower-energy, overbank deposits are finely laminated and crossbedded, are poorly to moderately sorted and much richer in organic matter (Plate VIIa).

6.2.3 *Hillslopes*

Fine-grained material on hillslopes can be eroded, transported and deposited in a variety of ways and on different scales. Large-scale (i.e., mass) movements involve processes and deposits such as mudflows and solifluction (including gelifluction, that caused by freezing and thawing), whereas more subtle effects include the results of creep, rainsplash and overland flow. Rockfalls, debris slides and talus deposits will not be discussed here because of their coarseness and their obvious nature in the field.

6.2.3.1 Mudflows

Mudflows are relatively rapid mass movements that result from the rapid saturation of fine-grained materials. The ratio of solid to liquid is high and the material moves down the slope as a large undifferentiated mass, commonly forming lobes or fans at the point where movement ceases. In the field and under the microscope, such deposits are massive, non-bedded, poorly sorted and composed of angular stony materials in a fine-grained matrix.

6.2.3.2 Solifluction

Solifluction entails the movement of water-saturated regolith (parent material, often including coarser rocks) on slopes as small as 2 degrees. Solifluction is commonly associated with colder environments (e.g., subpolar, mountain highlands) where it is more specifically called gelifluction (Embleton and King, 1975). Under these conditions a saturated topsoil overlying a permanently or seasonally frozen subsoil is subjected to seasonal thawing (the so-called active layer). The high water content, and the reduced compaction and cohesion of the soil materials produced by freezing and thawing provide the necessary conditions for downslope soil movement. Accumulations of such gelifluded material are known as head (in England), which is composed of massive, poorly sorted, angular stony fine-grained deposits; they can often be distinguished from glacial drift – of similar lithology – by the downslope orientation of the axis of the stones.

Solifluction also occurs in humid regions with clayey soils developed on slopes greater than 5 degrees (Butzer, 1976). Solifluction deposits are usually confined to the base of hillslopes and in comparison with mudflow deposits may be somewhat better sorted out and show some hints of stratification, due to the higher ratio of fluid to sediment.

The process of **creep** is much slower than those described above and essentially entails the slow (0.025 to 2.50 cm per year; Butzer, 1976) downslope movement of material under the influence of gravity (Chorley *et al.*, 1984). It is particularly effective in temperate regions with extensive vegetation cover and in periglacial regions, where it is traditionally ascribed to the effects of freeze–thaw and swelling. Recent work, however, suggests that it is a result of a complex of processes, including changes in porewater pressure, throughflow, solution/precipitation, hydration/desiccation, temperature changes and various forms of pedoturbation (Hole, 1961, 1981; Finlayson, 1985). Most of these processes are discussed in Chapter 9.

6.2.3.3 Rainsplash and overland flow

Much more localised processes are very prominent in the movement of slope materials. These are rainsplash and overland flow. Rainsplash represents the effects of individual drops of rain which tend to break down soil aggregates and move the material locally on the soil surface (Figure 6.4e), sometimes into the pores themselves. However, it is not responsible for moving relatively large amounts of material. Experiments on loess deposits showed in thin section that rainsplash resulted in non-layered material that showed no additional signs of sorting (Mücher and de Ploey, 1977).

Material transported by overland flow is carried by water, either within small

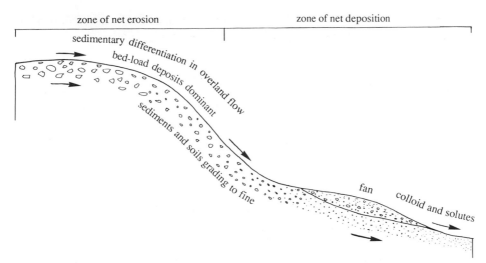

Figure 6.7   Schematic diagram showing sediment differentiation on hillslope.
(Modified from Walker and Butler, 1983)

gullies or thinly spread over the surface (sheetwash); the ratio of solids to fluid is
much lower than with mudflows. In the upper parts of the slope, the coarser
materials are concentrated as a lag deposit whereas downslope there is an
accumulation of finer material, often with a high proportion of soil aggregates.
Thus there is a net transfer of material from the head to the footslope (Figure
6.7). Deposits produced from flow without rainsplash display good layering
and very good sorting within individual lamina; clay (<2 μm) and silt (2–30
μm) laminae dominated. The effects of washing by rain result in poorly layered
deposits and poor sorting within individual laminae; the deposits show only
horizontal bedding and no crossbedding (Mücher and de Ploey, 1977). Thus the
effects of flowing water in hillslope deposits can be recognised in thin section by
distinct layering and good sorting within the laminae (Figure 6.8a). In sandy
materials, however, it may be difficult to differentiate micromorphologically
aeolian sand from that which has been reworked by overland flow, since they
have similar characteristics (Mücher and Vreeken, 1981).

6.2.3.4 Colluvium
The processes described above often act together on hillslopes and the presence
or predominance of one over any other will depend on several factors, among
which are climate, rock type, thickness and type of soil cover, slope angle and
vegetation cover. The total accumulation of deposits produced by these processes is called **colluvium**. Our usage of this term is rather broad and follows that
of Bolt *et al.* (1980:p 111) who employ it for 'non-consolidated slope deposits,
composed of macroscopically unstratified unsorted or poorly sorted heterogeneous material, containing coarse, mostly angular fragments of rocks and
materials present on the overlying slope'.

Colluvial deposits can be recognised in thin section by several criteria:

> Remnants of clay illuviation ('papules') or other features derived from soils, including rounded iron and calcareous concretions whose sharp boundaries contrast with the surrounding groundmass; as discussed in Chapter 9, nodules formed *in situ* have more diffuse boundaries.
>
> Charcoal and possibly anthropogenic debris, such as pottery fragments, slags and plasters. The occurrence of such materials may point to human endeavours that may have played a role in the accumulations of such deposits, including burning, deforestation or other clearing activities.
>
> Rock fragments that are typically set into a massive, undifferentiated groundmass.
>
> Fragments of previously developed mud crusts or clay curls that have been incorporated into the groundmass.
>
> As described above, sorting characteristics and the presence of laminations can serve to distinguish colluvium influenced by overland flow from that modified by rainsplash, for example.

Finally, it is worth mentioning that in the field clayey colluvial deposits in particular may display soil-like structures, which might suggest the interpretation that the deposit is in fact a paleosol. Such an interpretation may be verified (or rejected) on the basis of whether microscopic pedogenic features (e.g., 'stress cutans', development of b-fabrics) are present. In a strictly 'sedimentary' colluvium, they should not be present.

6.2.4 *Lacustrine environment and sediments*

Depending on the specific location (beach vs. lake bottom), the type of climate and hydrologic conditions, the lithologies of lacustrine sediment can vary greatly and include clastic, chemical and organic deposits. We will restrict

---

Figure 6.8 (a) Finely laminated silts and silty sands from laminated slope silts overlying interbedded deposits of decayed mudbrick and ashy silts (Chalcolithic site of Shiqmim, Negev Desert, Israel). PPL. (Bar = 300 μm)

(b) Photomicrograph of a limestone fragment rich in detrital quartz grains (shelter of la Micoque, Périgord, France). XPL. (Bar = 150 μm)

(c) Archaeological layer from la Micoque composed of dissolution residue of the limestone. The origin of the parent material can be inferred from the similarity of these grains with those found in the limestone. XPL. (Bar = 150 μm)

(d) Bio-anthropogenically induced sedimentation (Pre-Pottery Neolithic through Bronze Age) from cave of Nahal Heimar, Judean Desert, Israel. The fibrous grains are remains of decomposed goat/sheep droppings, the rounded speckled grains are composed of moonmilk (calcium carbonate). The whitish and grey areas are made up of secondarily precipitated sulfates and nitrates. XPL. (Bar = 300 μm)

(e) Photomicrograph of lacustrine sediments consisting mostly of diatoms mixed with calcium carbonate. PPL. (Bar = 50 μm)

(f) Photograph of a diatom taken with the SEM. (Bar = 15 μm)

(g) Field photograph of Late Pleistocene lacustrine deposits in the Sahara (Dayet el Mellah, Oriental great Erg).

(h) Photomicrograph of chemical lacustrine sediments rich in sodium chloride (infilling of NaCl crystals) mixed with calcium carbonate. PPL. (Bar = 150 μm)

ourselves to a discussion of clastic lakeshore sediments; lacustrine sediments of chemical origin are considered below in the section on chemical sediments.

There are several factors which influence the type of sediment found along the lakeshore. These include the composition and calibre of the material supplied to it by streams, the littoral vegetation growing on the lakeshore and the various agents and processes that continually modify these sediments, such as waves, currents and storms. It is evident that the lacustrine shoreline environment parallels in many ways that of the marine, beach environment although the variability in size of the former is much greater.

The composition of clastic lacustrine sediments is influenced principally by the types of sediments transported to it by streams and can therefore show great lateral variability along the beach. This is in contrast to marine beaches, which are compositionally more homogeneous. The grain size distribution is also a function of the source material but is, in addition, related to the size and hydrodynamic conditions of the lake. Beach sands are well to moderately sorted owing to the sorting action of the waves, which preferentially remove the finer material and carry it into the lake, where it settles as silts and clays. Although sorting varies in relation to mean grain size, such that coarser material is generally less well sorted than finer, sorting is somewhat poorer than in dunes because of the greater selectivity of the wind to transport certain sizes.

Beaches display several types of sedimentary structures which result in rapid hydrodynamic changes in the environment (storms, change in lake level resulting from strong winds). Thus the orientation of the laminae and the grain sizes show marked changes over shallow depths. In the area close to the action of the waves, low-angle planar crossbeds dominate, whereas trough crossbedding is more common in a landward direction. Ripple marks can occur in both areas and are generally oriented parallel to the shoreline.

Beach-sand grains are generally well rounded, though sphericity is much more variable. Quartz grains from the littoral (beach) environment are characterised under the binocular microscope by having rounded, shiny surfaces, unlike aeolian grains, which are rounded and matted. Surface features observed with the SEM are commonly illustrated from marine littoral environments where grains can be alternately exposed or submerged, resulting in the repeated precipitation and dissolution of silica globules. Also, both traces of impact and numerous V-shaped pits can be found; the latter increase in size with increased degree of agitation.

6.2.5 *Grain orientation*

Before we leave the subject of clastic sediments, some mention should be made of orientation fabrics, which can provide some detailed information about the direction of flow (Reineck and Singh, 1975). This is a subject that has received relatively little attention over the past 40 years since the early experiments by Dapples and Rominger (1945) which indicated that elongated grains in fluvial environments show an orientation upstream and occasionally display imbrication in this direction. On beaches, quartz grains appear to be aligned in the direction of the backwash (Curray, 1956). Grain orientation in aeolian sands is less well marked than in aquatic environments (Dapples and Rominger, 1945) though for some sands the prevailing wind direction may be indicated (Curray, 1956). For finer-grained loess deposits in the United States the orientation and imbrication of the silt grains matched those of inferred directions of palaeowinds (Matalucci *et al.*, 1969).

Evidence of orientation in fine silts and clays is more evident in thin section and can be more readily recognised by the general parallel orientation of the platy clay minerals, well exposed under crossed nicols. Visual understanding of the orientation of silt-size grains of iron minerals can provide a means of evaluating palaeomagnetic data obtained from sediments. Clearly, a sediment showing distinct grain orientation is preferable to one whose orientation has been modified or was never there.

In this regard, the lack of grain orientation – even though it may have once existed – can arise from a variety of primary and secondary effects. As discussed above, colluvium and mudflow deposits, as well as anthropogenic dumps and fills (see Chapter 8), are typically devoid of grain orientation. Furthermore, secondary processes such as compaction, shrinking and swelling of clays, diagenetic growth of crystals, animal burrowing and human disturbance (digging, trampling) can also result in disruption or annihilation of original grain orientation (see Figure 8.2a).

6.3 **Sediments produced by disaggregation phenomena**

A variety of sediments is produced as the result of disaggregation of bedrock. Although disaggregation might be strictly considered a process of physical weathering, it is discussed here, since it furnishes a group of sediments that are widespread in archaeological contexts, particularly caves.

The most commonly cited agents of bedrock disintegration are freezing and thawing (cryoclastism), growth of salts and dissolution; human influence has been recognised only recently. Under the activity of freezing and thawing, water percolating along an exposed cliff face or on the roof and walls of a cave seeps into the pores and cracks. If the ambient temperature drops below zero, the water freezes and the resulting ice expands thus enlarging the crack. If a sufficient number of cycles has taken place – especially during periglacial conditions of the Pleistocene – pieces of bedrock become detached and accumulate at the base of the cliff or on the floor of the cave. Such fragments, called rubble (*éboulis* in French), are generally fresh and range in size from sand up to coarse blocks, several centimetres in thickness. In prehistoric caves from southeast and southwest France they may constitute the major type of deposit (see Plate Ve), forming layers up to several metres thick (Laville, 1976). In the open air, they accumulate as stony talus deposits, known as scree (*grèzes litées* in French). It should be noted that aeolian and pedogenic processes as well as runoff can affect these sediments, both during and after their deposition.

The growth of salts by the evaporation of water found within cracks and pores works essentially in the same way in breaking down rocks, although the calibre of the resulting debris is much smaller. This process is also more prominent in arid and semi-arid areas where salts are more prevalent as, for example, in the Negev desert, Israel. There, the precipitation of halite or gypsum is responsible for the breakdown of limestone, chert or bones, and in the latter case is one of the principal reasons for poor bone preservation in prehistoric sites there.

Dissolution of bedrock can result in the accumulation of large masses of debris but the resulting pieces are smoother and generally show signs of being corroded. This corrosion is well expressed in thin section by dissolution of calcium carbonate and alteration of the less stable minerals, such as mica, pyroxene and amphibole. Moreover, solution is capable of liberating insoluble residues from within the bedrock. In the case of a cave developed in a quartzitic sandy limestone (common in southwest France), dissolution of the bedrock will yield a quartz-rich residual accumulation on the floor of the cave. This residue will have micromorphological characteristics (e.g., size, shape and sorting) similar to those found within the bedrock (Figure 6.8b, 8c).

The three mechanisms outlined above are the ones most commonly cited to explain the accumulation of the bulk of detrital material in prehistoric caves, particularly in temperate Europe. Recently, however, Hughes and Lampert (1977) have suggested that human beings might have played a significant role as sedimentary agents in several of the prehistoric caves in southeastern Australia. These caves are developed in friable sandstone and grains of sand can be easily dislodged by simply brushing against the bedrock walls. In the Neolithic cave of Nahal Heimar in Israel, goats and sheep penned within the cave enhanced sedimentation by dislodging large amounts of friable limestone and micritic crusts that had developed on the walls of the cave (Sandler *et al.*, 1988); they were also responsible for causing the precipitation of noticeable amounts of nitrates and gypsum (Figure 6.8d). Ordinarily, it would be difficult to make a case for such bio/anthropically induced sedimentation. However, in the case of Nahal Heimar Cave, this hypothesis is more than reasonable: the cave area is small (*c.* 50 sq m), the bedrock walls are extremely friable and the quantities of goat/sheep droppings are copious. Thus it is not difficult to imagine that even a moderate density of penned animals brushing against the walls could bring about deposition on the cave floor of wall material.

6.4 Biologically related deposits

6.4.1 *Diatoms*

Many marine, brackish and especially lacustrine environments contain accumulations of *diatoms* – aquatic algae with siliceous cell walls, roughly 5–400 μm in size. Some deposits of diatomaceous earth may attain thicknesses of up to several tens of metres and are commonly intercalated with plant remains, fine clastic sediments and chemical precipitates, such as gypsum (Figure 6.8e, 8f). Since different species tend to be sensitive to salinity and temperature and the supply of nutrients, they can be valuable palaeoenvironmental indicators.

6.4.2 *Mollusc fragments*

Gastropods and pelecypods (bivalves) form a common component in many terrestrial and shallow aquatic environments. They can be transported with the bed load or suspended load in streams, carried by the wind, or buried in living position, such as on a beach. In the case of the latter they are usually reworked by waves, resulting in well-rounded shell fragments. Certain terrestrial snails can also tunnel several metres below the surface.

In thin section, pelecypod shells are characterised by having long fibrous crystals composed of calcium carbonate (calcite or aragonite – aragonite is unstable and normally converts to calcite); fresh specimens of pelecypod shell are long and thin although they are commonly rounded by water action. Gastropods have a similar composition but their stacked tubular shape is diagnostic. The tests and spines of sea urchins, a common component of many middens, differ considerably from the above by being composed of single crystals of calcite.

6.5 **Organic deposits**

Organic deposits accumulate under conditions in which the oxidation of vegetable matter by bacteria has been slowed. This is accomplished by low temperature or by a chemical environment that is non-conducive to bacterial growth. Although many different types of organic deposits exist (peat, lignite, coal), we will consider only peats (Plate VIIa).

Peats are found in cold regions (**tundra peat**) as well as temperate ones, in which for the latter two types are usually recognised, **moorland peat** and **fen peat**. Fen, lowland or muck peats form by the gradual accumulation of vegetable matter in bodies of stagnant water. A typical vegetarian recipe would include such plants as rushes, sedges, trees, branches, seeds and leaves, mixed in with other organic remains including mollusc shells; dissolved mineral salts (calcium carbonate) and mineral detritus (silt and clay) also occur (see Chapter 18).

Peats are classified as oligotrophic acid and eutrophic base-rich, depending upon the type of parent materials and the quality of drainage, factors which influence the morphology of the decayed organic matter. Lowland peats relate to poorly drained systems, such as enclosed valleys, river valley cut-offs, and terrestrial areas which are below sea level.

6.6 **Chemical and biochemical sediments**

Chemical sediments – those precipitated directly from solution – are represented by an enormous volume of rocks on the earth's surface that include limestones, dolomites, cherts and evaporites. Of principal importance to us here are the chemical sediments associated with lacustrine environments and the calcareous (composed of calcium carbonate) material associated with caves (speleothems) and with springs (travertine). Forms of calcite produced in the soil are discussed in Chapter 9.

Chemical lacustrine sediments are generally associated with lakes situated in arid and semi-arid environments where high evaporation rates favour the precipitation of salts that are supplied by rivers and springs. The mineral composition of such salts varies widely from lake to lake, depending upon the geochemistry of the lake waters, which in turn is related to the local geology. The principal minerals are halite, gypsum and anhydrite and, less commonly, sodium and magnesium sulphates and carbonates (e.g., epsomite, trona, mirabilite). Some of these can be identified in thin section (Figure 6.8g, 8h) but more effectively by X-ray diffraction and microanalysis under the SEM. These minerals commonly show a lateral zonation with the most soluble ones being deposited around the lake margins and the least soluble toward the centre of the lake. Among the most noteworthy Pleistocene lakes are Searles Lake, California; Lake Bonneville (modern Great Salt Lake), Utah; Lake Lisan (modern Dead Sea); Willandra Lakes and Lake Eyre, Australia.

Calcium carbonate ($CaCO_3$) is present in virtually all naturally occurring waters, its solubility being controlled by the amount of carbon dioxide (CO_2) in solution. The latter is itself influenced by temperature (CO_2 becomes less soluble with increasing temperature) and other factors such as evaporation, in which the CO_2 content is lowered or it causes a change in partial pressure.

Surficial carbonate deposits take on a variety of forms that comprise travertines and tufas, stromatolites and cave dripstones (including stalactites and stalagmites). Although it was originally thought that most of these forms resulted from solely physico-chemical processes, recent evidence shows that the work of microorganisms such as bacteria and algae is instrumental in their formation.

The respective roles of bacteria and algae in the formation of calcium carbonate is a field of current research. Laboratory experiments have established that a close interrelationship exists between the two types of microorganism (Caudwell, 1987). Algae are primarily responsible for the fixation of sparitic calcite. At the same time, photosynthesis supplies both oxygen to attract bacteria – which are aerobic – and a carbon-rich substrate for bacteria. The growth of bacteria, on the other hand, lowers the pH, which results in the dissolution of the sparite. Continued metabolism of the bacteria in turn raises the pH and micritic calcite is reprecipitated. Thus the combined roles of algae and bacteria result in the formation of micritised sparite.

Natural environments are quite variable and the 'variations within them strongly influence both the physico-chemical factors affecting inorganic precipitation of carbonate (agitation, amount of solar heating, etc.) and the type,

abundance, and growth rate of organisms, thereby affecting the organic precipitation of carbonate' (Chafetz and Folk, 1984: 293). Several types of calcium
carbonate accumulations can thus be built in these ways. **Travertines** for
example are large masses of calcium carbonate that are precipitated as a result
of both inorganic and organic processes in areas with active springs (Figure
6.9a). A porous variety of travertine is **tufa** in which calcium carbonate has been
precipitated around twigs, reeds, leaves, algae and mosses (Figure 6.9d).
Travertines characteristically show horizontal or sub-horizontal bedding and
take on a variety of accumulation morphologies that include waterfall deposits,
lake-fill deposits, and steeply sloping mounds. In addition to laminated layers
of carbonate mud and porous 'foam rock', bacterial pisoids and bacterial
stromatolites are also formed (Chafetz and Folk, 1984).

An additional type of biogenic carbonate is that of **stromatolites**. These are
composed of laminated alternations (a few millimetres thick) of carbonate-rich
mud and dark, organic-rich layers formed predominantly by (decayed) blue-
green algae (Figure 6.9b). The alternations reflect repeated events of trapping
and binding of the carbonate and renewed growth of algae on this fresh
carbonate surface. Stromatolites commonly display small irregularities in
thickness and crenulations which help to distinguish them from those deposited
by physical processes.

Structures of algal sediments are variable and range from planar to dome
stromatolites which are tens of centimetres high. They can also be arranged as
roughly spherical algal balls – known as **oncolites** – that reach several
centimetres in diameter. Whilst marine stromatolites are the most common,
they are known from freshwater, hypersaline (e.g., sebkha) and terrestrial
environments.

In thin section, the laminations are composed of alternating layers of micrite
and mixtures of micrite and sparite, commonly with an aggregated, pellety
appearance and a laminated, vughy microstructure (see Figure 6.9b). They
differ from the bacterial travertines mentioned above by the presence of algal
filaments, which are best observed under the SEM.

Calcareous accumulations are well known from limestone caves, where they
take on a variety of forms and are composed principally of calcite and aragonite. Precipitation is strongly promoted by evaporation: evaporation of water
dripping from the roof forming icicle-like pendents (stalactites), and pillars
(stalagmites) built up from the floor. The former show bands disposed parallel
to the axis of the stalactite whereas in the latter a structure composed of cuspate
layers is observed. In a thin section cut normal to the axis of the stalactite,
radially disposed crystals of calcite appear. These comprise a variety of forms,
including columnar, fibrous and 'coconut meat' shapes (Kendall and
Broughton, 1978; Folk and Assereto, 1976). In addition to these columnar
forms, calcium carbonate may also accumulate as thin layers or sheets on the

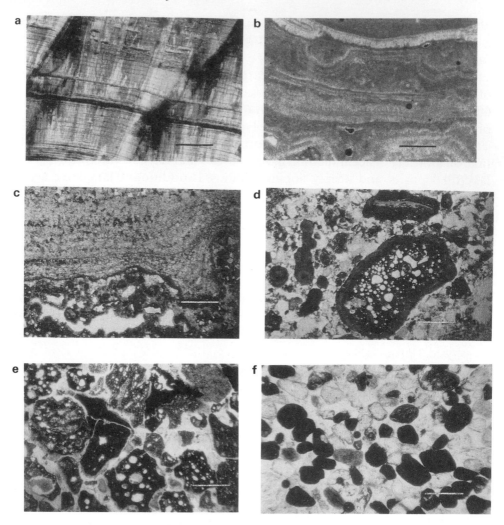

Figure 6.9   (a) Travertine from Herodian (*c.* 2,000 BP) aqueduct showing needle-like calcite crystals disposed in layers and precipitated as a result of strong evaporation of bicarbonate-rich springwater (Wadi Kelt, Jordan Valley). XPL. (Bar = 300 μm)

(b) Algal stromatolite from former shores of Late Pleistocene Lake Mungo (New South Wales, Australia), made up of layers of micritic calcite. The darker layers are relatively richer in organic matter. Note the few inclusions of quartz silt. PPL. (Bar = 300 μm)

(c) Last Interglacial stalagmitic cave floor formed of calcite laminae with detrital inclusions consisting of quartz, bones and soil fragments (Cave of Vaufrey, Périgord, France). PPL. (Bar = 150 μm)

(d) Photomicrograph of tufa reworked by flowing water (les Rivaux, Massif Central, France), showing detrital calcareous concretions of tufa mixed with rounded rock fragments. PPL. (Bar = 500 μm) cave floor (Figure 6.9c) or impregnate detrital sediments that have accumulated next to the cave wall. The latter deposits are common in prehistoric caves where they go by the name of 'cave breccia'.

Whilst stalactites are for the most part abiogenic in origin, other cave deposits seem more closely tied to biological activity. One such deposit is **moonmilk** (Figure 6.8d), which is found on cave walls of speleothems. It is generally powdery when dry and paste-like when wet and commonly has a nodular outer surface. Thin sections reveal it to be composed of very fine crystals of carbonate that occur as laminations or void infillings. Bacteria, algae and protozoa have been found in close association with moonmilk deposits (Thrailkill, 1976; White, 1976).

Many of these calcareous precipitates can also be affected by reworking, which markedly alters their form and overall aspect (Figure 6.9d).

The palaeoclimatic and palaeoenvironmental conditions associated with the precipitation and subsequent dissolution of these calcareous deposits is not straightforward, since a variety of factors is involved. In addition to ambient temperature, which can be both a climatic and a local feature, the concentration of carbon dioxide in the soil is strongly influenced by biological activity, especially by vegetation. A dense cover of vegetation, for example, can significantly raise the amount of CO_2, thus favouring the dissolution of calcium carbonate. At the same time, a greater amount of vegetation encourages greater evapotranspiration and results in less water being available to dissolve or precipitate calcite. Thus, it may be an oversimplification to equate the formation of cave carbonates (any or all of those described above) with a warmer or wetter phase, although onset or cessation of the growth of these speleothems on a regional scale may have palaeoclimatic implications.

A large variety of other minerals is known from cave environments, including other carbonates (notably aragonite), phosphates, nitrates and sulphates. Some of these are discussed in Chapter 9 (for additional information on cave minerals see Hill, 1976; White, 1982).

6.7 Pyroclastic deposits

Pyroclastic deposits are sediments which settle out of the atmosphere as a result of explosive volcanic eruptions. The coarser material settles closest to the source of the eruption and the finer materials are carried much further away,

---

(e) Pyroclastic airfall deposits from Qneitra, Golan Heights, showing variable lithologies of clasts as well as graded bedding. The yellowish intergranular material is generally isotropic to weakly birefringent in XPL and is probably associated with halloysite-type minerals. PPL. (Bar = 300 μm)

(f) Photomicrograph showing bedded, well-rounded charcoal grains mixed with grains of quartz beach sand. Iron Age occupation (Jutland Coast, Denmark). PPL. (Bar = 150 μm)

sometimes encircling the globe. In this respect, they bear many of the character-istics of aeolian sediments, particularly for the finest, dust sizes. The resulting deposits, being loose and porous, are commonly rapidly eroded and reworked by water.

A varied terminology is used to describe pyroclastic sediments, size being generally the first stage, although size boundaries vary according to author (Fisher and Schmincke, 1984). The coarsest material (>32 mm) (Moorhouse, 1959) is generally referred to as **blocks** (pieces broken from previously consoli-dated lava) and **bombs** (liquid lava that has cooled in flight). Because of their large size they will not be considered further. Smaller material (4–32 mm), known as **lapilli**, are essentially solidified droplets of lava and often have a twisted, rounded form.

The finest materials are called **tuffs** and consist of materials <4 mm. Several types of tuffs have been recognised but most are composed of materials with intermediate to acid composition (i.e., moderate to low amounts of iron and magnesium). Vitric tuffs are those composed principally of volcanic glass and consequently are isotropic in cross-polarised light. They are generally angularly shaped shards which have concave conchoidal surfaces and commonly show vesicles produced from escaping volcanic gases. Long transport dust is gener-ally of this type.

The lithic tuffs are composed of finely crystalline fragments of rock which are commonly rounded and vesicular (Figure 6.9e). Crystal tuffs are formed of crystals which had begun to form in the lava prior to the time of the eruption.

Texturally, pyroclastic materials range from fine-grained, well-sorted depos-its to coarse, poorly sorted ones. The former is typified by ash transported by air or water, whereas the latter is found in ash flows (Pettijohn, 1975). Moreover, when these deposits are reworked they commonly inherit bedding and sorting characteristics of the agent responsible, such as streams and waves.

6.8 Summary

In the first part of this chapter, we outlined some of the most common sedimentary environments – though by no means all – and some of their most important characteristics. Needless to say, the real world is never so simple and it is often a difficult task to unravel the sedimentary history of a geological deposit that has possibly been reworked by several sedimentary processes. For example, aeolian processes can easily pick up and remove loose sediment exposed on a flood plain. The reverse situation is also true, where aeolian sand encroaching on a fluvial system is reworked by water flowing in the channel.

Thus when examining a thin section, the observer must always be suspicious that what is being viewed is not the result of a single, simple process. A sediment composed of well-rounded and well-sorted quartz grains equally mixed with silt cannot be a typical aeolian deposit since the wind and its selectivity to transport only certain sizes will not produce such a concoction, although the sand grains may have been derived from an initially aeolian deposit. In the above case, a fluvial or colluvial interpretation would be more reasonable and should be checked with other data for confirmation. In a similar vein, finely bedded sands containing charcoal grains point to the reworking of some archaeological deposit even though such a phenomenon was not evident in the field (Figure 6.9f).

Finally, we point out that, because of the unpredictable and intrinsically vague nature of the geological world, it is simply not possible to present a set of microscopic criteria that will lead to an unequivocal (and correct) interpretation of the sedimentary features seen in a thin section. Each site and each geological or archaeological problem possesses its own individuality, though similarities with other sites do, of course, exist. Nevertheless, we hope that we have presented enough of the most common features that will enable a researcher to begin to sort out the material and history preserved in the slide.

7

ANTHROPOGENIC FEATURES

7.1 Introduction

This chapter is one of the most fundamental parts of the book, for it is here that we systematically present the micromorphological manifestations of various human activities and anthropogenic deposits, aspects that have not been previously discussed here or in the literature. The first part is devoted to more elementary features, such as ash and biological wastes, followed by a consideration of larger-scale archaeological features, in which they are often encompassed, including ditches and building materials. We conclude with a discussion of large-scale features relating to land use, such as clearance and cultivation.

Human activities can result in the production of new materials, the creation of an archaeological site, or they can more subtly change the environment such as by making a clearing in a forest. All these possibilities may be investigated micromorphologically and thus we consider that anthropogenic features include not only such archaeological elements as floors, hearths and ditches, and materials like pottery, mud brick and slag, but also ramifications of human manipulations of the soil landscape, the anomalous presence of imported geological materials, or microfeatures within a soil caused by cultivation. Thus a 'feature' for us can occur at any scale, and may involve, for example, the identification of single calcite ash crystals and phytoliths as elementary constituents of a burning episode.

As an example, we might imagine a virgin landscape first affected by minor clearance for subsistence cultivation. A dwelling is built. As time passes the population expands, additional housing is constructed, and the number of hearths and amount of midden material increase. As field systems are developed patterns of agriculture shift, resulting in the replacement of cultivation by pastoralism in some areas, perhaps tied to reductions in soil fertility; domestic industries start to produce large amounts of waste. All of the resulting structural remains, materials and human effects would be included within our concept of anthropogenic features.

In this chapter we present a repertoire of the most frequently occurring anthropogenic features. It should provide the necessary basis for understanding and interpreting the features from most archaeological sites or situations.

Features are dealt with systematically and where possible the processes responsible for them are proposed and some interpretation given. However, the details involved for specific reconstructions are presented in the case studies and these should be read as a complement to the individual sections referred to in the text. Naturally, each site has its own peculiar assemblage of anthropogenic features and it is therefore not possible to provide universal rules for the interpretation of each feature.

Moreover, as many of the interpretations are based to a large extent on our own experience, they should be regarded as proposals rather than definitive statements, especially since we recognise how much more work needs to be carried out. Nevertheless, many of the interpretations are based on arguments substantiated by modern experimental studies. For example, field and micromorphological features relating to modern agriculture have been studied in conjunction with examples of archaeological soils which are known from independent evidence to have been cultivated.

7.2 **Remains of human occupation**

In everyday life much waste material is produced by humans and by the animals living with them. In addition to ashes, there are many other forms of waste, which often constitute a large bulk of the anthropogenic deposits preserved at a site. Waste material mainly comprises organic refuse, such as cess, dung, plant remains, shells and bones, as well as mineral products (artifacts – flints and pottery sherds). These remains can be mixed with 'natural' sediments or can form individual layers, heaps (described as a midden) or consitute the principal material of pit fills. The same questions are repeatedly asked about these deposits: do such layers and pit-fills represent rubbish dumps, which implies a secondary deposition from a former location, or do they occur in their original location as a cess pit or as a stable floor, for instance? The aim of micromorphological investigations of such anthropic sediments is first to identify the constituents, and from their arrangement deduce how they have been deposited or emplaced and how they may have been modified.

7.2.1 *Burning phenomena*
7.2.1.1 Ashes and charcoal
Onc of the most striking indications of human occupation is burning and so we first describe its effects and the types of residues produced by this activity.

Burning on a site poses a number of questions for the archaeologist that may be answered by thin-section analysis. These include: What fuel was used? What was the fire for? What was the burning temperature? Were there one or many burning episodes? How did burning affect the surrounding sediments and has the fireplace been reworked or not? To answer these types of questions it is necessary to consider some of the elementary characteristics of ashes.

Wood ashes are identified in the field as pure white to whitish grey layers (Plate IIIa), which may be quite fragile. Although in thin section they show various degrees of homogeneity according to the history of the ashes, they are generally pale grey (PL) and highly birefringent (XPL) (Plate IIIb, c, Figure

10.3g). The latter characteristic is typical of calcium carbonate and variations in colour may be due to the presence of mineral inclusions other than calcium carbonate (e.g., phosphate). Fluorescence under blue light of wood ashes varies from pale blue to pale yellow when they consist mostly of calcium carbonate, but brighter colours up to orange are observed when the phosphate content increases. The ash, which is composed of fine-grained crystals of calcite (15–20 μm), may display relic plant shapes due to the replacement of plant material by calcite cell pseudomorphs; the cells of organic matter have been transformed by burning (Plate IIIb). In fact, whole plant pseudomorphs are quite rare because the ash is very fragile and easily dispersed into a mass of individual crystals, a phenomenon most typical of ash deposits.

Ash crystals from broad-leaved (deciduous) trees are lozenge shaped (Figure 7.1a, b), whereas those from coniferous trees are elongated rhomboids (Figure 7.1c); ash from pine cones has a particularly flaky morphology. In addition, relic fragments of charcoal, if they have been sectioned in the proper orientation, may also be used to ascertain whether an ash layer has been derived from mainly deciduous or coniferous wood; identifications down to the family and even genus level are sometimes, though rarely, possible.

In some cases the wood has been only half combusted or charred and displays dark or very dark brownish cellular material in PPL (Plate IIId). Under blue light various colours can be observed which appear to relate to the type of wood that has been burned and to the conditions of burning.

The calcite cellular pseudomorphs hold together until *c*. 500°C, above which they begin to fragment. With increasing temperature the calcite crystals become finely disrupted and have a droplet shape (Figure 7.1d) before they 'melt', altering to quicklime (CaO) above 650°C. In theory, the latter material undergoes further oxidation and is very short lived except when quicklime is being intentionally produced.

In sum, when wood ash has not been completely reworked, the arrangement, morphology and optical properties of the crystals provide good information on the fuel used and the intensity of burning.

*Grass (*sensu lato*) and leaf ashes.* Ash is almost always mixed with minor amounts of incompletely burned organic matter. Hence, layers of grass ash may be less than pure white in the field. Under PPL they differ from wood ashes by being less homogeneous and less grey, owing to the admixture of brownish (black to brown) charred grass and yellowish unburned organic matter (Plate IIIb). These characteristics result from the lower temperatures produced by grass burning. However, if burning has been maintained at high temperatures (> 600°C), all the organic matter is destroyed and the ashes consist primarily of the whitish grey residue of silica.

Under crossed nicols (Plate IIIb) the fabric of grass ash is very delicate and mainly isotic (i.e., an undifferentiated b-fabric) because what few calcium carbonate crystals are present are often finely dispersed. At medium to high magnification, however, grass ash can be seen to contain large quantities of poorly birefringent opal (silica) phytoliths, which in a sense provide the 'bulk' for this very thin material. Many readers may be familiar with phytolith extractions from soils and sediments, whereby numbers and types of phytoliths are counted. However, undisturbed phytoliths can be observed in thin sections, where they show up as 'skeletons' of relic plant material. Phytoliths which have rather rough surfaces when fresh become successively smoother with heating. At very high temperatures phytoliths from grass ash become melted and produce a specific kind of glassy, non-birefringent residue with a vesicular fabric (Figure 7.1e); in hand, a specimen commonly resembles slag or a strange type of green volcanic glass.

The presence of green ash may also be indicated by coarse charcoal, which often has a characteristic flaky or acicular shape.

Remnants of burnt leaves are often mixed with wood (Plate IIIe) or grass ashes and can be easily distinguished from them in thin section by their original fabric: poorly organised grey to dark brown (PPL) rounded crystals (*c.* 50 μm) that are highly to weakly birefringent (XPL). Under crossed nicols the crystals are always characterised by a dark cross (Plate IIIf) produced by calcium oxalate spherulites that are especially abundant in the flesh organs of angiosperms (Pobeguin, 1943). In contrast to wood ashes, these are a product of plant metabolism and may suffer mineralogical transformation during heating.

7.2.1.2 Effects of burning on soil constituents

Changes induced in the underlying surface during burning are related on the one hand to the intensity and duration of the combustion, and to the character of the subsoil on the other. In most of the fires observed, alteration effects are mainly concentrated in the upper 10 cm because the temperature gradient decreases rapidly with depth (Raison, 1979): in fires reaching 500–700°C only 50°C was measured at a depth of 5 cm. The changes that occur are non-reversible and their study permits reliable interpretations of a fire's history.

1. **Structural modifications.** In a soil with a coarse structure, heating causes cracks to appear and the soil surface disaggregates into finer structural units. At the bottom, the original subangular shape of the soil fragments is visible. Towards the top they are modified by heating to produce fine, highly desiccated aggregates which at the very top are injected into the ash.
2. **Colour changes.** These result from alteration in the composition and morphology of mineral and organic matter.
   (a) Organic matter. Roots and decaying organic matter in the humic horizon (A1 or Ah) are transformed, turning black under reducing conditions or reddish brown in an oxidising environment. Roots which were moist before being burned show charring mainly on their upper and outer parts.
   (b) Mineral matter

(i)   Carbonate materials. With heating, white limestone rock fragments and mollusc shells from the soil begin to crack and break up as well as become brownish grey; under UV light, fresh shell changes from blue to yellow. If some iron is present in the limestone, redder colours appear. Heating can also induce a change in the crystal morphology and crystal boundaries become poorly discernible. Finely crystalline limestones display a melted aspect. At very high temperatures (650–700°C) limestone alters to quicklime (CaO and has a fine grainy appearance).

(ii) Quartz (pure silica). At temperatures experienced in normal fires (400–600°C), quartz remains unchanged but above 800°C, alteration is noticeable at the grain edges, manifested by melting and the formation of a diagnostic dewdrop shape at 1,000°C. Above about 850°C and at low pressures, quartz is transformed to the mineral tridymite (Plate IIIg).

(iii) Clay minerals. In oxidising conditions reddening occurs whereas in reducing conditions blackening takes place. Heating also affects the optical properties and the clay becomes less birefringent; above 800°C obvious vitrification occurs (see ceramics, burned daub).

(iv) Bone is easily recognised by its colour and ropy pattern. Moreover, bone that has been altered by burning is readily apparent in thin section: fresh bone is pale yellow and has a low birefringence because of its phosphatic mineral content (hydroxyapatite). However, because burning destroys the organic part, bone undergoes structural changes when heated that modify its optical properties. The associated induced colour transformations are evident with the naked eye (Périnet, 1964; Bonucci and Grazziani, 1975) and have already been used to estimate the tempera-

Figure 7.1   (a) Photomicrograph of partially combusted branch of beech. Lozenge-shaped crystals are composed of calcite finely intermixed with carbon compounds. As a result they are darker than the lighter grey pure calcite ash diffused along the edges of the charcoal fragment (experimental hearth, Grignon Park, France). PPL. (Bar = 50 μm)

(b) SEM photograph of beech ashes, illustrating diagnostic lozenge shape and irregular surface of crystals. (Bar = 5 μm)

(c) Elongated rhomboids characteristic of calcite ash crystals from pine wood. The outlines of the original veins are discernible in the centre (experimental burning in oven). SEM. (Bar = 15 μm)

(d) SEM photograph showing droplet shape of melted ash from metallurgical hearth (Fort Harrouard, France). (Bar = 10 μm)

(e) Melted grass ashes with characteristic vesicular fabric (Potterne, England). PPL. (Bar = 550 μm)

(f) Highly burnt bone fragments mixed with ash. These show a typical grainy aspect (Neolithic sepulchre, Azirou – France). PPL (if viewed in XPL they would be totally white and highly birefringent). (Bar = 150 μm)

(g) Transformation of ashes by development of algal crust (centre of photograph) during period of temporary exposure prior to being covered with dump material (ceramic hearth, Kok Panim Di, Thailand). PPL. (Bar = 150 μm)

(h) Intimate mixing of microcontrasted particles and phytoliths with clay (Late Neolithic open-air site of la Fontaine de la Demoiselle, France). From dumped ashy material from a pit in which the ashes not only promoted the translocation of the clay but also maintained a relatively high pH within the deposits (pH 7 for dump vs. pH 4 for surrounding soils). PPL. (Bar = 45 μm)

ture of burning. Under the microscope, moderately burnt bone becomes brown at the edges and at higher temperatures (around 400–500°C), it is completely brown with darkish brown edges. Above 500°C, it undergoes strong mineral transformations and becomes paler with a higher birefringence. Above 650°C, it is completely white and has the birefringence of calcite (Figure 7.1f). There is some evidence to suggest that bone may have been especially chosen as a combustible agent.

7.2.1.3 Diagnostic types of burnt layers

Ashes and charcoals are commonly organised and associated in burnt layers or within hearths. The latter term commonly implies intentional preparation of the substrate upon which the fire has been built. For many Palaeolithic sites, however, this treatment is commonly difficult to demonstrate. Thus we prefer to discuss below the several types of 'burnt layers' rather than use the term 'hearths'.

1   **Simple burnt layer.** In this case an ash layer a few cm thick rests upon a burnt substrate. From top to bottom, the colour grades from grey to white to pinkish white near the soil interface. The grey layer results from charcoal inclusions mixed with the ashes, whereas the white one, when well preserved, may contain undisturbed, laminated remnants of wood or other combustibles. Finally, at the base, the pink layer may include reddened aggregates from the underlying soil, which were drawn into the ash during burning (Plate VIIId).

2   **Multi-sequence burnt layers.** These comprise undisturbed sequences of superimposed consecutive ash layers similar to the one described immediately above. At the contact zone between two ash layers, where former ash has been reheated and transformed by the subsequent fire, the calcite crystals are melted, resulting in fragmentation and cementation of the ash below.

3   **Charcoal layers.** These are characterised by abundant charcoal – often mixed with burnt bone – and result from low-temperature burning such as for cooking or in wood cinder fires for grilling. They could also originate from poor oxidising conditions, which occur when food is smoked. Where cereals have been roasted or somehow included in the fire, charred cereal remnants can be found.

4   **Ceramic hearths.** There is a large variety of such hearths, but as a group they can be recognised in thin section by their general grey colour, lack of charcoal and their vesicular aspect (Plate VIIIc). The fabric is often heterogeneous and includes the following diagnostic features: ashes are strongly disaggregated and disorganised; reheated ash is mixed with ashes that retained some of their organisation when the hearth was re-used; small, strongly reddened clay and ceramic (pottery) fragments, as well as vitrified or melted silica, are frequently present. The latter is non-birefringent (isotic) and in plain light may be dotted because charcoal has been altered to graphite.

5   **Metallurgical hearths.** Here again we can see the effects of high temperature by the dominance of vesicular fabrics (see Plate IIIe, f), indications of melted quartz (at 1,000–1,200°C), and the transformation of calcium carbonate to quicklime (CaO), which recalcifies somewhat on cooling. An important indicator of high temperature is the occurrence of melted 'dewdrop'-shaped quartz grains in silica aggregates, or 'bubbled' quartz. Ashes are poorly formed and badly preserved. When soil fragments are present and contain clay coatings, they become reddened because of their

iron content. Where limestone has been involved, burned 'calcium carbonate' – not recognised as such – produces small reddish dots, identified by X-ray diffraction as diopside ($MgSiO_3$) with the magnesium probably being derived from the limestone. Ashes can also be transformed into quicklime and when reprecipitation occurs, because the quicklime is so unstable, coarsely crystalline ashes are the result.

7.2.1.4 The alteration of ash layers

Ash layers can be altered by mechanical disturbance (either biological or anthropogenic) and by weathering. Although weathering and other post-depositional modifications are dealt with in Chapter 8, we discuss here the alteration of ashes since it is a thematic continuation of the subject of fires and burning as a whole.

Faunal and root activity may disturb the arrangement of the layers but the morphology of the individual mineral products of combustion is still recognisable. In contrast, these mineral products may lose their original properties when affected by weathering.

Mechanical disturbance. Mechanical disturbance can result from either biological or anthropogenic activities (Wood and Johnson, 1979). Among the most striking and dynamic examples of biological turbation is the rooting action of plants, whereby entire layers in a site or soil can be churned up (Limbrey, 1975).

Burnt layers and hearths can be disrupted by earthworms or by human and animal trampling, for example (Figure 7.2). Although the high levels of potassium in fresh ashes are toxic to earthworms, its rapid depletion enables them to invade the ashes within a few weeks.

Fragments of hearth layers – ash, charcoal and burned soil – are commonly mixed with bone, coprolites and local sediments to form ash middens. Within them, the ash is variously preserved in patches or is vestigial, according to local soil conditions. In the latter, especially in the case of grass (*sensu lato*) ash middens, relic ash material has a delicate, yellowish, phosphatic fabric, characterised by many phytoliths.

The more intensive the biological or human activity is, however, the more disrupted the evidence for burning becomes. Even in the base-rich urban sediments called 'dark earth' much mechanical disturbance, and dilution by other materials, is such that calcite crystals from ash are only rarely found.

With reworked ashes it is often useful to be able to differentiate between natural and human agencies. Various human activities, for example, may result in the transfer of ash to produce pit-fills or middens rich in ash. Because of their essential heterogeneity and disorganisation these deposits clearly differ from ashes reworked by wind or water, for instance, because the latter may exhibit typical sedimentary layering or the rounding of individual particles (cf. Figure 6.9f). It is also possible, even in harsh environments where all the ash has completely disappeared, to decipher evidence of burning from other

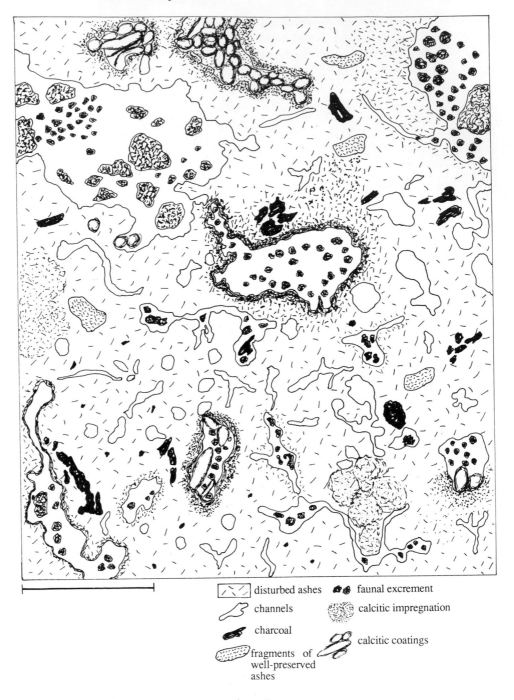

disturbed ashes   faunal excrement

channels   calcitic impregnation

charcoal

fragments of   calcitic coatings
well-preserved
ashes

Figure 7.2   Highly disturbed ash layer caused by dumping and biological activity, as shown by the fine intermixing of these materials with charcoal, and by the perforation by roots. The original arrangement of ashes is no longer distinguishable and in the field these ashes have a grey, homogeneous colour. Only a few fragments of the originally laminated ashes can be identified in thin section. Furthermore, secondary precipitation of calcium carbonate is observed within the groundmass and especially around channels (Neolithic fortified camp, Chassey, France). (Bar = 5 mm)

microfeatures, such as particulate dusty coatings, abundant phytoliths, burned soil fragments and specific phosphatic residues.

Weathering. The chemical weathering of ashy material, particularly in humid, temperate areas, constitutes a real problem relating to their subsequent recognition. Superficial alteration is often caused by plants, such as algae, lichens and mosses that may rapidly colonise an ash layer. Ashes become slightly cemented and greenish sometimes, producing some firm layers in otherwise loose deposits (Figure 7.1g). If weathering continues, the calcite crystals may be completely dissolved, leaving in thin section only a thin, yellowish, fine non-calcitic material, such as phosphate (P) in addition to the charcoal fragments.

Chemical dissolution is obviously more rapid and often total in acid soil conditions, whereas in a base-rich environment calcite may be well preserved. However, faunal working, as shown above, may be more active. Under alkaline conditions only ash rich in calcium carbonate is dissolved and reprecipitation of calcium carbonate can take place in the ash layer itself or in the underlying soil along channels (Figure 7.2), both combining to produce a cemented soil. When ashes have undergone extensive reprecipitation it is generally more difficult to identify their original morphology and even phytoliths may be altered if alkaline conditions are extreme.

In an acid environment, weathering may lead to the complete dissolution of calcitic ash. Under moderately acid conditions the weathering of ash composed especially of graminae often leads to the formation of clay coatings, probably because of the presence of large quantities of potassium (K), which encourages local clay movement with silica. These clay coatings are pale yellow, weakly oriented and show medium to low birefringence (Plate Ib, Ic), often similar to those formed around weathered lava flows and volcanic ash. Coatings associated with ashes, however, display very many dark patches consisting of pure carbon only a few microns in size (Figure 7.1h). The occurrence of abundant clay coatings has been tied to the presence of large quantities of potassium that has been weathered from the ash, and which has encouraged local clay movement in the form of coatings (Slager and van der Wetering, 1977; Courty and Fedoroff, 1982).

7.2.2 *Organic refuse*

As already mentioned in Part I, the study of organic components in thin section is much more complicated than that of minerals, as their optical properties vary according to their degree of ageing and specific composition.

Among the more easily identifiable organic components are **coprolites** – typically mineralised fossil excreta – which may be recognised by their particular composition and shape. Fortunately, they can often be related to the type of animal that produced them. Thus, there are major differences between the coprolites of 'full' herbivores (and rodents and mainly herbivorous pigs), and those of carnivores. Omnivorous animals such as dogs and humans produce wastes and coprolites that reflect their current, immediate diet, and it is sometimes safer to refer the identification to independent analysis of the host-specific parasite eggs contained in them.

Herbivore wastes and coprolites. The faecal residues of herbivores have a high porosity and contain many undigested plant fragments and amorphous dark brown organic matter that act as a type of binding agent. Large numbers of phytoliths occur in addition to relic plant pseudomorphs of calcium oxalate derived from grasses. Also present are detrital mineral grains that were either ingested from the soil surface if the grass was short or swallowed when the animal was drinking from muddy water holes.

Some differences between the main species can be highlighted. For example, in the coprolites of horses and cattle the coarse silica skeletons of plant stems are preserved, whereas sheep and goat coprolites are more compact and contain highly disorganised phytoliths and numerous crystals of calcium oxalate (Figure 7.3a, see Plate IIIf). Thus, for ancient stable layers it is possible to identify the animal species responsible for the specific shape of the coprolites and the nature and arrangement of the large quantities of phytoliths which they contain. Sometimes these coprolitic stable layers have been burnt during cleaning of the site, resulting in the preservation of their initial morphology (Figure 7.3b). Even if they are disaggregated, however, it may still be possible to interpret the remaining small fragments. A combusted stable layer produces many of the same features as those observed in grass ash, as shown by recent botanical studies of perfectly preserved, waterlogged, stable layers from a Scottish Bronze Age crannog (Clapham and Scaife, 1988).

Coprolites from omnivorous pigs (wild boar) are similarly rich in phytoliths but the groundmass seems to contain more amorphous organic matter.

Coprolites of carnivores and omnivores. The bone- and meat-rich diet of carnivores produces highly phosphatic coprolites, which are cemented when fossilised, and in the field appear whitish grey to whitish yellow. In thin section their predominant characteristics are a fine pale-yellow groundmass and a variety of inclusions which help to identify the major materials ingested (Plates IVa, IVb). The most common inclusions are bone, plant fragments, phytoliths, pollen grains, hair and mineral matter, such as quartz, silt and clay particles. The groundmass is generally amorphous, colourless to dark brown, non- to weakly birefringent and is highly fluorescent in UV light. In some cases whole layers can be formed from carnivore coprolites, such as those from hyaena dens or caves frequented by them.

Urine or solutions rich in soluble organo-phosphate, such as bat and bird guano, may produce specific features which can be associated with coprolitic material (*sensu lato*). However, because of their high solubility, these features are only preserved under specific conditions (Sandler *et al.*, 1988), where biological activity is very restricted, as, for example, in extremely arid caves or under deeply buried or waterlogged conditions. (The biogeochemistry of insular phosphate deposits related to excreta of birds and bats is discussed in detail by Hutchinson, 1950; see also Chapter 8).

In many cases, coprolites have been so highly transformed and intimately mixed with the natural sediments by the soil fauna that their original shape is no longer recognisable. Though their presence is difficult to detect at low magnifications, observations under blue light reveal numerous highly fluorescent particles which are finely dispersed organic residues. Vivianite is another product of organo-phosphate solutions either from ash or bone or cess itself (see Chapter 8).

7.2.3 *Inorganic plant remains: phytoliths*
Phytoliths are a common component of domestic wastes and can be either combined with other organic residues, such as coprolites, or be dispersed throughout the sediments. They are recognisable as having very low relief and may best be seen at low light intensity, using a closed diaphragm in order to outline their edges or using phase differential contrast (Plate Ie). They are often distinguished from other minerals by being isotropic and also by their specific shape. They are commonly either smoothly equant to prolate (rods and dumbells) or highly irregular acicular (spiny rods) (Figure 7.3c).

Phytoliths develop mainly within the grasses (including cereals) and equisetaceous plants which have an especially high silica content, although they occur at much lower concentrations in some trees and heath species. They are produced by the action of plant cells which take up silica, which results in the strengthening of the plant. Although few phytoliths are readily diagnostic at the microscopic level (Geiss, 1973), most of them can be identified with greater certainty using the SEM, which provides a three-dimensional image. Compared to identification classically carried out by bulk extraction techniques (Rovner, 1971, 1983; Bertoldi de Pomar, 1975, 1980; Smithson, 1958), phytoliths in thin sections from undisturbed samples can be observed in their original orientation. Thus it is often possible to study millimetre-sized plant remains whose silicified cells are still connected, sometimes permitting rough identification (Plates Ib, Ie, Figure 7.3c).

7.2.4 *Mineral products*
Flints. Flint is easily recognised by its petrographical properties, which include low birefringence and cryptocrystallinity. In thin section, however, it is exceedingly difficult to distinguish natural from human worked fragments of flints.

Ceramics. The study of ceramics using the petrographic microscope received a boost by the work of Peacock (1967, 1969; Peacock and Williams, 1986). Among the principal aims of ceramic investigations is the determination of

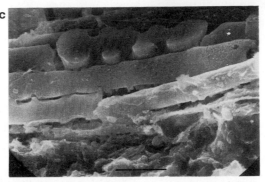

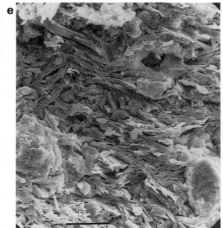

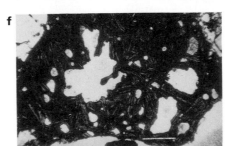

provenance, based on the mineralogical composition, particle-size distribution and morphology of the coarse fraction temper. Additional information can be gained about the technology and fabrication of the fired piece, particularly by observation of the fine fraction: orientation and arrangement of individual clumps (bedded fabric produced by compression is commonly observed) (Figure 7.3d, e), selective sorting for the fine fraction (levigation) and the transformations of clay during heating. The fine fabric of ceramics burned at low temperature (around 500°C) can sometimes be quite birefringent, whereas high temperatures induce important structural changes in the clay, which result in reddening (neoformation of iron oxides). In addition, as pointed out above (see Section 7.2.1.3), the destruction of $CaCO_3$ and formation of quicklime points to temperatures in excess of *c.* 700°C. Similarly, the vitrification of quartz and clay minerals also implies high-temperature firing (> 850°C).

These arguments are more generally true for a slice of pottery whose orientation to the original piece is known (e.g., perpendicular to the rim or through the handle). Unfortunately, many human waste deposits contain only a few scraps of millimetre size, and randomly oriented pottery, factors which constrain our ability to interpret these materials.

Slag. Slags are a common waste material from industrial sites. Iron slags are very dark grey in plain light and have a specific interwoven columnar form (PL), minor vesicular porosity and high-order red and green birefringence. Under reflected light (RL), slag is golden grey with minor opaque areas showing up as very red relic iron materials. Additional slags occur from other metal and glass working (Folk and Hoops, 1982) (Figure 7.3f).

Hammerscale. These 'rusty iron' fragments are opaque to faintly translucent

---

Figure 7.3   (a) Recent herbivore manure of cow, consisting of well-preserved plant fragments with opalised cells still maintaining their organisation. The dark brown staining of the groundmass is from the presence of organic matter. PPL. (Bar = 150 μm)

   (b) Well-preserved goat-sheep dropping surrounded by white wood ashes (Neolithic hearth, Saint Pierre de la Fage). PPL. (Bar = 150 μm)

   (c) SEM view of Graminae phyltoliths (dumbell and rod-shape silicified cells, most probably wheat (Late Bronze Age hearth, Fort-Harrouard, France). (Bar = 10 μm)

   (d) Fabric associated with ceramics:
SEM view of sample of hand-made Protohistoric ceramic from India, in which there is random organisation of individual clumps of clay. Layering that can be observed under the optical microscope is not apparent at this magnification. (Bar = 16 μm)

   (e) Fabric associated with ceramics:
Wheel-made pottery (Protohistoric site, India) viewed with the SEM. Note the regular orientation of clay particles forming platelets and weak clay orientation around voids. (Bar = 16 μm)

   (f) Slag. The dark opaque groundmass and vesicular fabric are characteristic of this material (Roman, Winchester Palace, England), PPL. (Bar = 150 μm)

(PL) and are very dark red at the edges and black in the interior under RL. The edges comprise fine (20 μm) laminae or scales originating from the repeated hammering out of the iron or steel tool.

7.2.5 *Human waste deposits: middens*

Middens are accumulations of much of the debris discussed above and usually take the form of a mound or a thick layer rich in organic debris and inedible food remains, such as shells, echinoderms and bones and those in coastal or palaeocoastal areas are interbedded with intertidal and beach deposits (Balaam *et al.*, 1987). Additional materials are charcoal, ashes and decayed vegetable matter, including cereals. Most of these elements are readily identifiable in the field and can be studied macroscopically or with the binocular microscope under lower magnification. In thin section, midden deposits display loosely packed fragments of mollusc shells, echinoderms (sea urchins), bones and aggregates of intimately mixed organic and mineral matter. Mollusc shells are easily recognised by their external shape, crystalline internal fabric, and the high birefringence (calcite or aragonite). Burning, however, induces cracking and a greyish colour with a reduction in birefringence. This association of elements, the overall angularity of the fragments, as well as the loose, porous nature of the deposit, set middens apart from 'natural' death assemblages that might have been thrown up on a beach, for example.

Post-depositional effects are poorly discernible in the field. In thin section, on the other hand, the activity of earthworms and the translocation of charcoal are clearly evident (cf. Stein, 1983, 1985). In secondary midden deposits, the admixture of natural soils and specific pedofeatures may indicate manuring for cultivation. In the case of grass ash middens, the midden material becomes diluted by soils and inclusions such as ash are dissolved – perhaps reprecipitating as calcite at depth – and phytoliths are finely broken up. Semi-cemented ash layers can be rounded and become part of colluvial deposits. In any case, resistant residues of fused ash and vitrified material are generally well preserved (Figure 7.1e).

Such observations might lead to important insights concerning the degree of post-depositional modification of the midden and the amount of time since abandonment (see for example Chapter 15).

7.3 **Construction materials**

Specialists have already carried out a great deal of work using common microscope techniques in order to study the petrography of building stones and related materials, to improve the preservation of monuments. This has resulted in good characterisation of cements, concretes, plasters and mortars, and a better understanding of the manufacturing technologies involved and the alteration these substances have undergone since they were first made. We refer the reader to the specific literature on this subject (for example *Proceedings of the International Congress on Deterioration and Conservation of Stones,* Lausanne 1985) and instead will focus here on the far less well investigated non-consolidated materials which have to be impregnated before being studied. Such materials include mud bricks, daub, mud floors, poor-quality cement, mortar and plaster, as well as any kind of soft material that has been employed for construction purposes, including organic materials (e.g., roof thatching) and soils (e.g., turves for walls).

The microscopic study of construction materials does not differ much from that normally carried out on archaeological soils and sediments and comprises the description of the coarse constituents (petrographical identification, sorting, particle-size composition, proportion of organic to mineral matter), the fine fraction in which coarse elements are embedded, the void pattern and, lastly, the geometrical relationships (or arrangements) of these three components. 'Arrangement' mostly refers to or reflects intentional human preparation. Mineralogical composition of building materials can be compared to that of the surrounding soils and sediments in order to identify the source(s), or to detect a certain preference for specific constituents. An estimate can also be made of the extent to which the original constituents were transformed by manufacturing processes.

Construction materials can be grouped according to their fabric, which is often related to their function, and below we discuss several types, including bricks, daub, clay walls, turves, mortar and plaster, and thatching.

7.3.1 *Mud bricks*

A very common and prominent characeristic of mud brick is the presence of elongated, tubular-shaped voids which are pseudomorphs of the plant temper that has been used (e.g., straw; see Figure 5.6). Remnants of these plants, such as phytoliths, can be often observed in the elongated pores.

The fabric of the brick is an indication of the *pugging* technique that has been used: a heterogeneous, poorly mixed fabric would indicate a moderate pugging, whereas a homogeneous and dense mixing of a large variety of different constituents would be evidence of a careful pugging (see Chapter 13).

The fabric of burnt brick appears to differ little from that of sun-baked brick, but the effects of burning – as in the case of ceramic, which is essentially the same material – can alter the petrological characteristics of the constituents to such an extent that the original character and provenance are difficult to decipher.

Sun-baked bricks may suffer important alterations by post-depositional processes. Poorly pugged bricks are less resistant to these processes than strongly compacted ones because they have a high porosity and their constituents are not strongly bound to each other. Consequently they may undergo complete disaggregation as a result of a variety of processes and agents: water, biological activity or salt weathering. The latter is particularly noticeable in arid and semi-arid environments where secondary impregnation by salt solutions or incomplete removal of salts from an original saline material can bring about exfoliation of the brick. When mud bricks break down and are reworked colluvially, their original heterogeneity is lost and they appear as better-sorted layered sediments (Figure 7.4a, b).

7.3.2 *Daub*

This material is very similar in composition to mud brick – it is often made of the same material – and the distinction between the two is commonly a cultural/geographical one. Daub, however, does differ from brick in its technique of manufacture. Daub is simply soil material – often including soil organic matter, fine charcoal, dung or any kind of fine refuse mixed with coarse temper and large plant fragments (cf Figure 5.6) – that is pressed onto a wattle frame. It is often characterised by voids with plant pseudomorphs. Its composition varies from very heterogeneous, with a variety of inclusions, to a more homogeneous kind where perhaps only local fine-grained soil material was utilised.

In areas of wet climates, daub is mainly only well preserved after baking (e.g., as a result of fire destruction) and the impression of the wattle may be quite pronounced. Clay void coatings, which formed as the daub was slaked during manufacture, will show up reddened by heating and thus can be differentiated from later clay translocation affecting the sediments in which the daub lies.

7.3.3 *Clay walls*

In contrast to the anthropic composition of mud bricks and daub, clay walls often comprise very pure geological materials which have been quarried and utilised with very little or no mixing, the clay being again reddened (oxidised) or blackened (reduced), when such structures are destroyed by fire (Figure 7.4c). Burnt clay walls commonly occur associated with fragments of the timber frame, preserved as wood charcoal and ash.

7.3.4 *Turves*

Turves are elements which have been cut from the soil surface, usually from a grassland 'prairie' soil or a heathland soil, where the high organic-matter content permits the removal of whole blocks. Soils covered with mosses have also been used without any addition or preparation because of their good consistency and heat-retaining properties. Turf walls are well known in Iron Age sites in Denmark, Ireland ('Soddies') and North America. Although turf materials have also been commonly used as foundations for some Roman fortifications, they are most famous for their use in tumuli (Drewett, 1985).

Because turves are essentially just the upper part of natural soils, they may not possess any especially recognisable fabrics, as do bricks. In addition, as they have a weak consistence, they are easily compacted and may be strongly affected by post-depositional processes. Well-preserved turves, however, can be easily recognised in the field by the alternation of black or dark brown and light bands within a structure.

In thin section, the dark bands can be seen to relate to the humic top-soil whereas the paler part of the turf represents the underlying lower part of the A horizon that is held together by roots. The type of soil that was initially used may be inferred from micromorphological features – the type of microstructure, features related to biological activity, and the nature and distribution of organic matter – and from chemical data (pH, organic-matter content). In addition, micromorphological observations can establish whether turves were laid face-up, face-down, or face-to-face, which can help us avoid situations where a pollen column would be unknowingly collected from a turf stack consisting of consecutive turves laid face-to-face, although this may be indicated by the pollen spectra (Scaife and Macphail, 1983).

7.3.5 *Thatched rooves*
Thatched rooves are not frequently preserved, except in cases where the house burned before the roof had decayed. Usually, however, it is possible to identify in thin section only relics of rooves, as is indicated by large amounts of wood-plant remains mixed with other kinds of construction materials (like daub) and also by the concentration of large fragments of straw.

7.3.6 *Mortar, plaster, cement*
The main characteristic of these materials is their calcitic nature, although weathering may lead to decalcification. In thin section, they usually have a very dark greyish (PPL) and highly birefringent crystallitic b-fabric (calcitic matrix) into which mineral inclusions are set (Plate IVd). Plaster primarily differs by having a finer sand-size temper that suggests a greater sorting of the material and a greater effort involved in its manufacture. Observation in thin section often reveals the presence of limestone fragments which have not been completely transformed to quicklime in the burning process. Equally, in destruction levels the calcite matrix may become dissolved by weathering, freeing the coarse inclusions into the surrounding sediment (see Chapter 15).

7.3.7 *Barrows*
Two main types of barrows occur: those made mainly of stone (cairns) and those made mainly of soil. Source materials, whether local or imported, can be determined for different parts of the barrow, including the mound, the burial(s) (when they occur), as well as for the associated ditch(es) when they have been identified. Specifically coloured, non-local sediments may have been used and can be shown to have been imported for possible ritual purposes. Anthropogenic materials, such as ashes, may have also been used.

Barrows consisting of soil materials may have been affected by subaerial

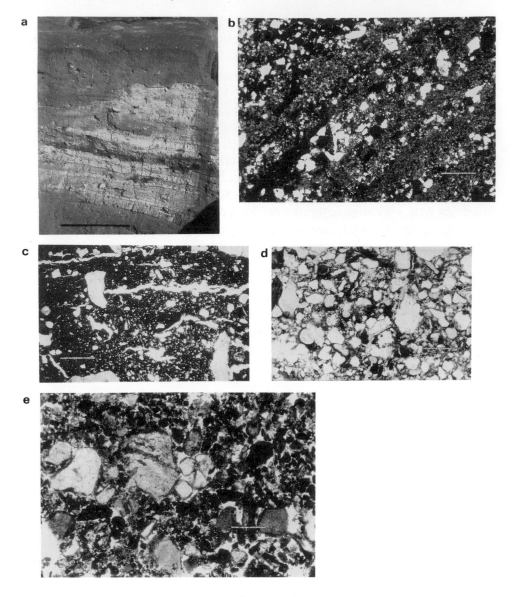

Figure 7.4   (a) Successive layers of decayed, washed and colluviated Late Bronze Age mud bricks and anthropogenic deposits from Deir al-Balah. (Bar = 1 m)

(b) Photomicrograph of colluviated and washed mud-brick materials, showing irregular bedding and sorting of coarse and fine constituents. XPL. (Bar = 190 μm)

(c) Fragment of burnt clay (brickearth) wall. Note the near absence of pugging of the soil materials used and the lack of plant temper. The horizontal fissuration is caused by heating (Roman, Courage, Southwark, England). PPL. (Bar = 150 μm)

weathering and soil formation, but a central, undisturbed core of the monument may be well preserved. Such conditions and materials permit us to study the methods of barrow construction and to determine the nature of the soil conditions prior to construction. Even cairns may contain environmentally useful contemporary turves (see above), now missing from the buried soil if it has been truncated prior to construction, thus sometimes enabling a full paleosol to be available for study.

7.3.8 *Inhumations and cremations*
Sediments, soils or anthropogenic materials associated with bone remains or ashes can be characterised in thin section. At the same time, it is possible to estimate the degree of bone alteration, which is related not only to the temperature of burning (Figure 7.1f) but also to those events which took place after burial (e.g., those associated with very acid conditions). In the case of cremation, the nature of the fuel used may also be identified. Finally, a few thin sections to study the relationship of the bones to the surrounding sediments should provide evidence concerning disturbances and may help solve such archaeological problems as relate to the discrimination of a primary cremation (burned *in situ*) from a secondary one (first burned and then buried or transported elsewhere).

7.3.9 *Ramparts*
The composition of ramparts can be studied in the same way as barrows, in order to establish the types of materials used and to distinguish different phases of construction. As ramparts are often associated with deep ditches, they may include small amounts of formerly existing surface soils, in addition to more deeply buried materials, such as sediments or bedrock (see Chapter 14). It is not uncommon that these rampart materials appear in reversed geological order, with more recent materials (e.g., former surface soils) at the base.

7.3.10 *Ditch fills, associated banks and postholes*
Ditch fills often include a primary fill accumulated shortly after it was dug, followed by various better-sorted fills, often mixed up with dumped materials.

(d) Occupation surface characterised by a dense porphyric related distribution caused by strong compaction (trampling). Note the occurrence of interconnected vughs infilled with dusty clay related to surface slaking (Cavour Iron Age floor, Piedmont, Italy). PPL. (Bar = 250 μm)

(e) Occupation surface strongly reworked by biological activity. The floor is from a collapsed pit-house (Keatley Creek, British Columbia, Canada) and consists of densely packed rock fragments and charcoal. The dense packing is partially a result of burrowing activity of cicadas; the rounding of the charcoal has probably been produced by aeolian activity while the floor was exposed. PPL. (Bar = 300 μm)

Accumulation of silt may produce very thin laminae of clay and silt, which may relate to reworking of the ditch faces and to deposition under standing water, as shown by graded bedding. Equally, juxtaposed banks may include the same, but disturbed, well-sorted sediments deposited after ditch cleaning episodes. For postholes, it may be possible to identify mortar or similar material that was used to hold the post in place (see Chapter 14). Thin sections may provide valuable information to differentiate man-related filling from natural ones, arguments being based both on the nature of the materials observed and on the kind of preserved sedimentary features.

7.3.11 *Floors and activity surfaces*

The concept of 'floor', as used here, refers more to a prepared or constructional surface rather than to the idea of the 'living floor' or 'occupation'. In thin section it is often possible to recognise former surfaces within a unit and to deduce from the features observed the past activities (Figure 7.4d; see Chapter 13).

Floors can be constructed of materials intentionally brought into the area or can consist of the local substrate purposefully prepared or modified by sweeping, by intentional compaction or by occupation trampling (Figure 7.4d). There is generally no problem in the field in identifying the first type and layers of plaster, gravel and sand are clear examples of floor constructions. The others, however, which are broadly speaking mud floors, and which lack strong lithological contrasts between the surrounding layers, may be extremely difficult to recognise during excavation.

A number of agencies can produce or modify a surface. Human or animal trampling sometimes acting together with natural puddling (after slaking of the floor material) are probably the most common agencies. Surface slaking can be considered as 'crust formation which is caused by the fact that structure elements at the surface are destroyed by the mechanical force of the precipitation and by the explosion of enclosed air' (Jongerius, 1970: 321, 1983). When well developed, the surface can be sealed by a fine laminated crust which is poorly or non-permeable and favours runoff. The features of trampling and associated slaking of a floor, while theoretically ubiquitous processes at archaeological sites, are rarely observable because of disturbances by further human activity and later by root and faunal working (Figure 7.4e). Furthermore, we wonder how much true 'trampling' actually occurs and is recorded at a site, in contrast to unintentional and contemporaneous deposition, homogenisation, sorting and mixing of materials at the floor surface. Dry, soft materials and intentionally hardened floors will compact poorly; both will result in the size reduction of soil aggregates, thus increasing their vulnerability to erosion by wind, for instance. Nevertheless, as a point of reference, micromorphological observations of soils compacted by heavy agricultural machinery show that soil compaction can be brought about by the mechanical action of heavy machinery affecting down to 80–100 cm (Jongerius, 1970). As a result, the larger vughs can almost be destroyed and planar voids form.

Returning to archaeological and prehistoric contexts, we should not expect to find striking effects and coarse features of heavy-machinery compaction as presented in the literature. On the contrary, it might be more reasonable to presume that in many instances – especially in prehistoric sites – human activities would destroy or partially disrupt stabilised surfaces such as slaking crusts, except where there is burial. In fact, the consequences of treading and trampling could explain the common occurrence at many prehistoric sites of lithic artifacts distributed through a layer of sediment several cm thick rather than concentrated at a 'surface'. Other explanations, involving bioturbation by termites or earthworms, for example, can also explain such vertical distributions of artifacts (Atkinson, 1957; Cahen and Moeyersons, 1978).

In any case, we have a long way to go to be able to infer the type of human activity (walking, scuffing, sweeping, cooking) associated with a given 'floor' from the micromorphological characteristics of a thin section. In order to accomplish this, detailed experiments would be needed to test the effects of different activities on substrates, whose micromorphological traits would then be checked, in ways similar to experiments on the taphonomy of artifact distribution.

Puddling effects are characterised by a vesicular porosity and a horizontally bedded fabric, which commonly displays dusty clay coatings in the pores. The vesicles, which indicate that the soil was saturated with water, are formed beneath the puddled, surface crust and may be later filled by fine material as water is drained from above (Figure 7.4d).

Some floors and activity surfaces may be quite 'pure' and be composed of only local soils and sediments (Plate VIIIa), whereas others may contain high quantities of charred organic matter derived from occupation activities, which were mixed into the floor. Different activities also produce various floor types. For example, stable floors and threshing floors can be characterised by thickly layered coarse phytoliths which are relics, respectively, of dung or cereals, the actual organic matter having been lost by oxidation (plate IVc).

7.3.12 *Final remarks*

Our experience has shown us that, regardless of the site and archaeologist digging it, there are several questions that are repeatedly asked. These generally revolve around the following issues:

> Does a certain material constitute a natural deposit, consisting of surrounding soils and sediments which have accumulated by natural processes?
> Is there evidence to suggest anthropogenic influences, as expressed either in the composition of the deposited materials or in the manner in which material has accumulated?
> How long has it taken for a pit or similar feature to fill up?

Finally, is there evidence that the accumulated materials have been altered since they were deposited (Figure 7.4e) and, if so, how does it contribute to our understanding of the original composition and of the geomorphic and palaeoenvironmental history of the site?

No doubt such questions will be asked well into the future, since they involve themes central to the thorough understanding of an archaeological site. We hope that this chapter will help make the solutions of these problems an easier task.

7.4 Land use and associated features

In recent years, both archaeologists and earth scientists (especially soil scientists) have been increasingly concerned with past and current human land-use practices and how these may have brought about changes in the landscape and soils. This interest stems principally from the realisation that, both in the past and at present, such human activities as the creation of small forest clearings, total deforestation or ploughing can irreversibly affect and destabilise soils and the landscape, ultimately leading to such problems as soil salinisation and soil erosion. The ramifications of these adverse environmental effects are particularly noteworthy for the archaeologist, since deteriorations in local conditions may bring about negative cultural feedbacks, which may be seen in changes in the type of archaeological settlement or even abandonment of an area (Proudfoot, 1958; Romans and Robertson, 1975a, 1983b).

It seems that the first clear signs of landscape manipulation on a detectable scale appeared in the Neolithic, if not possibly somewhat earlier, at the end of the Epipalaeolithic and Mesolithic (Keef *et al.*, 1965). We may suppose that in most parts of the world prior to that time, population density and social organisation were such that human activities left generally little impact in the geomorphic record and that soil/landscape changes were more likely attributable to climatic and geological causes. Thus most of the features discussed in this final part are drawn or illustrated from Holocene archaeological sites and not Pleistocene sites.

In spite of this keen interest in land-use change, we generally lack definitive and unequivocal criteria, methodologies and data that can be used to infer former land-use practices, though some claim that these can be garnered from phosphate analyses (Eidt, 1984). Although it is fair to say that more micromorphological work is needed to bond microscopic features with their human agents and activities, it must also be admitted that enough micromorphological data already exist – in many cases supported by independent environmental evidence – to allow us to infer with a reasonable degree of certainty past human activities. The effects of clearing, ploughing and grazing, for example, do possess their own micromorphological manifestations and hence these basic, generalised activities are described first. Furthermore, although direct micromorphological evidence for a certain feature may be lacking on account of destruction by subsequent events – well-sealed and datable buried soils being at a premium – certain micromorphological 'ghosts' may still remain to enable us to make inferences about the state of the original material, even if a series of events has been superimposed.

7.4.1 *Clearance and devegetation*

Partial disturbance or complete removal of natural vegetation can occur in the course of preparation of a land surface for a specific use, be it for exploitation of a forest, construction of a site or preparation of fields for cultivation (Butzer, 1982). The activities involved in devegetation are a function of local tradition – as shown by ethnogeographic examples – and the ultimate use that the land is being prepared for. Clearance, therefore, can be manifested in partial devegetation, where the humic layer between trees is removed, or in total devegetation, which is accomplished by uprooting and slash-and-burn practices.

7.4.1.1 Uprooting.

Uprooting of trees, either by man or by natural tree throw (Lutz and Griswold 1939), can induce important disturbances in the soil, especially in regard to soil horizonation. In a virgin forest with a continuous canopy, direct wind exposure is minimal and a dead tree can decay in an upright position for a long time. However, once clearings are made, wind-shake and wind-throw of trees becomes more important. Remains of tree hollows can be recognised in the field (Evans, 1971, 1972; Limbrey, 1975; Macphail, 1986) – both in plan and in section – by the way the lower subsoil and parent material adhere to the root plate and by the 'banana' shape of the soil pattern left after the fallen tree has decayed.

The microfabrics associated with this uprooting are related to the manner in which the tree hollow was subsequently infilled. A strongly and heterogeneously mixed fabric composed of material from different soil horizons indicates more of a rapid infilling, not affected by biological perforation (Figure 7.5a). Furthermore, the occurrence of coarse (i.e., forest) wood charcoal, flint or other artifacts can be used to substantiate the inference that anthropogenic activity is associated with the uprooting. On the other hand, the presence of a homogeneous microfabric highly reworked by biological activity – e.g., channels and fine integration of organic matter into the groundmass – will point to a rather slow infilling and a gradual recolonisation of the surface by vegetation. Finally, it should be remembered that, because of the open structure of tree hollow infillings, they are ideal places for burrowing (e.g., by rodents, moles, foxes) and they therefore serve as loci for preferential disturbance and mixing of the infill materials.

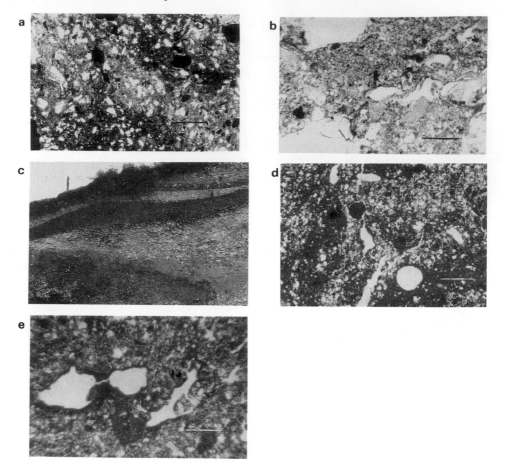

Figure 7.5   (a) Photomicrograph of the tree hollow infilling, showing the mixture of two different soil materials, caused by physical disruption by tree throw. The light patches belong to the calcitic subsoil and the dark brown patches to the decalcified clay soil. Note the closed void network indicating slow compaction (Atlantic forest soil, Hazelton, England). XPL. (Bar = 500 μm)

(b) Micromorphological evidence of clearance by burning is shown by the abundance of microdivided charcoal particles and dusty clay coatings around voids (Neolithic soil, Carn Brae, England). PPL. (Bar = 500 μm)

(c) Prehistoric lynchets of calcareous brown soil and chalky soil formed on the upper slopes of the Susssex downland after the decalcified brown soil had been eroded (near Lewes, Sussex, England).

(d) Colluvial mixture of decalcified subsoil clay (weathered from the chalk) and silty (loess cover) soil base of dry valley (Ashcombe Bottom, near Lewes, Sussex, England). PPL. (Bar = 550 μm)

(e) Present-day non-cultivated soil developed on loessic alluvium, showing structureless, disrupted silty clay micropans. PPL. (Bar = 150 μm)

7.4.1.2 Clearance by burning

Normally, the burning of trees or grasses directly affects only the upper few cm of the soil. The base-rich nature of the resulting ashes, once the toxic levels of potassium are reduced, tends to promote biological activity after the initial burning. With time, however, soluble nutrients and salts become increasingly leached, especially on coarse substrates, and biological activity decreases. Nevertheless, the net result is a microfabric characterised by the occurrence of finely mixed charred organic fragments (?originating from the buried Ah layer), in addition to a few remnants of charcoal and burned wood, as well as reddish-brown aggregates representing a rubified topsoil if the soil contains clay.

In addition to augmenting biological activity, the enrichment of K^+, Ca^{++}, Mg^{++} in ashes (see Section 7.2.1.1 on ash) can promote the translocation of clay. This, coupled with the fact that charcoal favours the dispersal of the clay, results in the formation in the lower topsoil of clay coatings, rich in fine charcoal (Figure 7.5b). All these features, however, are difficult to isolate if the soil is not rapidly sealed and thus put out of reach of continuing pedological homogenisation.

An example of prehistoric clearance comes from southern England, where trees covering a Neolithic landscape were probably pulled over and uprooted, thereby causing soil disruption features as noted above. Evidence also shows that the tree trunks were burned in place (Robinson and Lambrick pers. comm.).

7.4.2 *Grazing*

Grazing generally takes place on grass-covered soil surfaces, in which soil horizon development is less than that under forested conditions. Under grass, intensive fine rooting and biological activity form deep, stable, crumb-structured Mull horizons (Grieve, 1980; Barratt, 1964; see Chapter 8, biological features). In addition, structural modifications take place as a result of the mechanical action of pasturing animals. The latter are especially concentrated in stocking areas and droveways, which can commonly become puddled. Observations on present-day pasturage conditions show that intensive grazing on grassland brown soils by herbivores promotes the development of a platy structure near the soil surface (Figure 7.6). This appears in thin section as elongated and platy pores within a dense fabric. The formation of these pores is further exacerbated in grassland soils situated in temperate and cold-temperate climates where freezing also produces a platy structure (see Chapter 8, frost effects).

Animals associated with grazing produce an increase in phosphate and organic matter, again concentrated in stock pounds and droveways. In addition, 'fine' and 'coarse' fungal bodies have an inferred association with sheep and cattle grazing, respectively, the fungal ring becoming increasingly birefringent with age (*c.* 900 years; Romans and Robertson, 1983b).

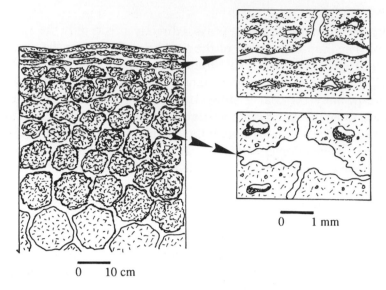

Figure 7.6   Structural changes induced by intensive grazing on grassland brown soil. Note the platy microstructure and dense fabric at the soil surface, and the vughy microstructure in the underlying subsoil, resulting from the compaction of the original soil fabric.

Briefly, evidence for differentiating buried pasture from forest soil include:

1   Deep homogeneous Mull A–horizons with intensive rooting and biological activity in regions where we would normally expect to find clearly developed surficial organic and A horizons. Moreover, as has been noted in cool, high-rainfall areas, a change from forest to grass can lead to surface waterlogging and peats.
2   Small mammal activity (e.g., moles, gophers, rabbits) in the top part of the buried soil.
3   Remnants of finely dispersed, humified fine matter of the grassy type; this includes high amounts of randomly distributed phytoliths mixed in with phosphatic-rich organic residues in stock concentration areas.

7.4.3 *Ploughing (including arding, hoeing, digging)*

The occurrence in the field of a sometimes overly thick homogeneous layer at the top of a buried soil may be an excellent indicator of past ploughing, especially when it is associated with lynchets, a hypothesis that the presence of ard-marks in the underlying subsoil (i.e., at the base of the 'plough soil') may confirm. On the other hand, ploughed layers may have been modified by subsequent human activity or recolonisation by natural vegetation prior to burial. In the latter cases, field evidence for former ploughing may be unclear and would have to be supported by information from other types of evidence. However, as a general rule, ancient field systems on sloping ground (where movement of ploughsoil under gravity is expected) can be ascribed to arable systems, where downslope ploughsoil accumulations are present, or to pasturage when soil movement has been minimal (Balaam *et al.*, 1982).

Clearly one of the first results of arable cultivation, by ploughing, for example, is to eliminate the upper soil horizons, especially the organic-rich layers, and to create a homogeneous Ap horizon. The latter includes, in the first instance, characteristics of the surface humic layer as well as mineral material reworked from the underlying A horizon. Further consequences are that devegetation for cultivation exposes the soil surface to direct rainfall impact and this will create soil features unlike those present naturally under grassland or forest. Equally, the use of irrigation in a desert area to aid cultivation will encourage greater biological activity (because of the increased moisture content) that again may be atypical for the regional soil.

Artificial soils such as plaggens or terrace accumulations created by dumping, which under normal circumstances would be dense, heterogeneous and 'sterile', become highly perforated and homogenised by biological activity that is favoured by cultivation and associated manuring. Thus, the impact of cultivation is to produce 'unnatural' features, which, when found in thin section, may be used to identify specifically an arable land-use pattern.

Micromorphological studies of modern cultivated soils (Jongerius 1970, 1983) show that, in addition to coarse mechanical disturbances and compaction caused by heavy machinery, the principal consequence of cultivation is the formation of textural features (see Chapter 8, particle translocation), grain coatings, void infillings and *pans* that appear in the **agric** horizon – the horizon formed under long-term, continuous cultivation. These agric horizons arc composed of fine-grained plasma, very fine sand grains and very fine-grained organic particles – collectively known as **agricutans** – that result from the structural breakdown and easy slaking of superficial soil horizons related to modern cultivation (Figure 7.7). Thus the same processes that operate for bare surfaces (floors) takes place here, except that the soil surface is endlessly renewed by ploughing.

Jongerius believed that these agricutans develop just below the Ap horizon or within deep cracks formed in heavy soils. It is now known that their distribution and degree of development is strongly related to the ability of solid particles to be translocated in the ploughed (cultivated) soil. This, in turn, depends upon both the chemical characteristics of the soil solution and the nature of the void patterns.

Though prehistoric and historic cultivation practices produced similar features, it is nevertheless possible to differentiate them, although there are a number of parameters which relate to:

  (i)   the kind of soils or archaeological deposits that were involved,
  (ii) the kind of cultivation that took place – shallow hoeing, deeper arding, digging with a spade or deep mouldboard ploughing, and
  (iii) the rapidity with which the cultivated layer was buried – quickly by a monument or slowly by colluvium; all give rise to anomalous features, which, as stated earlier, are clues indicating cultivation.

So far the best evidence comes from rapidly buried, moderately acid soils, and cases where there is independent supportive environmental data (charred

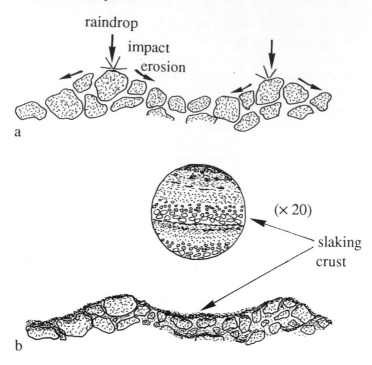

Figure 7.7   Splash effects of raindrops on the surface of a ploughed soil: erosion of the aggregates from the top part of the surface (a) and accumulation of the eroded particles in the small depressions, forming slaking crusts (b).

cereal grain and weed seeds, pollen and molluscs) or archaeological evidence (cultivation ridges, ardmarks, associated colluvium and lynchets) for on-site cultivation. An examination of the upper soil shows that the expected sequence of a biologically worked A horizon overlying an A2 horizon does not occur. Instead, a rather homogeneous fabric is present, characterised by a vughy porosity with very abundant textural features. (This layer is genetically not part of a Bt horizon, which may in fact occur as the subsoil horizon.) The textural features can be of all kinds, including intercalations, dusty clay coatings, and impure (i.e., with silt) clay coatings and infills (Plate IVe and IVf). These features are presumed to originate in the same way as discussed by Jongerius for modern cultivated soils: on the devegetated surface physical breakup of the soil produces a fine tilth that destabilises the soil and enables slaking by soil water after rain. The soil in this mobilised state is locally translocated to produce the above features.

On flat sites, where soil loss by erosion has been minimal, these features can be concentrated at different levels in the topsoil, as identified by semi-quantitative analyses, and the type of cultivation practised can be inferred because the various implements cause maximum disturbance at these different depths (Plate IVe and IVf) (Romans and Robertson, 1983a; Macphail *et al.*, 1987). At the point of greatest disturbance, the entire unsorted soil can be mobilised, but only the dusty clay may penetrate lower into the soil. Thus, a terrace sediment may feature coatings through the cultivation of an overlying layer whereas a subsoil Bt horizon may show these secondary coatings developed on textural features that were formed under an earlier forest cover. In contrast to modern ploughing, which penetrates to a depth of *c*. 40 cm and can affect B horizons, shallow arding will normally modify only the surficial horizons. Thus, if a prehistoric soil contains rounded fragments of B horizon material, it can be supposed that arding of an upslope area has caused erosion down to this subsoil level, thereby exposing it to erosion.

However, as a number of mechanisms may produce similar textural features (e.g., slaking on a floor), the final interpretation of such features requires close scrutiny of the context from which the samples were taken, such as by monitoring the pattern of coatings down the profile in a semi-quantitative way (Romans and Robertson, 1983a), and by sampling of the palaeolandscape in many locations.

With originally acid soils, such as those developed on sands with little or no clay, chemical changes induced by cultivation are too weak to increase the pH and change the soil solution – both of which favour translocation of solid particles. Consequently, we should not expect to find prominent textural features related to cultivation in these soils. The only evidence might be an anomalous heterogeneous mixture of microfabrics originating from different horizons that are at variance with those found in local soil formation (Plate IVg and IVh).

Experiments have shown that cultivation does not always lead to a surface Ap horizon characterised by textural features. In fact, when soil conditions are improved by a cultivation regime – with additions of manure for example – and where soil pH is neither too acid nor too alkaline, biological activity may become very intense. In these cases, textural or heterogeneous soil features can be rapidly lost, and added organic matter quickly humified. Thus in these circumstances, cultivated soils may only be recognised by their anomalously high biological activity. As well, abandoned cultivation plots or arable fields given over to pasture, that once had well-developed textural features, will have biological fabrics superimposed upon them.

7.4.4 *Manuring and related practices*
Mineral and organic matter are intentionally added to parent materials in order to diminish the depletion of certain nutrients (see Section 7.4.2) and to increase yields. The addition of farmyard manure to English soils, for example, changed both the structure of the soil and the distribution of pore sizes, leading to increased retention of available water (Pitty, 1978).

It appears that at the time of the earliest agriculture, manuring was not practised, and the organic matter of cultivated soils was possibly low (Macphail *et al.*, 1987), although seaweed, for example, as an organic manure may have been discovered rather early (Bell, 1981). The impact of manuring on soils is little known from a micromorphological standpoint. Evidence for manuring may include higher amounts of organic fragments, especially phytoliths, derived from animal dung. In thin section these can appear to be browner than those produced from decayed organic matter derived from a humic layer (Plate IVh). Where stable layers have been burned at low temperature, the resulting middens have a very pale, thin fabric except for included coprolitic material, derived particularly from scavenging animals. In some cases, intensive application of manure mixed with sediment has brought about a marked improvement of soils. These materials are ploughed into the soil and produce a homogeneous, dark-grey upper horizon, up to 1 m thick, rich in soluble phosphate. The resulting soils – known as **plaggen soils** – are known from historical periods in Ireland, the British Isles, Germany and the Netherlands (Figure 7.8a, 8b). In the latter case, horticultural soils were thus produced from otherwise infertile podzols, whose relic subsoil horizons can be found at depth.

7.4.5 *Terraces, lynchets and ploughwash colluviums*
In many places throughout the world field terraces were built in order to facilitate cultivation on steep slopes and to retain the soil. This was generally accomplished either by adding material – virgin soil or anthropogenic dumps – on the slope and stabilising it with a retaining wall or by cutting into the slope and using the excavated material to flatten the surface (see Chapters 14 and 17). In the cases where anthropogenic dumps were used, these horizons are very heterogeneous, generally poorly structured, commonly contain coarse fragments of charcoal and intra-ped porosity is generally low.

Terraces made up from virgin soil material display a heterogeneity of soil types mixed with A horizons. This results not only from human manipulation but also from colluviation, since deposits are accreted on the positive side from material found further upslope. Thus through time they may be layered if successive periods of land use are interrupted by abandonment and recolonisation by vegetation, accompanied by incipient pedogenesis.

Although the microfabrics associated with lynchets (Figure 7.5c) vary according to the soil types present and the history of the site under study, some main types can be presented. Prominent are heterogenous fabrics that reveal mixing of materials from various horizons colluviated from upslope. These commonly include well-rounded soil fragments, which give information about the ancient soils which were ploughed and perhaps now totally eroded from the modern landscape. In addition, pseudo-homogeneous fabrics occur, consisting of materials (Figure 7.5d) that have become thoroughly mixed by continuous cultivation. These include the abundance of organic fragments as well as various textural features associated with ploughing, as discussed above. In addition, stony horizons within colluvium (Allen, 1987), that could be inter-

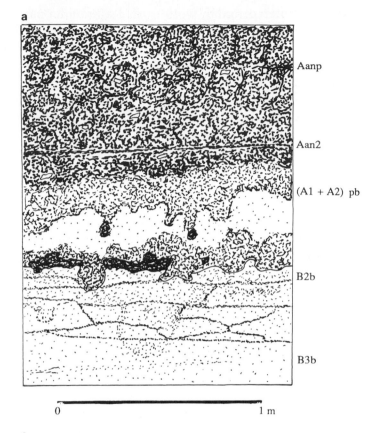

Aanp

Aan2

(A1 + A2) pb

B2b

B3b

0   1 m

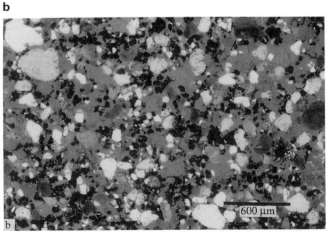

600 μm

Figure 7.8   (a) Sketch of a typical profile of a plaggen soil (sandy siliceous mesic Plaggept) in Netherlands (from de Bakker H., 1979: 141).

(b) Photomicrograph of the characteristic black moder-type of humus occurring in plaggen soils, comprising a loose mixture of sand grains (light grey and white) and black coprogenic, organic aggregates, mainly excrements. Circ. Pol. Light.

preted as plough phases interspersed by worm-sorted soils under pasture, have been shown to be stony fans when studied in three dimensions and are the result of high-energy runoff.

Various soil studies have now combined the archaeological dating of lynchet and valley-fill colluvium with snail analyses in order to study past environments. Similarly, acid substrates have the potential of yielding pollen for analysis, whereas fine materials can be dated by palaeomagnetism; magnetic-susceptibility enhancement can distinguish topsoil from subsoil colluvium. In all cases microfeatures provide their own independent evidence, showing, for instance in a chalk landscape, a change in soil erosion from decalcified to chalky soil materials.

7.4.6 *Irrigation*

There are several issues related to past irrigation practices which are of typical interest to archaeologists. One is concerned with the span of time that a particular system was used. Unfortunately, a direct response to this problem using micromorphological data is lacking or difficult to establish.

A more widespread phenomenon, and one which lends itself to microscopic study, is that of salinisation. Clear evidence exists to show that ancient civilisations may have faced problems of salinisation, as for example in the Mesopotamian Plain, around 2400 BC (Jacobsen and Adams, 1958; Goudie, 1981). Increased soil salinity, as is evident today, would have affected soil productivity and might have induced soil toxicity for those plants sensitive to salt – such as wheat – and would have been responsible for a gradual change in the use of cultigens, from wheat, to mixed wheat and barley, and ultimately to barley alone.

A major hindrance in recognising prior salinisation problems is that the accumulation of salts is a reversible phenomenon: salts that may have accumulated at one time have been leached out of the soil, leaving little or no evidence of their former presence (see Chapter 8, movements of in solution). In thin section, such salts may not be found or, if found, may have accumulated during some other, unknown period of time.

However, certain textural features can be found that aid in the recognition of salinity problems. Evidence of high amounts of sodium, which promotes the dispersion of clay, is indicated by dusty, poorly laminated, and weakly birefringent clays that are mixed with coarser particles. Another indication is represented by the presence of collapsed voids representing an unstable soil structure (Plate Va).

On the other hand, irrigation of arid and semi-arid soils does not always lead to salinisation, especially if the input of water is limited or the quality of irrigated water is good. A high input of water – as compared with non-irrigated soils – favours the translocation of particles, including clay and silt, and induces the formation of vesicles. These are characteristically produced from a rapid drying-out of the soil surface whereby, immediately under the surface, water and air are trapped in bubbles and silt and clay are deposited. When such an irrigated surface is buried, these features furnish clear evidence of former irrigation (Figure 7.5e). Similar coarse textural features and vesicles can, however, have been produced by natural flooding and it is only through a careful comparison of soils that are supposed to have been cultivated (corroborated by the archaeological context) and virgin soils (in areas never occupied by man) that interpretation of these features can be proposed.

7.4.7 *Effects of man on the soil ecology*

When human groups change the land-use practices of an area, the soil may be unaffected, degraded or even improved. High base status loams are quite resistant, whereas acid sandy soils may have most of their nutrients in the surface organic matter and vegetation. If these are lost by clearance, burning and subsequent leaching, poor soils such as podzols will result (Dimbleby, 1962). In such cases, thin sections of the subsoil horizons, which are too deep to be affected by acid leachates, may reveal relic features of the pre-podzolic, brown soil profile. Even on loams, the loss of the forest canopy may expose moderately sensitive soils to erosion on slopes, a process that would be exacerbated by the continual breakup of the soil by cultivation; pasture soils, well bound by roots, are the most stable.

In areas of heavy rainfall, the replacement of forest by pasture through grazing pressure and consequent decrease in evapotranspiration can also lead to surface waterlogging and peaty soils (Romans and Robertson 1975b; Keeley 1982). On the other hand, the destruction of montane conifers to develop pastures can increase soil nitrogen and biological activity at the same time that terracing inhibits soil erosion.

The above examples are not meant to be a complete discussion of all the various kinds of soil changes that could possibly be related to human activities but rather a selection of examples for which relatively clear inferences can be made from micromorphological observations. When possible, we stress that micromorphological interpretations of such human activities should be corroborated by archaeological and palaeoenvironmental data such as that from palynology and palaeontology. Furthermore, it should be evident that more empirical evidence will have to be gathered in the form of systematic micromorphological examination of features associated with present-day land-use practices in order to enable us to make firm interpretations from ancient settings.

8

POST-DEPOSITIONAL PROCESSES
AND RELEVANT FEATURES

8.1 **Introduction**

Post-depositional processes include a large variety of changes and transformations which affect a sediment after it has been deposited. Different disciplines, however, maintain different viewpoints as to what constitutes a post-depositional process and what it should be called.

For geologists post-depositional processes are lumped together under the term **diagenesis**, which refers to the changes that take place during the transformation of sediments into sedimentary rocks within tens of metres of the earth surface. Included under this umbrella are, on the one hand, physical transformations, such as mechanical alteration and compaction resulting from dewatering and, on the other, mineralogical and chemical changes such as alteration of clay minerals, silicification, decomposition of organic matter, dissolution and precipitation of calcium carbonate and segregation of metal elements to form iron pans, for example. For some, soil formation is regarded as a kind of early diagenesis (Retallack, 1983) and refers to the changes that take place once a cover of vegetation has developed. Since evidence for most of these changes can be obliterated by later diagenetic processes after burial, it is not surprising that the identification of fossil soils in terrestrial sedimentary rocks is rather difficult (Wright, 1986).

Pedologists studying post-depositional processes responsible for soil development group such transformations under the heading of **pedological processes**. These include such processes as eluviation and illuviation of solid particles, dissolution and precipitation of soluble components (e.g., decalcification/calcification, desalinisation/salinisation), pedoturbation, podzolisation, humification, rubification and hydromorphism. As discussed previously (see Chapter 2), the combination of these processes is essentially responsible for the development of the soil profile and most of these pedological processes are identical to the early diagenetic processes described by geologists. However, when attempting to explain the development of a soil profile, soil scientists will commonly include under the term 'pedological processes', effects which are geological or diagenetic (*sensu stricto*), such as mineral and chemical transformations induced by groundwater or mineral weathering at great depth. Furthermore, it should be kept in mind that the boundary between pedological and sedimentary processes should be kept operationally flexible: for example,

138

biochemical sedimentation that occurs at the soil surface (e.g., algal crust) can be regarded by soil scientists as a pedological process, even if strictly speaking a biogenic sediment is formed.

For archaeologists post-depositional processes are not so clearly classified as such but tend to be grouped just as 'disturbances', which include any alteration of an archaeological layer subsequent to its abandonment by humans. Disturbances by frost, animal burrowing and root cracking have been commonly cited (Wood and Johnson, 1978; Stein, 1983).

In order to understand fully the nature, history and development of an archaeological site and its environmental context, however, it is necessary to be able to recognise any form of change that affects a stratigraphic unit after its deposition. This central idea epitomises the approach we take here. (The transport and deposition of materials are considered in Chapter 6.)

In original sediments, post-depositional effects cause specific changes that can be recognised by the kind of features that they produce, as seen in thin sections. Each feature can usually be related to a process which is either physical (e.g., pure mixing), physico-chemical (e.g., clay translocation) or mainly chemical (e.g., iron oxidation). For the sake of convenience, we have grouped post-depositional processes into the following categories: biological activity and humification, mechanical effects of water, effects of frost, movements of solutions, and neoformation (which includes weathering *sensu stricto*), and hydration–dehydration.

When sediments have been transformed by only one agent, the resulting features are generally easy to recognise. Complications arise, however, when individual or successive post-depositional processes occur. This results not only in the super- and juxtaposition of features but also in the partial or total erasure of the effects of earlier post-depositional processes. Thus, one of the principal aims of thin-section study is to recognise, isolate and interpret all the post-depositional features recorded in a thin section and to organise them chronologically. In theory, this should provide all the data an archaeological team will need to comprehend their site: i.e., the characterisation of the virgin soil, description of the form of occupation and local land use, and examination of post-burial modifications.

In this chapter, we discuss different kinds of post-depositional processes and describe the relevant microscopic features associated with them, particularly those features which have diagnostic characteristics. Only the most commonly occurring post-depositional processes in archaeological contexts (e.g., biological activity) are emphasised here; less important ones (e.g., silicate weathering and neoformation of clay minerals) are only briefly presented because they occur so slowly that they are beyond the realm of archaeological time. The rate of rapid (a few years) or more slow (*c.* 100 years) processes may be commonly estimated with the help of archaeological data.

8.2 **Biological activity and biological features – humification**

8.2.1 *Importance in archaeological contexts*

Many archaeologists have been confronted with some striking examples of artifact dispersion by animal activity (see Butzer, 1982: 113; Cahen and Moeyersons, 1977). Animals such as porcupines, badgers or rabbits produce major disturbances that can be readily recognised. Except for strikingly recognisable structures such as termite mounds, most modifications induced by smaller soil fauna (e.g., earthworms) and by small roots or microorganisms may escape notice in the field, being observable only by slight changes in structure or colour that might otherwise be ascribed to chemical alteration. For such modifications, thin-section analysis is necessary to identify the processes responsible for such characteristics.

Because of their high nutrient content, archaeological sediments and soils constitute attractive loci for biological activity and the essence of the problem is to infer the correct biological agent that caused this disturbance (plant vs. animal) and its environmental significance. Modifications can be either physical (e.g., mechanical homogenisation) or biochemical (e.g., decay and degradation of organic matter) or a combination of both. Soil animals can permanently, periodically or accidentally reside in the soil and can comprise an elaborate community of herbivorous, carnivorous and coprophagous animals in addition to microorganisms living on organo-mineral complexes (Hole, 1981).

8.2.2 *Effects of large animals*

Pigs, foxes, rabbits, squirrels, gophers, moles, rats and mice strongly disaggregate soils and sediments when looking for food or 'shelter' and produce a soil with typically loose structure consisting of open-packed aggregates of varying shapes. In addition to this physical transformation, some material can be re-incorporated into the initial sediments in the form of excrements, stored food or displaced soil. The presence of these extraneous materials can be clearly recognised (Figure 8.1) and differentiated from the original sediments, even if the latter are present only as aggregates. If more than one archaeological unit has been mixed, this can usually be seen in the thin section, thus aiding the interpretation of artifacts found in reworked layers. Since disturbances can occur at any time after deposition and modifications can take place very quickly (e.g., daily changes), it is frequently possible to estimate the timing and relative sequence of 'disturbance events' by noting the composition of the different mixed materials.

Other relatively large animals, such as birds and bats, can have an indirect effect on underlying sediments and soils – particularly in caves and in coastal areas – as a result of guano accumulation on the surface below their living space (Hutchinson, 1950). These organic-rich accumulations can form thick layers, which are often brown and soft when fresh and may induce drastic changes of

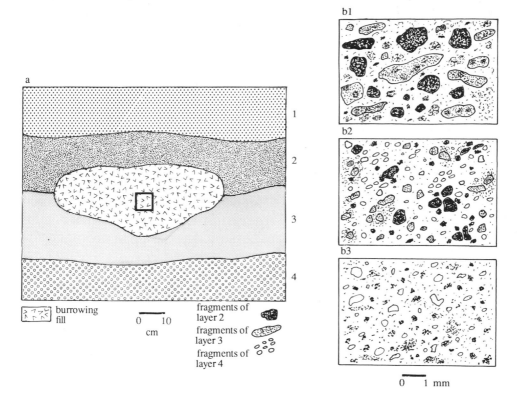

Figure 8.1   Effects of large animals on the mixing of archaeological layers:
   (a) Sketch showing the occurrence of a burrowing fill disrupting the archaeological sequence.
   (b1) The burrowing fill consists of weakly mixed materials from layers 2 and 3 (well-preserved coarse fragments from both layers).
   (b2) In this case materials from layers 2, 3 and 4 are finely mixed but the recognition of the different layers is still possible.
   (b3) The burrowing fill consists of strongly homogenised materials. The original characteristics of the reworked layers are nearly totally lost.

the initial characters of the underlying sediments. There are many examples from prehistoric caves, especially developed in calcareous rock, where archaeological layers have been deeply altered by the percolation of solutions enriched in organic acids and phosphates originating from guano (Peneaud, 1978; Goldberg and Nathan, 1975). In these instances, the most prominent features are the weathering of calcareous constituents, and the neoformation of various kinds of phosphatic minerals that can be optically identified but more effectively studied with the SEM (see Section 8.4). Different stages of transformations may be observed, from weak weathering of the still recognisable mineral constituents, to complete weathering, in which most of the original mineralogical characteristics of the sediments have been destroyed, including the bone. In spite of the striking features produced, much still needs to be learned about the specific environmental conditions necessary to cause these biogenic disturbances and alterations (climate, rate of development and edaphic conditions) (Plate VIIId).

8.2.3 *Effects of small animals, small roots, microflora and microorganisms*

Although these various agents may cause specific features in soil fabrics, it is quite difficult to isolate these actions individually since they generally occur in close association. Mesofauna, such as termites, contain symbiotic bacteria that are used for breaking down food prior to ingestion; various kinds of bacteria can be found living on the nutrients produced by roots. Because of these complex interrelationships, we will not attempt to discuss the detailed mechanisms of biological activity but will only describe in general terms those major effects and features recognisable in ancient soils that pertain to environmental reconstruction.

As with the larger animals, movements of smaller fauna produce disrupted soil fabrics, which may be grouped according to size (Toutain, 1981):

1   Greater than a few tens of cm (reaching up to a few metres), as found, for example, associated with earthworms. These move through different horizons, taking their food at the soil surface and living in the lower horizons.
2   Local movements of a few cm produced by microarthropods and enchytraeids living in proximity to roots.
3   *In situ* activity in which animals such as Oribatids live on organic residues.

When animals such as earthworms colonise soils or sediments, they produce voids of specific shapes called channels, whose walls may be lined by fine material brought by the animal itself. This is especially so in poorly structured soils (e.g., sandy soils), where an increase in the stability of animal pathways is required; at the same time, passage by the animal will produce compaction of the surrounding materials. When vertical movements are very intense, the action of soil fauna results in complete homogenisation and destruction of original soil or sedimentary fabrics (Figure 8.2a). In extreme cases the resulting fabric may only consist of criss-crossing channels and densely packed aggregates of biological origin; this is called a total biological fabric.

Other kinds of animals, such as enchytraeids and microarthropods, can only live in the organic-rich layers present at the soil surface. Their action is restricted to horizontal movements and does little to modify soil stratification. Whereas earthworms are more adapted to rich conditions (e.g., soils containing clay or calcium carbonate), enchytraeids and microarthropods survive in poor environments (e.g., acid sands) and resist unfavourable pedoclimatic conditions, such as cold and humidity.

The soil fauna plays an important role in the redistribution of organic and mineral particles through the production of excrements. Animals living solely in organic-rich layers and consuming only plant residues produce excrements

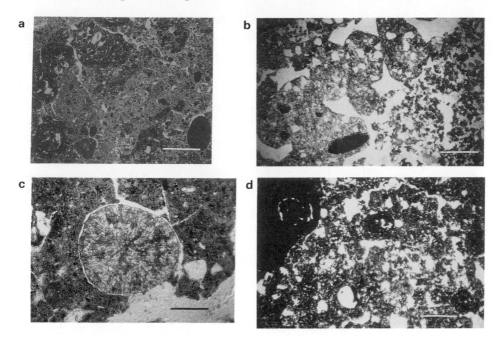

Figure 8.2   (a) Total excremental fabric resulting from a complete homogenisation by earthworms and insects of dumped constructional materials (Netiv Hagdud, Israel; see Chapter 13). PPL. (Bar = 8 mm)

(b) Specific shapes of soil fauna excrements: brown, large, mammilated, densely packed earthworm excrements with a low organic-matter content associated with dark, small, loosely packed enchytraeid excrements with a high organic-matter content. This association relates to an acidification process, such that earthworms are being replaced by enchytraeids (buried mull-like Dark Earth, Jubilee Hall, England). (Bar = 150 μm)

(c) Spherical calcite granule with a radial internal fabric representing the internal shell of slug (Arionid) (Dark Earth, England). PPL. (Bar = 150 μm)

(d) Diagnostic crumb microstructure of a mull related mostly to earthworm activity; base-rich soil (Atlantic tree hollow, Balksbury, England). PPL. (Bar = 150 μm)

consisting mostly of organic materials. On the other hand, animals living on mineral substances by the absorption of micronutrients in the lower soil horizon cast up excrements rich in mineral matter; animals eating both organic and mineral materials produce excrements consisting of finely mixed organic residues and mineral constituents. Furthermore, each kind of soil animal produces excrements of very specific shape and only slightly variable size, according to the age of the animal. Consequently, when the excrements are well preserved, their shape and internal composition can lead to the identification of the type of animal which may have produced them (Figure 8.2b). In some cases, excrements may include neoformed minerals produced by the organisms themselves. For example, infillings of loose calcite crystals are commonly observed in earthworm channels and are supposed to be produced by earthworms, (Bal, 1975). Mineral constituents can also be part of the decayed organisms themselves, as is the case of the internal shell of slugs (Arionids), which produce spherical calcite granules with a radial internal fabric (Figure 8.2c)

Biological disturbances can appear very quickly (*c.* within a few days) but their effects may be preserved over long periods, especially in soils which have a high structural stability, or in cases when biological fabrics have not been destroyed by other pedological processes. In poorly structured materials, such as loose sandy soils, biological fabrics are not long-lasting and channels will commonly have a collapsed appearance. In other cases, excrements will age and disintegrate through the mechanical effect of water; as a consequence, their initial shape will no longer be recognisable. In such compacted layers, biological channels – which can be more or less collapsed – will be the only features indicating that the soil was affected by biological activity (Figure 8.3).

In a way similar to soil fauna, roots create a void network within the soil, pushing away soil material, and in so doing create mechanical disturbances. This action is gradual, however, because roots grow slowly and compaction features are limited mostly to the environment very close to the root (Figure 8.4); moreover the compaction becomes increasingly important as the root diameter increases. The action of roots may sometimes be difficult to distinguish from that of microorganisms, with which they are always associated. Organic substances produced by roots and associated bacterial activity induce physico-chemical and chemical reactions, which result in the weathering of certain minerals and in the formation of stable organo-mineral complexes (see for example Dorioz and Robert, 1987). Some chemical changes, however, may be considered a consequence of root respiration and absorption only, without the interference of microorganisms. Such changes will vary in accordance with oxygen availability as well as moisture content. Along channels, for example, depletion and accumulation features of calcium carbonate or iron are considered to be the result of chemical reactions taking place locally at the soil–root interface.

The lower plants, such as lichens and mosses, possess great potential to develop on the surface of mineral soils or on unweathered exposed rocks, extracting nutrients from the substrate they have colonised (Robert *et al.*, 1983). Living symbiotically with various kinds of microorganisms, they are able to penetrate mineral elements by way of very fine pores. This results in a network of fissures and an alteration of the mineral structure, favouring further disaggregation. Rock fragments, especially limestone, which have been subjected to the activity of inferior plants before their incorporation into soil materials, may be identified in thin sections by the differential alteration of their edges, whereas fragments corroded *in situ* are more uniformly altered.

In the previous paragraphs we have tried to consider successively the specific effects of soil fauna, roots and inferior plants but the role of microorganisms on

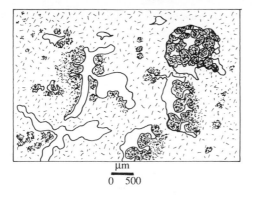

Figure 8.3   Collapsed biological fabric caused by water saturation. The original shape of the mammilated excrements can hardly be recognised; channels are partly closed and have a polyconcave shape (sketch from a Late Holocene buried Natraqualf, Ghaggar plain, India).

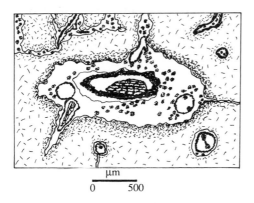

Figure 8.4   Biological disturbances created by root penetration, leading to slight compaction of the soil surrounding the root paths. Note the occurrence of small-sized excrements along the root that indicate activity of micro-organisms (sketch from a long-term exposure affected by recent plant colonisation, Camp de Chassey, Bourgogne, France).

the genesis of the features observed in thin section has also been mentioned on several occasions. Faunal excrements, as well as the vicinity of roots and lower plants, all provide a very suitable substrate for the development of soil microorganisms, which consequently control most of the chemical transformations of the affected materials. For example the impact of earthworms is restricted to the homogenisation of the soil, whereas microorganisms and chemical substances produced by earthworms are responsible for the degradation of ingested organic fragments.

The identification of organic substances and associated microorganisms is rather difficult in thin section, although use of specific stains may be helpful. This partly explains why analytical techniques have been preferred to the optical microscope for studying biochemical transformations. Electron microscopy has a greater potential for monitoring these transformations. With these instruments not only can microorganisms be viewed but the precise relationships between the substances produced and the mineral substrate can be characterised (see Dorioz and Robert, 1987).

Soil microorganisms include algae, fungi and bacteria. They produce enzymes which degrade organic constituents and exude hydrosoluble substances (sugar, amino acids, organic acids). Although they are not capable of moving far, proliferation along roots or within faunal excrements promotes their dissemination within soil materials. The various kinds of microorganisms are highly specialised in degrading specific substances under very specific conditions, and changes in soil conditions may strongly influence microbial activity.

Changes in colour, shape and internal structure of decomposed plant tissues as compared to fresh organic fragments are the only features observable in thin sections that may relate to microbial activity, although very similar effects, such as darkening by tannins, may also result from chemical reactions (Plate Vb) (see Babel, 1975; Loustau and Toutain, 1987).

Soil microorganisms, especially bacteria, are also able to extract very small quantities of nutrients from mineral substrates, occasionally resulting in the accumulation of mineral substances. For example, bacterial precipitation of iron may commonly occur in soil materials when affected by oxidising conditions (Houot and Berthelin, 1987) (see Section 8.6.4).

Our present knowledge of the specific features related to the activity of microorganisms in archaeological contexts is rather limited although microbial activity is known to play an important role in the alteration of bones (Baud and Lacotte, 1984) and excrements, the corrosion of copper objects, the degradation of building stones and even possibly the weathering of flints (see Section 8.6.6). We may suspect that microbial activity has been especially stimulated when high amounts of human-derived organic matter have accumulated. In the future it will not be surprising to find that features presently considered to result from chemical reactions *sensu stricto* are in fact biochemical in origin.

8.2.4 *Biological activity and humification processes*

In the previous paragraphs we briefly reviewed the respective role of the main biological agents that may affect both mineral and organic particles. As already mentioned, because the biological systems are strongly interrelated, it is commonly difficult to sort out the individual agent or factor responsible for producing a certain feature. In most cases we will describe a characteristic fabric that relates to a specific kind of soil ecosystem, for example a crumb microstructure characterising the A horizon of Dystrochrepts (brown acid soils). The degradation of fresh organic matter accumulated at the soil surface and its gradual integration into the underlying layers illustrate the complexity of the relationships that exist between the different components of each type of soil ecosystem.

These transformations, broadly known as humification processes, lead to the formation of humic horizons. Schematically, they represent the separation between insoluble residues and soluble organic substances, and the gradual mineralisation of the latter. Although mainly confined to the upper soil, humification may extend several metres into the parent material through deeply penetrating roots. Present-day knowledge of humification processes is concentrated upon chemical characterisation of the degraded molecules and of the new ones that have been synthesised, and in soil science humification generally refers to the physico-chemical and chemical reactions that may in some way be influenced by biological catalysts, among which microbial activity plays an important role.

The approach to the study of humification processes through optical microscopy, has led to a bias in favour of the role of biological agents because in most cases the chemistry of the organic substances cannot be precisely identified or localised in thin section. There is therefore a dichotomy between the theories based on chemical analytical data (molecules are identified by fractionation techniques) and the features observed under the optical microscope.

From a chemical point of view, humus consists of decomposed organic residues, humic and fulvic acids and insoluble organic matter, called humin. These different constituents are classified according to the way they react during chemical extraction. Under the microscope, organic residues can easily be distinguished and their degree of decomposition estimated according to their colour under plain light and their natural fluorescence under UV and blue light (see Bal, 1975). As already mentioned, specific staining can also be used to recognise the different kind of tissues.

Identification of soluble substances is more problematic in thin sections because in most cases they are combined with mineral constituents and form organo-mineral complexes in the upper horizons. The only exception is in podzols in which organic solutions do not lose their mobility in the upper part of the soil and accumulate at greater depth in the profile, forming coatings around grains and impregnating the groundmass (Plate Vc). It is only in the spodic (Bh) horizons of humus podzols with very low sesquioxide contents that coatings of pure humic and fulvic acids are thought to occur; in spodic (Bs) horizons the organic acids are usually combined with sesquioxides. Optical characteristics of these coatings suggest that many consist of pure organic acids but it is only by comparison with chemical data that their true nature can be confirmed.

It seems that humic acids have a lower fluorescence than fulvic acids (van Vliet-Lanoë, 1981), a factor which might facilitate their differentiation. The fibrous structures of these acids, as recognised from SEM observations of chemical extracts, have not been correlated with the characteristics observed in thin sections. In spite of these limitations, it is possible to correlate the humic layers recognised in the field on the basis of morphology plus chemical characteristics with the humification processes inferred from thin-section properties.

Mull is the most common type of deciduous forest humus and may occur under grassland. The vertical succession comprises an upper organic horizon, consisting only of well-preserved plant fragments (subhorizons O1 or L) overlying an organo-mineral A1 horizon. The *crumb microstructure* of the A1 horizon represents the diagnostic organisation of the mull (Figure 8.2d). Each aggregate displays a dense, homogeneous, fine mixture of organic and mineral particles that result mostly from earthworm activity. In fact, the majority of these aggregates are well-preserved earthworm excrements that display a typical mammilated shape (Figure 8.2b); excrements of smaller animals, such as enchytraeids, may also be observed. In addition to the intensive fragmentation and mixture by earthworm activity, fungi – and the associated enzymes that they produce – also play an important role in the rapid degradation of plant residues.

Because of the absence of fallen leaves, the succession of subhorizons differs slightly under natural grassland from that of mull under forest although microstructure of the A1 horizon is similar. A few non-humified organic residues may be recognised in the upper part of the A1 horizon or near channels (root fragments); the fine fraction has a typical reddish brown colour resulting from the impregnation of the clay by humified organic substances. Another important characteristic of the mull developed under prairie, and especially under tall grass prairie such as pampas, is the abundance of phytoliths.

Under mull conditions the soluble organic matter released is rapidly mineralised in the A1 horizon and forms organo-mineral complexes, which are responsible for the stability of the soil aggregates. This stability is further enhanced in calcareous soils because calcium carbonate acts as a very strong binding agent. Owing to their rapid mineralisation, the organic acids that are produced have little effect on mineral constituents and as a result weathering is limited both in the A1 and in the underlying horizons. This explains the good preservation of phytoliths.

A final characteristic of mull is the rapid turnover of organic matter as a consequence of the intense biological mixing.

In *moder* and *mor* soils conditions are not suitable for earthworms because of, for example, poor drainage or acid conditions, and instead microarthropods and enchytraeids proliferate at the boundary between the plant litter and the mineral subsoil. As previously mentioned, these organisms have limited vertical movements and their excrements accumulate mostly in the top part of the soil.

In moder, enchytraeids and microarthropods are very active and produce a characteristic microaggregated structure in the A1 horizon. Microaggregates comprise very fine mineral particles associated with partly humified organic residues whose morphology may still be recognisable. After their fragmentation, decomposition of the organic fragments by microbial and microorganism activity is slowed down and may require a few years to be completed. During this time soluble organic substances percolate into the underlying mineral horizons, where they precipitate (Plate Vc).

Under very acid conditions even the activity of microarthropods and enchytraeids is limited and consequently biodegradation of the organic matter is considerably reduced. In these circumstances a thick layer of weakly humified organic fragments (20 to 80 cm) accumulates above a non-structured A1 horizon in which only a few excrements are observed. This typifes mor which, because of this slow biodegradation, can be the progenitor of terrestrial peats (see for example Chapter 18).

8.2.5 *Environmental significance of biological activity and biological fabrics*

Biological activity can occur in a large variety of environmental conditions, except under extreme temperatures. Surprisingly, under climates with strongly contrasting seasons (e.g., alternating dry and wet seasons) biological activity can commence very quickly when conditions become favourable. In desertic areas, for example, a small amount of dew is enough to induce algal growth. In general, activity of the soil fauna and microflora is sensitive to seasonal variations as well as to slight changes in soil conditions.

Furthermore, under terrestrial conditions, biological activity is usually restricted to the interface between the earth's surface and the atmosphere. This means that, on the average, only a few tens of centimetres are affected, although in certain circumstances biological activity may penetrate to a depth of several metres, as for example in the case of deep tree roots or termite activity.

Because of the strong interrelationships between the different soil-forming factors (climate, parent materials, topography, biota and time), features related to biological activity and to humification processes can be considered in thin section as good indicators not only of soil microenvironments, such as pH and humidity, but also of land use (*sensu lato*, including 'natural landscapes'). The study of biological features may thus help clarify the dynamics of environmental changes (suggested by pollen or molluscan analysis) and may prove particularly useful in reconstructing successive land-use practices. However, some care is needed when a palaeosurface is not completely sealed, as the relic fabric(s) under study may have been disturbed by more recent biological activity. This 'biological contamination' can be recognised and put aside when interpretations are made because it can be relegated to a later stage event or to the effects of modern roots (see Figure 8.4).

In archaeological contexts, a good knowledge of the conditions of preservation of organic matter is an essential preliminary to palaeobotanical studies or ^{14}C dating. Reliable results may be expected from rather acid organic accumulations like mor or peat when they are well sealed under wet conditions or affected by localised waterlogging because of a perched water table. On the other hand, in a strongly aerated environment, in hot conditions or close to hearths, nearly all the organic matter can be lost by oxidation and only mineral residues (phytoliths, charcoal) remain. Localised post-burial oxidation–reduction can produce iron and manganese pseudomorphs of organic matter.

8.3 **Mechanical effects of water and related features**

Water plays an essential role in the dynamics of any post-depositional process and the correct interpretation of microscopic features that relate either to biological activity or to weathering can provide valuable information pertaining to the hydraulic behaviour of the soil in which those features were formed. Erosion, transport and deposition of solid particles within soils and sediments are among the more dominant processes representing mechanical effects of water. These can be tentatively subdivided into (a) wetting and drying effects that induce rearrangement of particles and soil microfabrics, and (b) the effects of water flow through the soil that bring about translocation of solid particles and mass movements.

8.3.1 *Wetting and drying*

Water can be retained in the soil at different levels, either within structural and biological pores, within packing pores between soil particles or as adsorbed water between layers of clay minerals. Thus, variations in the amount of soil water at all these different levels can generate alterations with soil fabrics. Simulation of wetting and drying for various kinds of soil materials has provided experimental evidence for interpreting soil microfabrics transformed in natural conditions (Dalrymple, 1972; Dalrymple and Theocharopoulos, 1984).

The importance of modifications induced by wetting and drying has been particularly emphasised in soils containing some clay because of its high activity with water. Transformations have been noted both in the arrangement and in the geometry of clay particles (e.g., size and shape) (Tessier, 1984). As previously mentioned, elementary clay particles cannot be isolated under the optical microscope and their arrangement and geometry can be precisely investigated only by using electron microscopy (cf. examples in Tessier, 1984). The reorganisation of soil microfabrics, especially of the fine fraction, can, however, be detected in thin sections under crossed polarised light by noting zones or streaks of elongated birefringence and striated b-fabrics. The extinction of the streaks – indicating the arrangement of fine particles and of domains of oriented clay particles – can be used as criteria to estimate the degree of reorganisation of soil microfabrics. The streaks can appear in the groundmass as well as along voids and their distribution provides indication of the intensity and the direction of the compressive stresses. The streaks are generally well expressed around sand grains (Figure 8.5a), which cannot be deformed, and also seem to exist around silt grains, even if scarcely perceptible because of their small size.

When the geometry of particles is affected, wetting and drying causes more drastic changes in the soil microfabrics, which are more commonly described as shrink–swell transformations. Hydration and desiccation of soils containing swelling clays (of the 2:1 type, see 8.6.7), and especially smectites, result in variations of the soil volume, which can generate considerable stress within the soil. In addition to the rearrangement of the fine particles, the major alterations caused by repeated alternations of swelling and shrinking are the fragmentation of friable soil constituents and the formation of fissures and cracks, both phenomena being the consequence of these stresses. The moulding of soil constituents and soil fabrics can be so intense that it has been compared to the effects of a grinding machine which produces a very homogeneous groundmass whose characteristics – microdivision and regular distribution of particles – can be easily recognised in thin section. Formation of fissures and cracks results in a blocky to prismatic structure. Coarse elements which cannot be fragmented because of their high resistance (e.g., quartzite pebbles or flints) have a propensity to move towards the soil surface and to be concentrated on the top of it. They may also fall into the fissures which open during drying (Yaalon and Kalmar, 1972), thus being recycled. Accumulation of coarse particles in fissures – including artifacts – can consequently be observed in thin sections from soils affected by shrink–swell. Fabric features embedded in organic matter commonly occur in the groundmass of soils strongly affected by shrink–swell. Called *matrans*, they originate during wetting and swelling from the incorporation of the upper soil horizon into the underlying subsoil.

In some cases shrink–swell appears to be the main soil-forming factor leading to the formation of vertisols. In addition to the high amount of swelling clays, the occurrence of hot and dry conditions and poor drainage are necessary for the development of these soils. Vertisols are sometimes considered to be 'naturally' ploughed by the intensive churning of both the fine and coarse constituents. The absence of horizonation, the uniform colour of the soil materials, and the structure (blocky to prismatic when dry or massive when wet) are some of the major field indications that archaeological sediments and soils have been intensively reworked by shrink–swell turbation. These field occurrences can be confirmed by thin-section observation, where the microscopic features differ significantly from those produced by homogenisation, fragmentation or other processes associated with biological activity or cryoturbation.

With low amounts of clay, especially in silty alluvium and in eluvial horizons, important changes are observed when the soil mass becomes saturated: packing of the coarse fraction and collapse of the aggregates bring about a decrease in pore volume. These transformations lead to soil compaction that can be identified in thin section by the absence of a microstructure and the polyconcave shape of unconnected voids. In soils containing some clay, the

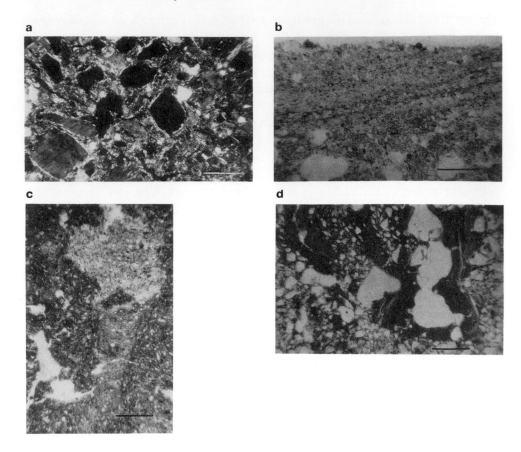

Figure 8.5   (a) Grano-striated b-fabric caused by repeated wetting–drying and resulting in rearrangement of clay domains around sand grains (Natric horizon, Spain). XPL. (Bar = 150 μm)

(b) Layered surface crust resulting from the impact of raindrops on a recently ploughed eluvial horizon developed on loessic materials. Layers are coarse (silty clay to sandy silt) due to the originally low fine fraction content. Note the occurrence of vesicles at the bottom of the crust (Alfisol, Paris Basin, France). PPL. (Bar = 500 μm)

(c) Loose, coarse clean silt infilling (light colour) in darker Bt horizon (paleosol, Kashmir loess). (Bar = 150 μm)

(d) Juxtaposition of textural features in a deep eluvial horizon. In chronological order: (1) microlaminated orange clay coatings related to deposition under calm conditions in a soil developed under vegetative cover; (2) coarse layered coatings resulting from rapid percolation of water provoked by the destruction of the natural canopy and by desertification in the area (Holocene soil, inner dead delta of the Niger, Mali). PPL. (Bar = 150 μm)

cohesion between particles prevents collapse of the structure. In sodic soils, however, features indicating structural collapse (polyconcave voids, massive structure) can be observed, since clays with attached sodium ions are dispersed and cohesion between particles is drastically reduced. When they are dried, soils, or at least horizons that have been affected by structural collapse, are highly compact and can scarcely be reworked by biological activity and can be penetrated by percolating water only with difficulty. The resulting collapse features are thus rather stable and may be preserved over long periods of time (Plate Va).

Soils with a collapse structure and weak cohesion between particles are known to be highly sensitive to **thixotropy**. Consequently, they are unstable when saturated with water. Deformations induced at this extreme stage are considered below (see Section 8.3.3).

8.3.2 *Translocation of solid particles*
8.3.2.1 Dynamics of the process
Mineral and organic particles can be both transported by water flowing through the soil and deposited in pores when competence decreases. At the maximal water-holding capacity of the soil, the movement of the water flow is controlled only by gravity and particles will be translocated from upper horizons into lower ones, or even laterally. The size of the transported particles depends on the energy of the water flow. Therefore, because of their small dimensions, clay-size constituents are the most commonly translocated but silt and sand-size grains can also be transported. Translocation of clay usually refers to the movement of chemically dispersed clays in the form of colloids, though non-dispersed clay-sized particles can also migrate. Dispersion of clay is influenced by chemical conditions and a neutral to weakly acid pH creates the most favourable conditions for clay dispersion and migration. Although most of the concepts presented in this chapter were developed in soil science – and we commonly employ the term 'soil' for brevity's sake – the reader should be aware that these processes affect not only soils but also sediments and archaeological materials and deposits.

Granulometric differentiation occurs as a result of particle translocation through a soil profile. This is expressed by a loss of particles in horizons from which they have been translocated and an enrichment of particles in horizons where they have accumulated (Figure 8.6). When translocation has affected mostly clays, the particle loss is called an **eluviation** process and produces eluviated horizons; the accumulation of particles is known as **illuviation** and is responsible for the creation of illuviated (or argillic) horizons. Because of this granulometric differentiation, mechanical analysis may assist in identifying horizons that have been affected by illuviation, although an increase in clay content can be brought about by neoformation (see Section 8.5). However, in cases where translocation has been rather weak or has not created very

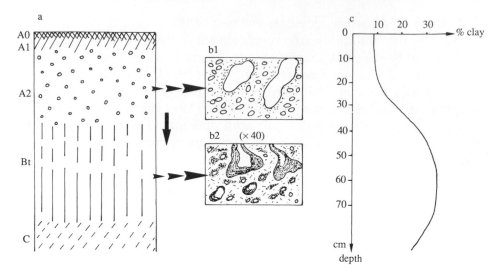

Figure 8.6   Schematic representation of the vertical translocation of clay particles through a soil profile:
(a) vertical succession of the horizons,
(b) diagnostic fabrics of (1) the eluviated horizon characterised by loss of fine particles and (2) the illuviated horizon with abundant laminated clay coatings in the voids,
(c) particle-size distribution with depth, showing the sharp increase in clay in the Bt horizon.

significant textural differences between soil horizons, its effects can be recognised only in thin section.

Units whose soil microfabrics are interpreted as resulting from particle translocation are grouped as *textural features* and can be identified by specific morphology, overall better sorting in comparison to the adjoining matrix and by differences of orientation and birefringence. They can be related to voids forming coatings or infillings or be integrated into the groundmass – through processes like shrink–swell or biological mixing – and then described as deformed textural features (see the typology of textural features in Chapter 9 of Bullock *et al.*, 1985). Their morphology, granulometry and optical properties are important criteria for interpreting the dynamics of the water flow and for determining the environmental significance of the translocation process.

The main factors controlling the characteristics of textural features are the following:

> nature of the soil surface (vegetation cover, kind of litter, effects of the soil fauna, land use);
> dynamics of the water input: for open-air soils this is a reflection of the distribution, intensity and amount of precipitation, and presence of a snow cover;
> soil stability;
> morphology of voids and the latter's relationships with the surface.

8.3.2.2 Textural features appearing on the surface

In comparison to soils stabilised by a continuous cover of vegetation, bare ground is particularly sensitive to surface erosion and particle translocation by water acting both horizontally and vertically. The dynamics of surface erosion in affecting cultivated lands have been well documented because of important soil loss in some regions (e.g., soils on loess in North-West Europe) (see Figure 7.7). Particles are detached by the impact of raindrops and eroded materials are simultaneously transported both laterally (accumulating in microdepressions) and vertically (moving in voids connected to the soil surface). Microscopic features resulting from such movements have been described (Boiffin and Bresson, 1987) and the occurrence of similar features in thin sections from archaeological sediments may allow the location of the position of ancient surfaces even when they have been subsequently reworked and destroyed by successive post-depositional processes.

Features which indicate that the surface has been affected by runoff are small areas (a few mm square) from which water has eroded fine particles and zones of deposition that seal the soil surface. Eroded areas have a low proportion of fine particles and the coarse residuum is densely packed and consists of washed grains whose surfaces are not coated by fine particles and have smooth edges.

Surface crusts (Figure 8.5b) consist of subhorizontal, millimetre-thick layers which generally display graded bedding. Clean silt and fine sand grains in coarse layers alternate with silty clay layers in which the clay is poorly oriented and may include small organic particles that impart a dusty aspect to the fine fraction; fragments from unwashed upper horizons may be also embedded in the fine layers. Vesicles are commonly associated with surface crusts, indicating sealing of the surface by fine particles and trapping of gas beneath it. Upon subsequent desiccation, fine cracks develop in the crust.

The above features are not only restricted to the soil surface but may also occur in the upper horizon where particles eroded by water infill large voids connected to the surface. The latter serve as conduits through which percolating water can transport the eroded particles. Coarse laminated textural features resulting from rapid deposition of particles have commonly been reported from cultivated horizons of sandy loam soils. These are described as agricutans (Jongerius, 1970) because they are considered to be genetically related to cultivation. The occurrence of similar features in the upper part of buried Holocene soils has provided evidence for identification of ancient cultivated horizons (see Plate IVe).

In arid and semi-arid regions, flood irrigation is known to generate erosion of fine particles from the surface and to create depositional crusts that include abundant vesicles and infillings of loose grains (see Figure 7.5e).

Except when rapidly buried, superficial crusts are in most cases strongly disrupted by subsequent events which may affect the soil surface, such as by biological activity or ploughing. Thus fragments of disoriented superficial crusts are commonly observed in the upper horizon(s) and cultivation colluvia (see Figure 6.4e).

In cemented soils, where calcium carbonate, for example, may prevent the detachment and dispersion of particles, formation of textural features at the surface is limited. Clayey soils and ones with a well-developed biological structure are also only weakly affected by this process.

Textural features formed in the various soil horizons are essentially comparable to those produced at the soil surface. The main differences concern better orientation and sorting of particles in the lower horizons, since turbulent water flowing through the soil gradually loses its energy and particles can settle more slowly in pores retaining stagnant, muddy waters.

8.3.2.3 Textural features formed throughout the profile

Eluviation results in the removal of fine particles in the upper horizons and in the accumulation in voids of clean, loosely packed grains at greater depth; these grains are particularly abundant in the A horizon, but may also penetrate into the B horizon (Figure 8.5c). Eluviation features are characteristically abundant when large amounts of water suddenly pass through the soil. Such a condition is common in semi-arid and arid regions with heavy rainstorms and in temperate and cold regions with the melting of snow or ice.

Illuviation in the underlying horizon results in the formation of microlaminated coatings consisting mostly of clay particles, though very fine silt grains are also present. Under crossed nicols these coatings are characterised by regular lamination, optical continuity with straight extinction, strong anisotropy and high birefringence (Plate IIb). All of these features point to good orientation of fine particles resulting from slow aqueous deposition under calm conditions. On the other hand, textural features generated under turbulent hydraulic conditions are weakly to poorly organised and show, in addition to poor sorting, irregular lamination, diffuse extinction, and moderate to low birefringence. The shape of textural features varies also according to the energy of the water flow. A crescentic shape, for example, indicates sedimentation related to gravity whereas fine clay coatings of regular thickness, occurring either around coarse grains or within fine pores, signify that clay was slowly deposited from weakly mobile water of capillary origin.

Though elementary clay particles cannot be singled out using the optical microscope (see Section 4.2), textural features consisting of pure clay minerals can be recognised by their limpidity and yellow colour under plane polarised light; the latter, however, varies with the type of clay mineral present. When clay is mixed with fine silt, textural features are described as impure; for coarser textures, elementary particles are clearly distinguished and their granulometric composition can be precisely described. Admixed fine microcontrasted particles (e.g., comminuted organic fragments) impart a dusty aspect to the clay and, when abundant, may mask its birefringence (see Figure 7.1h and 7.5b).

Iron oxides may have migrated together with the clay minerals; this not only darkens the colour of the clay features but also reduces their birefringence (see Section 8.5.2).

Though illuviation refers to the accumulation of fine particles, especially clay, coarser textural accumulations may also occur in the illuviated horizon. Each may be independently distributed or juxtaposed to form compound features (for example Plates IIa and IIb). Because of the close relationship between the particle-size distribution of textural features and their dynamics of translocation, a series of different textural features in the same thin section can provide valuable keys to unravelling the succession, history and environmental significance of 'illuvial events' that have occurred in a profile. These reconstructions are based on observations of natural soils coupled with experimental studies (Dalrymple and Theocharopoulos, 1984; Theocharopoulos and Dalrymple, 1987).

Formation of well-sorted, fine-textured, regularly laminated features has been shown to develop preferentially in weakly acid soils covered by forest, in which clay dispersion is enhanced and water loses its energy while percolating through the upper humic layers. As mentioned previously, coarse features are generated by turbulent water flowing rapidly through the soil and their abundance increases in soils which have bare surfaces or are only weakly protected by vegetation. When juxtaposed with illuviation features, they may indicate a change either in climate or in land use (Figure 8.5d). They can form very easily in any kind of soil or sediment when surface runoff infiltrates into the subsurface; they have also been observed in overbank deposits, which are periodically inundated during flooding. In all, these have limited pedological significance in comparison to illuviation features.

Silty clay coatings and infillings are commonly observed in sediments from caves and shelters which have never been colonised by vegetation and have thus not undergone pedological development *sensu stricto*. Poor sorting, weak organisation, diffuse extinction and the absence of lamination (although layering can sometimes be observed) are clear indicators of translocation under turbulent hydraulic conditions (Plates Ve, Vf). Thus they should not be confused with illuviation features. In calcareous environments, fine grains of detrital calcium carbonate can be transported in suspension, together with other particles, to form muddy micritic coatings (see Figure 14.5b).

A specific kind of coarse textural features, called **cappings**, occurs either on the top of large grains or on the upper side of aggregates or of coarse elements (Figure 8.7a). In addition, they may be continuous over a length of a few mm, linking aggregates and coarse grains; these are described as **link capping**. Cappings have a crescentic shape and are microlayered, displaying an alternation of well-sorted silty clay, silt and even sand layers; reverse graded-bedding is common. Cappings are especially abundant in boreal soils, and are present throughout the profile up to a depth of a few metres. They are also present in

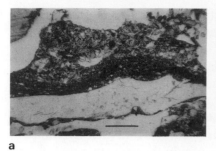

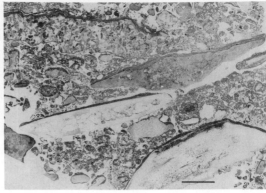

Figure 8.7   (a) Layered capping characterised by a reverse graded bedding developed on the upper side of a lenticular bone fragment: finely layered silt at the lower part is capped by weakly sorted silty sand (Mousterian occupation layer, Cave of Vaufrey, France). PPL. (Bar = 150 μm)

(b) Example of an archaeological layer strongly transformed by freeze–thaw processes. Both coarse limestone fragments and large-sized bones have a lenticular shape; interstitial finer material is formed of subrounded fragments and aggregates (Mousterian layer I, Cave of Vaufrey, France). PPL. (Bar = 500 μm)

mountain soils that are seasonally covered by snow. They are also common in sediments that have been subjected to periglacial conditions in the past. Overall, cappings seem to form under conditions of strong percolation associated with snow melting.

In summary, the above outline illustrates the capacity of water flow in the soil to bring about vertical textural differentiation in the profile that ultimately influences the formation of soil horizons. Lateral movements of water have very similar effects in redistributing particles on the surface, resulting in localised areas of erosion and particle accumulation.

It is not always a straightforward task to distinguish the vertical redistribution of particles – generally a pedological process – from granulometric differentiation within a layer or horizon achieved by lateral flow resulting from runoff or capillary rise. This can be approached, however, by detailed observation of the characteristics of the textural features and by comparison of the different textural features occurring in successive horizons or layers in order to establish their genetic relationships.

Textural features appear rather quickly in soils (a few hours to a few days) though it is usually accepted that the development of a well-expressed argillic horizon would require hundreds to thousands of years to be accomplished (Soil Survey Staff, 1975). They may remain undisturbed as long as they are not deformed or destroyed by subsequent post-depositional processes, such as biological activity or soil erosion. In most cases, however, fine-textured features are stable enough to be recognised after suffering some transport within the soil. They appear as rounded fragments within the soil mass and their typical internal fabric of textural features clearly differentiates them from the surrounding deposit. These *papules* (see Plate Vh) can be considered as remains of relic features of an ancient illuviated horizon. When soils have been buried, illuviation features may be preserved over very long periods (a few thousand or million years), and as such they constitute very useful indicators for palaeoenvironmental reconstructions, especially in soils developed on parent materials sensitive to translocation, such as loess. Translocation can appear under any kind of climate, but the most illustrative and successful reconstructions so far have been made in regions that now have temperate climates, although evidence indicates that fluctuations between cold and temperate conditions did occur (see Fedoroff and Goldberg 1982; Vazart, 1983). Complexities of similar magnitude (e.g., mixing and rotation of features) can be observed in floor materials and in reworked anthropic colluvia (see Chapter 7).

8.3.3 *Mass movements*

Water saturation of the soil may bring about a local or total collapse of the void system. When such saturation is induced by groundwater, mass movements in the deep horizons can create local sorting of the soil materials. Concentrations of particles can be observed in thin section, but these clearly differ from accumulations formed by translocation processes. They may include any kind of particles which are in general poorly sorted and weakly reorganised. Silty clay and clay concentrations show a generally discontinuous extinction pattern and, because they are not related to any void system, are described as intercalations.

In soils developed on slopes, mass movements can also affect surface horizons which are saturated with water resulting from heavy precipitation, or from melting ice and snow; the deep subsoil remains dry. The whole surface horizon may become muddy and begin to move on the slope, resulting in the formation of a mudflow. Such mass movement straddles the conceptual boundary between 'post-depositional processes' as described here and 'sedimentation', and results in homogenisation of the soil materials and strong disruptions in preexisting soil fabrics. Relic features, such as papules, may still be recognisable, thus testifying to previous phases of pedogenesis. Differentiation in the field between ancient colluviated soils and ones developed *in situ* is not always simple. Furthermore, analytical data are not always helpful because most of the chemical, physical and physico-chemical properties have been thoroughly modified or differences between horizons are not marked enough. In fact, the main disruptions between horizons involves soil fabric which is best studied by micromorphology and it would appear to be the most suitable technique for characterising and distinguishing *in situ* soils from colluvial deposits (see, for example, Plate Vh).

In sum, the mechanical effects of water are intimately connected with horizontal transport of material at the soil surface and with vertical movement of material within a profile. Furthermore, this mobility brings about textural differentiation, which is readily recognisable in thin section (if not in the field), and the textural features thus produced can be highly valuable in reconstructing the succession of the different events that have affected the profile.

8.4 Cryogenic alterations and related features

Cryogenic alterations and their features are widespread, not only in soils from present-day cold climates but also in temperate regions which have witnessed colder climates during glacial periods. Thus evidence of cryogenic processes recorded in fossil soils or landscapes can provide important information that can be used to reconstruct former environments.

When the soil temperature drops below 0°C, the transformation of soil water into ice results in a marked increase in the overall soil volume (1/10) and in the crystallisation of ice outside the soil groundmass. The latter takes the form of ice lenses that are more or less parallel to the soil surface. The strong stresses thus produced bring about fragmentation, compaction and deformation of the soil constituents.

These mechanical disturbances generate specific features whose nature and degree of development are related to the intensity of the frost, the water content and the characteristics of the soil materials (e.g., soil texture and porosity). Frost features may be evident in the field on a regional scale (polygonal network) or at the scale of the profile (ice wedge structure, cryoturbation). However, at the microscopic scale various transformations within the soil can be easily monitored to provide a better understanding of the dynamics of the processes involved.

The dynamics of the formation of present-day frost-related features on a microscopic scale have been thoroughly studied (Fedoroff, 1966; Bunting and Fedoroff, 1974; van Vliet-Lanoë, 1985a) and some of the observed structures have been reproduced experimentally (van Vliet Lanoë *et al.*, 1984). Similar features have been described in Quaternary sediments and fossil soils, and interpreted by comparison with features appearing under present-day conditions (synthesis in van Vliet-Lanoë, 1985b). Thus it has been possible to establish the intensity of successive cold events that have characterised the later glacial periods.

The duration of the freezing spell and the amount of ice produced are important environmental factors controlling the formation of frost-related features in different types of soils and sediments. In consequence, features appearing in seasonally frozen soils can be rather easily distinguished from those in profiles whose deep horizons remain frozen throughout the year (**permafrost**). The initial phases in the freezing process are similar in both cases and are marked by the segregation of the wet soil mass into plates of clear ice and relatively dry soil (ice lenses). The desiccation of the soil material is caused by water/ice transformation, which not only brings about the formation of a fissure network – comprising both planar voids and angular cavities with smooth walls – but also fragments the soil into lenticular aggregates. The diagnostic characteristic of this preliminary stage of frost deformation is a platy to lenticular structure, whose expression varies according to the particle-size distribution of the original materials (Figure 8.8). Moreover, the aggregates reveal weak disturbances of the original soil fabrics such that previously existing features (e.g., clay coatings) may appear finely cracked and deformed. Patches with a striated b-fabric may be observed, indicating strong stress during desiccation of the soil materials. High pressures induced by the crystallisation of ice favour the physical fragmentation of coarse elements which may also acquire a platy shape. Ice crystallisation commonly produces particle sorting and the uplift of the coarser elements.

In seasonally frozen soils, repeated alternations of freezing and thawing can modify previously formed frost structures and transform platy aggregates into lenticular ones (Figures 8.7b, 8.8). Simultaneously, fine particles extracted from the soil mass during ice crystallisation and abraded from the aggregates are transported by the melt water throughout the profile and accumulate as cappings on the upper part of aggregates and coarse grains or as infill cavities (see Figure 8.7a).

Repetitive freezing favours the fragmentation of coarse elements and the comminution of fine particles; after some time it may have irreversibly altered the initial characteristics of the archaeological layers, especially particle size and colour. Original pedological features, such as clay coatings, may be totally disrupted and recognised only as papules. Biological activity, which commences rapidly as soon as the ice has melted, may also intensively transform the structures created by frost and may greatly increase the homogenisation of soil materials (Figure 8.7b). Unusual features associated with specific kinds of materials may also be generated during the freeze–thaw alternations. For example, calcium carbonate precipitated during the thawing process can be present in the form of micritic (crystals $< 2 \mu$m) fine coatings at the upper part of the lenticular aggregates, or sparitic ($> 50 \mu$m) infillings of cavities (see Figure 9.2f). Laminated micritic pendents may also be associated with thawing, whereby a thin film at the base of aggregates and coarse elements provides favourable conditions for the possible growth of algae (see Figure 9.2e).

Alternations of freezing and thawing may also produce rotation of the lenticular aggregates and their lateral displacement, especially on slopes. This frost creep (**gelifluction**) results in attrition of the lenticular aggregates and the coarse fragments, which gradually become rounded (Figure 8.8c).

In sum, the distinctive microscopic criteria for identifying archaeological

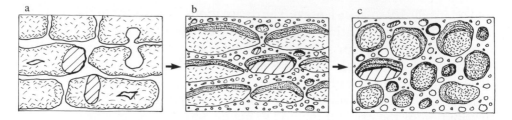

Figure 8.8　Evolution of frost-related microstructure with an increasing number of freezing–thawing cycles:
　(a) Platy microstructure – note the occurrence of uplifted coarse fragments.
　(b) Lenticular microstructure. Coarse fragments may also have a lenticular shape. Note the occurrence of cappings on both coarse fragments and aggregates, and the infilling of loose sand and silt within the fissure network.
　(c) Rounded aggregates resulting from attrition of the lenticular fragments caused by frost creep, in addition to repeated freezing–thawing cycles.
　f.l. varying between 2mm to *c*. 2 cm according to the nature of parent materials.

sediments and soils which have been affected by repeated alternations of freezing and thawing are:

　　a poorly expressed platy microstructure;
　　notable fragmentation of particles;
　　the occurrence of such textural features as cappings on structural elements and
　　　infillings in cavities; and
　　an intense disturbance of pre-existing soil microfabrics.

　　When the increase in air temperature during the warm season is not sufficient to thaw completely the subsurface ice formed in winter, deep soil horizons remain frozen throughout the year while the surface horizons undergo seasonal alternations of thawing and freezing. As a consequence of this depth differentiation, especially with regard to the depth of the thawing front, different kinds of frost-related features can be found within the profile. In the upper part, thawing is associated with biological activity and translocation of particles whereas below this these properties are absent. The intense desiccation that affects the permafrost soil induces considerable compaction of the soil materials, resulting in a high stability of the aggregates produced during freezing. Furthermore, the strong pressures generated at the time of desiccation create a network of vertical cracks, which fragment the lenticular aggregates into angular prisms. When sufficient moisture is available, segregations of ice develop along the vertical cracks, forming a network of ice wedges and a build-up of considerable pressures in the permafrost soil. These physical stresses result in large-scale disturbances such as injections, involutions and folds and the segregation of a specific class of soil constituents. Such deformations are usually easy to recognise in the field but micromorphology may help detect mixing of different source materials and clarify the nature of the boundaries between deformed layers. These boundaries may represent a previously developed limit between two soil horizons or two sedimentary layers, or may prove to be the result of frost-related disturbances that have affected an originally uniform layer. Recognition in thin section of such features as platy to prismatic structure, high compaction, absence of textural features and no detectable signs of biological activity provides strong evidence for recognising the former depth of the permanent freezing front. Moreover, micromorphology permits us to estimate frost intensity when local conditions of drainage are known. Under similar climatic conditions, a stronger development of permafrost can be achieved in soils with a higher moisture content. The position of the permanent freezing front may also be indicated by greater disaggregation of coarse elements as compared to the adjacent layers.

These various kinds of frost-related features are commonly observed in archaeological sediments and soils which have suffered the effects of repeated cold spells during the last glacial periods. The rather good preservation of frost-related aggregates is due to their high stability because they have been intensively compacted, especially in permafrost soils. In consequence, pedological development subsequent to the freezing event may have modified only the upper part of the soil, leaving frost-related structures in the deep horizons unaffected. Relics of freeze–thaw phenomena from the upper part of soils may be preserved when rapid burial has protected them from the effects of various agencies, especially biological activity.

When archaeological sediments or soils have been affected by one cold event – characterised by only weak variations of the frost intensity – the resulting features have a rather simple character and may provide valuable information for the reconstruction of palaeoclimatic conditions. Interpretation is more difficult when successive cold events of different intensities have repeatedly altered a layer. In the most favourable situations it is possible to recognise superimposed features relating to successive events and to suggest interpretations of such a polygenetic layer. More commonly, previously formed features are remoulded during the following cold stage(s) and palaeoclimatic reconstructions will be based mostly on the interpretation of the features produced last. Finally, the impact of local variations in environmental conditions, such as drainage, must also be considered when interpreting frost-related structures with a polygenetic character.

8.5 **Chemical weathering and related processes**
8.5.1 *Basic concepts*
The term *weathering* is applied to a number of processes occurring at the interface between atmosphere and lithosphere that encompass the chemical and physical disintegration and decomposition of rocks and minerals (Buol *et al.*, 1973). In this broad context, chemical weathering embraces such chemical reactions as oxidation–reduction, hydration–dehydration and hydrolysis,

which act in concert or over time to produce a collection of microscopic features. Fortunately, close relationships exist between these microscopic features and the processes which produced them, and in most cases it is possible to establish these interactions with the use of microscopic techniques. Thus, for example, we are able to study solution movements related to the hydrolysis of silicate minerals and the associated neoformation of clay minerals (see below).

The study of the weathering processes using microscopic techniques is accomplished in several stages. The first stage includes the identification of the weathered minerals and the associated neoformed components (both amorphous and crystalline) whilst the second entails the estimation of the intensity of the transformation. A final step concerns the search for evidence which may indicate the causal factors affiliated with the weathering. In most cases however, these objectives can be achieved only when the original shape and crystalline habit of the weathered mineral can be recognised. In this instance a five-stage weathering sequence has been proposed, extending from weak alteration of the optical properties of the mineral to total alteration: 'These transformations are derived from both a destruction of the crystallographic fabric by erection of fissures along which solution may circulate and by chemical transformations of the initial minerals by reactions with the percolating solution and formation of secondary mineral' (Figure 8.9a, b and c; Bullock *et al.*, 1985: 60).

In practice, estimation of the different weathering intensities can only be appreciated within the deep weathering zone (e.g., C horizon), or during the first stages of soil weathering or when weathering is the dominant post-depositional process. Apart from these few instances, other post-depositional processes may at the same time actively participate in the physical disintegration of the weathered mineral because of its weak resistance; at the same time any soluble crystalline and neoformed components can be leached and translocated. At this stage it is only through an overall comparison of the various features in the different horizons that the intensity, dynamics and causes of weathering can be surmised. In fact, when pedoturbation has produced a homogeneous groundmass, electron microscopy combined with X-ray diffractometry are necessary to characterise the degree of transformation of clay and fine silt-sized minerals.

The geochemical weathering (*sensu stricto*) that produces the deep weathered zone of a 'typical' soil profile is considered to be a very slow process achieved over a few thousand to millions of years, although it may be accelerated under specific aggressive conditions (e.g., tropical climates, percolation of phosphate-rich solutions). Because of these slow rates, the role of this type of weathering on the evolution of archaeological soils and sediments can often be considered negligible.

In archaeological contexts the recognition of weathering features is important. First, biochemical agents are powerful factors of weathering and their impact on minerals is rapid (Robert *et al.*, 1983; see Section 8.2). Secondly, as a result of colluviation, materials derived from deeply weathered zones may commonly be mixed up with fresh or weakly weathered sediments. This association of variably weathered materials occurring in the same unit may help reveal multiple sediment sources, a result that can barely be achieved by applying X-ray diffraction techniques to the clay fraction of bulk samples. In cases where *in situ* weathering was suspected in the field, the recognition of inherited weathering features is also effective in averting misinterpretations concerning the climatic significance of the weathered unit.

8.5.2 *Dehydration–rehydration*
An important weathering process is that of **hydration**, which can create structural and volume changes in rocks and minerals. Water molecules or hydroxyl groups may enter the mineral structure and be adsorbed at the surface or within the mineral. In most cases hydration does not modify optical properties of the disrupted minerals but for highly soluble minerals, such as salts, hydration may induce ultrastructural changes resulting in modifications of the initial optical properties. The hydration of anhydrite ($CaSO_4$, birefringence of second order – blue to red) to produce gypsum ($CaSO_4.2H_2O$, grey birefringence of the first order) should be of interest in archaeological contexts, where excavated gypsic plasters may represent anhydrite that later became rehydrated. Increased temperatures lead to dehydration or the reverse changes.

A more commonly observed process that involves alternating cycles of dehydration–hydration is *rubefaction*, which involves the mineralogical change of goethite ($aFeOOH$) into a haematite (aFe_2O_3). When they are finely integrated into the clay, these iron oxides are responsible for the colour of the groundmass. When goethite crystals are the dominant iron oxides, the resulting colour is yellow to ochre, whereas haematite imparts a red colour to the clay (Plates Vg, Vh). The very fine size of both goethite and haematite crystals (a few nm) cannot be distinguished under the optical microscope and use of the TEM is necessary to separate them from those of the clay minerals. Even at high magnification, structural differences between goethite and haematite are not obvious, and X-ray diffraction is necessary to differentiate both species. The colour of the groundmass however, is a dependable criterion to follow the transformation of iron oxides.

Warm climates with contrasted wet and dry seasons – particularly of the Mediterranean and tropical regions – are known to be the most favourable for rubefaction of iron oxides. Consequently the red colour observed in paleosols has been considered as the classic indication of an earlier humid and hot phase. Reddening, however, may also appear under temperate conditions, when soils having received large amounts of moisture during spring suffer strong dehydration during summer. In this case, rubefaction *sensu stricto* only concerns the upper soil horizons in which dehydration has induced transformation of goethite into haematite. With time, the red colour gradually penetrates the

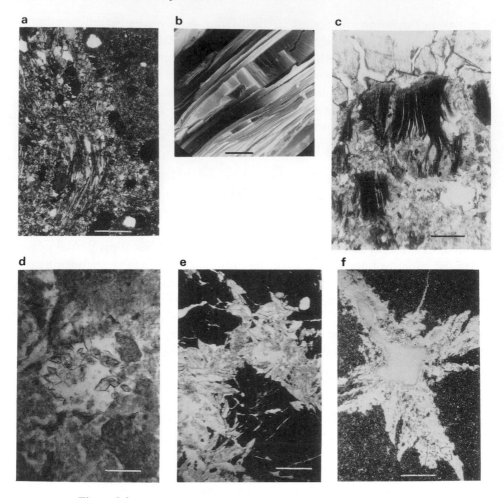

Figure 8.9
Examples of weathered minerals and estimation of their degree of alteration:
   (a) Weakly weathered biotite in Late Pleistocene petrocalcic horizon.
Disruption of the mica flakes is caused by crystallisation of calcite. In this very
first stage of alteration the original high birefringence of the biotite is not affected
(Thar desert, India). XPL. (Bar = 80 μm)
   (b) SEM view from (a), showing radially crystallised calcite crystals disrupting
mica flakes. (Bar = 10 μm)
   (c) Moderately weathered biotite in a deep weathered zone developed on
granite. The original shape of mica is still recognisable although the edges of the
biotite are strongly disrupted; phyllites are expanded and darkened.
Neoformation of secondary silicates (kaolinite) can be observed in between the
phyllites as shown by the lighter colour in PPL and by the first-order birefringence
as observed in XPL (Algeria). PPL. (Bar = 150 μm)
Salts:
   (d) Examples of highly soluble salts are shown by the partial infilling of halite
(NaCl) crystals (upper horizon of a saline soil, Ghaggar Plain, India). PPL.
(Bar = 150 μm)

underlying horizons through the vertical translocation of iron oxide-rich clay (Figure 8.10). After a few hundred years the field characteristics acquired in a profile by these two mechanisms are very similar, although the first concerns true rubefaction whereas the second is a combination of rubefaction and illuviation. The climatic significance of these two processes is rather different and micromorphology can be used to identify the relevant features. A homogeneously red groundmass is evidence of the first mechanism, whereas textural features incorporating red clays in the pores characterises the second.

True rubefaction has to be distinguished from reddening inherited with the sediments from a previous period, possibly of geological age. These earlier red layers may have been transported and redeposited, thus obliterating the climatic significance of the red colour. In thin section, when the colour has originated from rubefaction–illuviation cycles, colluviated red layers may be identified by the textural features consisting of red, finely disrupted papules (Plate Vh).

In some cases, the convergence between features derived from *in situ* rubefaction–illuviation and inherited rubefaction–illuviation can be nearly complete: previously red clay can be translocated from the sedimentary red layer into the underlying sediments (Plate Vf). Only careful observation may permit recognition of evidence that can support one or the other of these hypotheses.

When reddening is the result of only *sensu stricto* rubefaction, distinction between an *in situ* rubefied layer and a sedimentary one is difficult – especially if the red layer has been deposited by colluviation – because both are characterised by a homogeneous, undifferentiated red groundmass. Field observations, such as layering, inclusions of coarse components of possibly colluviated origin, may provide evidences to suspect inherited reddening.

The timespan necessary to obtain a homogeneous rubefied layer through rubefaction *sensu stricto* and rubefaction–illuviation is highly variable, since a combination of factors is involved, such as drainage, temperature and organic matter. A suggested, tentative average timespan is on the order of a few hundred to a few thousand years. This is small in comparison to the long duration necessary for complete mineral weathering, with which rubefaction has been so commonly associated, since both processes are active in tropical conditions.

Pedological rubefaction should not be mistaken for the sudden reddening produced by high temperatures, as in layers underlying a fire place or buried by a lava flow. Although in the field the red colour is generally more pronounced

---

(e) Gypsum crystallisation: Crystallisation of lenticular gypsum within cracks, causing disruption of the original soil fabric (gypsic soil, Aragon, Spain). PPL. (Bar = 150 μm)

(f) Ghost of gypsum crystals. Originally formed during a semi-arid phase, these ghosts of gypsum crystals were later dissolved during an episode of increased humidity (loessic paleosol, Xifeng, central China). PPL. (Bar = 150 μm)

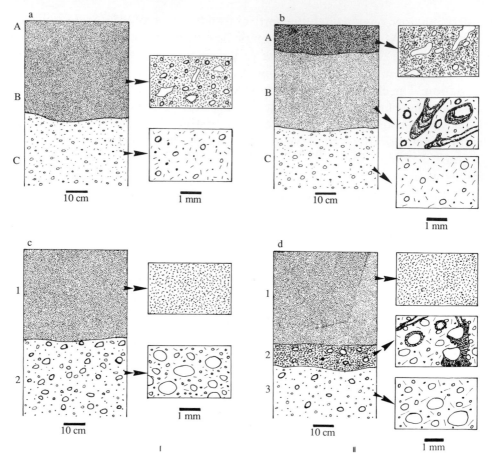

Figure 8.10   Sketch illustrating several possible origins of a rubefied unit and related micromorphological features.

(a and b) *Sensu stricto* rubefaction: in (a), rubefaction of the groundmass takes place through dehydration of iron oxides; in (b), the red colour of the B horizon reflects the occurrence of reddish clay coatings around voids, whereas the overlying organic-rich A horizon is dark brown.

(c and d) Inherited rubefaction: layer 1 represents colluvium whose reddish colour is inherited. (c) illustrates a sharp boundary between the two stratigraphic units which clearly have a different textural composition. In (d) a gradual transition between the red colluvium (layer 1) and the underlying coarse sands (layer 3) is observed (layer 2). This intermediate unit has the overall textural characteristics of layer 3 but the red colour is caused by the occurrence of reddish clay coatings which are translocated downward from layer 1.

(c) Same as (b) but in XPL showing the high birefringence typical of calcite.

(d) Dark brown charred organic fragment embedded in pure white wood ashes. Same layer as (a). PPL, f.l.: 0.9 mm.

(e) Pale grey structureless ashes consisting mostly of burnt leaves mixed with some wood ashes (stabling layer, Neolithic levels, Cave of Arene Candite, Liguria, Italy). PPL, f.l.: 0.9 mm.

(f) Detail of the burnt leaves showing remains of calcium oxalate crystals in the form of spherulites characterised by a dark cross. XPL, f.l.: 300 μm.

(g) Specific features of ashes associated with metallurgical hearths. These include abundant melted ashes and partially melted grains of quartz sand whose outer rims have been transformed into tridymite. Note the red dots, which are the result of the transformation of silicate and the formation of diopside (Bronze Age Fort Harrouard, France). PPL, f.l.: 300 μm.

Plate IV

(a) Human coprolite: yellowish phosphatic organic matter, including abundant plant remains and phytoliths (Middle Saxon levels, Maiden Lane, London, England). PPL, f.l.: 0.9mm.

(b) Dog coprolite: opaque, non-birefringent phosphatic groundmass with bone and quartz inclusions. Note the presence of yellow, weakly birefringent clay coatings caused by post-depositional translocation of clay (Late Bronze Age midden, Potterne, England). XPL, f.l.: 0.9 mm.

(c) Stable layer characterized by the high amount of grass remains and organic matter finely mixed with sand grains. Effects of trampling are here indicated by a weakly expressed layering. Note the occurrence of brown coatings in the vughs caused by the percolation of organic-rich solutions derived from urine (Late Bronze Age, midden, Potterne, England). PPL, f.l.: 3 mm.

(d) Mortar fabric: coarse mineral inclusions embedded in highly birefringent crystallitic b-fabric caused by heating of the limestone powder taken as a source material. Soil inclusions are non-birefringent as a result of overheating. XPL, f.l.: 0.9 mm.

(e) Agricutan in a buried soil (1–2 cm deep in the buried soil): laminated infilling consisting of silt, silty clay and clay layers. These features are clear evidence of hoeing cultivation before burial. Presence of charcoal may indicate addition of manure to the soil (Strathalham Neolithic mound, Perthshire, Scotland). PPL, f.l.: 3 mm.

(f) Dusty clay coatings (10 cm deep in the buried soil) providing evidence of ard cultivation (henge Neolithic site, Strathallan, Perthshire, Scotland). PPL, f.l.: 3 mm.

(g) Ard marks well preserved in the A2 horizon of a buried podzol. The 40 cm thick dark grey horizon represents the cultivated soil homogenised by repeated ploughing and subsequently buried by aeolian sands (Iron Age fields at Lodbjerg, Denmark; see Liversage *et al.*, 1987).

(h) Fabric of the cultivated buried podzol illustrated in (g). The fine fraction between quartz sand grains consists of yellowish-brown organic-rich clay mixed with fine charcoal (evidence of manuring) and humified organic fragments (remains of the original peat upper horizon). PPL, f.l.: 300μm.

Plate V

(a) Polyconcave voids and massive structure indicating structural collapse subsequent to water saturation of a sodic soil (high amount of exchangeable sodium is responsible for loss of cohesion between particles and dispersion of clay). Note the strial b-fabric (grano and porostriated) resulting from rearrangement of clay particles during wetting–drying events (buried Natraqualf, Ghaggar plain, India). XPL, f.l.: 0.9 mm.

(b) Degradation by the combined action of microorganisms and microfauna of organic fragments in a mor type humus (A horizon of a spodosol, Vosges, France). PPL, f.l.: 0.9 mm.

(c) Microfabric of a Bh horizon on sandy loam till in Boreal conditions: the groundmass is impregnated by spodic organic matter resulting in this brownish-yellow colour (Laurentides, Quebec). PPL, f.l.: 300 μm.

(d) Charred peat (Prato Mollo, Liguria, Italy). PPL, f.l.: 1.3 mm.

(e) Field view of the top of the stratigraphic sequence at La Micoque (prehistoric shelter with Micoquian prehistoric industries, Perigord, France): brownish-red layer L, at the bottom of the view (interpreted by F. Bordes, 1984, as a Riss–Wurm palaesol), cemented light colour layer M, at the upper part, consisting of coarse limestone blocks.

(f) Photomicrograph from layer L showing poorly sorted, weakly layered, brownish-red silty clay infilling juxtaposed to rather fresh limestone fragments. These textural features clearly differ from *sensu stricto* illuviation clay and only relate to a rather rapid percolation of solution transporting reddish silty clay particles, probably eroded from red soils covering the plateau. PPL, f.l.: 0.9 mm.

(g) Juxtaposition of yellow ochre clay and red clay (on the right side). The following interpretation can be proposed: (1) illuviation of yellow clay, (2) rubefaction of this clay (shown by the darkening on the right side of the view), (3) illuviation of rubefied clay forming laminated clay coating (seen on the left of the view) (Middle Pleistocene paleosol, northwestern Morocco). PPL, f.l.: 0.9 mm.

(h) Red paleosol consisting of totally rubefied clay. Note the strong dark red colour and the moderate birefringence related to the presence of iron oxides finely mixed with clay particles. Signs of disturbances are expressed by the occurrence of papules (fragments of clay coatings) (colluviated Middle Pleistocene paleosol, northwestern Morocco). PPL, f.l.: 300 μm.

Plate VI

Photogramme of thin section from Kebara cave, sample 84.28 (example no. 1). The basal part displays a complex spongy microstructure composed of charcoal fragments and aggregates of organic matter. The pale grey irregular aggregates are probably composed of poorly crystallised leucophosphite.

In the middle part there is a large subhorizontal mass of light grey leucophosphite precipitated into a spongy mass of charcoal and organic matter. Note how the blobs of phosphate disrupt both the overall horizontal layering and the pieces of charcoal. PPL. (f.l. = 5 cm).

Plate VII

(a) Boxgrove, West Sussex. Silty clay alluvial sediments containing high amounts of detrital organic matter (partially replaced by iron and manganese) in clay-rich laminae. They probably represent overbank deposits of renewed, but significantly more organic, alluviation (base of Unit 5a) and mark the inundation and burial of ripened soils (top of Unit 4c) occupied by an Acheulian culture in the Middle Pleistocene. PPL. f.l. 3.3 mm.

(b) Laminated calcareous crust developed on a Neogene piedmont. The yellow band is an algal mat. Beneath it, the dense reddish part is a fine mixture of clay and secondary calcium carbonate produced by the algae. Above it, the material is more detrital, and quartz-rich, resulting from the mechanical breakdown of the crust and aeolian additions. Krabeg en Nam (the Western Great Erg, Algeria). PPL. f.l. 3 mm.

(c) Complex cave sediment development in the Upper Yellow Breccia at Westbury-sub-Mendip, Somerset. Peds of fine cave soil have been formed, probably by freeze/thaw activity, but the soil itself has become phosphatised as the result of bone dissolution in these highly fossiliferous deposits. Secondary movement of phosphate has also formed pale yellow coatings (apatite?) that cement the peds together. At the top, a later phase of micritic calcium carbonate growth is juxtaposed to a final infilling by sparite. PPL. f.l. 1.6 mm.

(d) As (c), but XPL. Note non-birefringence of phosphatised cave soil except for quartz silt. The phosphate coatings have a low birefringence (but high fluorescence under UV), compared with the micrite and sparite.

Plate VIII

(a) Intentionally prepared loamy floor in a Bronze Age alley (northwest India). The characteristic here is the elongated subhorizontal porosity resulting from repeated trampling. Note, in the lower cavity, a dark thin coating produced by movement of organic-rich solutions derived from the accumulation of animal wastes in the alley. PPL. f.l. 3 mm.

(b) Thin fine fabric of very abundant fine charred organic matter (skeletal grains of fine quartz and weathered glauconite) typical of anthropogenic soils and sediments. Charred organic matter has become intimately mixed with mineral matter by occupation activities. Dark earth, Southwark, London. PPL. f.l. 0.16 mm.

(c) Bronze Age ashes from an open ceramic hearth (northwest India). The fuel used consists essentially of cow dung which has been burned at a high temperature resulting in partial melting of the silica. The temperature seems to have been around 700–800 degrees C since there is no vesicular fabric. PPL. f.l. 3 mm.

(d) An enigmatic cave horizon containing few flint artefacts and poorly burned layers. The finer material comprises lightly charred plant fragments, sometimes stained by yellowish amorphous material of a coprolitic/phosphatic character. This is believed to be birds' nest material. A slightly crushed grey eggshell is present. Regurgitation by predatory birds has produced the leached (digestive action) bone fragments at the top of the slide and the rodent tooth on the right. The layers in the cave which were thought to be hearths have now to be accepted as the results of bird occupation, although the slight burning could either be from spontaneous combustion or reflect occasional visits by humans. Upper Palaeolithic (c. 20,000 yrs bp.), Arene Candide, Finale, Liguria, Italy. PPL. f.l. 5.54 mm.

Publisher's Errata

Plate II b Picture is upside-down; orange fine clay coating should be seen in the upper half of the frame.

Plate V d Picture is on its right side; charred peat should be seen to be horizontally layered.

Plate V e Picture is on its left side; in field photo brownish layer should be seen to be at the base of the sequence.

Plate I

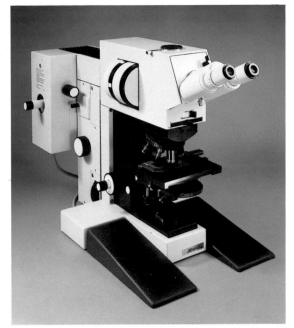

a

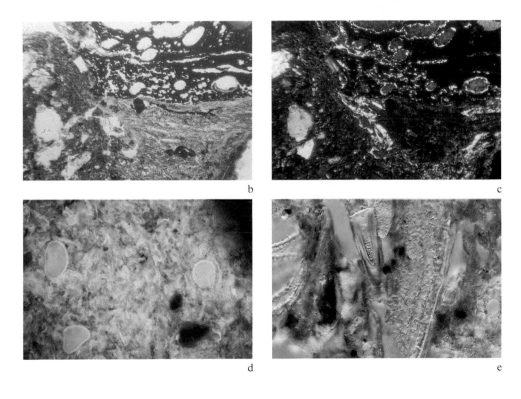

b

c

d

e

Plate II

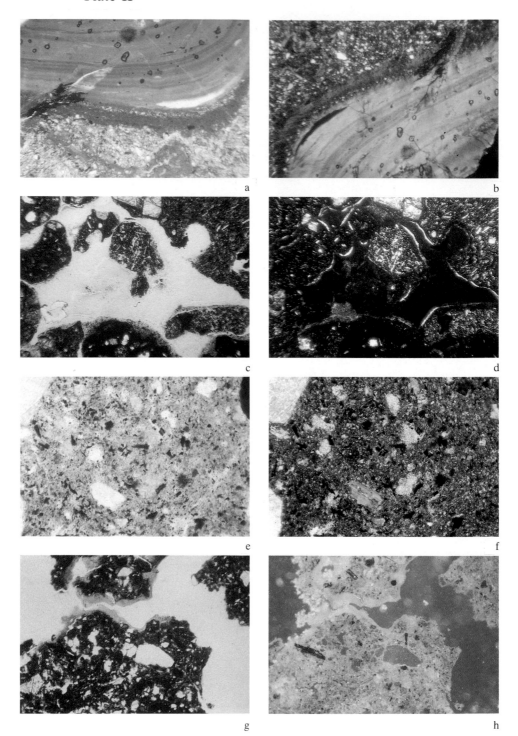

Plate III

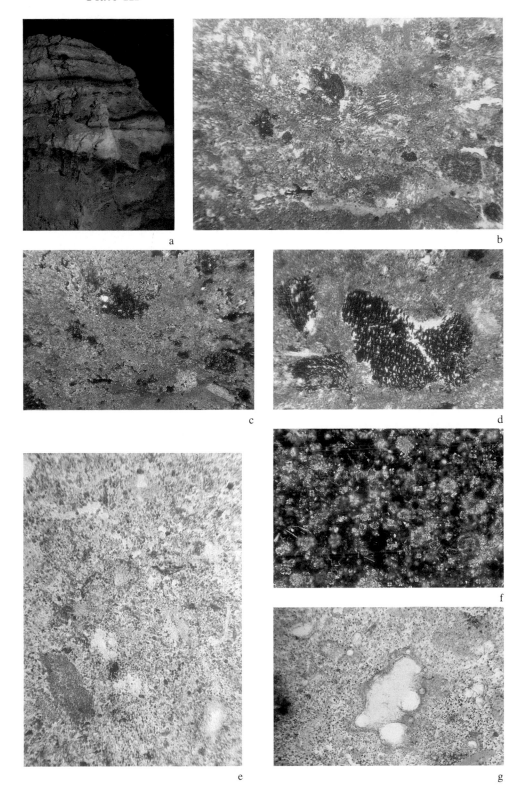

Plate IV

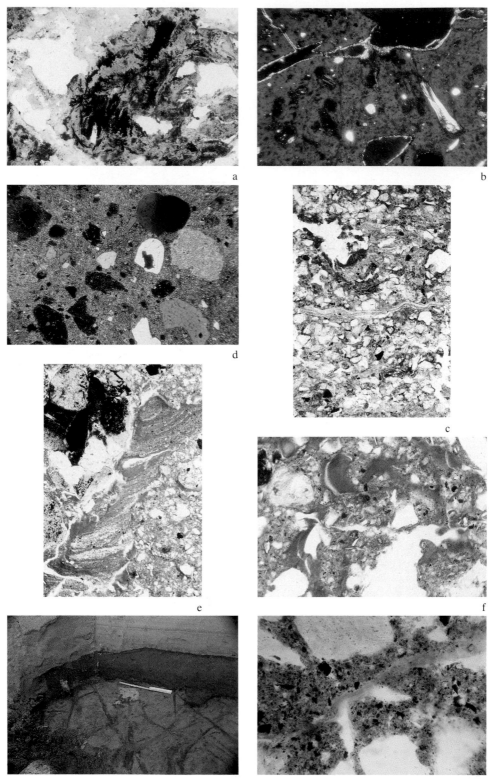

Plate V

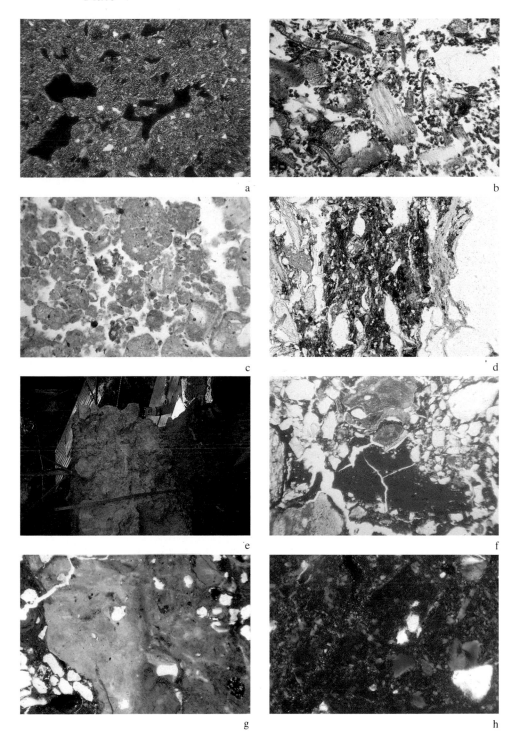

Plate VI

Plate VII

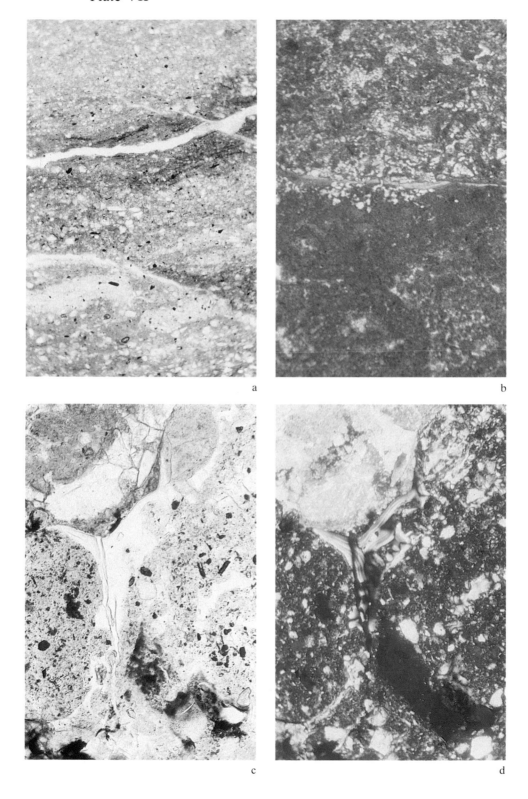

a

b

c

d

Plate VIII

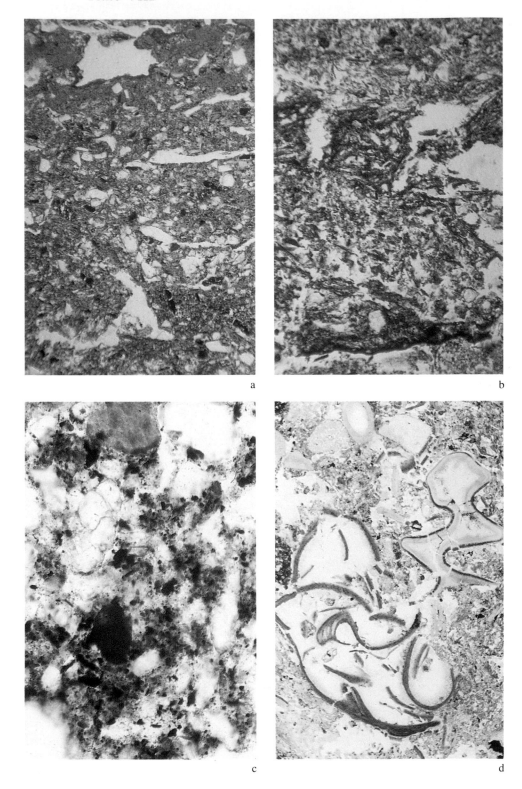

a

b

c

d

than that produced by low temperature rubefaction, clear differences are observed in thin section. This is illustrated by a marked decrease in birefringence caused by the structural disruption during heating and the resulting segregation of iron oxides (see Plates IIIb and IIIg).

The multiplicity of factors that may create a red unit in archaeological contexts explains why their origin is so commonly open to question. In this regard, a final consideration concerns the intentional use in earthworks of red soil or sediment, which were probably selected and imported because of their colour. Field and microscopic features are not very different from those that characterise naturally deposited red materials. Nevertheless, indications of importation may comprise mineralogical composition unlike that found in the surroundings, the impossibility of a natural input, based on the field context, or the absence of sedimentary features.

8.6 Movement of solutions and related features
8.6.1 *Dynamics of the process*
In contrast to the translocation of solid particles, which affects soil constituents without altering their original chemical and mineralogical characteristics, water may also be chemically active and react with mineral and organic constituents that are no longer in equilibrium with the solution. In order to establish an equilibrium at the interface between the liquid and the solid phases, soil constituents are dissolved into the soil solution.

The dissolution of the various soil constituents is highly variable and depends upon their crystalline structure and their specific reactions with the solution. Silicate minerals, for example, are generally known for their weak solubility or inertness, especially quartz, which can be put into solution only under particular chemical conditions. Salts (e.g., gypsum, sodium chloride), on the other hand, are highly soluble and can easily and rapidly pass into the soil solution. When the solution becomes sufficiently concentrated, precipitation of a solid phase occurs – either mineral or organic – resulting in the **neoformation** of these components.

Dissolution and reprecipitation may take place alternatively in the same location when the chemical equilibrium is endlessly disrupted and re-established, as for example in the case of fluctuations of the water content in arid regions where alternating evaporation and wetting control the dissolution–reprecipitation of salts. With its suspended load, water may migrate through the soil either downward or upward, reaching a zone where dissolved elements become concentrated and then precipitate. Such a redistribution may strongly modify the original composition of the materials and represents a major pedogenic process, the formation of soil horizons.

As with particle translocation, microscopic evidence for the movements of solution are illustrated by features indicating chemical loss by dissolution in one location within the profile and by chemical enrichment through the reprecipitation in another. These features are respectively termed **depletion** and **accumulation** features. The chemical nature of depletion features can be inferred from observation of the surrounding matrix by searching for the remains of mineral or organic elements that have been depleted. These elements, of course, are not always there. Accumulation features, on the other hand, are much easier to observe and identify under the optical microscope. Accumulation zones are commonly related to the pre-existing void network, forming hypocoatings, coatings or infillings. They may also be independent of the structural and biological pores and impregnate the soil mass, resulting in the formation of nodules which have distinct shapes (see Bullock *et al.*, 1985, Chapter 9).

Accumulation features are usually grouped according to the crystallographic structure of the neoformed components recognised under the optical microscope. Two main classes are distinguished:

> crystalline features, including neoformation of soluble salts, such as gypsum, carbonates, phosphates, clays and aluminous oxides (e.g., gibbsite);
> cryptocrystalline and amorphous features comprising essentially neoformed iron and manganese oxides and, to some extent, the accumulation of amorphous organic matter, although the origin of the latter has yet to be clearly established.

The above size distinction is necessary when the optical microscope is used, since the SEM is capable of revealing the crystalline structure of apparently amorphous mineral substances, especially iron oxides. As a consequence, in the following section we tend to play down this size differentiation and review features associated with solution movements principally in terms of their mineralogy.

8.6.2 *Accumulation of soluble salts*
8.6.2.1 Origin of salts

Salts in archaeological sediments and soils may have a geological, pedological or an anthropic origin. Parent materials may have a high content in soluble salts as a consequence of their geological evolution (e.g., evaporites or lacustrine sediments formed under arid conditions). Salts may also have precipitated from saline groundwater flowing through parent materials or they may be of aeolian origin, having been derived from a beach or from salt lakes in desertic environments.

Salts of pedological origin are believed to be produced through mineral weathering under very alkaline conditions. In arid and semi-arid regions high amounts of sodium and calcium ions are derived from the weathering of feldspar; cations forming soluble salts can be generated during plant respiration. Soluble salts, however, may be easily and rapidly leached out of the profile because of their high solubility, draining into the percolating groundwater, with consequent alteration of the original properties of soils or sediments.

When the evapotranspiration is very high, especially in arid and semi-arid regions, vertical drainage is limited and soluble salts concentrate in the soil solution and accumulate within the soil. This is particularly the case where salts are concentrated on the surface by seasonally active capillary water arriving at the soil surface.

8.6.2.2 Precipitation of highly soluble salts

The micromorphological observation of salt accumulation is difficult to monitor in thin section. This arises during thin-section manufacture when, unfortunately, the most soluble salts are dissolved in the resin solvent added during impregnation and are only preserved when initially present in high quantities. The use of the SEM on unimpregnated samples is therefore recommended to study their morphology. Normally, however, it is possible to recognise crystals of halite (NaCl) concentrated at the soil surface or formed as coatings around structural soil units (Figure 8.9d), indicating that chloride ions were present in the soil solution. The accumulation of sodium carbonate – impregnating the soil matrix or infilling pores – is observed when carbonate ions are dominant and exchangeable calcium is nearly absent. The first situation characterises saline soils where surface concentration of salts results in the formation of a white, millimetre-thick powdery crust, consisting of mostly halite. In the second case, which is specific to alkaline soils, a dark brown layer is formed at the soil surface, consisting of sodium carbonate mixed with organic matter.

The accumulation of highly soluble salts may appear rapidly, on the order of a few days, but may strongly fluctuate throughout the year, with salts being leached during the rainy season and accumulating in the dry season when evapotranspiration is very high. Moreover, salts can be totally leached from soils when conditions have changed subsequent to their accumulation, as for example by an increase in humidity or by a change in land use. In thin sections, remnant features testifying to a prior stage of salinisation are not likely to persist although previous alkalisation will be easier to identify because the release of sodium from clay induces irreversible structural changes (Plate Va).

8.6.2.3 Precipitation of gypsum

Moderately soluble salts, such as gypsum, may be more easily preserved over longer periods of time. Gypsum in soils most commonly occurs as lenticular crystals of various sizes but other shapes may be present (e.g., featherlike) when environmental factors such as impurities and drainage control its crystallisation. The accumulation of gypsum usually starts as infillings of large voids (e.g., channels and fissures) as well as individual crystals within the groundmass (Figure 8.9e). Crystallisation of gypsum from the soil solution causes a significant volume increase, which results in pressures within the soil mass and ultimately in disaggregation of the soil fabric. At an extreme stage of evolution, gypsum may become the dominant component of the thin section at the expense of the original material. Such an organisation is typically observed in massive gypsic horizons (see Table 2.2) and in gypsiferous crusts formed, for example, on alluvial terraces in arid regions, especially in North Africa. There, repeated dissolution–reprecipitation of gypsum results in the formation of interlocked crystals that are thought to bring about the cementation observed in gypsum accumulations (Halitim and Robert, 1987).

In arid and semi-arid areas, the role of crystal growth and expansion on the disruption of consolidated materials, such as rocks or mud-brick structures, can be considerable (Goudie, 1977, 1981) and in some cases invasion of an archaeological layer by gypsum may totally transform the original material into a powder. Even if at a later time there is sufficient moisture to dissolve them, traces of former gypsum crystals can still be recognised in thin section by the characteristic lozenge shape of voids. Such 'ghosts' can testify to changes in past environmental conditions (Figure 8.9f).

8.6.3 *Dissolution and precipitation of calcium carbonate*
Because they are so widespread, the transformations of calcium carbonate in soils and sediments have been especially well documented. Although magnesium carbonate can also occur in sediments and soils (e.g., when derived from dolomitic limestone), we will restrict ourselves to the more commonly occurring pedogenic form of calcium carbonate.

8.6.3.1 Dissolution
In general, naturally formed carbonic acid is essential to the dissolution of carbonate. Carbon dioxide (CO_2) may be produced by a great many processes, among which are the respiration of plants and the activity of microorganisms. Both play a major role in the dissolution of carbonate in any environment affected by biological activity. Dissolution of carbonate may be enhanced by the presence of acidic substances, such as humic acid produced under moder or mor surface horizons or deeper at the root soil interface. Hydrothermal reactions as well as specific geochemical alteration processes may also produce carbonic acid and, as a consequence, dissolution of carbonate may occur at any depth in the substrate. Such diagenetic, geological processes will not be examined in this chapter.

Calcium carbonate in sediments and soils possesses a large diversity of forms, varying from single fine-grained calcite crystals to large fragments of calcareous rocks. Crystal size and the number of impurities may strongly influence the dynamics of dissolution and the resulting kinds of features recognisable in thin sections. The main pathways of the dissolution process can be summarised as follows.

Dissolution gradually attacks the calcite crystals simultaneously at the edge of each individual crystal and along fissures and cleavages (Courty, 1986; Delmas *et al.*, 1987) (Figure 8.11a). This dissolution is readily observed in large-

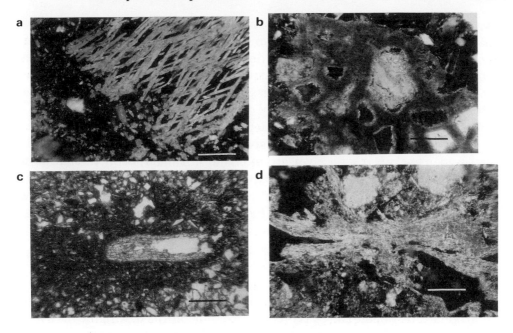

Figure 8.11 (a) Highly dissolved calcite fragment showing remnants of calcite along cleavages. the isotropic groundmass mostly consists of poorly crystallised phosphate minerals (layer VII, Cave of Vaufrey, France). XPL. (Bar = 150 μm)

(b) Dense micritic fabric associated with quartz sand grains.This characterises amygdaloidal nodules related to pedogenic accumulation of calcium carbonate (Late Holocene soil, Ghaggar plain, India). XPL. (Bar = 50 μm)

(c) Micritic hypocoating and calcite pseudomorphs of root cells (buried, weakly expressed BCa horizon on alluvium, Ghaggar plain, India). PPL. (Bar = 150 μm)

(d) Coatings of needle-shaped calcite crystals (or lublinite) producing a light grey, weakly cemented layer (Neolithic cave of Bellefons, Charente, France). XPL. (Bar = 50 μm)

sized (a few hundred microns) calcite fragments which appear highly corroded and with possibly a lower birefringence. When the corrosion is very intense, calcite fragments lose their cohesion and split into very fine grains, commonly needle-shaped, which may then be completely dissolved. When finely crystalline (less than 5 μm) the process is similar, though the transformation of each elementary crystal is not recognisable in thin section and the resulting features are indicated by darkening (PPL), loss of birefringence and increased porosity.

For heterogeneous limestones (e.g., those consisting of micritic clasts cemented by sparite), the less stable sparite cement may be preferentially dissolved, thereby liberating the finer-grained, more resistant clasts. In addition, calcium carbonate fragments containing small amounts of insoluble elements may be slowly dissolved, leaving a residuum.

As mentioned above carbonate dissolution may be stimulated in zones of high biological activity and dissolution cavities may be produced by the penetration of root hairs as well as by microorganisms. Such dissolution cavities are easily distinguishable from those related to chemical dissolution *sensu stricto* because their edges are outlined by organo-mineral substances resulting from the activity of microorganisms. These substances form a yellow-ish-brown to brown rim at the edges of dissolved crystals and fluoresce strongly, whereas carbonate normally displays weak fluorescence.

Dissolution of carbonate results in depletion features distinguished by a loss in carbonate from the surrounding soil. For example, when it is partially dissolved, a fine calcareous clayey groundmass with an originally crystallitic b-fabric will display patches depleted in calcite and a b-fabric which is dominated by the arrangement of clay. Such depleted patches commonly result from the intense activity of microorganisms at the contact between roots and calcareous soils, along the walls of channels, or at the contact between an algal and a calcareous soil.

8.6.3.2 Reprecipitation of carbonate

Reactions and controlling factors When solutions are saturated in dissolved bicarbonate, carbonate can be reprecipitated or neoformed, with the release of carbonate gas and water. In most cases only calcium carbonate reprecipitates because magnesium, which migrates easily, has been leached out of the active zone. Moisture and biological activity are two essential factors controlling the neoformation of calcium carbonate and two different paths of reprecipitation are usually distinguished. The first refers to a chemical reaction occurring when evaporation brings about saturation of the solution. In the second case, precipitation results from a complex interaction between chemical and biological factors. These two different courses may produce different microscopic features although the morphology of the reprecipitated carbonate may not always permit recognition of the process that produced them. This is shown by the formation of the microlaminated crust. This was originally thought to be solely of chemical origin but recent experiments and technical improvements show its formation is often controlled by biological factors, especially algae (Vogt, 1987) (Plate VIIb).

The high sensitivity of calcium carbonate to slight environmental changes (e.g., an increase in soil pH or a higher evaporation) make neoformed carbonates valuable indicators of a large set of post-depositional events that have affected calcareous sediments. Moreover, cementation, commonly from secondary calcium carbonate accumulation, has generally favoured good preservation of these features and partly explains why they have been so abundantly studied.

Morphology, distribution and significance The large variety of calcium carbonate accumulations occurring in sediments and soils has been extensively studied in the field, with a special emphasis on concretions (or nodules) and crusts (also described as caliche or calcrete). Both are striking features and considered to be significant environmental and climatic indicators. In prehistoric caves, careful attention has been given to stalagmitic accumulations which result in cemented layers. In cave sites from southwestern France they are supposed to form during moist, temperate, interglacial periods.

Both the optical microscope and the SEM have proved to be very efficient tools for studying the various kinds of calcium carbonate accumulations and how they were formed, since the characteristics of crystalline fabrics are in most cases very clear.

Calcitic features consist predominantly of calcium carbonate crystals of varying sizes and shapes, including mineral and organic constituents that were in existence before calcium carbonate was precipitated. Distinction is first made according to crystal size : micrite ($< 10 \, \mu$m) and sparite ($> 50 \, \mu$m) (Folk, 1959). An intermediate class (between 10 and 50 μm) is called microsparite. Individual microsparite and sparite crystals are clearly observed in thin sections, whereas individual micritic crystals are difficult to distinguish. Pure micritic fabrics appear grey in PPL and have a grainy aspect because of the density of fine crystals. Large-sized crystals generally have the typical rhombohedral shape of calcite but other geometric shapes can also be observed, for example cubic or quadrangular when crystals are pseudomorphs of plant cells; needle-shaped crystals (a few microns in diameter) are also a common type. Observation under the SEM is recommended for studying the precise size and shape of crystals, especially when they are smaller than 10 μm (e.g. Figure 8.9b).

Generally speaking, the size of the neoformed crystals may reflect upon the conditions under which crystal growth took place. Large-sized crystals are generated from solutions containing only dissolved calcium carbonate and are further encouraged by the lack of physical or chemical constraints on crystallisation. Upward and lateral movements of groundwaters rich in dissolved calcium carbonate are known to induce the precipitation of sparite that cements sediments or soils. This process forms a typical mosaic fabric, which clearly differs from the finer-grained fabrics produced by downward migrations of solutions (Figure 8.11b). Infillings of sparite crystals may also occur in large cavities in which solutions were preferentially flowing, giving rise to millimetre-thick cemented layers intercalated between non- or weakly cemented materials, e.g., in caves. When the evaporation rate is very slow very large-sized sparite crystals may also form from a water film. Thick accumulations of layered calcium carbonate can thus be produced in limestone caves as the result of repeated episodes of sparite precipitation (cf. Figure 6.9c).

Pedological accumulation of calcium carbonate is associated with downward migration of solutions that yield a large variety of micritic and sparitic features. Micritic coatings consisting of needle-shaped crystals (or lublinite) are the most common feature to appear as soon as soil solutions dissolve small amounts of calcium carbonate. These are classically described as **pseudomycelia** because of their fungus-like aspect in the field (Figure 8.11d). The presence of organic and mineral impurities, transported in solution with calcium carbonate, is supposed to prevent the crystallisation of well-shaped calcite crystals (Vergès, 1985). The environmental significance of needle-shaped micritic coatings is limited because they may form and disappear very rapidly. Neoformation of calcium carbonate along bio-pores in association with plant respiration produces micritic and microsparitic hypocoatings and coatings; pseudomorphs of roots can also be observed, with each pre-existing cell being replaced by an individual sparite crystal (Figure 8.11c). Compared to pseudomycelia these are more permanent features and can be considered as good indicators of a previous phase of biological activity, in particular the colonisation of the soil by roots.

Calcitic features along bio-pores may develop below the zone of maximal root activity since biological production of organic acids in the overlying layers favours the dissolution of calcium carbonate. In a homogeneous calcareous parent material this simultaneous dissolution–reprecipitation results in the formation of a carbonate-depleted upper A horizon and a carbonate-enriched B horizon (Figure 8.12). When the dissolution affects a layer originally rich in calcium carbonate, e.g., an ash unit, the underlying layer is gradually invaded by neoformed calcium carbonate and the occurrence of calcitic features along bio-pores modifies to some extent the original characteristics of the parent materials, producing a greyish colour and weak cementation.

More intense dissolution–reprecipitation of calcium carbonate increases the vertical differentiation of the profile, and neoformed calcitic features appear not only in bio-pores but also as impregnations within the groundmass. This impregnation may be irregularly concentrated in some patches or in nodules, or may impregnate the entire soil mass. Repeated cycles of dissolution–reprecipitation produce nodules with a complex internal fabric, whose characteristics are often useful in the reconstruction of their genesis (Figure 8.13). Calcitic nodules are sensitive to (slight) changes in soil conditions and can be good indicators of past environmental conditions.

The hardness of some calcitic nodules fosters their own preservation even when cemented layers have been reworked or partially eroded. They may be concentrated *in situ* when all the non-cemented sediments have been eroded or they may be transported. Good evidence of allochthonous origin is provided by rounded shape, sharp edges (Figure 8.13) and differences in the mineralogical composition of the non-calcareous inclusions in comparison to that of the surrounding matrix. In some extreme cases pre-existing calcitic nodules have been so intensively disrupted and reworked that the only relics are individual micritic and grains or crystals, whose origin can only be guessed at from context. In most cases it is hardly possible to differentiate these inherited post-depositional features from mineral grains of geological origin.

The most obvious changes resulting from calcium carbonate precipitation are changes in colour, structure (cementation) and mineralogy; textural changes are also commonly produced by the fragmentation of mineral grains in

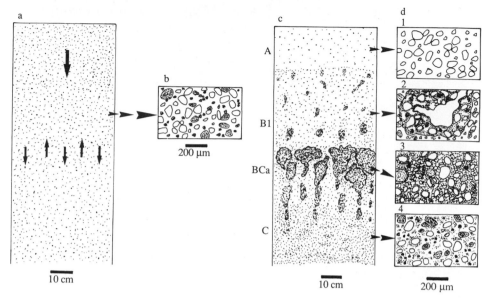

Figure 8.12   Schematic representation of the effects of pedogenic dissolution–reprecipitation cycles on a soil profile:

(a) Original fine sandy soil profile, arrows indicating the downward migration of solutions and the theoretical position of the evaporation front.

(b) Characteristics in thin section of the original calcareous structureless fine sands.

(c) Typical soil profile with a moderately expressed BCa horizon characterised by amoeboidal-shaped, well-cemented calcite nodules.

(d) Related micromorphological features:

1 decalcified upper part consisting of loose, structureless, fine sands,

2 micritic hypocoatings along channels forming poorly cemented elongated nodules,

3 microsparitic and micritic, well-cemented nodules (note the regular orientation of calcite crystals around sand grains),

4 structureless C horizon enriched in fine calcite particles.

which calcite crystals gradually grow. Calcium carbonate may also replace pre-existing silicate minerals when soil solutions become alkaline (pH 9 to 10), thereby favouring dissolution of silica. Combination of these mechanical and chemical effects of crystallisation have been invoked in arid regions – especially in North Africa – to explain the development of thick calcareous crusts at the expense of outcropping rocks during the Pleistocene.

Neoformation of calcium carbonate controlled by biological activity falls within the realm of both post-depositional and sedimentary processes, ascription to one of these processes depending upon the scale (i.e., volume) of precipitated calcium carbonate. The formation and significance of cemented calcareous layers occurring in desertic regions (calcrete) have been actively debated from this point of view and two hypotheses have been proposed: (1)

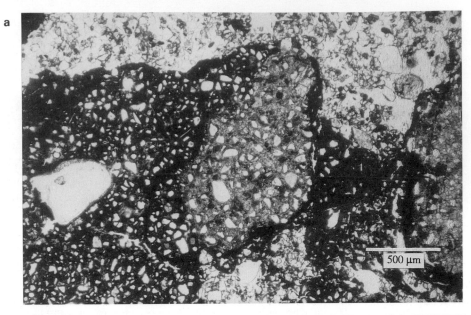

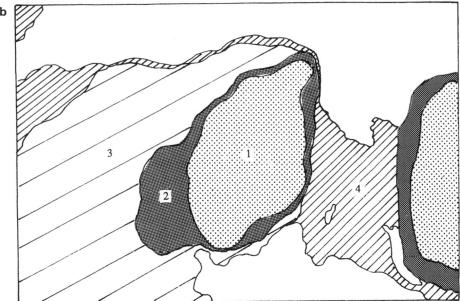

Figure 8.13   Calcrete band with a complex internal fabric:
   (a) Middle Pleistocene petrocalcic layer (Didwana, India). PPL. (Bar = 500 μm)
   (b) Interpretation of the different fabrics:

1 Microspartic inner part with a rounded shape: this represents the first stage of calcium carbonate accumulation related to vadose crystallisation. Nodules were subsequently reworked as indicated by their sharp edges.

2 Brown micritic rim: dissolution of previously formed nodule.

3 Micritic and microsparitic fabric relating to pedogenic accumulation of calcium carbonate.

4 Last phase of micritic cementation.

gradual formation resulting from lateral and vertical migration of calcium carbonate leading to a horizon of accumulation; and (2) bio-sedimentary accumulation from the combined action of runoff and organisms that are able to precipitate calcium carbonate.

In semi-arid conditions, micromorphological work has revealed that the formation of massive and strongly cemented calcrete (the 'petrocalcic horizon') is tied to the prevalence of repeated surface erosion; tufa-like layers and crusts, on the other hand, are essentially generated by algae in association with microorganisms that are able to precipitate calcium carbonate and to stabilise the soil surface under limited moisture conditions (Vogt, 1984). The above is illustrated in thin section by the juxtaposition and imbrication of features indicating algal formation and others produced during erosional phases.

Calcareous crusts may also occur in cold deserts, though to a lesser extent than in hot, arid regions, and develop preferentially on the underside of surface stones. They have been related to surface dissolution and downward precipitation of calcium carbonate arising from the percolation of relatively acidic solutions formed in summer (Bunting and Christensen, 1978). A succession of dense micritic layers with various detrital inclusions and calcite layers forms on the underside of coarse fragments producing typical festoon-like features called **pendents** (cf. Chapter 9, Figure 9.2e).

In archaeological contexts, the dissolution and precipitation of calcium carbonate is particularly important since it is commonly associated with human activities, either in the form of wood ashes (see Chapter 7) or as building materials (e.g., mortar, plaster). Consequently, its response to natural modifications that may alter its original characteristics must be extensively known, before interpretations of archaeological sediments and soils can be made.

The debate regarding the time needed to effect these modifications is not finished. Some processes seem to be seasonal, such as colonisation by algae. Others, like the development of hard, thick, cemented calcareous crusts would require that the soil surface remain bare and exposed to high evaporation and runoff for at least a few hundred years. A similar span of time would lead to a well-differentiated Bca horizon where vertical leaching is involved. These, however, are only rough estimates because various factors – either internal (such as texture and mineralogy) or external (such as moisture content and temperature) – may inhibit or accelerate the dissolution. Hence, the respective role of these factors has to be carefully determined before any definitive interpretation can be made.

8.6.4 *Movements of iron and related features*
When iron is not combined with silicates, it has the potential to move within the soil in response to chemical changes and may modify the original characteristics of the parent material, especially colour and chemical composition. Free iron (i.e., iron that is capable of being moved) is highly mobile only when present in the ferrous state (Fe^{2+}) which occurs under reducing (anaerobic) conditions.

When sufficient oxygen is maintained in the soil, free iron is oxidised (Fe^{3+}) to form stable crystalline and amorphous components of the iron oxides. Movements of iron in sediments and soils thus involve processes of **oxidation–reduction** which are controlled by several factors:

> **biological activity:** respiration by plants and microorganisms effect alternate uptake and release of oxygen;
>
> **water content and circulation:** permanent waterlogging creates anaerobic conditions whereas circulating soil or groundwater maintains an oxidising environment.

Mobile forms of iron can occur as detrital elements in sediments and soils, or can be dissolved from silicate minerals by chemical and biochemical agents. The release of free iron derived from silicate weathering is particularly notable under acid and reducing conditions, and has been shown to be controlled by microbial activity and by the production of organic substances.

Insoluble oxides and hydroxides (amorphous or crystalline) represent the most common forms of iron accumulations although under highly reducing conditions ferrous iron may also occur, combined with sulphur or phosphate, as in vivianite (ferrous phosphate), for example.

Accumulations of amorphous oxides and hydroxides generally result from the presence of high amounts of acid organic matter, whereby iron is finely integrated with organic molecules to form organo-mineral complexes. During the humification of organic matter amorphous substances are gradually transformed into cryptocrystalline and then crystalline oxides and hydroxides; crystalline oxides may also be formed directly, especially in the case of low amounts of soluble organic matter.

Movements of iron generally produce colour changes that can be easily traced in thin section. In layers affected by fluctuations of the water table, clays that have been depleted in iron because of reducing conditions are characterised by paler colour (PPL) and lower birefringence (whitish grey to yellowish white) than those from non-altered zones. In contrast, iron developed under oxidising conditions takes the form of diffuse impregnations of the groundmass that differs from unaltered matter by its darker colour and loss of birefringence (Figure 8.14b). The latter is brought about by absorption on clay minerals of neoformed iron compounds, which mask the previous arrangement of clay particles. Impregnated zones are commonly observed along biological and structural voids, where oxidation–reduction processes which are mostly related to plant respiration and activity of microorganisms are concentrated. In some cases, the masking of clay by neoformed iron may be so complete that pre-existing fabrics cannot be recognised and any earlier manifestations of iron accumulation, such as weak clay illuviation in podzol B horizons, is very difficult to detect.

Plant fragments within soil materials are often preferential traps for iron accumulations, which may create pseudomorphs of the plant cells. The impregnated fragments thus have a dark brown, blackish colour or a charcoal-like aspect. However, under oblique reflected light, these iron compounds have a metallic lustre and reddish hue. Iron may also create pseudomorphs of weathered silicate minerals, such as biotite or olivine, whose original shapes and cleavages can still be recognised even after they have been completely weathered.

Localised accumulation of iron within the groundmass results in a large variety of **nodules** or **concretions** if it becomes cemented. Nodules exhibiting a complex internal fabric point to polygenetic development composed of alternate phases of iron accumulation and non-accumulation or rounding during transportation (Figure 8.14c). As with calcitic nodules, iron nodules – because of their indurated nature and high resistance – can remain intact after being eroded and may undergo some transportation before being deposited. A final phase of iron accumulation may then bind the nodules together, resulting in cemented ferric crusts called 'ferricrete', plinthites and petroplinthites. Formation of well-developed and abundant iron concretions and ferricrete requires marked alternations between highly oxidising and reducing conditions. Such situations are particularly prevalent in tropical climates, where abundant moisture and high temperature encourage iron dissolution. More rarely they may also appear under semi-arid Mediterranean climates in small depressions or 'dayas', where repeated fluctuations between dry and humid phases produce ferruginisation.

The high preservation potential of ferruginous nodules makes them a very common inherited feature in Quaternary sediments and paleosols, including those from archaeological sites. The climatic significance of these reworked nodules is much diminished in comparison to iron concretions that have developed *in situ*. Sharp edges and good rounding of nodules in thin section are significant criteria for suspecting that iron concretions have been transported (Figure 8.14c).

When reducing conditions are permanently maintained at some depth within a profile (e.g., waterlogging associated with a high water-table), iron reduction brings about total or partial discolouration of the groundmass. This produces typically homogeneous grey layers, which may occur in both sedimentary environments or in soils; in the latter case they are described as **gley** horizons. The usually sharp limit between the gley and the overlying materials may be interpreted in the field as a sedimentary contact but observation in thin section will reveal only a colour difference between the two juxtaposed units, which are in fact the same layer. If the front of the permanent water-table coincides with a sedimentary limit, micromorphological evidence (e.g., texture, composition) can demonstrate a sedimentary change associated with post-depositional transformations.

Discolouration is often incomplete, resulting in a reddish-grey mottling. This state can arise from fluctuations between oxidation and reduction conditions or when formerly gleyed units have been subsequently reoxidised. Horizons

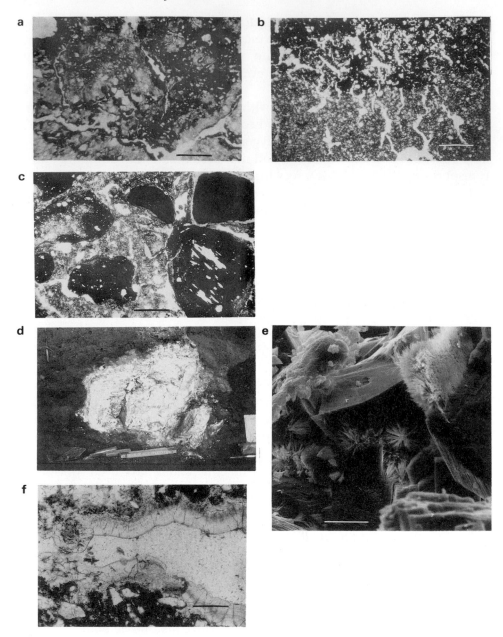

Figure 8.14   (a) Ferruginous features: dark ferruginous impregnations and hypocoatings of the groundmass within B horizon of a glossic Albaqualf (Marly forest, France). PPL. (Bar = 150 μm)

(b) Iron and manganese impregnation of a Neolithic buried soil surface containing pseudomorphs of roots, interpreted as a short-lived grassland vegetation (turf) invading after cultivation (Hazelton long cairn, Gloucestershire, England). PPL. (Bar = 500 μm)

affected by this transformation are described in soil science as **pseudogley** and commonly originate from conditions of poor surface drainage (also known as 'surface gley'). In this case, thin sections are also helpful in showing that the colour heterogeneity is related to *in situ* iron depletion and accumulation, and not to other processes which may have mechanically mixed reddish and grey materials.

Gley and pseudogley features may develop rapidly because of drainage modifications. The recognition of the sequential relationship between the formation of ferruginous features and others developed previously is necessary in order to determine the actual causes responsible for producing the hydrological changes. For example, the superimposition, or juxtaposition, of clay coatings and subsequent iron accumulation commonly characterises some lessivé soils (luvisols) formed during the Holocene in temperate regions (cf. Figure 8.14b). This association can be interpreted as the consequence of a decreasing velocity of percolating water subsequent to the accumulation of clay in voids, thus leading to temporary waterlogging and localised iron movements.

The discolouration of soils from red to pale yellow and even to white takes place with the opposite mineralogical change of haematite into goethite, though the transformation necessitates the establishment of an intermediate soluble form of iron. Acid conditions and temporary waterlogging may cause the partial or total degradation of red soils. In the latter case microscopic evidence for an earlier red stage has totally disappeared. If, on the other hand, the superimposition of these hydromorphic (i.e., water-saturated) conditions is only partial, it is then possible to pinpoint in thin section the location of deferruginised zones and their relative distribution with respect to other features which either pre- or post-date the period of discolouration. This in turn permits the determination of the relative timing of the deferruginisation and the pattern of voids through which the soil solution circulated.

Beyond the basic inference that archaeological sediments and soils have been once affected by waterlogging, more elaborate interpretation regarding the

---

(c) Loosely packed ferruginous nodules related to repeated phases of iron accumulation and erosion. Note the various fabrics of iron nodules and their subrounded shape, indicating some transportation (Saalian paleosol developed on loessic material, Paris Basin, France). PPL. (Bar = 500 μm)

(d) Alteration of a dolomitic limestone related to percolation of phosphatic solutions, presumably derived from bat guano: block of weathered dolomite from Kebara Cave, Israel. The greyer inner core is unweathered dolomite which is surrounded by a lighter, cream-coloured weathering rind $\sim$5–10 cm thick, consisting of phosphate minerals, principally taranakite (potassium–aluminium phosphate; see Table 8.1). Ruler is $\sim$20 cm long.

(e) SEM view of weathering rind shown in (d) showing acicular taranakite crystals growing on rhombs of dolomite. (Bar = 15 μm)

(f) Apatite coating of a void (Tabun Cave, Israel). PPL. (Bar = 230 μm)

chronological position of this transformation – including its environmental significance and its relationship to the entire stratigraphic sequence at hand – is more problematic and requires a good combination of both field and micro-scopic data. If necessary, additional analytical data (e.g., microprobe) may be gathered. In any case, alteration of iron minerals through biological activity can enhance the magnetic susceptibility (MS) of a soil, particularly the topsoil. Post-depositional hydromorphism, however, can alter the state of the iron, yielding MS values that are unrelated to the original ones (Allen and Macphail, 1987).

In conclusion, among post-depositional processes, solution movements of iron are significant since they may strongly affect the original characteristics of the soil or sediment, particularly colour, which may lead to misinterpretations of the stratigraphy in the field. The optical microscope is able to detect iron depletion and accumulation although observation in thin section does not permit the discrimination between the different neoformed iron oxides and hydroxides, be they amorphous, cryptocrystalline or crystalline. The use of electron microscopy – both SEM and TEM – is recommended to improve the location and characterisation of iron oxides and their relationship with other soil particles, such as clay.

8.6.5 *Solution movements of aluminium and neoformed features*

Weathering of clay minerals under acid conditions releases aluminium ions into the soil solution. These ions form hydroxylated polymers that play an impor-tant role in the formation of stable organo-mineral aggregates. These polymers are of course not discernible in thin section because of their very small size (nannometres). However, their fine integration into plates of clay has been recognised with electron microscope techniques.

Aluminium oxides, the most common being gibbsite, may crystallise when conditions remain weakly acid, organic matter content is low and good drain-age favours the elimination of soluble silica. Formation of gibbsite is primarily associated with soils developed on basic rocks under tropical humid conditions and gibbsitic features may occur in the weathering zones as well as lower down in the profile, in the upper oxic horizons. These features are present mostly as irregular coatings and infillings in voids but also as discrete crystals in the groundmass; they also develop as nodules which are in most cases pseudomorphs of silicate minerals, especially feldspars.

Weathering under alkaline conditions may also release a high amount of aluminium, which creates strong chemical bonds with organic acids, chiefly fulvic acid. This occurs when the clay content is low, in a soil rich in organic matter. This reaction is particularly active in soils developed on volcanic ash (andosols) in which the fine fraction consists of highly stable amorphous compounds (named allophane), formed of aluminium and silica polymers combined with organic acids. True andosols consist predominantly of allophane and have a very low clay content; with time poorly ordered clay minerals develop, such as halloysite. Under the optical microscope they are characterised by very low birefringence resulting from their granular arrangement and weak crystallinity. Moreover, the abundance of organo-mineral complexes in these soils results in the formation of a microaggregated structure, commonly described as a silt-like texture. These aggregates have a yellow to brownish yellow colour and contain both mineral inclusions (basaltic glass fragments, phytoliths) and humified organic fragments (Hetier *et al.*, 1974).

8.6.6 *Solution movement of manganese and neoformed features*

Like iron, manganese can be put into solution during the weathering of silicates and may precipitate as oxides in environments characterised by alternating cycles of oxidation–reduction. In fact many concretions may be composed of both iron and manganese oxides but the two species cannot be differentiated. In the field, these ferro-manganiferous concretions are blue–black and should not be mistaken for charcoal or humic bands. In thin section they are generally opaque with a black lustre under oblique incident light (OIL). Like iron concretions, these nodules can impregnate the groundmass or form pseudomorphs of organic matter. Normally, it is only through chemical extraction that the relative proportions of each element can be quantified.

8.6.7 *Solution movement of silica and neoformed features – neoformation of clay minerals*

Under conditions of permanent humidity and intense drainage, soluble silica released during silicate weathering is continuously leached out of the profile at the same time as aluminium and iron hydroxides precipitate (see gibbsite above). This extreme dissolution and leaching of silica leads to total **hydrolysis** (reaction of mineral salt and water) of silicate minerals, notably quartz sand. In the absence of silica the neoformation of clay minerals is not possible and soils formed on parent material impoverished in silica consist predominantly of aluminium and iron hydroxides and oxides.

Soluble silica may be only partially eliminated. This occurs when strong humidity and intense drainage are seasonally interrupted by a well-marked dry season or because there is too much silica to be dissolved. As a consequence, the available silica reacts with amorphous aluminium present in the soil solution, resulting in the neoformation of 1:1 clay minerals (kaolinite and halloysite types). Although clay mineral types cannot be specifically identified in thin section, neoformed kaolinite and halloysite (not mixed with other clays) can be recognised by their typical pale yellow colour and weak birefringence (cf. Plates IIc and IId).

Under limited drainage conditions all the released silica remains where it was dissolved and forms 2:1 clay minerals (illite, smectite and vermiculite types) with soluble aluminium, iron, manganese and basic ions present in the soil solution. Neoformed 2:1 clays can be identified in the weathering zone where pure species occur (Figure 8.9c).

When weathered minerals have been integrated by pedoturbation to the solum overlying the weathering zone, identification of neoformed clay mineral species is normally impossible and requires the combination of X-ray diffraction and electron microscopy techniques.

High amounts of organic matter and permanent humidity may prevent the neoformation of clay from amorphous silica, which precipitates. These amorphous components can barely be recognised in thin section because of their very low birefringence, though silica globules can be observed on the surface of quartz grains under the SEM. Reprecipitation of amorphous silica may also form a cement of silica gel. This occurs particularly under arid, highly alkaline conditions (pH > 9) and when the aluminium content and availability of basic ions is very low. A considerable amount of time is then necessary for the silica gel to evolve into quartz crystals, which explains why only weakly developed silcretes may have formed during the Quaternary (Hutton *et al.*, 1977).

When aluminium and magnesium are present, fibrous, magnesium silicates crystallise (palygorskite and attapulgite type clay minerals).

Silica dissolution may play an important role in the post-depositional alteration of flint artifacts. Modifications may first appear in the formation of a thin patina of precipitated silica, which to some extent protects the flint from further corrosion. If conditions remain unstable, silica dissolution can attack microcrystalline quartz, creating intergranular pores. In extreme conditions, the flint may completely disappear. The optical microscope is not a very efficient tool for pursuing the successive stages of this alteration because corrosion of opal crystals cannot be detected on account of their small size. For the same reasons, dissolution cavities and amorphous silica cannot be observed.

8.7 Phosphates

The origin and geo-pedochemistry of sedimentary phosphates have been studied by geologists and agronomists for many years because of their value as fertilisers. As a tangential outgrowth of this, a marked interest has been shown over the past two decades in phosphates from archaeological sites and is manifest in two broad types of studies being carried out. The first deals with phosphates from the point of view of site survey and land-use practices, where samples are collected from various sections over an area and different organic and inorganic forms of phosphate are monitored (Eidt, 1984); this is essentially a pedochemical approach. The second, which is carried out on a microscopic scale and considered in further detail below, concerns the various types of phosphate minerals and transformations that occur particularly within the cave environment (Table 8.1) (Goldberg and Nathan, 1975; Martini and Kavalieris, 1978), although minerals such as vivianite can be found in bone, ash or cess deposits.

Table 8.1. *Some of the more common phosphate minerals from caves (after Nriagu, 1984)*

Phosphate minerals	Colour-lustre	Habit
Brushite $CaHPO_4 \cdot 2H_2O$	Colourless to ivory yellow; transparent to translucent; vitreous.	Crystals needle-like or prismatic to tabular; earthy powdery or foliated.
Crandallite (Pseudowavellite) $CaAl_3(PO_4)_2(OH)_5 \cdot H_2O$	Yellow, yellowish white to white or grey; transparent to subtranslucent; vitreous; also dull and chalky.	Crystals as minute prisms, or as rosettes of fibres; commonly massive, as nodular masses or spherules with fibrous, fine-granular, or chalcedony-like structure.
Hydroxyapatite $Ca_5(PO_4)_3 \cdot OH$	Colourless, white, grey, yellow to yellowish green, pale to dark green, pale to dark bluish-green, pale to very dark blue, violet-blue, violet, purple, various shades of red and brown; transparent to opaque; vitreous to subresinous; often fluorescent, phosphorescent.	Crystals short to long, prismatic or thin to thick tabular, often complex. Also massive, compact to coarse granular; globular; stalactitic; fibrous, oolitic; earthy.
Leucophosphite series $K_2(Fe^{3+}, Al)_4(PO_4)_4(OH)_2 \cdot 4H_2O$	White to greenish; dull.	Crystals usually short prismatic; also lamellar or as fine-grained chalk-like masses.
Millisite $(Ca, Na, K)Al_3(OH, O)_4(PO_4)_2 \cdot 2H_2O$	White, light grey, greenish.	As chalcedonic crusts or spherules with finely fibrous structure.
Montgomeryite $Ca_4MgAl_4(PO_4)_6(OH)_4 \cdot 12H_2O$	Deep green, rarely pale green to white; transparent to translucent; vitreous.	Crystals minute, lath-like, often in subparallel growths; also massive, as subparallel aggregates of coarse plates.
Strengite (variscite–strengite series – dimorphous with metastrengite) $FePO_4 \cdot 2H_2O$	Colourless, pale to deep violet, red; transparent to translucent; vitreous.	Crystals, thin to thick tabular, stout prismatic; as small spherical aggregates with radial fibrous structure and drusy surface, and as crusts.
Taranakite $H_6K_3Al_5(PO_4)_8 \cdot 18H_2O$, more likely $K_x[Al_{2-y}(H3)_y](OH)_2$ $[Al_xP_{4-x-y}(H)_zO_{10}]$	White, grey or yellowish white	As minute lath-like crystals; also massive, clay-like, pulverulent to compact.
Wavellite $Al_3(OH)_3(PO_4)_2 \cdot 5H_2O$	White to greenish white to green, also yellowish green to yellow and yellowish brown, brown to brownish black; transparent to translucent; vitreous to resinous or pearly.	Crystals minute, rare, stout to long prismatic; usually as acicular radiating aggregates, often distinctly spherical; also as stalactitic crusts.

In caves, phosphates are represented both by detrital elements, generally in the form of bones, and by several types of secondary (diagenetic) forms that are produced by a complex series of chemical reactions. Bone, which represents the most common form of detrital phosphate, is composed of the mineral apatite (generally hydroxyapatite). In thin section bone apatite can be readily recognised by its low birefringence (grey, or more yellowish if fresh) and its ropy texture.

In many sites, however, transformations of phosphates occur, which result in the precipitation of a variety of new phosphate minerals. The type of neoformed minerals depends upon several factors, which include moisture, pH, carbonate and organic-matter content, location within the cave, and the composition of sedimentary substrate (i.e., clay-rich vs. clay-poor). By and large, however, the principal driving agent is the presence of guano and the acidic, phosphatic solutions derived from it. Solutions passing through guano (predominantly from bats) are quite acidic (pH as low as 2) (Martini and Kavalieris, 1978) and can follow a variety of reactions depending on the location of the bats and the directions the solutions themselves take. In a simple case, solutions can flow along the cave walls and ceiling, a phenomenon enhanced if there is a chimney in the cave, as is commonly the case. When these solutions come into contact with Ca^{++} and Mg^{++}, the pH increases and calcium phosphate (generally apatite) is precipitated. Such apatite in the field can take the form of chalky, yellowish-amber layered crusts (Figure 8.14d, 14e), whereas in thin section it is expressed by pale yellow coatings (PPL), which are isotropic under crossed nicols (Plate VIIc, VIId). In many instances the apatite essentially invades the host rock, producing isotropic ghosts of dolomite rhombs. In a similar manner, the mineral brushite can be formed.

When the phosphatic solutions pass into the sedimentary substrate itself, different paragenetic sequences take place, resulting in the formation of several types of phosphate minerals. In sediments rich in carbonates, for example, pH remains high and few transformations occur. As a consequence, any bones present will remain intact, effectively 'protected' from dissolution. However, once all the carbonates have been removed, acidity increases, in which case apatite from bones can be totally or partially dissolved and the phosphate re-precipitated as apatite or as another phosphate mineral. In many cases, apatite is found as well-crystallised vein fillings (Figure 8.14f) or as diffuse impregnations, which render the groundmass completely isotropic.

In cases where the substrate is rich in clay, aluminium and iron phosphate minerals can be formed (Table 8.1). A typical sequence of formation involving groundwater as a source of moisture results in the 'replacements of apatite by hydrated calcic and alkali calcic aluminium phosphates (crandallite and millisite), which are in turn replaced by the hydrated aluminium phosphate, wavellite' (Altschuler, 1973; see also Flicoteaux and Lucas, 1984):

groundwater + apatite + clays − > millisite − > crandallite − > wavellite − > augellite

in which, progressively, the amount of alkalis and the degree of hydration decrease, and the ratio of Al-Fe/P increases. These replacements may take place both by phosphatisation of clay or the attack of apatite by aluminium-bearing solutions. If there is an excess of alkali, a different set of reactions takes place, with a different suite of minerals:

$$\text{clay} + \text{guano} = \text{leucophosphite} - > \text{strengite} - > \text{crandallite}$$
$$\text{or}$$
$$= \text{taranakite} - > \text{barrandite} - > \text{crandallite}$$

In materials deficient in iron, aluminium-rich taranakite will form.

Because of their small size and the fact that several minerals can occur within the same void, most of these minerals are difficult to identify in the field. Many, however, are typified by whitish or bright greenish, yellowish and orange colours, with dull to vitreous lustres (Table 8.1). Furthermore, since in thin section many are colourless and have similar crystal shapes, it is generally desirable to confirm the presence of these minerals with X-ray diffraction and SEM/EDXRA techniques.

8.8 Concluding remarks

In this chapter we have attempted to provide a survey of the most important post-depositional processes that are pertinent to archaeologically related situations. As we tried to show, these processes can affect not only soils and sediments but also any material situated at the interface between the atmosphere and the earth's surface. Although we have discussed them individually, they more often than not take place simultaneously or successively. Consequently they can impart an overprinted signature which is commonly quite blurred and difficult to read. Nevertheless, the microscopic responses to these processes must be sought after and isolated in thin section in order to be able to reconstruct as completely as possible the individual events that constitute the history of the soil or sediment in question.

III

CASE STUDIES

INTRODUCTION

In the previous chapters we have presented the fundamental aspects of field and microscopic strategies and have discussed most of the sedimentary, anthropogenic and post-depositional processes likely to be encountered in geoarchaeological research. In this final part of the book we wish to demonstrate how such knowledge and skills can be applied to solving problems arising in actual archaeological contexts. We do this by furnishing a series of case studies chosen from a variety of sites situated in different environments and settings.

The first set of studies touches upon different types of problems associated with cave sediments. Examples are provided from:

> Vaufrey Cave (Southwestern France), where the effects of chemical transformations and periglacial activity are shown;
>
> Kebara Cave (Mt. Carmel, Israel), in which the micromorphological aspects of burnt layers provide evidence of the types of depositional and post-depositional processes (including phosphatisation) that have modified these layers;
>
> Taforalt Cave (Morocco), where the post-depositional effects of water on the original sediments can be clearly demonstrated.

The remaining case studies are from open-air sites. At Berekhat Ram (Golan Heights) micromorphology demonstrated multiple sedimentary and pedogenic events that were responsible for the formation of an apparently uniform red layer that contains Acheulean artifacts and is sandwiched between two basalt flows.

At the Pre-Pottery Neolithic site of Netiv Hagdud (Jordan Valley) we discuss the nature, origin and technological aspects of building materials, including mudbricks, floors and plasters.

In the more temperate regions of northern France, broadly similar issues are considered from the Neolithic/Bronze/Iron Age site of Fort Harrouard. Here, in addition to clarifying construction techniques associated with Neolithic and Bronze Age ramparts, we could clearly demonstrate the combined pedogenic–anthropogenic origin of a 'dark layer' found near the base of the site.

The ability of micromorphology to study the source and nature of urban sites is illustrated through the study of Medieval deposits known in Europe as 'dark earth'.

A final set of examples deals with regional problems, first from northwest India, where the relationships between the evolution of physical landscapes and

193

patterns of human settlement were established through the light of micromorphology, then in northern Italy, where micromorphology was effective in monitoring the effects of land use on the amelioration and degradation of natural soils in the region.

Whilst these examples are by no means exhaustive (in reality they represent summaries of more detailed works), they serve to provide a reasonable sampling of the types of information that can be gleaned from micromorphological studies of archaeological soils and sediments. The scope and breadth of application of the technique are, of course, virtually unlimited.

Micromorphological aspects of prehistoric cave sediments

Sediments and sedimentary environments from prehistoric caves and rock shelters are peculiar in many ways and are considerably different from those associated with most 'open-air' sites. Caves serve as traps for a variety of sedimentary types, and normally, whatever is deposited within the cave system remains there and is commonly modified or reworked in place; material is rarely transported out of it. In other words, caves are semi-closed systems where there is a delicate balance between autochthonous and allochthonous sedimentation, and syn- and post-sedimentary modifications. Thus, sediments within this system can have multiple origins that result from combinations of physical, chemical, anthropogenic and biological processes which operate at the same time.

In the next few chapters we present a broad sampling of some of these processes by providing illustrations from three prehistoric caves located in different parts of the world. Needless to say, these examples do not cover all the possible scenarios of sedimentation and post-depositional modifications that occur in caves. Nevertheless, they should provide enough material to illustrate the types of observations and the scope of implications and interpretations possible from such complicated sedimentary environments.

9

THE CAVE OF VAUFREY (PÉRIGORD)

9.1 Introduction

For over a hundred years the region of Périgord in southwest France has been well known for its numerous prehistoric sites, especially caves and rock shelters. On the basis of the findings from some of these sites (e.g., Le Moustier, La Micoque, Pech de l'Azé, Combe-Grenal), prehistorians – among whom are Vaufrey, Peyrony, and more recently F. Bordes and his team – have established a chronological succession of Lower to Upper Paleolithic cultures, which has been recognised in other parts of Europe and beyond.

This region now enjoys a temperate climate (in spite of commonly cold winters and cool summer temperatures), and the green landscape offers a large variety of ecotones, including riverine, hillslope and plateau environments. Palaeoenvironmental investigations carried out on the sediments of prehistoric sites by geologists, palynologists and palaeontologists have shown that over the last few hundred thousand years climatic conditions have fluctuated between temperate (interglacial periods) and cold (glacial periods). Sedimentologically, this succession in prehistoric sites has been deciphered from the alternation of cryoclastic calcareous deposits (cryoclastism being responsible for the fragmentation of the cave walls – see Chapter 6) and of finer-grained layers, rich in red clay; the latter are generally regarded as resulting from runoff and pedological illuviation under humid temperate conditions (see Chapter 8). Both are commonly intermixed with layers of secondary calcium carbonate, (called **planchers**), which are associated with the processes of stalagmitic or stalactitic growth and indicate a strong increase in humidity.

In addition to the recognition of these three main classes of deposits, which is mainly based on field observations, minor intermediate geological and environmental events have been discerned using laboratory analyses, including granulometry in particular, complemented by X-ray and total chemical analyses. As there are inherent limitations in these kinds of standard geological analyses from 'bulk samples' (see Chapter 2), a complete reconstruction of the succession of sedimentary and pedological events affecting these sites has yet to be made. For this reason palaeoclimatic inferences from these prehistoric sites, based mostly on such sedimentological analyses, have not gained full acceptance.

The first attempt to correlate standard sedimentological analyses of cave sediments with their micromorphological study was carried out on the

195

Mousterian site of Pech de l'Azé II (Goldberg, 1979a). In spite of the very limited study undertaken, micromorphology was shown to be a highly useful tool for interpretating sedimentological analysis by offering a clear distinction between sedimentary events and post-depositional processes. Unfortunately since that time micromorphology has been little applied to other Palaeolithic sites of Périgord, with the exception of a very small study at the rock shelter of La Micoque and the recent work on the cave of Vaufrey.

Micromorphology was only one aspect of the environmental studies carried out at Vaufrey in an effort to reconstruct the geological and environmental history of this site: sedimentological analyses, studies of the fauna and pollen were also performed on the different layers (Rigaud, in press). Our purpose in this chapter is to illustrate, by way of some chosen examples, the potential of micromorphology to interpret effectively prehistoric cave deposits from the temperate region of Périgord; it is not the intention here to provide extensive details on the results of these investigations.

9.2 **Presentation of the site**

The site of Vaufrey is a wide karstic cave developed in Coniacian limestone, whose main part was connected to an internal karstic network, which has since collapsed. Excavations were first carried out by R. Vaufrey in the 1930s and were continued in the 1970s, with extensive investigations undertaken by Rigaud and his team, who showed the complexity of the stratigraphy. The stratigraphic sequence was tentatively dated from the Mindel–Riss Interglacial for the lowermost deposits to the early Würm Glacial near the top, on the basis of the cultural sequences, faunal associations and sedimentology, and by comparing these data to similar ones from other sites in the Périgord area. Cemented calcific deposits present near the top were dated using Uranium-series techniques (Rigaud, 1982; Figure 9.1). Artifacts related mostly to Mousterian cultures were discovered throughout the whole sequence.

Field observations indicate that the uppermost units consist of yellowish brown sand layers, containing a variable amount of coarse calcareous fragments. These seem to have been slightly reworked by cryoturbation and are intermixed with a cemented calcareous layer (*plancher stalagmitique*).

The underlying units comprise an alternation of brownish yellow sand layers and accumulations of coarse calcareous fragments ('plaquettes calcaires'). The latter display in most cases the specific morphology of cryoturbated pockets. The lowermost units, the base of which has not yet been reached, consist of thick, reddish sands (Figure 9.1).

For illustrating the original characteristics of the deposits of this cave we have selected layers VIII and V from the middle part of the sequence, but the features observed in these two layers can only give a partial picture of the large variety of features occurring throughout the whole sequence. It should be kept in mind, however, that for such a stratigraphically complex sequence the

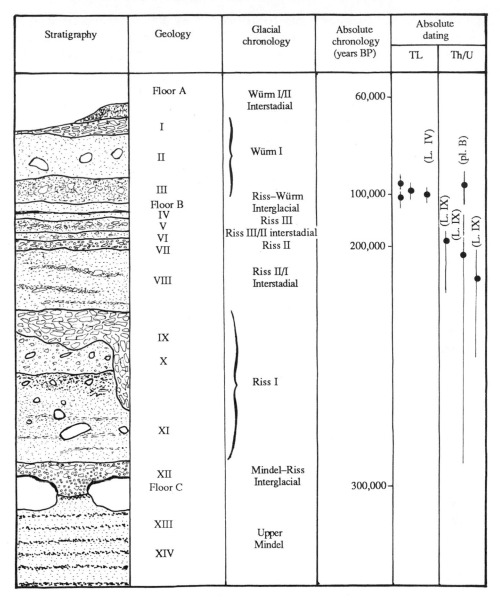

Stratigraphy	Geology	Glacial chronology	Absolute chronology (years BP)	Absolute dating	
				TL	Th/U
	Floor A	Würm I/II Interstadial	60,000		
	I	Würm I			
	II			(L. IV)	(pl. B)
	III Floor B IV V VI VII	Riss–Würm Interglacial Riss III Riss III/II interstadial Riss II	100,000 200,000		(L. IX) (L. IX) (L. IX)
	VIII	Riss II/I Interstadial			
	IX X	Riss I			
	XI				
	XII Floor C	Mindel–Riss Interglacial	300,000		
	XIII XIV	Upper Mindel			

Figure 9.1   Schematic representation of the stratigraphy of Vaufrey and some chronological data.

complete interpretation of each stratigraphic unit can only be made by comparing its characteristics with those of the underlying and also overlying units in order. For example, if the cave is closed, stable temperatures are maintained inside and cryoclastic events will not be recorded in the sediments. However, if the cave opens up, it will become more sensitive to external factors and slight changes in environmental conditions outside the cave can be recorded in the sediments. As a consequence the occurrence of weakly expressed cryoclastic features in a layer can signify not only that the intensity of the cryoclastism was moderate but also that the cave was dry or not open enough. This 'differential' behaviour of caves, and to a lesser extent of rock shelters, is a characteristic more associated with caves in comparison to open air sites.

The micromorphological study presented below concerns two samples from Layer VIII and two from Layer V. During excavation, both layers showed lateral and vertical variations in the abundance of coarse elements, texture, colour and consistence. Though hypotheses were proposed in the field to explain these variations, more detailed sedimentological characterisation was needed to confirm them and micromorphology formed part of this analytical approach.

9.3 **Layer VIII**
9.3.1 *Field characteristics*
During excavation (Rigaud, 1982), Layer VIII was recognised as a homogeneous, yellowish-brown, coarse sand unit, *c.* 20 cm thick, characterised by strong compaction and good coherence even though it possessed a loose grain structure (Figure 9.2a). In spite of the overall homogeneity of this unit, calcareous gravel was more abundant towards the entrance of the cave. In addition, lenticular sub-units a few cm thick occurred locally, either having a higher clay content and a finely aggregated structure or appearing microlayered, whitish and powdery. The clayey subunits were interpreted as being the consequence of water stagnation, whereas the whitish ones, situated in the upper part of fissures in the limestone ('diaclases') were thought to indicate water dripping from the roof of the cave.

Boundaries with the adjacent layers were sharp and both layers showed a clear increase in coarse calcareous elements and a lighter colour of the sands.

9.3.2 *Micromorphological description*
Sample VIII–I
In the top few centimetres, the sediments consist of loosely packed, sub-rounded, centimetre-sized aggregates composed of poorly sorted sand grains, including a few of rounded, highly dissolved, calcareous sand. The fine fraction is light yellowish-brown and is generally isotropic, in spite of a few randomly dispersed calcite crystals with jagged edges, and abundant, flaky, micaceous particles. Towards the top of the layer the structure gradually grades from a loose packing of well-rounded aggregates (Figure 9.2a) to a laminated microfabric with well-developed channel porosity. Concomitantly, the proportion of calcareous components decreases in both coarse and fine fractions, whereas other mineral sand grains are more abundant. The latter consist of poorly sorted quartz sand grains (200 to 500 μm), corroded quartzite rock fragments, micas and some grains of basalt. A few grey, well-rounded, Coniacian sand grains can also be observed.

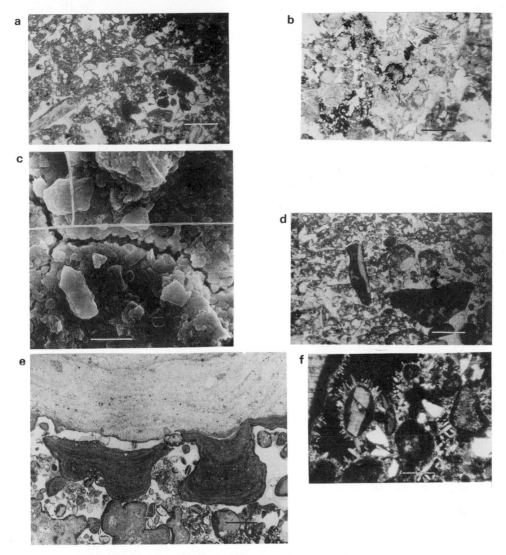

Figure 9.2   (a) Rounded microaggregated structure (bottom) related to cryogenic events. PPL. (Bar = 500 μm)

(b) Strongly corroded calcite fragments. They appear finely cracked with diffuse edges and a pale to lightish grey colour. PPL. (Bar = 500 μm)

(c) Fissuration of a corroded calcite fragment seen under the SEM; the granular and altered outer parts consists of phosphate minerals. (Bar = 5 μm)

(d) Sample VIII—2: ice lens microstructure. The coarse, dark grey fragments are Coniacian limestone. Note the occurrence of loose, fine sand infillings within the inter-aggregate voids. This sample shows an abundance of weakly dissolved calcite grains and fine calcite particles in the groundmass. PPL. (Bar = 500 μm)

(e) Microlayered pendent at the base of a calcite fragment. Silt grains and organic inclusions, as well as partial infilling by rhombohedral crystals, can be distinguished at higher magnification. PPL. (Bar = 5 mm)

(f) Microaggregated structure of sample V–2: rounded calcite fragments and micritic aggregates associated with quartz sand grains, cemented by microsparite. PPL. (Bar = 150 μm)

Coarse components are roughly organised as millimetre-thick layers intermixed with layers of white, angular, disrupted fragments of bones, and millimetre-sized layers of microaggregated reddish-brown, dusty, isotropic clay, rich in fine organic particles. The whitish sub-units identified in the fields are composed chiefly of highly corroded calcite fragments which have undergone strong chemical transformation, resulting in a notable decrease in birefringence (Figure 9.2b). When similar fragments are observed under the SEM, they appear strongly corroded and are embedded in a groundmass rich in phosphate (Figure 9.2c). As the microprobe analysis confirmed, the presence of phosphates in thin section was also shown by the bright yellowish fluorescence; fresh calcite fragments and pure calcitic fine fraction have low, bluish fluorescence.

Sample VIII–2
An evolution similar to that found in VIII–1 was observed in this sample though some differences were observed in the higher amount of sand grains, especially calcareous ones, and the abundance of fine calcite particles in the groundmass (Figure 9.2d). Calcite fragments were only weakly dissolved and they displayed a microlaminated capping of calcitic silty clay; interaggregate voids and channels were partly filled by loosely packed fine sand grains, free of fine fraction.

Interpretation of Layer VIII
In order to understand the history of Layer VIII, we must first explain the occurrence and significance of calcite coarse fragments. As discussed previously (see Chapter 6), calcareous fragments are a common component of limestone caves and shelters and result principally from cryoclastic disaggregation of the limestone walls and ceiling. In the case of Vaufrey this generalised scheme is only partially applicable because the limestone walls are covered by a calcite film a few centimetres thick, produced by secondary precipitation of calcium carbonate from solution percolating along the limestone. The calcite film is only weakly bound to the underlying limestone wall and is loosened by the action of microorganisms and percolation by solutions rich in organic matter. Alternating cycles of wetting and drying may also favour the detachment of the calcite film, which results in the accumulation on the floor of angular and partially dissolved calcite fragments. These processes cannot be observed under the present-day conditions because the walls of the cave are no longer covered with calcite, although in Cave XVI (situated a few hundred metres further along the same cliff), which possesses the calcite film, the fragmentation described above resulted from the present-day action of lichens and mosses, enhanced by freezing during severe winters.

In the deposits underlying Layer VIII, the major parts of the coarse calcareous fragments were of pure calcite and only rare fragments of Coniacian limestone were observed. The occurrence for the first time in Layer VIII of limestone fragments in significant amounts, associated with calcite elements, suggests the wall of the cave was then only partly protected by the calcite film and exposed in patches. The rounded shape and the grey colour of the limestone fragments indicate that the Coniacian was strongly resistant to alteration and its fragmentation could be achieved only after deep corrosion.

The high degree of dissolution of most of the calcite and limestone fragments suggests that chemical alteration has greatly accelerated the disaggregation of the cave walls and that evidence for a cryoclastic fragmentation is rather weak. The subangular and rounded aggregated microstructures as well as the cappings on the coarse fragments, however, are clear indications of freezing having affected Layer VIII in the early phases of its history. These structures are related to ice-lens microfabrics (see Chapter 8), and to the rounding of angular aggregates produced by alternate freeze–thaw cycles. The action of soil fauna – shown in the upper part of Layer VIII by the channel microstructure – seems to be responsible for the partial disappearance of cryoclastic features there. This inference is supported by the high amount of organic matter finely integrated into the groundmass, indicating conditions suitable for the development of mesofauna and microorganisms in the upper part of Layer VIII.

The occurrence of calcareous fragments that exhibit various degrees of dissolution shows that alteration was initiated on the walls of the cave and then followed by physical disintegration of the weathered fragments, as indicated by the dispersion of fine calcite particles nearby. Solutions rich in organic matter, especially phospho-lipids, reacted with calcium released during the dissolution process to form amorphous calcic phosphates. In the rear of the cave, this alteration also affected small bones, and caused a high porosity and a lightish colour; towards the entrance, the continuous output of calcite fragments offset dissolution by maintaining high pH values. Such differential behaviour from various parts of a cave may easily generate lateral facies variations.

As noted during the excavation, the localised lenticular subunits resulted from the puddling of water and affected the sediment in two ways. In some places, the effects were only chemical and calcite fragments were dissolved *in situ* though their original shapes were preserved. In other places, the mechanical effects of water are displayed by layered accumulations of the residual dissolution products, produced by low-intensity runoff.

The succession of events which affected Layer VIII can thus be summarised as follows. Sedimentary processes are represented by physico-chemical alteration of both the limestone and its calcite film, by highly dissolved fragments and by accumulation on the floor of insoluble and weakly soluble components. This alteration seems to be initiated by the action of acid-rich solutions running along the cave wall and microorganisms colonising the cave wall, which indicate that temperate and humid conditions were affecting the cave at this time.

During the early stage of its formation, however, Layer VIII was affected by cryoclastic phenomena (possibly representing some severe winters), which enhanced the disaggregation of the previously altered wall. Moisture content remained high and promoted biological activity and *in situ* alteration of the calcareous components. Some kind of 'cave soil' (essentially related to the action of the soil fauna and microorganisms) was developed on the top of Layer VIII, but because no macrophytic vegetation cover was able to colonise the cave, post-depositional processes could not lead to the development of a true soil profile. Thus we should not expect to find soil horizons associated with the types of processes described above.

The occurrence of features associated with repeated runoff (e.g., laminated sand layers) and to intense percolation (e.g., silty clay textural features) indicates periodic increases in humidity.

The most striking aspect of this layer, however, is the importance of synsedimentary dissolution processes, which are principally responsible for the apparent homogeneity described in the field. Moreover, the high amount of insoluble residues in the form of sand grains indicates that a large amount of calcareous material had been dissolved.

Consequently, the original thickness of Layer VIII–1 was probably substantially greater than what is observed today. Determination of the amounts and rates of dissolution are unknown and would require an estimate of the average insoluble residue content in the bedrock and modelling of present-day solution rates of the limestone, corrected for changes in temperature and vegetation cover. Last but not least, these results clearly show that archaeologists must keep in mind the loss of the original deposits when studying the distribution of artifacts within this layer.

9.4 Layer V
9.4.1 *Field characteristics*
Layer V forms the uppermost part of a succession of three units overlying Layer VIII. All three are characterised by a high content of calcite fragments and a low content of fine-grained sediment. The bottom of Layer V differs markedly from the underlying Layer VI by being lighter in colour and locally cemented. From the bottom to the top of this 15-cm-thick unit, coarse calcite fragments become smaller and more angular; the middle part of the unit is in places totally devoid of fine fraction.

This layer has been recognised only in the rear of the cave and gradually pinches out downstream. In addition to questions regarding mode of deposition and post-depositional processes, the most pressing points regarding Layer V centred around the significance of the cementation at the base and the downstream wedging out of the layer.

The low amount of fine material precluded sampling of undisturbed sediment from many of the deposits. Consequently, samples were taken from consolidated parts of Layer V in two localities where lithological differences in the field were clear. Sample V–1 comes from near the back of the cave, where angular coarse fragments were abundant, the fine sediment content was low and cementation irregular (in millimetre-thick layers). Sample V–2 was selected nearer to the entrance, where Layer V was thinner, well cemented and contained no angular coarse fragments.

9.4.2 *Micromorphology*
Sample V–1
This consists mostly (*c.* 80%) of slightly rounded, weakly dissolved calcareous coarse fragments, comprising both pure calcite fragments and grains of stalagmitic concretions in addition to quartz sand grains and rounded millimetre-sized aggregates of calcitic silty clay. All the coarse fragments display coatings of greyish-brown, microlaminated, calcitic, silty clay, which is a few microns thick on the upper part (see Figure 8.7a: capping) and some millimetres thick and coarsely layered at the bottom (Figure 9.3: pendent). In the pendent, the coarser layers commonly include silt-sized particles and organic inclusions (Figure 9.2e) with various orientations. The void space between the coarse elements is partly filled by large-sized (40 μm), rhombohedral, sparite crystals (Figure 9.3).

Sample V–2
The number of calcareous fragments decreases abruptly and the fragments concomitantly show an increase in rounding. They are associated with millimetre-sized, well-rounded, calcitic silty clay aggregates, whose internal fabric is identical to that of the pendent described above (Figure 9.2f). Gastropod shells embedded in calcitic fine fraction are also common, as well as a few radial sparite concretions (probably remains of slugs), rounded grains and fragments of bone and metamorphic rocks. Aggregates and coarse fragments have a banded fabric and intergranular pores are nearly totally filled by large-sized, rhombohedral, sparite crystals. One biological channel was seen to be filled with yellowish-brown, non-calcareous, silty clay derived from Layer IV. It is worth noting that, with regard to the occurrence of sparite crystals, no discontinuity was observed between the channel and the surrounding matrix. This means that the crystallisation of sparite crystals – which is responsible for the cementation of Layer V – occurred after the deposit of layer IV.

Interpretation of Layer V
The origin of sediments in Layer V differs clearly from that of the underlying layers (VI and VII), which contained only calcite fragments as coarse elements. The abundance of calcareous concretions shows that *in situ* fragmentation of cemented layers is also responsible for the production of coarse elements.

The angular shapes of the coarse elements and the occurrence of pendents

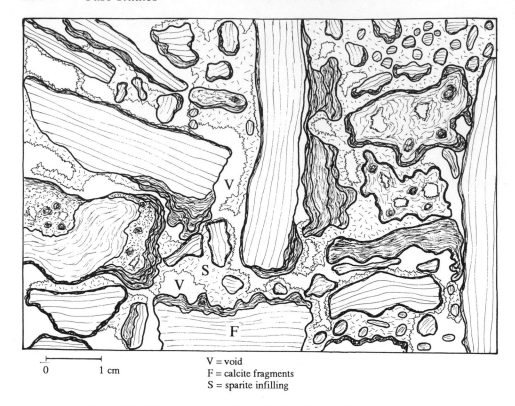

V = void
F = calcite fragments
S = sparite infilling

Figure 9.3   Microstructure of sample V–1 showing formation of pendents on cryoclastically broken calcite fragments (see text for discussion).

and cappings are features which are tied to periglacial conditions. Similar microlaminated pendents have been observed under dry, very cold deserts (see Chapter 8), in which each microlayer can be related to the movement of fluids charged in fine mud and calcium carbonate. The abundance of fresh, angular, coarse elements that were primarily fragmented *in situ*, and evidence for limited seasonal moisture, indicate that the formation of Layer V took place under very dry and cold conditions, in which calcareous fragments were not chemically altered.

Considering only sample V–1, the irregular position of the pendent compared to its original genetic position and its degree of fragmentation (Figure 9.4), we can conclude that this layer was affected by cryoclastic fragmentation subsequent to the development of the pendent and prior to its cementation by calcite.

The nature of coarse fragments in sample V–2 contrasts sharply with those described from sample V–1. Angular fragments are no longer observed and the occurrence of rounded fragments derived from the pendents (Figure 9.4c) shows that, subsequent to their formation, calcareous fragments were re-worked, resulting in the detachment of the pendents, which were only weakly

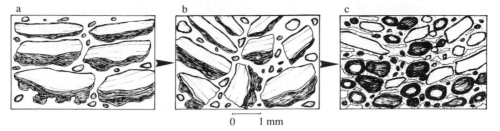

Figure 9.4   Evolution of the microstructure of Layer V during a succession of cryogenic events:
   (a) fragmentation of calcite coarse elements and formation of pendents,
   (b) disruption of the calcite fragments,
   (c) transformation by frost creep of calcite fragments and pendents, resulting first in rounding and then cementation by sparite.

bound to the fragments. Fragmentation was probably initiated by cryoclastic phenomena, indicated by the disruption observed upsteam, but fragments were later reworked by water, as shown by their rounded shape. Stagnation of water also attracted gastropods and slugs, as is illustrated by the presence of radially crystallised sparite. The last phase of the evolution of Layer V is indicated by the formation of the ice-lens microstructure and the cementation by rhombohedral sparite crystals; both of these took place subsequent to the deposition of Layer IV (see arguments given above). The latter layer also has a microbanded fabric. This cementation may possibly be related to the development of the stalagmitic deposit ('plancher') situated between Layers III and IV.

The gradual change observed in the characteristics of Layer V from the back of the cave towards the entrance is thus explained by gradual abrasion of both calcareous coarse fragments and their pendents, resulting from repeated cycles of freezing and thawing (see Chapter 8). The absence of fragmented sparite crystals proves that this cementation took place very late in the development of Layer V and probably came about after burial as a result of circulation of underground water in this porous medium. Thus it seemingly has no palaeoclimatic significance.

This example illustrates the complexity of events which may affect a layer, not only during its formation, but also after its burial. Furthermore, an apparently insignificant detail, such as the biological channel in this case, can be shown to convey its own valuable message and may help to avoid misinterpretation in unravelling the sequence of events.

9.5 Conclusion

The study of these two layers of the cave of Vaufrey has been presented to illustrate the large variety of subtle aspects of periglacial phenomena. In contrast with soil-profile development under a vegetation cover, it was difficult here to establish a clear separation between depositional and post-depositional processes. Micromorphology allowed us to establish a relative chronology of events, including those which took place penecontemporaneously. This relative chronology of simultaneous and successive processes provides the key to a fuller and more accurate understanding of the palaeoenvironmental and palaeoclimatic history of these cave sediments.

KEBARA CAVE (ISRAEL)

10.1 Introduction

The prehistoric cave of Kebara is one of several caves found in the Mount Carmel area of northern Israel and is situated about 13 km south of Tabun at an altitude of *c*. 60 m above sea level (Figure 10.1). It overlooks a 2.5 km wide coastal plain on which heavy, clayey alluvial soils partially cover a series of Quaternary calcareous sandstone ridges (*kurkar*). Terra rossa soils occur in partially eroded patches on the surface of Mt Carmel.

The cave is developed in Cretaceous dolomite and consists of a large chamber with several vaulted domes (Figure 10.2a), of which only the innermost is open to the surface of Mt Carmel. These elevated vaults are apparently mirrored at depth by solution cavities or 'swallow holes' formed in the underlying bedrock (Bar-Yosef and Vandermeersch, 1972; Goldberg, 1978). The swallow holes and the karstic activity associated with them are responsible for the dipping layers observable in many parts of the cave (Figure 10.2a).

The sediments are well exposed in profiles recently excavated and cleaned as part of the Franco–Israeli project, *Evolution of Modern Humans in the Southern Levant* (Bar-Yosef *et al.*, 1986; Goldberg and Laville, in press). In these profiles – referred to as the west and south profiles (Figure 10.2) – a sequence of Mousterian and Upper Palaeolithic units can be observed beneath the Kebaran and Natufian levels that were largely removed by Turville-Petre (1932).

Although there are many interesting features of the Kebara sediments – their study is still in progress – we will here touch upon only a few of them. These comprise characterisation of the types of deposits present in the cave, geogenic as well as anthropogenic, and clarification of the syn- and post-depositional modifications that have occurred, including phosphatisation and biological disturbances.

For the sake of simplicity, we will consider only the Mousterian deposits.

10.2 Field characteristics of the Mousterian deposits

The Mousterian sediments are best exposed in the west profile (Figure 10.2). Their most striking aspect is the presence of a series of superimposed lenticular burnt layers, which vary in thickness between a few to tens of cm and are *c*. 0.30–1.50 m wide; in certain localised areas within the cave they are quite massive and reach thicknesses up to *c*. 30–50 cm. In the field they are characterised by a sequence of brownish black organic-rich silts overlain by grey ashy material that grades progressively upward into whiter ash (Figure 10.3a); in general,

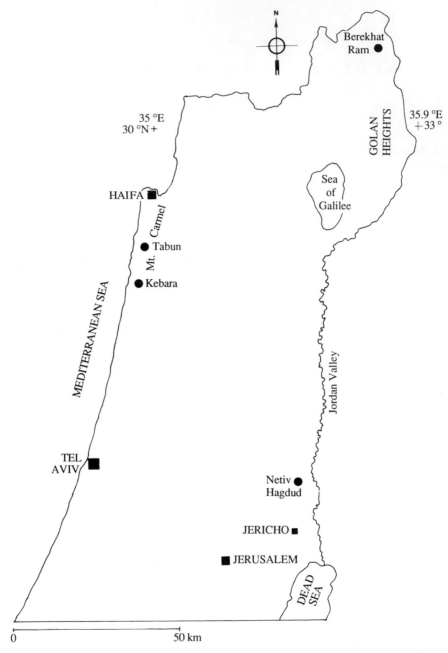

Figure 10.1   Location of Kebara and other sites in Israel, including Netiv Hagdud (Chapter 13) and Berekhat Ram (Chapter 12).

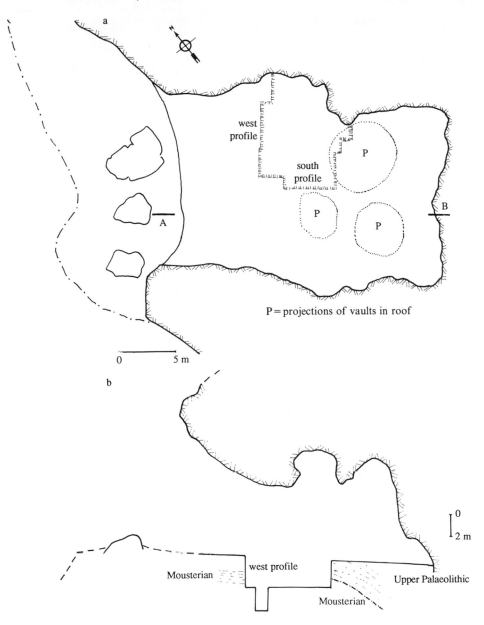

P = projections of vaults in roof

Figure 10.2   (a) Generalised plan of Kebara Cave showing position of west profile mentioned in the text.

(b) Simplified longitudinal profile along line A–B of (a) in which excavated portions of the deposits have been projected. (Modified from drawings of D. Ladiray, CNRS)

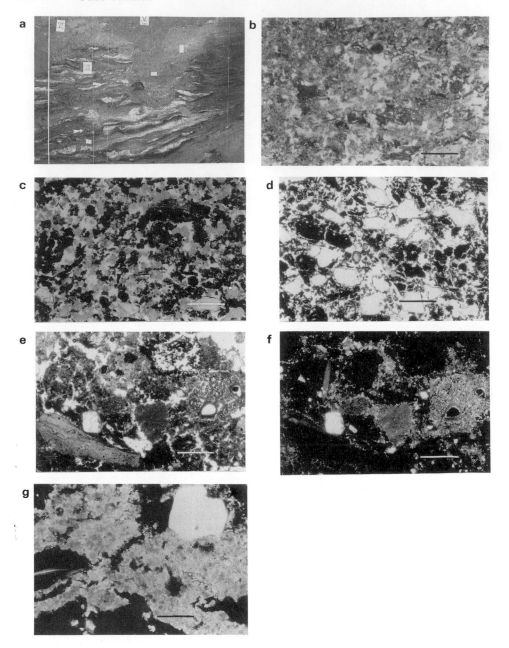

Figure 10.3   (a) Photograph of southern part of west profile, showing series of lenticular burnt areas locally disturbed by rodent activity and slumping (upper part of photograph).

(b) Upper part of Keb–84–28 (example no. 1), showing pale yellow to greyish-white spongy mass consisting of numerous plant remains that, along with the groundmass, are isotropic in XPL and are composed of silica. PPL. (Bar = 230 μm)

each burnt complex truncates the one immediately below it. Such burnt sequences are most prominently exposed in the west profile, either along its southernmost portion or at the base of the central part.

In contrast, in the northern part of this profile these burnt lenses give way to broader, more diffuse, horizontal bands of bone and ashy material that generally lacks the appearance of having been burnt in place. Moreover, unlike the others, they are calcareous, probably as a result of their proximity to the bedrock walls.

Evidence of burning activity is not very common in Mousterian deposits and it is important to know the function and activities associated with these burnt layers as well the types of materials that were burnt. Although the micromorphological study of these layers is still in progress, some preliminary observations and hypotheses can be presented.

Whilst many of these burnt layers look broadly similar in the field, we know that in thin section they are quite different in terms of composition, internal organisation and structure, and history.

10.3 **Micromorphology of the Mousterian deposits**
10.3.1 *Example no. 1* (Keb–84–28)
In the field this sample appeared as simply banded hearths with thin laminations 1–2 m thick, some apparently decomposed limestone fragments. A similar aspect is shown in the photogramme of an *c.* 11 cm thick sequence of this same material (Plate VI). In this view we are able to see subhorizontal layering of whitish 'ashy' material at the top and lower 3–4.5 cm, as well as horizontally bedded charcoal pieces at 5–6 cm and at the top. The remainder is represented by mm-sized charcoal pieces dispersed throughout a more massive and apparently homogeneous-looking matrix. How do some of these different zones look in thin section at higher magnifications?

(c) Example no. 2, showing fragmented and microaggregated nature of the sample, charcoal and fluffy red clay mixed with quartz silt. PPL. (Bar = 230 μm)

(d) Example no. 2. Two diffuse layers of subrounded grains of quartz sand. These grains originated outside the cave and were probably deposited in this position by the wind, since aqueous deposition would have produced better defined laminae. PPL. (Bar = 230 μm)

(e) Photomicrograph of sample Keb–85–6 (example no. 3), showing a heterogeneous mixture of bone, charcoal and organic matter, quartz sand and aggregates composed of red clay and quartz silt. The aggregates are commonly welded to produce compound grains. Note also the fine micritic cement which in part is associated with the proximity of this sample to the cave walls. PPL. (Bar = 230 μm)

(f) As (e), XPL. (Bar = 230 μm)

(g) Sample Keb–85–6. Ash consisting of bundles of square micritic crystals produced by the burning of wood and not grasses as in Figure 10.3b. PPL. (Bar = 230 μm)

Basal, homogeneous part consists of a variety of elements with an intergranular to complex structure and a porosity of *c.* 25%. There is considerable local variability but on the whole the bulk of the grains is charaterised by:

> quartz silt, randomly distributed throughout and not showing any distinct layering (*c.* 3–5%);
>
> charcoal fragments in various stages of disintegration and ranging in size from *c.* 100–250 μm;
>
> various size grains (*c.* 250 μm) of whitish grey, spongy material that are isotropic in polarised light (most probably plant remains), commonly rounded;
>
> the remainder of the groundmass consists of loose, aggregated flecks of red and dark yellow-brown organic matter and aggregates of red clay mixed with fine silt.

Post-depositional features locally constitute a large proportion of the area. The one with the greatest area is represented by pure, amorphous (isotropic in XPL), globular, light-yellow to yellow-brown nodules that range in size from 0.10 to 1.5 mm. They are commonly rounded with serrated-edged boundaries that are sharp and prominent. In general, they disrupt the other grains and groundmass, thus showing that they accumulated after the latter were emplaced. X-ray analysis revealed a very poorly crystallised substance, possibly leucophosphite (hydrated potassium iron aluminum phosphate) associated with bat guano (Flicoteaux and Lucas, 1984).

The second feature is represented by 100 μm thick bright-yellow void coatings and hypocoatings whose inner surfaces are generally smooth to weakly mammilated. In polarised light they show low birefringence (grey) and locally appear pseudomorphic after the leucophosphite (?) nodules; elsewhere, they coat voids which cut these nodules, thereby showing the relative ages of these two substances.

The *middle part* of the slide on the whole shows similar basic features. Notable exceptions are:

> The groundmass is less fragmented and maintains greater integrity. Charcoal fragments are more massive and seem to be somewhat layered. They also show clear signs of having been attacked by microfauna, as indicated by the circular to elliptical excretion features.
>
> More striking, however, is that leucophosphite is less disposed as discrete rounded nodules or nodular aggregates and more as irregular and patchy veins, *c.* 70–100 mm across. Further up the slide, the leucophosphite is more spatially concentrated into splotchy masses, 2–3 mm thick, and in one case seems to be a partial hypocoating associated with a large (*c.* 4 mm), elliptical void.

The *top* centimetre of the sample is characterised by a pale-yellow to greyish-white, somewhat spongy material, which is isotropic in XPL and contains numerous shreds of plant remains, presumably silica (Figure 10.3b). These could have been produced by the burning of grasses. In addition, they contain numerous angular, light-grey aggregates, 0.2–1.0 mm in diameter, that contain fine quartz silt in a dense isotropic matrix.

Discussion

In the light of the observations presented above, it is clear that the bedded burnt layer or burnt 'complex' is in reality a more complicated feature. With the exception of the upper siliceous layer and the two bands of charcoal, most of the materials are not in their originally pristine context and have been modified by a variety of post-depositional processes that include:

(a) The precipitation of poorly crystalline leucophosphite, followed by that of void coatings of another yet-to-be-identified phosphate mineral. Moreover, since leucophosphite is commonly associated with the reaction of phosphates derived from guano with soil material, we might infer from its occurrence here that these sediments were situated beneath a location where bats were congregating. Furthermore, since bats and humans usually do not occupy the same place at the same time (E. Tchernov, personal communication), the presence of these guano-derived minerals indicates that the cave was abandoned at some time for at least a period of a few years. In any case, much of the mesoscopic 'bedding' seen in the field and under low magnifications is tied to the precipitation of leucophosphite, probably along weakly defined, subhorizontal layers.

(b) The precipitation of the phosphate in the voids is clearly later than leucophosphite formation. Although the exact conditions of formation at Kebara are currently being studied, evidence from other prehistoric caves, such as Tabun (Goldberg and Nathan, 1975) and Arago (Péneaud, 1978), suggest that this precipitation is tied to the dissolution of phosphate from bone and guano and is associated with several mineralogical transformations.

(c) There is clear evidence of local reworking by insects on a microscopic scale, as shown by the elliptical and circular excrement pedofeatures within the large pieces of charcoal in the centre of the slide.

10.3.2 *Sample 2 (Keb–85–25)*

A somewhat similar picture occurs for another burnt layer in Kebara. In the field (cf. Figure 10.3a), this appeared as interbedded creamy-white ash at the top and bottom with darker-brown burnt silt with speckles of ash and appeared to have been reworked 'hearth' material, but it was not possible to discern with certainty. In mesoscopic view, there is a broad, diffuse layering with whitish material at the base, overlain by reddish-brown and grey bands.

In a thin section of the lower part, however, we see that the whitish layers at the base are very similar in aspect to that of leucophosphite described above and that they in fact impregnate a different type of groundmass.

In contrast to the above example, the grains and matrix as a whole are much more fragmented and microaggregated, resulting in a porosity of *c*. 50%. There are large variations in size of fragments: shreds of charcoal range between 0.2 and 1.5 mm at the base to *c*. 10 mm at the top, whereas aggregates of fluffy-red clay mixed with quartz silt and fine organic matter are between 20 and 40 μm (Figure 10.3c).

Also striking is the presence of subangular to subrounded grains of quartz sand (100–200 μm), that is concentrated in two broad bands in the upper and lower thirds of the slide (Figure 10.3d). This material, undoubtedly originating from outside the cave, was most likely deposited here by wind and not water, since the layering is not distinct enough and the grains/matrix are too poorly sorted. Wind deposition would account for the fine comminution of the particles observed here: a gust of wind from the cave mouth (note that there is a chimney) would not only carry sand from the outside but would also pick up, rework and redeposit any fragile fragments of ashy burnt material lying on the surface.

Thus in sum, it would seem that the 'burnt layers' observed in this sample result from a combination of aeolian reworking of an original charcoal- and clay-rich burnt material, whose layering has been enhanced by the secondary precipitation of phosphate.

10.3.3 *Sample 3 (Keb–85–6)*
In the northern part of the section, layers occur that are overall laterally equivalent to the example described immediately above. These are composed of broad calcareous bands that are rich in bone, flint and ash.

The sample is also micromorphologically different from those described above, particularly in terms of structure and composition. Firstly, it is a heterogeneous mixture of a variety of components that include (Figure 10.3e, a & b):

> bone, both burnt and unburnt (*c.* 3–5%);
> angular chips of flint (*c.* 2%);
> subangular to subrounded quartz sand (*c.* 2%);
> charcoal and organic matter ranging in size from 150 to 600 μm and in various stages of disintegration, from whole pieces to shreds;
> fine to coarse sand-sized aggregates consisting of red clay and quartz silt.

Most of these components are heterogeneously mixed and take the form of loose, compound aggregates or, commonly, densely 'welded' aggregates. These components are frequently bound together in a fine micritic cement, which forms braces between the aggregates and weakly cements the sediments as a whole.

The most striking feature of this sample is the remains of calcareous ash which takes the form of square bundles of micritic calcite, *c.* 40 μm on a side, typical of wood ashes (Figure 10.3a). In the burnt layers described above, any traces of such calcareous material were lost by decalcification of the sample. It is only here, near the calcareous environment of the wall, that such originally ashy accumulations can be preserved. Moreover, unlike the materials in sample 1 (Keb–84–28), where the upper ashes are siliceous and probably from the burning of grasses, here we have clear evidence of wood ashes.

There is evidence, however that some post-depositional modifications have taken place. These are related to phosphate precipitation and expressed as:

local golden-yellow patches of ash that are isotropic in XPL;

a phosphatic reaction rim 200–300 μm thick produced on a single grain of *kurkar*, 1 cm in diameter (in this case, the micritic cement and some of the calcareous microfossils have been replaced by phosphate);

the identical amberish material is precipitated and fills cracks within some of the chert grains.

In this sample, the phosphate is hydroxyapatite (calcium phosphate), which was probably derived from bat guano and liberated by the weathering of bones.

Thus, looking at the above three ash-rich samples in perspective, we see that the first represents burnt material that has been disturbed only slightly (on the scale of mm to cm) and the second, aeolian reworked burnt materials; both have been subjected to decalcification and precipitation of one or two different types of phosphate material. The third is composed of the original calcareous ash and has not been decalcified. Interestingly, the siliceous plant remains found in the first sample are not present and certainly would have been preserved if they were present. It seems likely, therefore, that the presence of wood ash in the last sample is not a chemical artifact but suggests that the former inhabitants were burning a different kind of material in this part of the cave and that this material was not organised in the form of discrete burnt layers but rather broad bands of ashy sediment. Why this was so is currently being investigated.

THE CAVE OF THE PIGEONS AT TAFORALT (ORIENTAL MOROCCO)

11.1 The archaeological problem

The succession of Mousterian, Aterian and Epipalaeolithic lithic industries is a special characteristic of the Maghreb regions and has been documented from a large number of open-air and cave sites (Balout, 1955; Debénath *et al.*, 1986). The Mousterian and Aterian are thought to be culturally related because of similarities in the lithic assemblages. The Epipalaeolithic (also locally called Ibero-Maurusian) is considered to be an extraneous culture in the Maghreb, although its exact origin is still under discussion.

The transition of Mousterian to Aterian occurred in Morocco around 40,000 years ago, possibly under wetter climatic conditions than today's. On the other hand, the gradual spread of the Epipalaeolithic, starting around 20,000–18,000 BP, is supposed to be more or less contemporaneous with a marked increase in dryness (Debénath *et al.*, 1986).

The debate in archaeology regarding the effects of environmental changes on the dynamics of human populations continues. Investigations of multicultural sequences which can be linked to environmental changes may provide substantial arguments to the debate. These sequences are not so common in Morocco, and the present micromorphological investigation reports the results of such a palaeoenvironmental study for the cave of Taforalt.

11.2 Site setting and stratigraphy

The Cave of Pigeons at Taforalt is located 40 km inland from the Mediterranean coast in the north-facing side of the Bni-Snassen mountains in eastern Morocco (Figure 11.1). The cave opens to the east at 750 m a.s.l. and is developed in a massif of Plio-Pleistocene travertines bordering on Dogger dolomitic limestone. A spring flows nearby, forming a waterfall on its northern side. The cave is spacious, open and well lighted.

The Bni-Snassen mountains fall within the Mediterranean climatic zone, which is characterised by a well-marked moisture gradient from east (subhumid) to west (semi-arid). Increased aridity is also observed from the interior of the mountains to the lower Moulouya basin. A Mediterranean forest consisting essentially of *Pinus halepensis* associated with *Quercus ilex* and *Juniperus*, is the natural vegetation, although it has been considerably reduced by human overexploitation.

Thick red calcareous soils cover the slopes of the surrounding limestones,

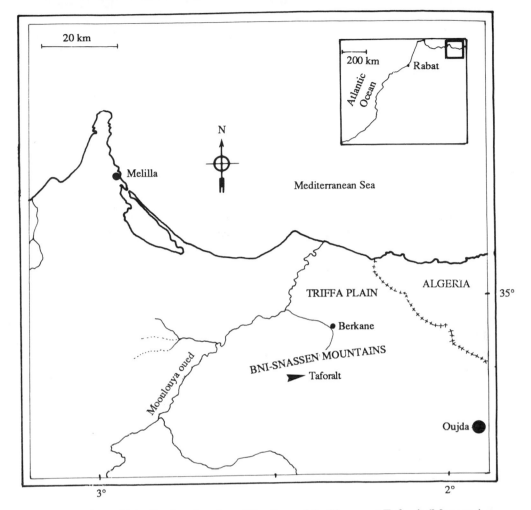

Figure 11.1   Regional setting of the Cave of the Pigeons at Taforalt (Morocco).

although lithosols are also common, owing to recent erosion. Vertical redistribution of calcium carbonate is supposed to have repeatedly affected the soil cover during the Quaternary period, resulting in the formation of decalcified red clay horizons and thick calcareous crusts (Ruellan, 1971).

Excavations in the cave have been coordinated by the French Archaeological Mission and the Archaeological Service of Morocco (Roche 1963, 1976; Raynal, 1978) and a sampling survey was carried out in 1982.

The Aterian layers were excavated in the back part of the cave and comprise massive, yellow-orange (7.5 YR 7/8), sandy loam, rich in coarse travertine fragments. They are occasionally cemented by calcium carbonate and are interbedded with powdery, light-grey ash layers (*c.* 10 cm thick).

The Epipalaeolithic layers overlying the Aterian consist of subhorizontal,

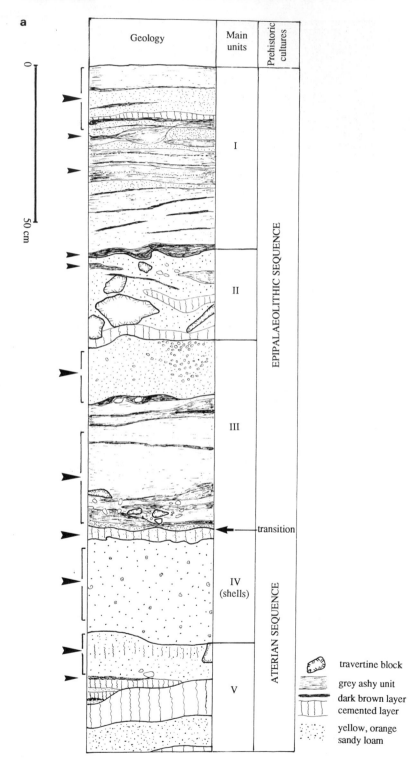

Figure 11.2   Stratigraphy of the site:
(a) Sketch showing the major characteristics of the Aterian and Epipalaeolithic sequences.
(b) Transition between the Epipalaeolithic sequence (down to sample 18 in a grey ashy layer) and the Aterian sequence (up to sample 19 in yellow–orange sandy loam containing coarse travertine fragments and gasteropod shells).

interlayered units (10 to 15 cm thick), that are either massive, dull orange sandy loam (7.5 YR 7/4) with calcareous coarse fragments, or powdery light brownish-grey (7.5 YR 7/1) ashy loam and dark-brown (7.5 YR 3/3) sandy loam rich in powdery charcoal (Figure 11.2a and b). Grey cemented layers, a few cm thick, may also occur interbedded with these units. Most of the archaeological artifacts were found horizontally displayed in the dark ashy layers and most of them were burnt (J.P. Raynal, oral communication). In the middle part of the cave, in a slight depression situated below a drip line, laminated, centimetre-thick layers of dark-brown, brown, light dull orange, light yellow-orange and light-grey sandy loam are observed over a few square metres (Figure 11.3).

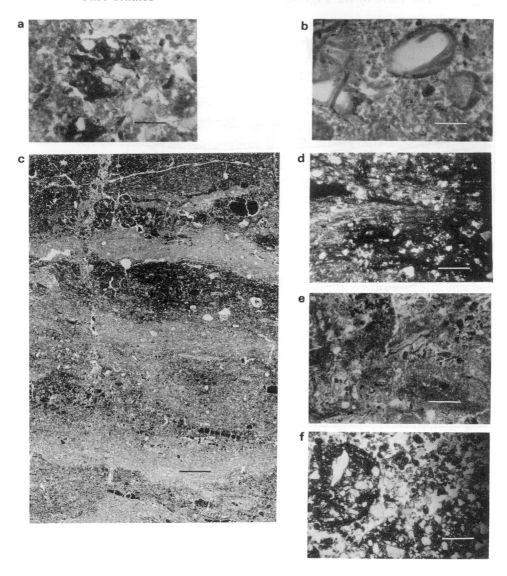

Figure 11.4   (a) Aterian sediments. Enlarged view of the groundmass showing
fine micritic aggregates (in pale grey) and dark terra rossa subrounded fragments.
Overall, the sample has a micro-aggregated micritic fabric with a well developed
channel porosity. PPL. (Bar = 50 μm)

(b) Aterian ash layers. Coniferous wood ashes. PPL. (Bar = 50 μm)

(c) Photogramme showing the layering of the middle Epipalaeolithic sequence
in the middle part of the cave. The darker layers consist predominantly of finely
disrupted charcoal associated with yellowish brown fine fraction. The grey layers
are yellowish brown and the pale grey layers are dull orange. PPL. (Bar = 3.6 mm)

biological activity, weak dissolution–reprecipitation processes periodically modified the micritic fine fraction. The limited amount of water and possibly the rapid evaporation prevented vertical leaching of calcium carbonate and cemented layers formed locally from *in situ* recrystallisation of calcite.

11.3.2 *Ash layers*
The grey ash layers consist predominantly of loosely packed and poorly organised cubic and rhombohedral calcium carbonate crystals originating from deciduous and coniferous woods respectively (Figure 11.4b). Carbonate crystals are finely mixed with both the pale-yellow fine fraction and abundant calcium oxalate crystals resulting from the burning of tree leaves. A few fragments of red soils, charcoal, burnt bones and burnt travertine are also observed. The high birefringence of mica flakes in the red soil, as well as the mild alteration of the travertine, suggest a combustion at moderate temperature averaging 500°C, and the scarcity of charcoal shows that oxidising conditions were sufficient to burn the wood completely. The absence of layering and lack of a structural porosity such as channels eliminates water or biological activity as possible factors of post-depositional disturbances, though trampling would have been sufficient to cause the observed disorganisation of ashes.

11.4 **Micromorphological characteristics of the Epipalaeolithic layers**
11.4.1 *Basal part of the Epipalaeolithic sequence*
Sediments forming the lowest 20 cm of the Epipalaeolithic layers are very similar to those of the underlying Aterian sequence.

The most obvious change is the gradual depletion in calcium carbonate of the groundmass, which results in a relative enrichment of both coated quartz sand grains and red soil fragments, the consequence of which is a darker orange colour. Although calcareous coarse fragments are as abundant as in the underlying units, they show clear signs of dissolution, expressed in thin section by greyer colour, low birefringence and by a diffuse limit with the surrounding matrix caused by penetration of the orange fine fraction into fissures; near the top some fragments are strongly dissolved.

The channel microstructure is well expressed and even more pronounced, as shown by a higher density of fine channels, though quartz sand grains and red clay aggregates of the groundmass are only loosely packed.

(d) Partially decalcified ash layers that have been somewhat reworked by runoff (indicated by the irregular lamination) and slightly modified by secondary accumulations of calcium carbonate (thin dark grey lenticular units). PPL. (Bar = 150 μm)

(e) Mildly disturbed calcitic ashes forming thick accumulations in the upper part of the Epipalaeolithic sequence. PPL. (Bar = 150 μm)

(f) Brown micro-aggregated fabric resulting from intense mixing by biological activity. Epipalaeolithic layers near the porch of the cave. PPL. (Bar = 50 μm)

The transformations affecting the lower part of the Epipalaeolithic sequence are reflected mostly in chemical alteration of the deposits compared to the underlying Aterian sediments. The gradual increase in the density of channels and quartz grains, as well as the darkening, are changes directly related to an increase in moisture.

11.4.2 *Middle Epipalaeolithic sequence*

In contrast to the lower part of the middle Epipalaeolithic sequence, only strongly altered travertine fragments and the fine fraction may be observed. In thin section, fine layering is the most notable feature of the middle Epipalaeolithic sequence and characterises even units which appeared homogeneous in the field, except for the massive layers near the porch. However, only in the slight depression in the middle part of the cave do the layered units present clearly different characteristics (Figure 11.4c); in the rear of the cave the layering affects homogenised materials and consequently was poorly expressed in the field.

In the laminated units of homogeneous colour, the coarse fraction consists predominantly of quartz sand grains coated with red clay and these are very similar to the ones described in the underlying layers. They are associated with abundant, rounded, orange bone fragments which have been moderately burnt. The fine fraction is always formed of loosely packed, weakly birefringent microaggregates (100–150 μm), which may be dark brown, brown, orange or light yellow–orange.

In the uniform light yellow–orange units, only a few mica flakes and fine articles of iron oxides are recognised within the microaggregates, which have a grainy aspect and are amorphous. The presence of non-crystallised calcitic phosphate, suspected from their orange colour and the low birefringence, was confirmed by microprobe analysis (EDXRA). Amorphous, light-grey thin laminae occasionally occur embedded within the dull orange units.

Mica flakes, red clay and quartz sand grains are more abundant in the orange units, whereas the dark-brown ones contain a high amount of fragmented charcoal. The brown units have a highly heterogeneous composition. Microaggregates of various colours are finely mixed with flaky charcoal, burnt bones, strongly altered travertine fragments, phosphatic nodules and burnt decalcified plant residues, in addition to quartz sand grains and red soil fragments.

In the rear of the cave, lighter-coloured lenses composed of fine calcitic particles have been recognised within the non-calcified microlaminated units (Figure 11.4d), although their birefringence is notably lower than calcium carbonate which has not been altered. Local impregnation by secondary calcium carbonate results in channel hypocoatings and centimetre-thick cemented lenses.

It is only in the upper part of the Epipalaeolithic sequence in the thick layered ash units at the base of the necropolis that calcium carbonate ash crystals become abundant (Figure 11.4e). There they form an essential constituent associated with abundant, highly burnt sheep droppings and fire-cracked exploded travertine fragments.

Fine lamination is totally absent in the thick units occurring near the porch. They show a well-developed channel microstructure and consist of densely packed, well-rounded aggregates (300–500 μm). Associated with the dense clay-rich fine fraction are travertine fragments of various degrees of alteration, well-rounded phosphatic nodules, quartz sand grains and fragments of red soils (Figure 11.4f).

11.4.3 *Discussion*

Microscopic observations show that sediments from the lower part do not differ much from the Aterian layers, though a prominent change in sedimentation occurs in the middle of the Epipalaeolithic sequence. The latest sediments were produced basically by physical disaggregation of the walls of the cave, then repeatedly reworked by low-energy runoff, as shown by their fine lamination and massiveness.

Although there are clear differences in the composition of sediments between the lower and the middle Epipalaeolithic layers – especially in the high amount of quartz sand grains in the latter – the sources of sediments remain the same: travertines and local red calcareous soils. Considering the similarity existing between the decalcified yellowish-brown aggregates in the lower Epipalaeolithic layers and the non-calcareous aggregates forming the bulk of the middle Epipalaeolithic units, we may infer that most of these latter materials were derived from the decalcification of travertine. The good preservation of the shapes of the microaggregates underneath the drip line suggests only mild reworking of sediments following the decalcification. In the rear of the cave the great mixture of constituents and the fine lamination indicate a more intense reworking by runoff. Near the porch, decalcified sediments have been intensively disturbed by biological activity, probably earthworms, whereas effects of runoff are not discernible.

In the light of the lateral variability of microfabrics we can conclude that running water has affected the cave only locally. Moreover low-energy features point to continued dripping from the roof that formed puddles, especially in the rear and middle parts of the cave. We can also conclude that water which accumulated on the ground was mildly acidic and capable of decalcifying the sediment, releasing high amounts of soluble phosphorous, either from the travertine or from organic matter on the ground.

The middle Epipalaeolithic sequence is thus characterised by a clear increase in humidity. The increased degree of decalcification in the lower

Epipalaeolithic units, as compared to the underlying layers, might be interpreted as an initial stage in the onset of these wetter conditions. In fact
observations of thin sections clearly show that decalcification of the earlier
Epipalaeolithic units was contemporaneous with the deposition of the middle
Epipalaeolithic sequence.

   Micromorphology has revealed the scarcity of calcareous wood ashes in the
Epipalaeolithic layers, though they were abundant in the Aterian hearths. A
hypothesised change in the type of fuel used can be rejected because most of the
numerous silica plant residues found in the different Epipalaeolithic units (both
burnt and unburnt) were clearly derived from the decalcification of travertine –
where they are abundant – and not from the burning of grasses. The thin lenses
of altered calcium carbonate crystals observed in the middle Epipalaeolithic
units are undoubtedly the remnants of more important ash accumulations,
which have been strongly decalcified and are preserved because of their great
initial abundance.

   Although fires seem to have been repeatedly lit in the cave during the earlier
and middle Epipalaeolithic occupations, the fine lamination of ashes is essentially the result of low-energy runoff and can not be considered as a characteristic of multilayered hearths.

   The composition of ashes changes only in the upper Epipalaeolithic layers
where abundant sheep droppings are associated with wood ash. Moreover, the
latter are very well preserved. This permits the detection of a change in human
activities.

11.5 Conclusions

In conclusion, we see that the only significant sedimentary change did not take
place at the transition between Aterian and early Epipalaeolithic layers but
within the Epipalaeolithic sequence. A rough estimate of the chronological
position of this change would be approximately 15,000 BP (based on ^{14}C dating
on charcoal, Debénath *et al.*, 1986) which in North Africa roughly coincides
with the end of the Late Palaeolithic dry period. Complementary dates and
comparison with other sites, however, are necessary before a regional correlation can be proposed, since the study of only one sequence does not permit
differentiation between local and regional events.

   Although wetter spells seem to have affected the Aterian sequence, their
influence was weak compared with the humidity effects recorded during the
middle Epipalaeolithic. This seems to be explained by moderate acidity of the
water that percolated through the cave during the Aterian inducing moderate
dissolution in addition to the repeated reprecipitation of calcium carbonate. On
the other hand, the latter process had negligible effects on the Epipalaeolithic
layers.

   The decalcification which affected the cave during the middle Epipalaeolithic
has considerably modified sediments accumulated earlier, as well as anthropo-

genic deposits (ashes). Thus what could have been interpreted as a gradual increase in humidity at the transition between the Aterian and the Epipalaeolithic is essentially the result of post-depositional processes having erased part of the information recorded in the sediments.

The data presented in this case-study again illustrate the necessity for understanding fully the nature of post-depositional processes operating on archaeological deposits.

THE ACHEULIAN SITE AT BEREKHAT RAM, GOLAN HEIGHTS

12.1 Introduction

Exposed in the vicinity of the extinct volcanic crater of Berekhat Ram – now partially filled by a natural lake – are two basalt lava flows with a red clayey layer between them (Figure 12.1). This red clay varies in thickness from 1 to 3 m and contains in its middle portion an abundance of Acheulian artifacts concentrated in a diffuse layer *c.* 30–40 cm thick. Such a rare occurrence of Acheulian material, sandwiched between two basalts, required a detailed excavation of the site (Goren-Inbar, 1985).

12.2 Site setting and stratigraphy

Situated on the Golan Heights at an altitude of *c.* 960 m, the crater of Berekhat Ram is one of many Pleistocene volcanoes that dot the landscape. Just north of it flows the Nahal (Hebrew for ephemeral stream) Sa′ar, whose valley today forms a natural separation between the crater and Mt Hermon, which is composed of a variety of Jurassic and Cretaceous limestones, dolomites, chalks, marls, sandstones and some basalts.

The climate is cold Mediterranean, with mean precipitation averaging over 800 mm per year. This falls as both rain and snow, mostly between November and March.

Exposures of the clay unit are particularly good in the inner part of the crater and it was here that archaeological excavations were undertaken and the samples used in this study collected. The following field description is a synthesis representing samples collected from the area of the excavation and from an exposure *c.* 25 m to the north (Figure 12.1) (Goldberg, 1987).

At the base of the section is the Lower Kramim Basalt, which was dated to *c.* 800,000 yrs BP by the ^{40}Ar/^{39}Ar technique (Feraud *et al.*, 1983). It is locally sphaeroidially weathered and is overlain at various heights by the clay layer, from which five samples were taken. These are stratigraphically, from bottom to top (Figure 12.1):

> No. 1   (from archaeological excavation, *c.* 25 m to south and stratigraphically below No. 4; not shown in Figure 12.1). Dark reddish-brown (5YR3/6 d) sandy clay containing sandstone and limestone fragments and iron pisolites. Occurs only in isolated pockets that overlie irregular surface of the Lower Kramim Basalt.

> No. 2   (from profile, north of site) 60–110 cm: Yellowish-red (5YR5/6 d) clay, similar to above but slightly more massive.

228

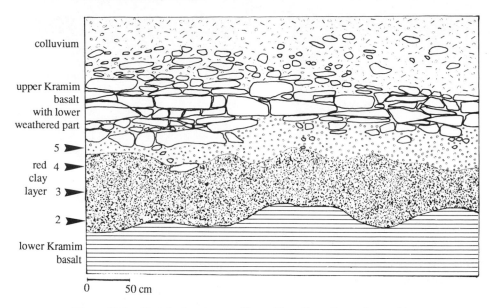

Figure 12.1 Sketch showing profile and location of samples used in micromorphological study. Sample no. 1 is from area of excavation *c*. 25 m to the south and lies stratigraphically between sample no. 2 and the contact with the Lower Kramin Basalt.

No. 3   45–60 cm: yellowish-red (5YR4/6 d), hard, coarse, crumbly to massive, slightly gritty clay with fresh basalt pebbles and scoria fragments.
No. 4   30–45 cm: yellowish-red (5YR5/1 d), hard, coarse, gritty, crumbly clay.
No. 5   0–30 cm: grey (5YR5/1 dry), crumbly, weathered basalt with small pieces (*c*. 2 cm) of fresher material.

This profile is capped by the Upper Kramim basalt, which yielded a date of 233,000 ± 3,000 yrs BP (Feraud *et al.*, 1983).

The fundamental problem presented by the Berekhat Ram profile concerns the geological history of the layer and its palaeoenvironmental significance and, more specifically, the relationship between the origin of the red layer and the prehistoric materials which were found in it. Although similar layers had been interpreted as weathering horizons (paleosols) or hydrothermal alteration zones, the same clay layer at Berekhat Ram had been interpreted as both colluvial and pedological in origin (Singer, 1983). Nevertheless, the relationship between the clay layer and the archaeological horizon at Berekhat Ram remained unclear. Moreover, it seemed to us that previous conclusions relating to the historical development of the clay layer – based on granulometry, X-ray diffraction and selected chemical analyses – lacked a certain definition and that these techniques were not capable of revealing the complex history of the profile that we believed existed. Clearly, an understanding of the origin of this layer should influence the archaeological interpretations of the site. Thus, with these goals in mind, a micromorphological study of the clay layer was undertaken (see Goldberg, 1987 for details).

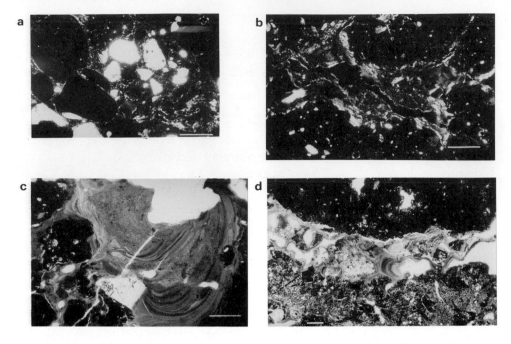

Figure 12.2   (a) Photomicrograph of sample no. 1 showing well-rounded quartz grains and opaque iron pisolites. The bright ropy fabric in the lower right-hand corner represents coatings of red-brown (initially formed) and bright-yellow clay (formed later); these two clay coatings are not resolved in the photograph). XPL. (Bar = 400 μm)

(b) Sample no. 2 illustrating a markedly different sediment from that in (a): absence of quartz sand and pisolites, and a greater amount of fine fraction, which is relatively rich in quartzitic silt. Clay coatings are very well developed, mostly in channels. XPL. (Bar = 400 μm)

(c) Near the top of the red clay layer (sample no. 4). The photomicrograph shows a large void infilled with regularly bedded and cross-laminated light yellow-brown and dusty yellow-brown clay. Note the rounded aggregation of the groundmass. PPL. (Bar = 400 μm)

(d) Sample no. 5 from base of Upper Kramin Basalt. Exfoliated basalt clast with infillings of clay and allophane(?). Note the similarity of the crossbedded infilling to that in Figure 12.2c. PPL. (Bar = 200 μm)

12.3 Micromorphological results

The thin sections described below follow the same stratigraphic order as the field description (Figure 12.2).

Sample No. 1

The coarse fraction is characterised by *c.* 20–30% subround to round, sand-sized quartz grains and *c.* 2–3% angular quartz silt (Figure 12.2b, c). Also present are *c.* 2–3% rounded, sand-sized iron pisolites and concretions that contain quartz silt; weathered fragments of tuff, volcanic glass and angular chert grains also occur (Figure 12.2a).

The fine fraction consists mostly of red- and orange-brown clay and shows granostriated b-fabric. It is also expressed as well-rounded aggregates composed of clay and quartz silt.

The most prominant type of clay coating is represented by moderately oriented, microlaminated red-brown clay, which fills thin irregular cracks and, more rarely, packing voids between pisolites and quartz sand (Figure 12.2a). The second type of coating is markedly different and is developed over the red-brown type. It consists of thin, discontinuous films of bright yellow, limpid clay.

Samples from the overlying materials differ strongly from that described above, and with the exception of No. 5 are basically similar to each other. Thus, a general description for No. 2 will be given and will be followed by comments pertaining to Nos. 3 and 4; No. 5 will be treated separately, with exceptions being noted.

Sample No. 2

Only traces (< 2%) of fine quartz sand are present, although finer quartz silt is more abundant (*c.* 5%) (Figure 12.2b). In addition, there is a greater abundance of weathered volcanic fragments, including scoria, basalt and tuff. These are generally weathered. Particularly interesting is the presence of rounded, sand-sized papules of red-brown clay and pellets consisting of quartz silt and clay, which are similar to those observed in the underlying layer and have presumably been reworked from them.

The fine fraction is also different from that in No. 1 and is represented by finely divided and dispersed silt-sized grains of weathered volcanic materials mixed within a dark red-brown clay, and having an undifferentiated b-fabric.

In contrast with No. 1, clay coatings are very well expressed (Figures 12.2b, c) and take the form of non-laminated to regularly and cross-laminated limpid, light yellow-brown and dusty, dark yellow-brown clay. On the whole, they are well oriented and moderately birefringent. On the other hand, the red-brown type is distinctly absent.

Samples Nos. 3 and 4

Samples No. 3 and 4 are similar but show an upward increase in the presence of fine to coarse sand-sized aggregates (Figure 12.2c). In addition, the yellow clay coatings are more abundant and not only fill voids but form bridges between the aggregates (Figure 12.2c). Finally, red-brown clay/silt balls and rounded quartz grains of quartz sand decrease and are rare in No. 4. In the latter sample, the matrix takes on a dark brown colour, with an undifferentiated b-fabric, even with the substage condenser in place.

Sample No. 5

Sample No. 5 again differs from those previously described and is composed of exfoliated vesicular and massive basalt from the Upper Kramim Basalt. The detached exfoliation shells are well weathered, although the basalt cores from which they were derived are relatively fresh (Figure 12.2d). Most striking, however, is the abundance and distribution of clay coatings and infillings, which not only fill vesicles within the basalt and cracks between exfoliation shells (Figure 12.2d) but also fill voids within masses of weathered basalt. As in the underlying samples, the coatings are composed of bright-yellow, limpid, well-oriented, microlaminated clay; in certain areas the clay is darker brown and more birefringent. Finally, in many cases the vesicle fillings are isotropic and presumably represent amorphous material, such as allophane.

12.4 Interpretation and discussion

These micromorphological observations should show that the clay layer is in fact composed of two markedly different lithological units. The lower unit (represented by sample No. 1) – occurring in isolated pockets – is composed of quartz sand and ferruginous pisolites in a red-brown matrix. These coarse grains were no doubt colluvially derived from the nearby slopes of Mt Hermon, *c*. 0.5 km to the north (also pointed out by Singer, 1983). In the absence of bedding or other sedimentary features – observed both in the field and under the microscope – alluviation seems a less likely mode of deposition. As a consequence, this sedimentation would have occurred before the incision of the modern channel of Nahal Sa'ar. The finer quartz of silt size is ultimately of aeolian origin as this material is a well-known imbedded component in many soils in Israel.

In addition to its colluvial origin, the lower layer experienced some pedological activity, as shown by the red-brown illuvial clay found in voids; the origin of the yellow, limpid clay, which in turn coats the red argillans, is dealt with below.

These observations moreover show that the upper part – and bulk – of the section is also sedimentary in origin, since its strikingly different composition of predominantly weathered basaltic materials not only indicates that it could not have developed from weathering of the underlying layer but that it was also derived from another and different source. Although the source is related to one or several Plio-Pleistocene basalts, it is not possible to pinpoint which one since they all have essentially the same composition. In any case, it too is likely to be of local (on the order of a few kms) colluvial origin, since traces of rounded quartz sand and red-brown clay papules reworked from the lower layer are present in the base of this unit.

This upper unit was also modified by post-depositional processes. Although we initially interpreted the abundant yellow argillans as resulting from pedological development beneath subaerially exposed surface, we had to aban-

Table 12.1. *Summary of depositional and post-depositional events at Berekhat Ram*

Period	Depositional event	Post-depositional event
Present	6a Downcutting of N. Sa'ar to present depth	6b Weathering of Upper Kramim Basalt by groundwater and vertical and lateral translocation of yellow-brown clay to top of the lower unit
233,000 BP	5 Emplacement of Upper Kramim Basalt	
	4 Slight erosion of lower unit and colluviation of upper one, including papules and quartz sand reworked from lower unit	
		3 Alteration of lower layer corresponding to red-brown clay coatings.
	2 Weathering of basalt and colluviation of lower layer containing quartz sand, iron pisolites and red clay derived from Mt Hermon	
800,000 BP	1 Emplacement of Lower Kramim Basalt	

don this interpretation on the basis of the observations made from the uppermost sample (No. 5). These observations indicate that the clay infilling in both the clayey sediment and in between the weathered exfoliation leaves of the Upper Kramim Basalt is contemporaneous and that both are associated with subterrestrial weathering of this upper basalt flow. The deposition of this 'illuvial' clay is most probably tied to the presence of groundwater, which is concentrated at the contact between the clay and basalt (cf. Singer, 1983). Similarly, an interpretation tied to hydrothermal activity associated with the upper basalt is not satisfactory, since the clay accumulated within the weathered basalt only after it cooled.

To sum up, the clay layer at Berekhat Ram in fact represents two sedimentary units, with pedogenesis affecting the lower layer and groundwater the upper one. The sedimentation of both is clearly younger than the age of the Lower Kramim Basalt, whereas the yellow clay coatings postdate the Upper Basalt; the latter may represent an ongoing process that has continued until the present. These events are summarised in Table 12.1.

12.5 Implications

This study has implications for both earth scientists and archaeologists alike. It should demonstrate to the former that such a 'red clay layer' is neither a simple paleosol nor a simple sediment but a complex of both sedimentary and post-depositional events interdigitated through time at the same locality.

By understanding the origin and nature of this complex unit, the archaeologist is in a much better position to interpret the lateral and vertical distribution of the artifacts. The general colluvial nature of the sediments may explain to some extent the fact that the artifacts are distributed through a vertical thickness of over 30 cm. Consequently, the location in which they are found today may not correspond to that in which prehistoric man originally left them.

THE NEOLITHIC SITE OF NETIV HAGDUD AND THE SALIBIYA DEPRESSION, LOWER JORDAN VALLEY

13.1 Introduction

Netiv Hagdud is a Pre-Pottery Neolithic A (PPNA) mound, situated some 13 km north of Jericho (Bar-Yosef *et al.*, 1980) (Figure 10.1). It is located at the base of the Samarian foothills to the west, which are composed of Cretaceous limestones, chalks, cherts and phosphorites, and overlooks the Salibiya depression which has an eastward slope toward the main part of the Jordan Rift Valley. This sloping depression is interrupted by a small rise, upon which is found the roughly coeval PPNA site of Gilgal I (Noy *et al.*, 1980). The climate of the area is arid, with *c.* 150 mm of mean annual rainfall that falls during the winter (November–March).

The Salibiya basin was the subject of intensive geoarchaeological research, which documented the distribution of prehistoric sites in their stratigraphic and palaeogeographic contexts around the time of the Pleistocene/Holocene transition (Schuldenrein and Goldberg, 1981). As a background to our micromorphological study, which illustrates the use of a variety of locally available materials for construction, we will briefly describe and outline the most important stratigraphic units and events of this history.

At the base of the Salibiya depression – and distributed over much of the Jordan Valley – are Lisan marls consisting of interbedded chemical sediments (calcite, aragonite, gypsum, diatoms) and fine-grained clastics (Begin *et al.*, 1974). These were deposited in Lake Lisan (the Pleistocene ancestor of the Dead Sea), which extended from the Sea of Galilee in the North to *c.* 20 km south of the present Dead Sea, and attained a maximum elevation of 180 m below sea level (Neev and Emery, 1967). Although the size of Lake Lisan appeared to have fluctuated throughout its lifetime, it retreated definitively – and rapidly – about 13,500 years ago.

This retreat was accompanied by successive prehistoric occupations, such that younger sites are generally found at progressively lower elevations within the basin. For example, Epipalaeolithic sites (Kebaran and Geometric Kebaran *c.* 17,000–13,500 BP) are found above − 180 m, whereas early and later Natufian sites (*c.* 12,500–10,500 BP) are found at − 218 m and − 230 m, respectively. These latter sites tend to be situated in subaerially eroded gullies and pockets that were developed on the Lisan marls as Lake Lisan retreated. In turn, this erosion was halted by the deposition of pinkish brown (7.5YR5/4)

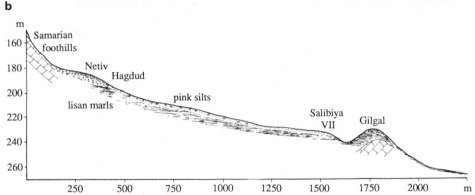

Figure 13.1   (a) View of Salibiya depression facing west towards the Samarian Hills. The site of Netiv Hagdud is indicated by the arrow.
(b) Generalised cross-section of Salibiya depression from Netiv Hagdud in west to Gilgal in east.

silts that infill this partially eroded terrain and contain the early Neolithic (PPNA?) site of Salibiya IX (Bar-Yosef *et al.*, 1980; = Gilgal III of Noy *et al.*, 1980). Significantly, localised in the lowermost few cms of these silts and clearly overlying Late Natufian sites, are predominantly *in situ* pieces and masses of algal tufa that formed from water seeping out of small, localised depressions. Silt deposition ceased some time after the PPNA (possibly Chalcolithic), with the formation of the badlands that characterise the Salibiya depression today (Figures 13.1a and b). A summary of these events and their inferred climatic significance is given in Table 13.1.

Netiv Hagdud forms a distinct topographical mound at *c*. 190 m and is more

Table 13.1. *Late Pleistocene/Holocene events and inferred climates from Netiv Hagdud/Salibiya area (modified from Schuldenrein and Goldberg, 1981)*

Date	Prehistoric site	Event	Inferred climate
0–5,000 BP		Erosion and development of badlands	Dry
5,000–10,000 BP	Netiv Hagdud, Salibiya IX (PPNA)	Deposition of pink fluvial silts and algal tufas	Moist at beginning & drier later
10,000–13,500 BP	Salibiya I (Late Natufian) Salibiya XII (Early Natufian)	Erosion of Lisan gullies and local depressions	Drying
13,500–pre 14,500 BP	Geometric Kebaran/ Kebaran	Lake Lisan fluctuating around maximum level of *c.* − 180 m deposition of Lisan marls	Moist

or less contemporaneous with the formation of the travertine and the deposition of the orange-brown silts. In contrast, however, it is associated with coarser gravels since it lies closer to the apex of the alluvial fan built by Wadi Baqar as it exits from the Samarian Hills into the Jordan Valley (Figure 13.1). Two samples of charcoal yielded radiocarbon dates of 8230 ± 300 BC (RT − 502 C) and 7840 ± 380 BC (RT − 502A), which are comparable to dates from PPNA layers excavated at Jericho (Bar-Yosef, 1980).

After several seasons of excavation it appears that the site covers an area of *c.* 10,000 m² and has at least 3 m of archaeological deposits (Bar-Yosef *et al.*, 1980). These deposits and those of the surrounding Late Pleistocene sediments form the focus of our micromophological study.

13.2 Description of the site

The site consists of several superimposed archaeological levels expressed by oval to circular semi-subterranean structures. In most instances, their lower courses were built of undressed limestone slabs, cobbles, etc. (Figure 13.2), while the upper courses were built of mud bricks. In one structure the walls were constructed of yellowish-brown (10YR5/6) plano-convex mud bricks, whose shape was poorly defined and often it was difficult to isolate an individual brick (Figure 13.2). Nevertheless, these formed well-defined walls (about 30 cm high and *c.* 5 cm thick), which were readily recognisable from the surrounding sediments because of differences in colour and consistence. In addition, we could observe lateral colour changes from the outer part of the brick – light

Figure 13.2   Netiv Hagdud, showing oval and rounded structures and mud-brick construction. (Bar = 2 m)

brown (10YR6/3) to yellowish-brown (10YR5/6) – in the direction of the centre of the structure. The innermost part of the brick seemed to be covered with a thin (5–10 mm), limey, mud-like coating.

The structures are filled with greyish-brown (10YR5/2), structureless, crumbly, locally compacted material in which we could identify pieces of decayed mud brick. These compacted materials could be distinguished during the excavation from what appeared to be discrete surfaces, consisting of millimetre-thick compact crusts which were thought to be intentionally prepared living floors.

Along the northern part of the site, which was damaged by the building of a modern water-reservoir, it was possible to recognise well-preserved, brownish-yellow (10YR6/6), loaf-shaped bricks in spite of the fact that they tended to peel off in layers, *c.* 3–5 mm thick. These bricks rested upon a pronounced, undifferentiated, powdery ashy layer (10YR5/1) that is mixed with various kinds of archaeological materials. These bricks clearly differed from those forming the walls in Loci 21, 22 and 27 (Figure 13.2), in their greyer colour and in having striking imprints of straw temper.

The essential problems at Netiv Hagdud are centred around the sources and nature of the archaeological materials, manufacturing techniques involved at the site, and the effects of penecontemporaneous as well as post-depositional changes. We begin with a discussion of the bricks.

13.3 Mud bricks

As in many sites where mud bricks are found, the archaeologists wished to know which raw materials were used in the manufacture of the bricks and whether the former inhabitants preferred one particular constituent over another. Furthermore, they wanted to know whether the observed differences in mud bricks was the result of preferential selection of raw materials or other anthropogenic activities, such as burning, which we suspected from the reddish colour of some of the bricks?

13.3.1 *Composition*

Several types of material were identified in the bricks and all have a local origin. The yellow bricks, regardless of their location in the site, are composed of the same fine components as found in the finer wadi deposits: abundant coarse, rounded calcareous sand and quartz-sand grains, associated with a poorly sorted calcitic groundmass containing clay, which is dispersed in the groundmass or is in the form of individual aggregates (Figures 13.3a, b). Unlike these wadi sediments, however, the bricks contain numerous mm-sized limestone and chert fragments and also traces (2–3%) of finely dispersed, flaky charcoal (*c.* 20 μm). Nevertheless, the limestone temper is finer and better sorted in the bricks from the surrounding walls than those from the house itself.

In addition, the lighter layer that covers the house bricks differs markedly from the above brick composition in that clay is essentially absent and the sorting is much better. Moreover, the high amount of Cretaceous foraminifera testifies either to a source material in the Samarian Hills or to the Lisan marls which contain reworked Cretaceous sediments (Figures 13.3c and d).

13.3.2 *Fabrics*

Although variations in the composition of the brick material are on the whole insignificant, differences in fabrics are striking. The inner bricks (Figure 13.3a) are characterised overall by the presence of elongated voids typically found in mud bricks and which are a result of the decay of the original straw binder. Large cracks and fissures are also associated with these voids and are commonly filled with lenticular, well-crystallised gypsum. This void network emphasises the crumbly microstructure and high porosity that are readily apparent in these bricks.

In contrast, the bricks from the surrounding wall (Figure 13.3e) have a

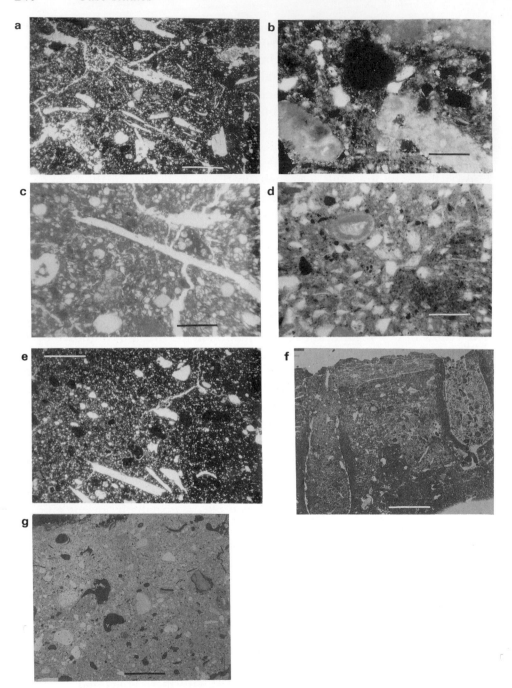

Figure 13.3   (a) Yellow part of house mud brick: microstructure formed of elongated voids resulting from the decay of the original straw binder. Note the abundance of coarse elements and the abundance of fine fissures indicating weak resistance to disaggregation. PPL. (Bar = 150 μm)

relatively low porosity, mostly in the form of elongated fine fissures and vughs. Furthermore, the outlines of original aggregates were recognisable only locally. A final difference in these bricks is the intimate blending of the finer material that results in a homogeneous fabric.

13.3.3 *Discussion of the brick material*

Not surprisingly, all the bricks have been made from local materials. In spite of the volumetric abundance and widespread availability of the Lisan marls, we find no bricks made solely of this material. Rather, all the bricks have a high proportion of fine alluvium even though it is relatively scarce in the vicinity of the tell. This alluvial source hypothesis is supported by the overwhelming abundance of aquatic pollen found within the bricks (Darmon, 1984, 1986, 1987). Thus, it is obvious that a certain selectivity was practised. Furthermore, the whitish plastering material represents a clearly intentional selection for the calcareous deposits (Lisan/Cretaceous chalks).

Technically, the bricks were manufactured from raw, unfired materials and owe their yellowish colour to the admixture of coloured alluvium. Furthermore, the differences in brick types seem to be related to the degree of processing of the material. The dense and homogeneous fabric of the bricks of the surrounding walls results from careful preparation, thus producing a 'melted effect' of the original aggregates. These finely blended bricks appear to have been more resistant to post-depositional effects than the house bricks.

The manufacturing techniques used for the house bricks were noticeably different, as shown both by the greater heterogeneity of the basic raw materials,

---

(b) Yellow part of house mud brick: rounded calcareous sand and quartz sand grains embedded in a poorly sorted calcitic groundmass containing clay and fine charcoal. XPL. (Bar = 50 μm)

(c) Plaster material and grey colour layer of the house bricks: elongated void microstructure similar to 13.3b but note the better sorting of coarse components and abundance of microfossils derived from Cretaceous chalk. PPL. (Bar = 150 μm)

(d) As (c); detail of the calcitic groundmass at higher magnification. Addition of localised fine powdery charcoal can be observed. PPL. (Bar = 50 μm)

(e) Compacted mud brick from the surrounding wall. A few elongated voids are observable but they are very small in comparison to those shown in 13.3a and only generate very fine fissures. Note the very dense fabric and the good sorting of sand and silt. PPL. (Bar = 150 μm)

(f) House floor from Locus 26. The original mud brick-like structure can be observed between the two insect channels. Note the intense disaggregation and homogenisation of the underlying materials related to both trampling and biological activity. Later turbation caused by insect burrowing results in total disaggregation. PPL. (Bar = 10 mm)

(g) House floor from Locus 21. Very dense fabric similar to that in 13.3f. Note the vesicular porosity (subrounded voids not related to each other) and absence of straw prints. Dark field, PPL. (Bar = 2.5mm)

indicating less care in their preparation, and by the addition of straw. These two manufacturing processes have induced a higher degree of fragility in the bricks, since water solutions were able to penetrate via the voids, thereby favouring dissolution–reprecipitation of gypsum that exists in the source materials. Numerous fissures and cracks have thus developed from pre-existing fissures and voids and enhanced the disruption of the brick.

13.4 House floors and infillings
13.4.1 *Characteristics*
Surfaces of greater resistancy were recognised in most of the houses during the excavation and appeared to be quite different from the underlying and overlying loose materials. They formed a 2–3 cm-thick, grey to brownish-grey layer and were identified as house floors.

In thin section, these compacted surfaces appear to be significantly different according to their location. In Locus 26, the thin layer appears to be very similar to the bricks forming the surrounding walls of the house, consisting of a light grey-coloured upper part and a reddish-brown lower part. Elongated voids are also abundant but are more or less displayed parallel to the soil surface (Figure 13.3f). They are finely cracked and strongly disrupted by the nesting activity of insects. The lower boundary is clear and smooth and the underlying loose materials consist mostly of disaggregated mud bricks.

These characteristics indicates that such a surface was intentionally prepared following a similar technique to that used in the manufacture of the bricks forming the surrounding walls. Abundance of straw temper and a moderate pugging explain why this house floor was later finely cracked and easily disturbed, not only by biological activity but also by trampling.

On the other hand, the millimetre-thick cemented crust sampled in Locus 26 is yellowish-brown, homogeneous, massive and contains a few vesicles and vughs (Figure 13.3g) and in these features resembles the fabric of the bricks from the walls surrounding the site. Moreover, a rough layering can be observed, that is expressed by lamination of the coarse grains. This crust material was most probably purposely prepared from material similar to that of the carefully pugged mud bricks but shows even better sorting. It was prepared from a moderately loose slurry, which would explain its characteristic layering. Because of its dense fabric, this layer was not affected by secondary effects, such as splintering related to the growth of gypsum crystals.

We may conclude by noting the following points:

> All the bricks and construction materials were made from locally available re-
> sources, but a preference was exercised for the clayier, calcareous wadi alluvium.
> The plastering material was made principally from chalky substance, which was
> selected from either the Lisan marls and/or Cretaceous chalks and was probably
> chosen because of its lighter colour and its properties of cementation.
> Floors are indeed intentionally prepared surfaces.

The differences in the types of mud bricks and house floors can be explained by differences in preparation techniques. These, in turn, have influenced the quality of preservation of the different construction materials. No evidence of heating of the bricks was found.

Finally, we point out that, although partial conclusions pertaining to composition might have been reached with the aid of other techniques (e.g., X-ray diffraction for determining mineralogical composition), it would have been very difficult to make inferences concerning techniques of preparation from the fabrics of these materials. This is especially so in light of the generally homogeneous mineralogical composition of the various materials checked. With a few thin sections, the geometrical arrangement of the components that make up each sample is readily apparent and the geological and archaeological implications of these observations are soon evident.

THE BRONZE AGE/NEOLITHIC SITE OF FORT HARROUARD (EURE ET LOIRE)

14.1 Introduction

The important site of Fort Harrouard (Figure 14.1) was excavated during the 1930s by Abbé Philippe, who demonstrated not only the presence of Neolithic and Bronze Age activities associated with metallurgy and large rampart constructions but also evidence of Iron Age and Roman occupations (Philippe, 1936, 1937).

It was formerly thought that the latter were responsible for most of the large building constructions found at the site and it was a surprise to find that the landscape had been so extensively modified in Neolithic times and that it had been preserved so well. While these early excavations concentrated on establishing the stratigraphy, recent efforts by Mohen, Roussot-Laroque and Villes (Mohen and Villes, 1984) have adopted a broader scope, stressing palaeoenvironmental studies and greater understanding of human activities at the site, such as metallurgical technology, types of construction materials used in the fortifications and habitation areas. Our objective here is to show how micromorphology can contribute to such an understanding.

14.2 Background

The Middle Neolithic Period in the Paris Basin is characterised by large enclosed settlements, some situated on the edges of higher plateaux. These settlements, as is the case for Fort Harrouard, were commonly fortified to maintain lowland pastures or to keep watch over agricultural areas on the adjacent loess-covered plateau; both are seen as a response to increased competition for available agricultural land at this time (Scarre, 1985). These defensive, fortifications typically consist of a large fortified rampart surrounded by a large ditch. The interior of the settlement was presumably bare and used for grazing, whereas habitation was generally concentrated close to the fortifications. The habitation areas were probably wooden structures and locally derived materials, such as mud daub. These defensive-type settlements continued into the Late Neolithic, and up to the Iron Age. With the Bronze Age we see the introduction and development of metallurgy and its consequence manifested in environmental and land-use changes.

14.3 Location and strategy

The site of Fort Harrouard is situated on a chalk plateau along the Eure River, near the small community of Sorel Moussel (Eure et Loire) (Figure 14.1). The

1° N 10° E
+

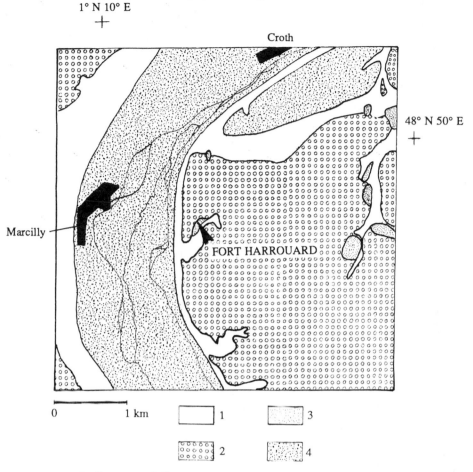

0   1 km   □ 1   ▒ 3

           ⊙ 2   ⬚ 4

1   Cretaceous chalk
2   Early Quaternary alluvium and colluvium
3   Plateau loam
4   Recent alluvium

Figure 14.1   Schematic geological map of the Eure valley near the site of Fort Harrouard. (After n. 180 "Saint-André de l'Eure, 1–50,000 BRGM sheet no. 180)

plateau is partly covered with remnants of Tertiary weathered material consisting of the '*argile à silex*' (cf. clay-with-flints), and more locally the Sables de Fontainebleau (Dewolf, 1982). Further east and in a few restricted localities, such as on slopes, more recent deposits of Pleistocene loess occur.

Our efforts were localised in the area of the site known as Area II (Figure 14.2). This locality is characterised by a soft, loess-like sediment at the base (Middle Neolithic), abruptly overlain by a chalky talus deposit (Late Neolithic) (Figure 14.3a). A few metres to the south, resting upon the talus, is a large, bedded rampart construction dating from the Bronze Age.

Several specific questions were posed by the archaeologists concerning the

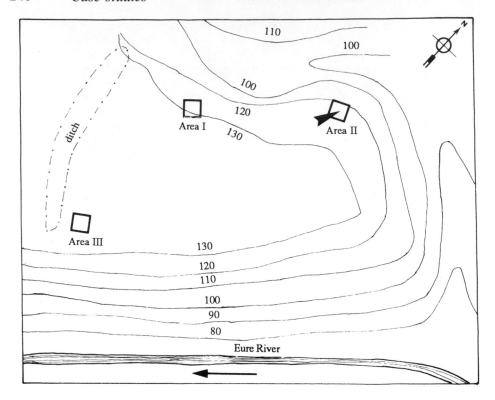

Figure 14.2   Detailed topographical map of the site of Fort Harouard indicating the areas under excavation in 1985. (After Abbé Philippe)

nature and origin of many of these materials and the methods of construction. Below, we attempt to demonstrate how micromorphological analyses can help resolve these issues.

14.4.1 Field descriptions (Figure 14.3a)

Profile X

X1 bottom unit – 50–75 cm. Very pale-brown (10YR7/4), fine silt, massive structure, fine porosity with well-expressed whitish coatings on pores (pseudomycelia) and strong effervescence with HCl; flat, regular, gradual boundary characterised by a change in colour.

X2 – upper unit – 0–50 cm. Brownish yellow (10YR6/6) to reddish yellow (7.5YR6/6) at the top, fine silt, massive structure, abundant very fine porosity and a few millimetric channels at the upper part with whitish coatings, no effervescence with HCl (except near the latter coatings); presence of archaeological materials (sherds, bones, flints) in the upper 15 cm, sharp upper limit due to human truncation.

Profile Y

Y1 – bottom unit – 60–75 cm. Very similar to A1 but with flat, irregular, sharp boundary characterised by a change in colour and an increase in fine pores.

Y2 – middle unit – 15–60 cm. Yellow-brown (10YR5/6) to light yellowish-brown (10YR6/4) silt with a few coarse flint fragments, massive structure, abundant fine pores and tubules filled with darker material (10YR5/4), no effervescence with HCl; flat, regular, clear boundary, characterised by a change in colour. A few sherds and bones occurred throughout the unit with some charcoal in the upper part.

Y3 – upper unit – 0–15 cm. Yellow-brown (10YR5/4) to dark yellowish-brown (10YR4/4) coarse silt with abundant coarse fragments of flints, many mm-sized charcoal fragments and sherds, massive structure, many fine pores, no effervescence with HCl; flat, sharp, regular boundary as the layer is truncated by the talus deposit. At the contact, penetration of lime from the talus can be observed at a depth of 1 cm.

The problems presented by these profiles relate to characterising the nature of each and the relations between the two juxtaposed upper layers: the reddish-brown one of X2 and the dark one of Y3. Is the latter, for example, a soil, an anthropic horizon, or possibly both? Linked with this is the clarification of their relationships to the underlying lighter loessic material and the overlying, clearly anthropic talus deposit. Observation of thin sections from the different units reveals that they consist of the same basic material (i.e., the original loess deposits) but the observed variations result from both pedological and human transformations. In the following part we present only the characteristics essential to the detailed reconstruction of this part of the site.

14.4.2 *Micromorphological description*
1 Bottom loess (X1 and Y1)

Structure varies from massive to spongy and crumbly with high total porosity (25%), mostly expressed by channels (Figure 14.4a). The coarse fraction is essentially composed of calcareous and quartz silt (30 μm; 20%) and quartz sand (200–300 μm; 1%) mixed with a fine fraction consisting of calcitic clay (40%). This fine fraction is somewhat dusty and a few pieces of charcoal were observed only in A1. Pedofeatures are expressed by coatings of needle-shaped calcite and micritic hypocoatings (impregnation of pores by finely crystallised calcite; 15% calcitic features in total). There are no signs of illuvial clay.

The weak development of pedological features and the quasi absence of anthropogenic features indicate that this lowermost unit consists of weakly altered loessic sediments, whose micromorphological characteristics are similar to those from loesses deposited at the end of the last glacial period.

2 Upper reddish brown loess (X2)

This superficially resembles the underlying unit but variations do occur. Traces of carbonate appear only in the coarse fraction and the fine fraction consists of reddish-brown silty clay, with medium birefringence and wavy extinction; thin, poorly laminated clay coatings occur in fine, intergranular voids (Figure 14.4b). Large-scale voids are much less common, especially in the lower part, though there is a marked increase in channels at the very top, which results in the disruption of the void coatings. Here in the upper part, thick bedded

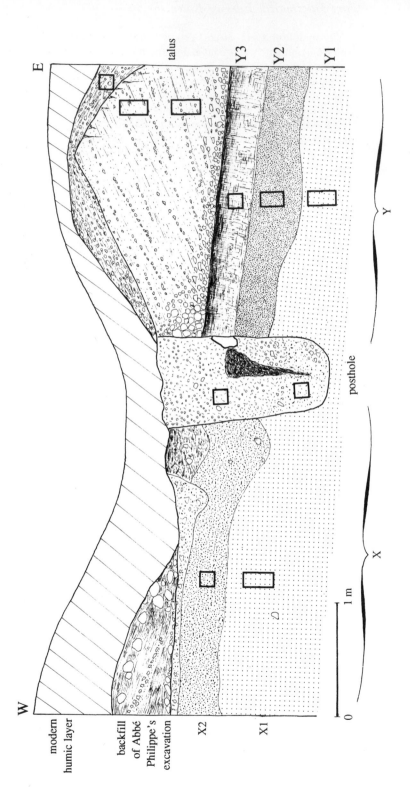

W E

modern
humic layer

backfill
of Abbé
Philippe's
excavation

X2

X1

posthole

talus

Y3

Y2

Y1

X Y

1 m

0

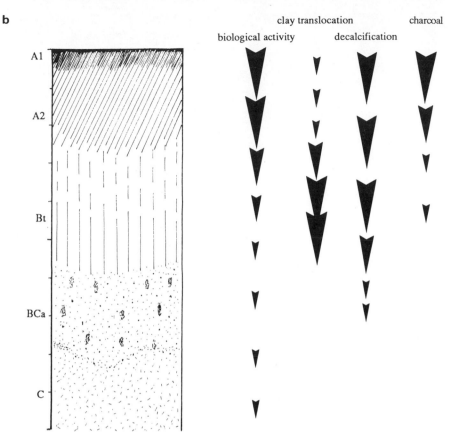

Figure 14.3   (a) Section exposed during 1985 excavations in Area II showing the location of some of the samples studied in the Neolithic layers. (After J.-P. Nicolardot)

   (b) Schematic representation of the soil profile on loess in Area II and vertical distribution of the most important pedological features.

textural features composed of silt-sized detrital calcite partly fill the voids (Figure 14.4c).

Thus, in profile X, differences within the profile result from pedological differentiation of an initial loessic parent material.

3 Middle Loess (Y2)

A mild transition could be recognised in the lower part of the middle loess and was most marked by a colour contrast between yellowish-brown, coarse aggregates and a very pale brown groundmass. Compared to the bottom loess, the calcitic fine fraction is less abundant and calcite appears more as grains; the yellowish-brown aggregates consist of partially decalcified loess and are richer in fine microcontrasted particles.

Figure 14.4   (a) Massive calcitic loess at the bottom of the profile studied (areas X1 and Y1). Note the calcitic b-fabric and the occurrence of calcitic hypocoatings around vughs. XPL. (Bar = 230 μm)

(b) Upper reddish-brown loess (X2): weakly disturbed argillic horizon and totally decalcified fine fraction. Thin, poorly laminated clay coatings are observed around vughs. PPL. (Bar = 230 μm)

(c) As (b), calcitic coatings consisting of silt-sized detrital particles. PPL. (Bar = 500 μm)

(d) Middle loess (Y2): view of an illuvial zone characterised by abundant clay coatings around fine sand grains. At lower magnifications it is possible to see a massive microstructure with channels and vughs and a decalcified groundmass which contains a few charcoal particles. XPL. (Bar = 500 μm)

(e) Upper part of the talus profile: association of chalky fragments (in grey) with a red laminated papule derived from '*argile à silex*' (on the left) and decalcified loess (isotropic fabric and abundant silt). XPL. (Bar = 230 μm)

(f) Middle part of the talus profile illustrating the melted aspect of the chalk grains caused by secondary precipitation of calcium carbonate. A decalcified loessial fragment is observable at the upper right. XPL. (Bar = 230 μm)

Most of the unit shows clear differences with the bottom loess. The structure is homogeneous and massive to spongy with a total porosity of 20%, composed of a few channels and abundant vughs. The very coarse fraction is more abundant (3%) and contains some flints and abundant charcoal. Silt (30–40%) is irregularly distributed and heterogeneously mixed in with the fine fraction, which is reddish brown to yellowish brown and distributed as aggregates (100 μm) with low birefringence. It is totally non-calcified and contains abundant microcontrasted particles (5%), producing a dusty aspect. Pedofeatures are expressed by dusty, reddish-brown clay coatings with moderate birefringence and are poorly to non-laminated. Their degree of integration into the ground-mass is moderately good but they also tend to be localised around voids or to infill small pores and are irregularly distributed around the surface of aggregates and around fine sand grains (5%) (Figure 14.4d).

4 Upper unit (Y3)

This exhibits a massive to spongy microstructure, slightly fissured, and a porosity (15%) represented by fine fissures and vughs. The coarse fraction (7%) is composed of very coarse elements (0.2 to 10 mm), represented by numerous grains of flint and abundant pieces of disaggregated charcoal. Other elements in the coarse fraction are quartz sand, traces of bone, coarse silt/very fine sand and fine silt (40%). The fine fraction is darkish brown, dusty, has low birefringence and contains abundant, very fine (< 5 μm) phytoliths. The dust (30%) of the fine fraction, represented by charcoal and microcontrasted particles, is poorly sorted and very localised, and forms small aggregates (100 μm in diameter) mixed with eluviated portions. Pedofeatures include excrement and, in the lower part, reddish-brown, dusty, non-laminated clay coatings on the faces of elongated fissures; in this same part very thin, dark grey calcitic coatings (a few microns thick) of the textural type also occur.

The vertical distribution of the most important elements described above is summarised in Figure 14.3b.

14.4.3 *Interpretation*

The thin-section observations show that the units described in the field are essentially soil units that have been partly affected by anthropogenic activity (Table 14.1). Moreover, beginning with a natural deposit of calcareous loess at the base, the profile had developed in stages.

In the initial stages of development, the upper part of the profile began to be decalcified at the same time that the entire profile was being subjected to biological reworking. The latter is well illustrated by the well-developed spongy and crumbly microstructure and porosity (channels). This phase was soon followed by illuviation of the clays that are best expressed in Y2. However, compared to a typical Holocene soil profile that forms under forest cover, this one displays certain features, such as clay coatings, that are too poorly expressed and others, such as biological activity, that are too abundant. Thus, the

Table 14.1. *Summary of the evolutionary sequence at Area Y*

	Event	
Sedimentary	Pedological	Anthropogenic
1 Deposition of loess		
	2a decalcification	
	2b biological activity	
	3 illuviation	
		4 clearing, burning and terracing
	5 dusty illuviation and biological activity	
		6 burial
	7 translocation of calcitic silt	

type of pedogenesis inferred here seemed to have developed under more of a prairie grassland pastural environment – with some trees but predominantly grasses – than under a forested one.

Towards the end of this pedogenic sequence, we see the effects of anthropogenic activity clearly shown in Y3 by the abundance of charcoal and the mixing of both eluviated and illuviated horizons but also marked in the top part of X2 by the disturbance of the original illuviated fabric. Furthermore, while the Y soil profile is fairly complete because of the occurrence of an upper organic-rich layer, the latter is absent in profile X. Comparison of these various lines of evidence, together with the field characteristics, suggests that in this location the loessic soil was levelled by men. For this purpose, organic-rich loessic horizon occurring in areas such as X seems to have been removed for preparing some kind of subhorizontal platform. The levelled soil was then exposed for some short period of time before the overlying talus was emplaced and simultaneously affected by pedological processes and anthropogenic activities. Abundance of woody and herbaceous charcoal indicates episodes of burning. The fine fragmentation of the charcoal and its dispersion throughout the unit can be strongly correlated with the biological activity of plants (e.g., roots) and animals (worms, insects, etc.). In addition, the fact that dusty illuvial clay occurs within the groundmass and lightly coats some of the charcoal grains and the surface of aggregates and voids demonstrates that the illuviation took place after the phases of burning and biological activity. We may link these various features with a possible phase of cultivation of the levelled soil but there is no other evidence to support this hypothesis, since pollen grains are yet to be found in this profile.

Translocation of calcitic silt marks the end of the evolution of the sequence and most probably relates in profile Y to water percolation after the talus was built, while in profile X the calcitic silt seems to be derived from talus backfill of Abbé Philippe's excavation, which has sealed the upper reddish-brown loess.

14.5 **Talus profile**
14.5.1 *Field description and relevant questions*
As shown in Figure 14.3a, a massive chalky unit sharply truncates Y3, as described above. This talus, related to the Late Neolithic fortification, is described as follows:

> *Upper part – 0–30 cm* – Light brown (7.5YR6/4) to pinkish-grey (7.5YR7/2) gravel and coarse sand, comprising chalk fragments, chert and reddish-yellow grains (10YR5/3). These are loosely packed and overlain by greyish-brown (10YR5/2) coarse sand, rich in charcoal. Many fine roots penetrating from the upper layer. Strong effervescence. Inclined, sharp, regular boundary.
>
> *Middle part – 30–65 cm* – Microlaminated white to very pale brown (10YR7/6) gravel and coarse sand, composed mostly of chalk fragments, a few pieces of chert and brownish, loess-like materials. Local pockets of highly fragmented charcoal or humified organic matter. Massive structure with slight cementation at the upper part. Clear, irregular boundary, more or less inclined.
>
> *Lower part – 65–85 cm* – Pale brown (10YR7/4) gravel composed of chalk fragments and chert; with massive structure and horizontal, sharp and regular boundary.

The problems expressed in this talus section are several-fold: (a) What is the origin of these chalky deposits and, specifically, is there any evidence of burnt lime being used to construct the rampart? (b) Is the red colour in the upper part a result of burning or some other process, such as pedogenesis? (c) What is the nature of the black 'organic fragments' locally mixed with the chalky talus material? Do they represent charcoal, either burned in place or mixed in a later time, or are they plant residues that have been partially humified after burial?

14.5.2 *Micromorphological results*
Upper Part
This is composed of moderately to poorly sorted and loosely packed aggregates, consisting of subangular chalk fragments (2–10 mm), mixed with red clay and silt derived from the Tertiary *argile à silex*, and with aggregates of Pleistocene loessial soils, similar to those just described in the loess profile (Figure 14.4e); the latter are marked by pieces of pale yellow-brown argillic coatings (papules). In addition, there are several compound grains, composed of mixtures of the above lithological types. Some of the aggregates have been broken as the result of biological activity, such as root growth and mixing by earthworms. Biological activity is also responsible for the integration of fine charcoal within the cracks. Chert is moderately abundant (1%). The top part of the sample is noticeably enriched in charcoal and the clay has been slightly rubified by burning.

Middle and lower parts
Compared to the sample previously described, the overall composition is similar although proportions are different. Firstly, apart from nearby localised zones rich in charcoal, clay is not rubified and has a brighter yellow colour. In addition, there is an increase in the amount of clay from the *argile à silex*. Furthermore, the sorting is better and the clay components are smaller. The individuality of the chalk grains is less well-expressed due to secondary precipitation of calcium carbonate, which produces a 'melted' appearance (Figure 14.4f). The latter aspect changes with depth, however, where the grains are distinctly coarser and more individualised, and the 'melting' effect is less prominent.

14.5.3 *Interpretation of the talus profiles*

From the above descriptions, it is evident that the bulk of the material in the talus profile is derived from the chalk bedrock that makes up the surrounding plateaux. Although the specific source within the area of the Fort could not be determined, it is clear that the quarrying operation used to exploit the chalk also took with it both the Neogene *argile à silex*, as well as the Pleistocene loess, since both are mixed with the chalk. Thus, it seems that the chalk was not deeply excavated at its source but, rather, was scraped off the top, resulting in contamination with these brown and redder sediments.

The red colour in the upper parts is a result of this admixture, coupled with the effects of mild burning, which enhanced the reddening. From the weakness of the burning – the *argile à silex* becomes red when even mildly heated, whereas the chalk is not transformed – it seems that the heating resulted from one burning episode of a very localised nature and of short duration. In addition, there are no signs of the chalk having been deliberately heated for the preparation of quick-lime in building the rampart (limestone takes on a dull yellowish-grey colour after heating). On the other hand, the chalk fragments from the middle part do show some signs of secondary cementation (calcareous bridges between fragments). This weathering is associated with pedogenesis, since the talus was exposed in the Late Neolithic, but the weathering has no specific significance as it can develop very rapidly (tens of years) when calcareous materials are exposed at the surface.

Finally, the layering within the talus points to the deliberate efforts of the inhabitants in building the rampart and could easily represent tip lines, which are not uncommon in constructions such as these. Moreover, the moderate sorting of the fragments indicates either a selected preference for this size material (which may result in greater stability of the rampart), or is indicative of the size of the raw material available from where it was quarried; jointing of the chalk and its subsequent weathering or even the manner in which it was extracted (e.g., picks and sticks) could have produced fragments of this calibre.

14.6 **The posthole**

14.6.1 *Field characteristics*

A large posthole, *c.* 25 cm in diameter, separates profiles X and Y discussed above (Figure 14.3a). Two samples were collected from material that filled the posthole in order to characterise the type of construction materials associated with the posthole, and to explain their origin.

At the base is material resembling Y2 and having a weakly expressed, fine, granular structure, with a few coarse elements, and a spotted, lightish-brown colour. Above this, the material is light brown, more massive, with coarse granular structure and has fewer coarse elements.

14.6.2 *Micromorphological descriptions*

Lower sample

This sample, with a granular to channel-type microstructure and total porosity of 30%, consists of a mixture of two types of materials: (1) predominantly dark, yellow-brown (similar to underlying loess), (2) with centimetre-sized aggregates of light yellow-brown loess closely mixed with dark brown decalcified loess; pieces of chert (3–5%) also occur. The most striking feature of the sample is its degree of disaggregation, and the extensive intermixing of eluvial and illuvial loess, and chalky aggregates (Figure 14.5a).

Upper sample

This constitutes a radically new type of material, being massive and very compact, and containing numerous planes and some vughs. It is characterised by a bimodal coarse fraction: (a) 100–200 μm, consisting of rounded quartz and fragments of calcite, chalk, fossils and chert. These are irregularly distributed, commonly in pockets; and (b) fine silt (30 μm) that occurs in relatively small amounts (*c.* 5%). The fine fraction is highly calcareous, with high birefringence and is marked by a high abundance of brownish-red to black shreds and fragments of plants that vary from dust size up to 100 μm (Figure 14.5b). A few mildly heated bones can also be observed.

14.6.3 *Interpretation of posthole samples*

For the lower sample, its chaotic aspect, poor sorting and its varied composition suggest an anthropogenic filling of materials present in the local surroundings. The upper sample, however, is noticeably different. The density and compaction and highly calcareous nature of the sample suggest that it represents some type of intentionally prepared lime mud (non-baked mortar) used in the construction of the posthole. It is in fact the high carbonate content which produces the lighter colour of this sample in comparison to the lower one. The good sorting of the material is an additional argument that the deposit was purposely treated to achieve a specific aim and, perhaps not coincidentally, it resembles the interstitial filling between the talus fragments described above.

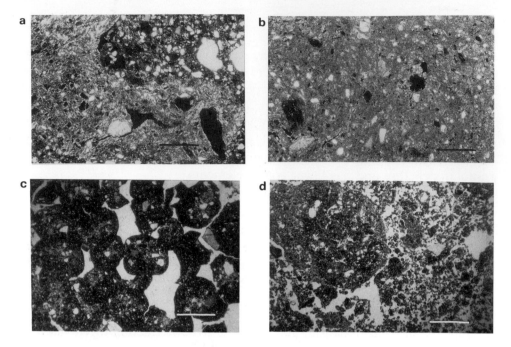

Figure 14.5   Materials found in the posthole:

(a) Lower part: extensive intermixing of eluvial (left and right side) and illuvial (middle) loess. Note the polyconcave voids (in black) resulting from strong compaction. XPL. (Bar = 230 μm)

(b) Upper part: dense calcitic fabric mostly derived from chalk, finely mixed with some loess (fine grains in white) and associated with abundant charred particles and charcoal (in black). Note the rather low porosity as a result of careful pugging. XPL. (Bar = 230 μm)

(c) Sample 161 (a in Figure 14.6): dense packing of rounded aggregates which are mostly earthworm excrements. PPL. (Bar = 500 μm)

(d) Sample 165 (upper part of d in Figure 14.6): very loose, fine granular microstructure. These materials in fact represent backfill from previous excavation and cannot be mistaken in thin section for a Bronze Age layer. PPL. (Bar = 500 μm)

The most intriguing aspect of the material, however, is the abundance of the intimately mixed organic fragments. They are not of recent origin, since they are commonly highly fragmented and very well incorporated into the calcareous matrix. One interpretation of these phenomena is that they were purposely mixed into the sample for some unknown reason. Alternatively and more likely, they were inherited from the process of mud preparation. For example, if the mud were mixed in a wooden container, such as a hollowed-out log, pieces and fibres of wood would certainly have been mixed in. A wooden paddle, used to mix it, could have also contributed some organic material. Wood is preferable to a ceramic or stone container, since the mud would not have adhered to the sides of the vessel and would not have required repeated cleaning. (We are grateful to Dr J. Gunnweig for suggesting this explanation.)

14.7 **Bronze Age rampart**
14.7.1 *Field characteristics*
A few metres to the south and resting upon the Late Neolithic talus deposit described above are the remains of a large, well-bedded Bronze Age rampart (Figure 14.6), consisting of light grey coarse layers with abundant chalk fragments and block of flints alternating with brownish-grey to black, homogeneous, structureless loam, rich in Bronze Age remains (sherds, bones). Five units were sampled from this construction (Figure 14.6) and for the sake of clarity we will present the interpretation of each unit immediately following its micromorphological description. Although the lighter, chalky units looked similar to the talus material and therefore invited comparison, the intercalated darker units differed among themselves and from those observed elsewhere in the site. What were they and how did they get there?

14.7.2 *Micromorphological descriptions*
(a): Sample 161 (base of exposure)
This has a granular structure (Figure 14.5c), with a total porosity of *c.* 30%, consisting of planes and vughs. The coarse fraction is represented by a few big pieces (> 1 cm) of chert and abundant, smaller pieces (< 1 cm) of chalk, burnt bones and sherd. The finer part of the coarse fraction is composed of quartz sand (10%), calcareous loess aggregates (1–3%), and varying amounts of calcite and microfossils derived from the chalk. The fine fraction is yellowish brown, rich in both calcite and notably microcontrasted particles, particularly charcoal. In spite of the masking effect of highly birefringent clacite, many phytoliths were observed. Occurring in small amounts are light yellow grains, 500 μm in diameter, that are isotropic and highly fluorescent; they contain 5% quartz silt and phytoliths and are partially impregnated with iron around the outer rim. They most probably represent remains of herbivore coprolites. One sherd fragment was observed, consisting of quartz sand and silt, chert and calcareous fragments in a slightly calcareous clay matrix. Moreover, some pottery fragments appear to have formed part of the temper, which was also rich in straw and phytoliths.

Interpretation of sample 161
The origin of the material is quite clear, consisting essentially of calcareous loess intimately mixed with brown clay, quartz sand and microcontrasted particles. It seems that the unit was locally derived from nearby loess exposures but was 'contaminated' *en route* by substantial additions of anthropogenic materials of bone, pottery and burnt organic matter. The hows and whys of its deposition, however, remain elusive, though simple dumping of occupational debris from within the fort is probable. Nevertheless, it is clear that the

W   E

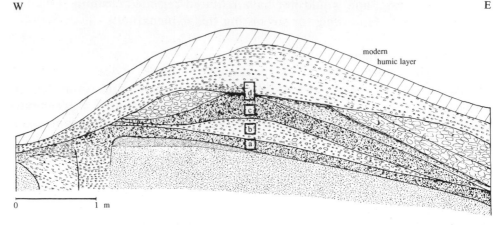

Figure 14.6   Field section from the Bronze Age rampart, showing location of the
samples studied.

'homogeneous' appearance of this sample in the field is no doubt related to the
intense biological mixing by earthworms.

(b): Sample 162

This sample consists mostly (50%) of subrounded chalk fragments (1–3 cm)
and rare chert pieces with finer interparticle aggregates composed of
disaggregated chalk mixed with fragments of *argile à silex*. At the contact
between grains, slight cementation between particles can be observed, as in the
middle part of the talus profile and it is this cementation that produces the
spongy microfabric. The upper part is finer grained, with a greater quantity of
aggregates, as in the bottom layer (no. 161). Noteworthy here are pieces of
bright yellow, angular clay papules, tightly mixed with some fine calcitic
material.

Interpretation of sample 162

The mixture of chalk and *argile à silex* is similar to that observed in the talus
profile, but here it is not as well sorted, thereby indicating that they were less
carefully selected. It is also possible that they were quarried from a slightly
different source or at a different depth.

(c/d): Samples 163/164

These have subangular–blocky to coarse–granular and open–spongy structure
with very high porosity (40%) formed by planes broadening into large vughs.
There is an abundant coarse fraction that includes mainly angular chert
fragments, bone, rounded chalk grains, decalcified loess and clay (from *argile à
silex*). The latter shows some reddening, probably from heating. The very fine
part of the coarse fraction is quite similar to that of the bottom unit (no. 161),

although the finer fraction here is much richer in charcoal (a few to 100 μm), which is responsible for imparting the dark colour to the unit. Under fluorescent light the fine fraction displays many finely divided yellow fragments and filaments.

Although the upper part grades perceptibly into a finer and darker material in the field, the change in thin section is much more marked. The finer coarse fraction is here a mixture of calcareous and non-calcareous loess, such as that observed in the loessial profile. In addition, this is much chalkier than the sediments at the bottom and there is no secondary cementation.

Interpretation of samples 163/164

As described above, these two units are basically similar to each other but differ from the basal unit. The greater amount of organic matter, some charcoal and decalcified loess, and less clay, point to a slightly different origin for this material. Furthermore, this lithological assemblage suggests a source close to an activity area within the site, where charcoal and organic matter would be concentrated and where partly decalcified loess would be exposed or available.

(dwyer): Sample 165

Loose, fine granular and generally fine-grained with compound packing voids. Though homogeneous in the field, it is microscopically quite heterogeneous, consisting of very loosely packed red clay balls, pieces of charcoal, bones, sherds, chalk fragments, quartz sand (some partially vitrified), clay papules, melted grass ashes, burnt fragments of paleosols and decalcified loess (Figure 14.5d).

Interpretation of sample 165

The grey colour of this unit results from the contribution of both the calcareous fine fraction and ashes. Noticeably, however, and unlike the units below, which contain mostly organic materials, this one represents a distinct variant, illustrated by the increased proportions of charcoal and the presence of typical ashes. It is also marked by the occurrence of burnt clay and melted ashes, which could have been derived, for example, from metal processing, such as found in Area I. Finally, the very loose, granular fabric, large compositional variety of coarse elements, lack of bedding in the field and total absence of pedogenic features suggest that it has been recently emplaced and possibly represents the backfill of Abbé Philippe's excavations. Such deposits were recently exposed during the 1986 field season.

In conclusion, it seems that the builders of this rampart used a variety of substances, which included fine, anthropogenically modified loessial sediments (no. 161), chalky materials, similar to those used in the rampart (no. 162), and mixtures of the two, enriched with charcoal in the fine fraction (no. 163/164). The uppermost layer (no. 165) is somewhat exceptional by its fabric and ash

and charcoal component which were presumably derived from a source different from those of the underlying rampart sediments, probably one associated
with metallurgical activities that have been recognised elsewhere at the site (e.g.,
Area I, which is not discussed here).

14.8 Concluding remarks

With these examples from Fort Harrouard we have attempted to illustrate how
micromorphology can be used to elucidate any number of issues involving
constructional activities associated with a large-scale settlement: talus and
rampart section and materials, metallurgical materials and associated dumps.
In addition, we could unequivocally clarify the nature and development of the
dark layer within the loess profile.

The wider ramifications for the archaeologist await fuller excavation of the
areas discussed and new loci yet to be excavated.

DARK EARTH

15.1 Introduction

This case study is presented as an example of how difficult it can be to investigate successfully, by standard analytical methods, heterogeneous human occupation deposits that occur so frequently in archaeology and how the application of soil micromorphology is the only way to interpret them properly.

'Dark earth' is the name given to urban occupation deposits which are dark-coloured and seemingly homogeneous. They are common to most cities with long histories, especially those in Europe of Medieval and earlier ancestry. Where urban sediments are waterlogged, the excavation of well-preserved wood structures and dumped refuse have provided a wealth of information for both archaeologists and palaeontologists concerning the lifestyle of early city dwellers, as at York (England) and Bergen (Norway). The origin and significance of such dark earth deposits in well-drained urban situations is less easy to explain, because the sediments are usually unstratified, c. 0.5–2 m thick and contain very few archaeological features. However, they are important, as they may represent 400–700 years of life in the city, spanning the Roman, through Saxon, Viking and Medieval periods in England (Brooks, 1986).

Dark earth commonly rests upon relic Roman floor levels and continues upwards into overlying post-Medieval deposits with little obvious layering (Merrifield, 1965; Grimes, 1968). The basal part may contain Roman coins, Roman burials and be cut through by later Roman buildings. Thus this part of the dark earth is undeniably of Roman date and cannot be dismissed purely as a Dark Age deposit (Sheldon, personal communication) and its understanding is therefore essential to the study of continuity in Roman towns and cities. Equally dark earth can be found to commence on mid-Saxon (c. 700AD) floors in London.

15.1.2 Archaeological character

Dark earth, called 'made earth' or 'dark-made earth' by Norman and Reader (1912), was found burying Roman surfaces and abutting Roman walls during early excavations of Roman London. Recently some attempts were made to excavate dark earth carefully, in its own right, but again only an occasional Saxon Grubenhausen or possible tip lines and spreads of concentrated inclusions and building debris were found (Roskams and Schofield, 1978; Roskams, 1981), probably because the dark colour of these deposits makes the identification of features difficult, although pottery assemblages do indicate accretion of the deposit (Orton, 1978).

Archaeological interpretation has variously ascribed dark earth to flood deposits, and to within-city-wall market gardening as the Roman city declined in the third to fourth centuries AD (Reece, 1980).

15.1.3 *Previous study methods*
Environmental analyses of dark earth have been exceptionally unrewarding, except to show that they contain some food waste (bone, oyster shells and rare charred cereal grains) and have sparse pollen spectra indicating waste ground (the strongly alkaline and oxidising conditions of the sediments causing very poor pollen preservation; Scaife in Macphail, 1981). However, the deposits can include moderately high quantities of phytoliths. Standard soil science analytical methods did not produce diagnostic results either. They showed only that:

> dark-earth sediments are exceedingly uniform in colour, being generally dark greyish-brown (10YR4/2) when dry and very dark grey (10YR3/11) when moist;
> the deposits display a mildly alkaline pH (7–8) and contain calcium carbonate (1–7%) and small amounts of organic matter (1–2% organic carbon);
> phosphate is commonly present and sorting is poor.

This characterisation of dark earth has not been of much use for either confirming or refuting clearly the archaeological interpretation for these ubiquitous sediments so far attempted.

15.2 **Present approach**
The major failing of the previous study methods was that they were incapable of overcoming the problems inherent in studying heterogeneous deposits typical of intensive human occupation, as here represented by dark earth. Such basic analyses could only produce average assays of all the constituents that can result from building, building decay, dumping and other waste disposal and human occupation in general, so that even the essential composition of the deposit was still very poorly understood. As a result, micromorphology was applied to overcome this problem of heterogeneity and to answer a series of major questions on the dark earth (Macphail and Courty, 1984).

15.2.1 *Unsolved questions*

(i)   What are the constituents of dark earth – for example, what makes the deposit so dark?
(ii) How uniform is dark earth from site to site and what mechanisms cause this apparent homogeneity?
(iii) How are these deposits related to the local geology and soils, and to the immediately underlying Roman deposits (*sensu stricto*); floors, walls etc.?
(iv) Does dark earth contain evidence of water sedimentation, cultivation or other environmental clues?

15.2.2 *Strategy*

Because it can be used to study undisturbed samples, micromorphology is the ideal technique for the investigation of these questions and, unlike some of the case studies that have been presented, it is clearly the best interpretive tool, probably benefiting little from other analyses. For example, coarse anthropic inclusions can be characterised and distinguished from the fine fabric, which itself can be interpreted in terms of formation by post-depositional – including pedogenic – processes that modify the original constituents. Similarly, materials such as calcium carbonate, which are measured in total in bulk analyses, can be divided into several groups – mortar/plaster, ashes from fires, biogenic calcite and neoformed calcite – to help understand the deposit. Also, as thin sections can sample across boundaries, the essential relationship between the Roman levels and the dark earth can be examined, and the cause of the dark colour isolated.

15.3 **Results**

A number of sites have now been studied in the City of London and in Southwark (the Roman London suburb south of the river Thames) and the sampling strategy can be summed up as follows.

Thin sections are made of (a) local parent materials, (b) imported building materials, i.e. clay floors, *opus signinum* ('concrete floors'), mortar, clay walls and associated plaster and daub, (c) deposits at the contact between the dark earth and the underlying identifiable cultural levels (floors, well-preserved collapsed walls, paths etc) and (d) the overlying dark earth. A number of sequences would be studied on a large complex site.

A hypothetical section would comprise (Figure 15.1):

> Nineteenth-century foundations
> Post-Medieval and Medieval layers and pits
> Dark earth
> Pale dark earth of Roman floors, wall foundations and wall collapse
> Natural sands and gravels

15.4 **General field characteristics**

1 0–70 cm Dark earth: very dark grey (10YR3/1 moist, 10YR4/2 dry) moderately weak sandy clay loam; weakly developed coarse subangular blocky structures; apparently humose; 20% gravel, oyster shell, bone, pottery, brickearth and mortar fragments etc.; common charcoal; common root holes and earthworm channels; clear, generally smooth boundary.
2 70–85 cm Pale dark earth: discontinuous very dark greyish-brown (10YR3/2 moist, 10YR4/3 dry) weak to firm, massive sandy loam; abundant brickearth and mortar fragments; few biological channels; generally sharp, smooth boundary.
3 85–95 cm Distinct Roman levels: strong brown (7.5YR5/6) massive silt (brickearth) floor (known as 'clay floors'), walls or pale brown (10YR6/3) *opus signinum* or mortar foundation (for tesselated floor) or mixed collapse; generally sharp, smooth or wavy boundary.

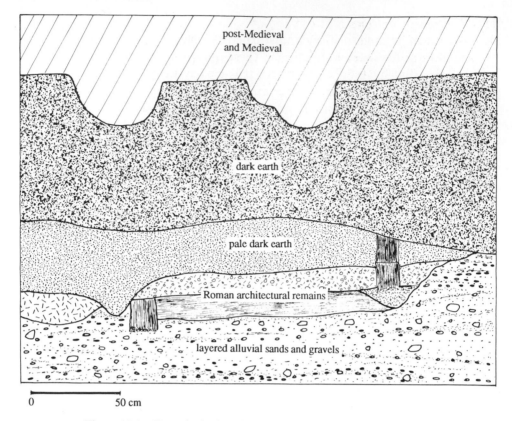

Figure 15.1   Hypothetical section at a dark earth site.

4   95–130 + cm Truncated soil (Bg horizon): light brown (7.5YR6/6) very weak sand with common ferruginous mottles; mainly free of anthropic materials except for small amounts of charcoal; structureless; common gravel; common root holes.

15.5 Micromorphology

1   *Dark earth* (Figure 15.2a; Plate VIIIb): Moderate homogeneity; structure is subangular blocky with intergrain microaggregate. Porosity is high (30%), compound packing pores, coarse channels and fine intergranular vughs and channels. C:F 55:45. coarse mineral as 2. Fine material is very dominant, very dark brown (PPL) commonly moderate to high birefringence (XPL) with dark brown or grey (ashy) in OIL; very thin pale brown, low birefringent areas, or greyish-brown highly birefringent features with 'loose' gravel inclusions, clear fragments of pottery, burned brickearth etc. Organic matter is very abundant as fine 'gramineae' charred material (Figure 15.2b), phytoliths common. Fine ash crystals can be present. Pedofeatures in addition to nodules and vivianite, few dusty clay coatings occur. Fabric is strongly homogeneous, with common fine organo-mineral (probable Echytraeids) excrements. Few pale earthworm excrements. Slug granules also present.

2   *Pale dark earth:* Strongly heterogeneous; intergrain microaggregate structure, 25% porosity as coarse packing voids (around large inclusions), few coarse faunal

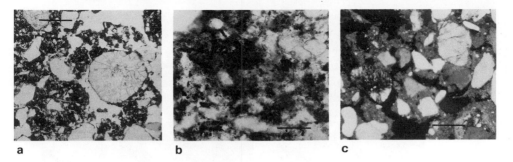

a   b   c

Figure 15.2   Dark earth:
(a) Microaggregate fabric of very dark brown fine mineral material containing silt; mineral skeleton consists of fine and medium sand and coarse biogenic radial calcite, probably a slug granule. PPL. (Bar = 550 μm)

(b) Dark earth: detail showing 'thin' mineral fine fabric and very abundant fine charred organic matter which gives this deposit its characteristic dark colour. PPL. (Bar = 250 μm)

(c) Pale dark earth: fragment of mortar comprising medium and coarse sand grains set in a highly birefringent calcitic cement; dissolution of this cement is responsible for the development of the porosity and ultimately will lead to the liberation of coarse skeleton grains to the deposit. XPL. (Bar = 550 μm)

channels; low porosity (10–15%) within fine fabric. C:F,65:35; coarse material as dominantly fine and medium sand-sized quartz, with this size sand also present in common inclusions of brickearth (see 3), whereas fragments of mortar contain gravel and coarse sand, and plaster contains very fine sand (Figure 15.2c). Fine fabric is mainly brown, moderately low birefringence, brown (OIL), although within coarse channels it is dark brown, moderately high birefringence (crystallitic), dark brown (OIL). Both mortar and plaster have high birefringent (crystallitic) characters. Fragments of brickearth and daub can have pseudomorphic porosity of plant tempering and show reddish colours (OIL) from being burned. Wood charcoal and associated calcite ash crystals can be related to burned brickearth. Fine 'gramineae' charcoal occurs in the darker fine fabrics, together with common phytoliths. Coprolitic brown amorphous organic matter can also be present between floors and collapse. Pedofeatures include dusty clay coatings associated with charcoal and ash areas; extreme fabric heterogeneity; amorphous ferruginous nodules and crystalline vivianite present. Two types of excrements occur: few pale brown coarse mammilated mineral (probable earthworm) excrements and dark brown, organo-mineral (probable Enchytraeids) excrements. Biogenic radial calcite features (*Arionid* – slugs) also occur.

3   *Distinct Roman levels e.g. brickearth floor* (see Figure 15.3a): Mainly homogeneous; massive microstructure; low (10%) porosity of smooth wall medium vughs and few fine channels. C:F is 6:4; coarse material is very dominantly silt-sized quartz; fine is dark reddish-brown, moderately birefringent, pale yellow (OIL). Pedofeatures comprise void clay coatings not oriented to present-day vertical way-up (coatings are therefore relic and relate to the original brickearth source), and fine ferruginous nodules. Occasional coarse channels contain large mammilated earthworm excrements of fine soil resembling dark earth (from above) but it is paler because organic matter other than charcoal has been digested.

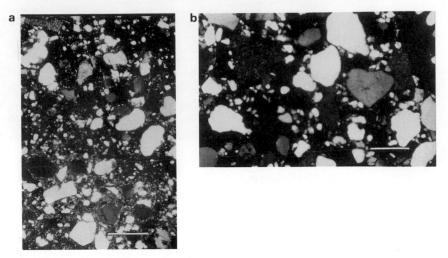

Figure 15.3   (a) Junction of dark earth and underlying Roman brickearth floor. The birefringence of the dark earth is masked by organic matter as compared to the speckled and granostriated birefringence of the clay-rich brick earth. XPL. (Bar = 550 μm)

(b) Bg horizon (local parent material alluvial sands); note fine and medium sands of quartz and flint separated by compound packing pores, and marked absence of any birefringent fine fabric. XPL. (Bar = 550 μm)

4   *Bg* (local parent material–alluvial sands, Figure 15.3b): Homogeneous; structure is single grain to microaggregate, with 20% porosity mainly of compound packing pores. Mineral fraction comprises 90% coarse material; fine and medium quartz sand, with fine brown non-birefringent, pale orange (OIL) coatings and infills of ferro-manganese character. Only occasional organic matter and charcoal. Main pedofeatures are rare impure clay coatings and abundant amorphous ferruginous nodules and coatings.

15.6 Discussion

15.6.1 *Sediment source*

These include (a) from the underlying alluvial geology: sands and gravels; (b) from the anthropic mineral materials (see below): silts and clays from the breakdown of imported brickearth 'clay' floors and wall-building materials, so-called 'pea-grit' or gravels from the local geology and also liberated from mortar as the calcite cement weathered (also pale yellow-brown thin fabrics, which appeared to be relic of weathered [decalcified] plaster); and (c) from the organic anthropogenic constituents: coarse wood charcoal, fine flaky 'grass' charcoal, phytoliths, oyster shells, bones and coprolites.

15.6.2 *Anthropogenic materials*

These are: (a) mortar or *opus signinum* composed of large sand to gravel-sized mineral inclusions (flint, rock, quartz, brickearth and pottery fragments etc.)

set in a calcite cement; (b) plaster, which differs by having only fine sand-sized inclusions in a calcite matrix; (c) 'clay wall' and 'clay floor', which are in reality a silt loam brickearth material quarried in the City of London but imported into Southwark (for substantial timber-framed buildings; Sheldon, 1978), that may feature pseudomorphic porosity of coarse plant tempering (textural pedofeatures in this are mainly relic to the origins of this natural sediment); (d) mud daub fabrics, which, unlike the brickearth, are rich in included fine 'grassy' organic matter and charcoal, but essentially have the mineral composition of brickearth and thus are interpreted as anthropically reworked brickearth; (e) charcoal and ash from collapse and destruction by burning and regular domestic fires in an occupation area – perhaps some fine charcoal blowing around as found in 2 cm of dark earth between a floor and wall collapse (continual anthropogenic reworking of 'brickearth daub' with local organic matter, much of it charred, for the building of insubstantial mud huts contributing to the overall dark colour of the deposit); and (f) coprolitic materials, including both organic-rich rodent-like and phosphate/bone-rich probable human (associated Nematode egg analysis, De Rouffignac, personal communication) coprolites found on old floor surfaces preserved by collapse.

15.6.3 *Biological activity*
The waste ground (as inferred by pollen) and domestic refuse environment was frequented by slugs (*Arionid* granules) and Enchytraeids, and probably rooted by small shrubs such as elder (*sambucus*; seed evidence); such biological action reworked the organic-rich daub material producing the typical dark micro-aggregate structure of the dark earth. In contrast, earthworm activity appears to have been less important at the time of initial accumulation, but was later more effective as a post-depositional mechanism, perforating through the rather organically 'sterile' Roman and pale dark-earth levels from Medieval gardens. Its effects are distinguished by the total removal of non-charred organic matter in the coarse mammilated excrements.

15.6.4 *Weathering*
Although the dark earth has a mildly alkaline environment, minor decalcification was noted in the biogenic calcite of *Arionid* granules, which showed some evidence of dissolution. Equally, the fine calcitic cement of some mortar was seen to be dissolving around the coarse mineral inclusions and, as noted earlier, liberating gravel and sand into the deposit as a whole. Weathering effects in addition produced decalcification and local mobilisation of phosphates from ash (also bone and coprolites), producing neoformed vivianite in less well-drained situations.

15.6.5 *Sedimentary features and site usage*
There is no evidence of water sorting or sedimentation, although urban soils were dumped as embankments against the river Thames. There is also little

clear evidence of cultivation. At its base the dark earth undoubtedly originates from building decay and destruction, local clay coatings being ash-related. Further up, the dark earth is uniquely homogeneous through biological mixing, Enchytraeids seemingly the most important agency. Phases of garden-soil digging may have been contributary, but only as a secondary effect.

15.6.6 *Summary*

Local parent materials were recognised from the underlying sands and gravels, whereas relatively pure building materials dominated the distinct Roman levels. It was in the pale dark earth that these primary constituents could be seen juxtaposed to the more organic daub fabrics and all the materials and features deriving from the anthropogenic usage of the site, e.g., burning and building collapse. These were only moderately reworked by human and other biological factors. In the dark earth proper, repeated anthropogenic re-use of earlier building materials with increments of organic matter for insubstantial huts, and intensive on-site faunal activity and some weathering, have produced the dark earth as we now see it. Unlike the pale dark earth, which may vary in detail both across a site and from site to site, the dark earth itself is extremely uniform. A sample from Southwark is identical to one from the City of London, as presumed Roman dark earth is the same as known mid-Saxon dark earth. The mechanisms responsible for dark earth as discussed above are therefore also likely to be ubiquitous, telling us a great deal about city life during some periods of its history.

15.7 **Conclusions**

Dark earth on many London sites can be shown to have arisen as the result of the accretion of building decay materials from timber-framed buildings and insubstantial mud huts in an environment in which occupation refuse materials were mixed with them, mainly through biological activity. Of especial archaeological significance is that on many sites in London the deposits, when dated by coins and various building constructions to the third to fourth centuries AD, suggest a rather intensive but poor lifestyle in this city, when many of the richer Romans had left urban areas for villa life during the latter part of Roman England (Reece, 1980).

Micromorphology identified the source of the mineral and organic components and classified them as debris of both substantial and insubstantial buildings. The dark homogenised fabric resulting from the mixing of domestic wastes, including 'gramineae' charcoal and airborne charcoal from fires, with decayed mud-walled and mud-floored huts, occurs through rooting and faunal mixing, garden cultivation perhaps a later effect enhancing the biological activity.

HUMAN SETTLEMENT PATTERNS AND HOLOCENE ENVIRONMENTS IN THE GHAGGAR PLAIN (NORTHWEST INDIA)

16.1 The archaeological context

Around the third millennium BC, agrarian protohistoric societies started to spread extensively across the fertile alluvial plains of the Indus Basin; earlier agriculture, however, had been mainly practised on the hilly piedmont and in small valleys. This gradual expansion reached its peak with the Harappan civilisation, nuclear sites being dated to *c.* 2300–2000 BC (Agrawal and Sood, 1979). Although the most prestigious Harappan cities are located along the course of the Indus river (e.g., Mohenjo-Daro) and its tributaries (e.g., Harappa), a large number of Harappan settlements have also been found in the Ghaggar plain, a region which is not presently crossed by Himalayan rivers. Palaeobotanical records, however, suggest that Harappan populations were mostly dependent upon winter cereals (wheat, barley), which cannot tolerate semi-arid monsoonal conditions (present climate of the region) because of insufficient moisture at the seeding period. The preferential location of Harappan settlements along two supposed major water courses (Figure 16.1) – called in the Holy texts the Sarasvati and the Drishadvati – has provided arguments to suggest rivers originating from the Himalaya were flowing across this area during the protohistoric period (third and second millennia BC), offering a perennial water supply essential to settled agriculture. Indeed, observation of aerial photographs and satellite imagery have confirmed the existence of two large palaeochannels crossing the Ghaggar plain (Pal *et al.*, 1981), although no old water courses were traced in the field, probably because of masking by extensive spreads of sand dunes which cover this alluvial plain.

The well-organised social system of the Harappan civilisation deteriorated around 1800 BC, as suggested for example by the observation of an architectural decline, and a retrogression into small farming communities (Leshnik, 1973). At the same time, population movements to the east (Ganga–Yamuna basin) and south (Rann of Kutch) also seem to have occurred (Leshnik, 1973). These social changes have been explained by deterioration of the hydrographic network, starting with rivers changing their courses at the end of the protohistoric period (possibly because of tectonic activity), and finishing with them totally drying up during historical times (*c.* first millennium AD), (Agrawal, 1982). In addition, the spectacular extension of the Harappan civilisation has been correlated with a supposed period of climatic amelioration, whereas its

269

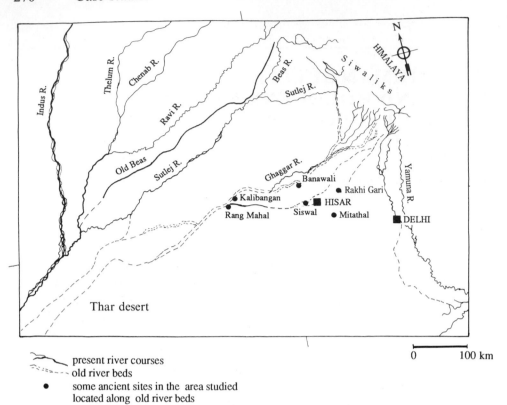

Figure 16.1   Present river systems and traces of old river beds (using satellite imagery) in the eastern Indus Basin. (After Pal *et al.*, 1981). The arrow indicates the general study area.

decline has been associated with a reversion to dry, semi-arid conditions (Singh, 1971). The different alternative explanations have given rise to impassioned debates but so far insufficient evidence has been collected to distinguish clearly the influence of environmental parameters on protohistoric populations.

16.2 Study strategy

16.2.1 *The questions*

The aims of the investigations carried out by the Franco–Indian archaeological mission (1983–1987; in Francfort, 1985) were to gain more information on the protohistoric farming systems and to evaluate the influence of natural constraints (hydrographic network, climate) on human settlement patterns in the Ghaggar plain.

More specific issues involved the following:

> Recognition of the fossil hydrographic network: When were these rivers active? How and when did they dry up?
>
> Reconstruction of the Holocene climatic events: Were the climatic fluctuations known elsewhere from similar latitudes recorded in the Ghaggar plain? Had these

changes any influence on the evolution of the hydrographic network? What is the evidence that supports the theory of an increase in desertic conditions during the late Holocene?

Estimation of the agricultural potential of the protohistoric soils: Were there any differences from the present-day soils? Were they capable of maintaining a suitable moisture regime for the growth of winter crops?

16.2.2 *Approach*

A detailed archaeological survey has permitted the history of human settlement to be reconstructed and this has provided the essential base for approaching these questions logically. In addition, geoarchaeological data have been collected in close association with the archaeological findings, including, for example, physical characteristics (hydrographic network, nature of sediments and soils) of the region in areas both rich and nearly devoid of protohistoric settlements.

Numerous deep unbricked tube-wells (*c.* 10 m) have provided access for surveying the entire area in order to reconstruct both relative and chronological stratigraphic sequences of Holocene sedimentary events. Present-day soil profiles from the various landform units were compared with soils buried below archaeological sites belonging to both historic and protohistoric periods. Deposits from ancient canals and occupation layers were also studied to help identify sediments, soils and organic materials related to human activities.

Micromorphology provided the means of characterising rapidly the different sedimentary facies and recognising post-depositional processes which have affected Holocene sediments in this area. Only the main results necessary for understanding the interpretations are given.

16.3 **Physical characteristics of the area**

The area is situated at the border zone between the northern alluvial plain *sensu stricto* and the southern sand area (northeastern margin of the Thar desert) (Figure 16.1). This partly explains the complexity of the stratigraphic sequences, since the whole region has been alternately influenced by the Himalaya mountains and the Thar desert. This explains the evolution of stratigraphic sequences from northeast to southwest. We discuss here only the sequences from the alluvial plain itself.

The alluvial plain is bounded by two Himalayan rivers, the Sutlej and the Yamuna, which are supposed to have crossed the Ghaggar plain during the protohistoric period (see above and Figure 16.1; Agrawal, 1982). This hypothesis would only be confirmed by the recognition of alluvium in the Ghaggar plain similar to that of the active Himalayan rivers. The Ghaggar, which is now flowing in the northern part of the plain, has its origin in the Siwaliks, the southern piedmont of the Himalaya. Unfortunately, there is little mineralogical difference between Himalayan and Siwalik alluvia, since both were derived from the Himalaya. Both consist mainly of sand derived from metamorphic rocks, although micaceous silts and cemented calcareous bands are specific features of the Siwalik formations. The main contrast between the two river systems is their differing hydraulic regime: Himalayan streams are perennial whereas piedmont systems have an irregular hydric regime dependent on the summer monsoons.

16.4 Reconstruction of sedimentary events

In the alluvial plain three major stratigraphic units were recognised in the studied sequences (Figure 16.2).

16.4.1 *Lower unit*

In the deepest sections, massive, grey sands are present at an average depth of 10 m, varying between 8 to 10 m. (1) Through micromorphology it was noted that the proportion of quartz sand grains is always high (*c.* 40%), and the significant characteristic is the abundance of weatherable minerals (biotites, hornblende) and of grains derived from schistous rocks; grains of calcite are nearly absent (Figure 16.2b). Within the deposit sand grains are loosely packed and randomly distributed. They are moderately sorted and their size averages 150 μm. Subangular grains predominate. Under SEM, quartz sand grains exhibit a fresh but irregular surface with fractures.

Mineralogy and shape of the grey sands show that they are of metamorphic origin and were deposited by the stream under high flow velocities. They also have the same characteristics as sediments forming in the active flood plain of the Yamuna. We can thus conclude that the grey sands have been deposited by Himalayan rivers with a hydraulic regime similar to the present Yamuna.

Unfortunately, in the absence of large exposed sections of this basal sequence we cannot give more information on this earlier river system.

16.4.2 *Middle unit*

The overlying sedimentary deposits form a 6-m thick sequence consisting of alternating massive bands of variable grain sizes. These sediments may be roughly grouped into three subsets:

1   At the bottom, densely packed, massive grey micaceous loamy sand (100 μm) that may also include centimetre-thick layers of micaceous silty clay.

   The sands are angular, generally well sorted and are noteworthy for their abundance of detrital calcite particles and the high proportion of bedded, long (250 μm) mica flakes, both biotite and muscovite (Figure 16.2c). Their minimum thickness averages 4 m but may increase where grey sands are deeper.

2   In the middle are loosely packed, structureless yellow to grey fine sands (100 μm), which differ from the underlying sediments by the smaller quantity and the marked rounding of sand grains, especially calcite and mica grains, and by the random orientation of sands (Figure 16.2c). They form a well-expressed band (*c.* 2 m

---

[1] Their exact thickness is unknown but these sands have been observed by well-diggers down to 60 m.

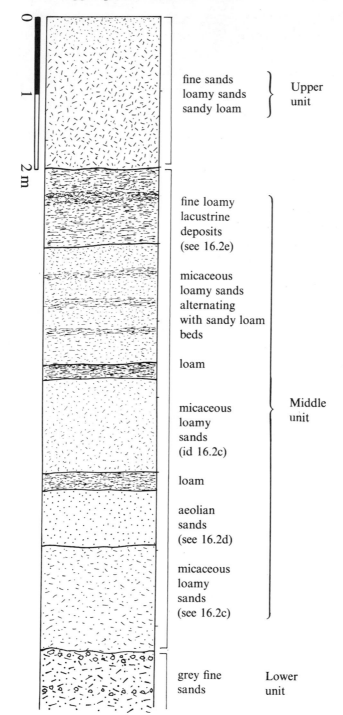

Figure 16.2   (a) Schematic representation of the stratigraphic sequence in the alluvial plain *sensu stricto*.

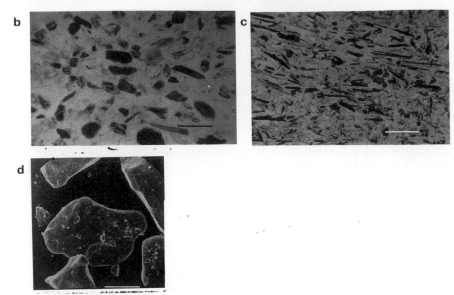

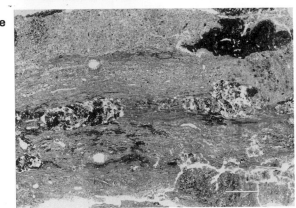

(b) Microscopic characteristics of the grey fine sands occurring at the bottom of the sequence. PPL. (Bar = 150 μm)

(c) Massive grey micaceous loamy sand, bottom of the middle sequence. Note the clear difference with (b): in this case abundance of long mica flakes suggests short-distance low-energy transport, thus eliminating a Himalayan origin of the alluvium. PPL. (Bar = 150 μm)

(d) Alluvial sands similar to (c) reworked by wind, seen under the SEM (quartz, mica and feldspars). Note the rounded edges although the original angular shape can still be recognised. (Bar = 50 μm)

(e) Fine loamy lacustrine deposits highly reworked by biological activity. PPL. (Bar = 5 mm)

thick) in the southern part of the plain (Hisar area), where they have a yellow field colour, which is due to the scarcity of calcite and mica particles, but their thickness decreases to the north, where they are grey because mica and calcite sand grains are more abundant.

3 The last subset at the top consists of an alternation of massive micaceous sandy loam (*c*. 40 cm thick) and silty clay bands (*c*. 20 cm thick), which, in spite of their finer texture, have a mineralogical composition similar to that of the lower loamy sand. Mica flakes are always abundant and commonly horizontally bedded (see Figure 6.4d).

Loam rich in calcite and in fine sand-sized mica particles forms the transition with the overlying sediments. Locally they may grade to thin silty clay beds (20 cm thick), rich in secondary gypsum and interbedded with fine-grained calcareous lacustrine sediments (Figure 16.2e).

The hypothesis of a direct Himalayan origin of these sediments is unlikely when we consider the abundance of fragile minerals (calcite and micas) and their small size in the lower and upper subsets. On the other hand, an alluvial nature finds support in the horizontal orientation of mica particles. Furthermore, the interbedded character of this alluvial sequence reflects a variability of flow intensities and complements the mineralogical arguments that these sediments were deposited by rivers originating in the Siwaliks.

Can the reconstruction of the hydrographic network be taken any further at this time? Although the succession of the alluvial beds varies from site to site, these alluvial deposits have always been observed, which would indicate that the Ghaggar plain was swept by numerous wandering channels.

The aggradation of the alluvial plain was interrupted by an aeolian episode, as shown by the rounded shape of sands forming the middle subset. One obvious question is: Do these sand dunes result from a penetration of the Thar desert into the plain? The similar mineralogy of the lower and middle subsets would more strongly support the hypothesis that the earlier alluvium was locally winnowed, while there is no real argument for long-distance transport. The former theory is more reasonable, considering the high content of easily weatherable minerals, which are only a little finer than more resistant mineral types.

The sequence ends with sedimentation in low-energy environments, highly charged in calcium carbonate. Drainage was limited and water accumulated in slight depressions, where chemical precipitation of gypsum and calcium carbonate could occur with evaporation.

16.4.3 *Upper sequence*
Description
The sediments forming the upper four metres are very variable, though the most common features can be outlined.

1 Where the Ghaggar plain is regularly flat, the upper sequence consists predominantly of massive brown sandy loam and loamy sand with a variable amount of

calcium carbonate (from 5 to 10%), which occurs as detrital micritic sand grains and fine calcite particles. Mica flakes are abundant but commonly have rounded edges and are smaller than those in the underlying alluvium. In contrast to the latter, fine sand grains are subrounded. The sandy loam grades upwards to weakly structured calcareous yellowish-brown loamy sands characterised by increasing roundness of the fine sands and by a decrease in the amount of mica and micrite sand grains. This evolutionary trend ends as structureless fine sands (Figure 16.3a) in dune areas. At the base they still retain a few mica and micrite sand grains which, moreover, are well rounded, whereas these fragile grains are nearly absent in the top part.

2 In what was considered to be the dry beds of ancient rivers, massive, non-calcareous loams are present, although they always contain fine subrounded quartz sand grains similar to the coarser fraction of the surrounding sandy loam. In slight depressions, loam (Figure 16.3b) and sands are horizontally bedded and features indicating high moisture content such as polyconcave walls of biological channels showing signs of structural collapse, can be observed in thin section.

All the layers of the upper sequence have been intensively reworked by biological activity.

16.4.4 *Interpretation*

In contrast to the regularity characterising the succession of the previous sequences, the variability of the facies over the entire area shows that the earlier alluvial plain was slowly shaped through the combined action of floods and wind, which gave rise to the geomorphological units now forming the present-day landscape.

Effects of floods were prominent only along two major depressions, which in fact correspond to what have been described as the ancient courses of the Sarasvati and Drishadvati. Silting up of these water courses, which preferentially drained monsoonal rains, is combined with the gradual infilling of the depressions by aeolian activity, as shown by the addition of subrounded sand grains to the flood loam.

Between the depressions, effects of floods are considerably reduced while earlier-deposited alluvium was reworked by moderate winds. The gradual scarcity of mica flakes, their decreasing size and their worn edges supports the conjecture that input of fresh alluvium from the Siwaliks has ceased. Thus the wind action results in the physical destruction of less resistant minerals.

16.4.5 *Relative chronology of the recent sedimentary events recorded in the Ghaggar plain (Table 16.1)*

The dating of the Ghaggar plain sequence is essentially relative. Only calcium carbonate nodules, which are present in the upper sequence, could have been dated by the radiocarbon method, but abundance of detrital calcite particles has rendered them unsuitable. Nevertheless, we note the following relationships between well-dated cultural entities and the stratigraphic sequences.

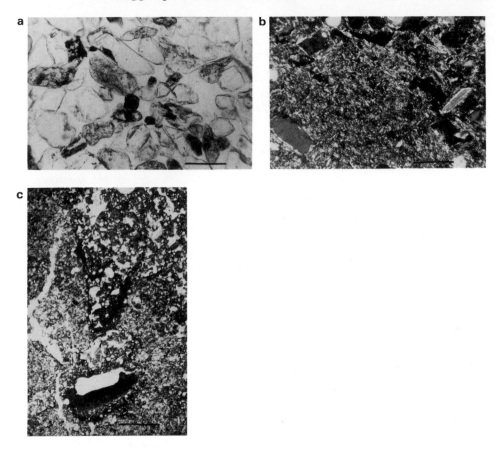

Figure 16.3   (a) Structureless fine sands from dune area: note their clearly expressed subrounded shape and the smaller size of easily weatherable minerals such as mica (dark grains). PPL. (Bar = 70 μm)

   (b) Latest sediments deposited in the depressions: non-calcareous micaceous silt mixed with fine sands characterised by a striated micaceous b-fabric formed by repeated wetting–drying. Latest flood deposits filling the south depression (called Drishadvati or Chautang), which were possibly deposited during the historic period (based on the archaeological remains occurring in these sediments). XPL. (Bar = 150 μm)

   (c) Microlayered textural feature formed in a biological channel in a sandy loam soil. These features are also called flood coatings because they appear when soils are flooded (natural floods or under flood irrigation). Although indicating vertical translocation of solid particles, no significant loss is recorded in the upper horizon because of the continuous biological mixing. The situation is rather different in lighter textured soils (see next). PPL. (Bar = 500 μm)

Table 16.1. *Relative chronology of the recent sedimentary events recorded in the Ghaggar plain*

1 Regular fluvial activity (rivers originated from Himalaya)
2 Gradual drying of the rivers and increasing aeolian activity. Major extension of the Thar desert (probably during the Late-Glacial maximum)
3 Fluvial activity (rivers originated from the Siwaliks), simultaneous aeolian reworking of the inter-fluvial flood plain
4 End of the regular alluvial activity, seasonal floods along two major depressions. Increasing wind activity (phase occurring just before the protohistoric period).
5 Gradual decrease of the floods up to complete filling of the two depressions. Continuous wind activity.

Sediments observed below protohistoric sites of the Harappan tradition are always found in the upper part of the stratigraphic sequence, although the settlement may have been situated in a variety of environments (Banawali in an area of stablised flood plain slightly reworked by wind, Siswal on juvenile sand dunes, Mitathal in a dried-out depression, for example; see location of these sites on Figure 16.1).
Aeolian fine sands forming the topmost part of the upper sequence were recognised below historic sites.
Deposits more than 7 m thick always separate protohistoric sites from Yamuna-like alluvium derived from large and perennial Himalayan rivers. The sequence in between has already been ascribed to an irregular and lowered alluvial activity, interrupted by a major aeolian event (see above). The latter could possibly correspond to the maximum aridity recorded in the Thar desert at the end of the late Pleistocene (Allchin *et al.*, 1978). In addition to the more sluggish hydraulic regime indicated by the change in alluviation, the formation of sand dunes seems to have played an important role in the disorganisation of rivers, forcing them to shift either further west or further south. The two transversal dry river courses observed would relate to this event, when waters flowing from the Siwaliks would have been diverted further west. Most importantly the study shows the two depressions have never been Himalayan rivers.

The occurrence of grey Yamuna sands just below the present-day flood plain in the surrounding of Mitathal, reported by Bhan (1975), led to the erroneous conclusion that Yamuna was initially flowing; the area has now been explained with the help of micromorphology. The typical alluvial grey sands present at the base of the sequence cannot be mistaken in thin section for the thin grey loamy sand beds produced by seasonal floods during the formation of the upper sequence.

The protohistoric populations thus colonised a rather well-stabilised alluvial plain. It is believed that proximity to the soil surface of fine alluvium helped in maintaining a high level of fertility and good water retention necessary for a settled agriculture. This gave a high agricultural potential to the soils covering the region at this time.

Subsequently, the alluvial plain was continuously reworked by moderate winds which gradually modified the character of superficial sediments. The influence of this sediment and landscape evolution on the properties of soils formed since the protohistoric period is now considered.

16.5 **Holocene evolution of soils and their agricultural potentials**
The abundance of pedological features in sediments forming the upper sedimentary sequence demonstrates that the alluvial landscape stabilised just before the protohistoric period. Comparing buried and present-day soils, we see no significant differences in the nature of pedological processes, which always comprise biological activity, accumulation of calcium carbonate and, to a lesser extent, translocation of solid particles.

Although significant differences in the abundance of the related kinds of features and in the degree of soil development are commonly observed in thin section, they always seem to be influenced by the nature of parent materials upon which soil profiles were developed. This interrelationship is highly important in understanding the genesis of calcium carbonate nodules, whose occurrence has commonly been considered in the region as the testimony of semi-arid conditions, more humid than present-day ones (Agrawal and Sood, 1979).

16.5.1 *The secondary accumulation of calcium carbonate*
Calcic horizons with well-expressed calcium carbonate nodules are present in soils buried below protohistoric sites and also at moderate depths (*c.* 1 m) below the present soil surface. In both cases, micromorphology reveals a sedimentary discontinuity at the calcic horizon boundary, which is scarcely recognisable in the field or by standard analytical techniques because the junction is strongly affected by biological mixing. Secondary accumulation of calcium carbonate preferentially influences the calcareous loam underlying the sandy loam (Figure 16.4) because water percolating easily through the well-drained upper solum is trapped in the lower fine-textured layer and evaporates there.

In fact, the development of calcitic nodules is more poorly developed as the sediments coarsen. For example, soil profiles formed on thicker sandy loam still contain a few calcitic nodules, whereas in loamy sands and fine sands, only weakly expressed calcitic features – mostly hypocoatings and small nodules in biological pores – occur. This decrease is correlated with the gradual loss in calcium carbonate noted from the sandy loam to the upper fine sands as the result of wind winnowing. Thus, soil profiles developed on sand dunes buried below historic sites (e.g., Agroha dated 400 BC for the bottom part; Courty and Fedoroff, 1985) may present a weakly developed calcic horizon because the parent material still contains *c.* 10% detrital calcium carbonate grains but the absence of this calcareous material in the most recent sand dunes – caused by complete wind ablation – explains the non-existence of calcitic features here. The occurrence of well-developed calcitic nodules in dumped clearing materials from later historical canals dug in calcareous loam is further confirmation that

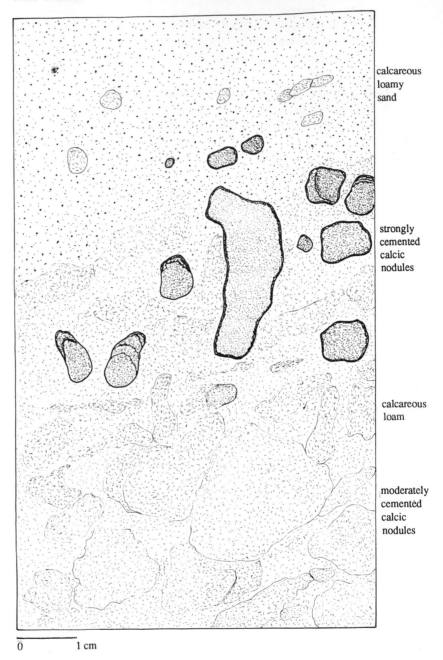

calcareous
loamy
sand

strongly
cemented
calcic
nodules

calcareous
loam

moderately
cemented
calcic
nodules

0   1 cm

Figure 16.4   Contact between the calcareous loam (latest flood events recorded in the interfluvial plain) and the upper weakly calcareous loamy sand: preferential retention of water in the lower fine-grained sediments induces the formation of calcitic nodules at the boundary between the two layers (caused by strong evaporation under these semi-arid climatic conditions). These are not pedogenic nodules *sensu stricto*, although their formation is influenced by pedological processes.

secondary accumulation of calcium carbonate may develop rapidly and is strongly influenced by local factors (soil moisture, calcium carbonate content) (Courty *et al.*, 1987).

16.5.2 *Role of biological activity*
The most prominent effects of biological activity are observed in sandy loam soils. These exhibit well-developed channel microstructures throughout their entire profile, pointing to the repeated passage of the soil fauna. Primary sedimentary layering has been completely obliterated and most of the ground-mass has been transformed by the soil fauna into rather highly cohesive fine aggregates that explain the good structural stability of these sandy loam soils. Biological mixing also plays an important role by counteracting the effects of vertical translocation of solid particles, as shown by the occurrence of textural features in some channels (Figure 16.3c). Therefore no significant loss in fine particles was detected in the upper horizons, which consequently maintain a high level of fertility.

Biological features are also abundant in loam soils but the channel microstructure commonly appears collapsed (see Plate Va). In addition, ferruginous impregnations of the groundmass and ferruginised biotites are present. Because of their fine texture and their preferential location in slight depressions where rains accumulate, these loamy soils are seasonally affected by waterlogging. Although they are fertile, these soils are highly compacted and thus suffer from oxygen deficiency.

The number of biological features is significantly lower in light-textured soils by comparison with sandy loam soils. In soils developed on fine sands only a few channels commonly infilled with loose sands occur. The decline of biological activity in these soils may be interpreted as the consequence of a rapid drying of sandy upper horizons after the wet season, which reduces movements of the soil fauna to the deep, perennially humid subsoil. Concomitantly, less excrement is produced and cohesion between soil particles is only moderate to weak, thus affecting soil stability and lessening resistance to wind erosion. Thus the sandy loam soils are the most biologically active and also the most stable. In the case of lighter soils, biological activity can no longer ameliorate the soil structure and can sometimes lead to the reverse effect, as suggested by the presence of loose sandy infilling of biological channels. Any accumulation of fine sands at the soil surface caused by wind winnowing also seems to be integrated into the underlying horizons by biological activity (Figure 16.5).

16.5.3 *Evolution of the agricultural potential of soils since the protohistoric period*
In summary, the combined role of aeolian winnowing and soil-forming pro-cesses has resulted in textural degradation of soils formed since the protohis-toric period. This has reduced the fertility and the water-retention capacity

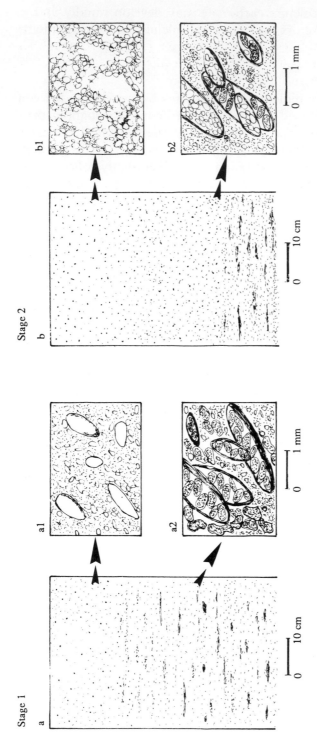

Figure 16.5   Textural degradation of loamy sand soils caused by the combined effects of wind winnowing and biological activity:

(a) Stage 1: thin loamy sand mantle overlying fine-grained flood deposits. Although light in texture, the upper sandy horizon is well structured (biological channels coated with fine fraction) and rather resistant to the action of wind (see a1). The lower part (see a2) has a very well-developed channel microstructure (this would be called in agronomy a 'self-mulching' soil). The underlying fine-textured horizon has a high moisture retention and evaporation loss is reduced by the presence of the upper loamy sand layer. This kind of soil offers rather good potential for dryland farming (no water supply) because it can retain for several months moisture accumulated during the monsoon period.

(b) Stage 2: following an increase in wind action and subsequent accumulation of aeolian fine sands on soils similar to (a). The light-textured upper horizon (see b1) has a channel microstructure but is weakly resistant to wind action (compared to a1) because of the low fine fraction content (absence of fine fraction plastering channels and weak bounds between fine sand grains). The underlying loamy sand horizon (see b1) has an abundance of fine fraction and well-developed channel microstructure; however, abundant channels are filled with loose sands coming from the upper part and integrated to the lower part by biological activity. Compared to (a), the vertical losses of water and fine particles are considerably increased and resistance of the soil surface to wind is consequently reduced.

because of the loss of fine particles. Thus, since the protohistoric period, when most of the Ghaggar plain was covered with sandy loam soils of high agricultural potential, lighter-textured soils have gradually gained ground, inducing local populations to utilise artificial irrigation in order to balance the water deficit.

16.6 Conclusions

To what extent was the study able to answer the questions initially posed?

Field observations and micromorphology have provided clear arguments on the non-contemporaneity of the protohistoric populations with Himalayan rivers. The latter have indeed been active in the past in the Ghaggar plain but the depth of this alluvium suggests that they are some tens of thousands years older than the protohistoric period.

The gradual desiccation of this hydrographic network has yet to be correlated with late Pleistocene climatic events, although this is beyond the scope of the present chapter.

The palaeochannels were indeed active before the protohistoric period, draining water derived from the Siwaliks and monsoonal rainfall. Thus they were seasonally flooded.

Since the protohistoric period, depressions in the previously formed alluvial plain were gradually filled by the combined effects of silting up and wind activity. Although dunes have gradually formed since then, no evidence exists to suggest the influence of a significant environmental change to account for the degradation of the soils. Micromorphology indicates that this soil degradation is self-accelerated because of the combined effect of wind and biological activity. The resulting loss of fertility is, however, moderate because wind strength is too weak to eliminate totally the weatherable minerals, but the poor water retention of the fine sandy soils is a more important limiting factor for agricultural exploitation.

RURAL SETTLEMENT AT CASTELLARO DI USCIO, GENOA (LIGURIA) ITALY

17.1 Introduction

The unique nature of the Castellaro di Uscio is manifested in the rare sequence of multiphase prehistoric deposits that occur on this mountain-top site in the severely dissected and steeply sloping Ligurian Apennines. Uscio contains the only stratified sequence of Chalcolithic, Late Bronze Age and Iron Age sediments and is probably the most important late-prehistoric open-air site in eastern Liguria (Maggi *et al.*, 1982, in press; Maggi, 1983; Melli, 1983). Previously, Apennine occupation has been mainly described from the Castellaro di Zignago (*c.* 700 m; Bronze Age/Iron Age; Mannoni & Tizzoni, 1980) and from Suvero (600 m; Neolithic/Bronze Age; Maggi 1984) (Figure 17.1). In addition, recent palynological studies (Cruise, 1987) from newly found Apennine peat sites (e.g., Prato Mollo, Lago Nero) are providing a regional environmental background, especially to the dramatic events of the Chalcolithic (see Chapter 18). Although soil micromorphology has been applied to the deposits at Zignago and Suvero (Macphail, 1987, in press), the nature of these sites has so far permitted only spot sampling. Uscio, on the other hand, provides a catena of archaeological deposits suited to semi-continuous sampling of various occupation phases and buried soils from a number of locations across this mountain-top rural settlement.

17.2 Archaeological and environmental background

The location of Uscio on a ridge top that runs 12 km south to Portofino on the Mediterranean has always suggested that the Castellaro is situated on a major prehistoric routeway inland (Maggi *et al.*, in press), its mountain-top position making it secure but still allowing access to local woodland and pastoral resources. Mesolithic and Neolithic flints and Roman finds occur at the site but the major archaeology comprises Chalcolithic (here *c.* 1800 BC), two late Bronze Age (*c.* 1000 BC) and Iron Age (*c.* 400 BC) sequences. Charcoal analysis by Nisbet (Maggi *et al.*, 1982) and a survey of the local area (Maggi *et al.*, in press) show that the former woodlands, which were a heterogeneous mixture of light-demanding xerophyles and mesophyle types often reflected man's presence (e.g., hazel), and that cereals and legumes were consumed on site. The survey also found that there is a spring only 100 m downslope, used until recently for pastoral practices. The interpretation of the site, based purely on the archaeological evidence, suggests that Chalcolithic occupation, which

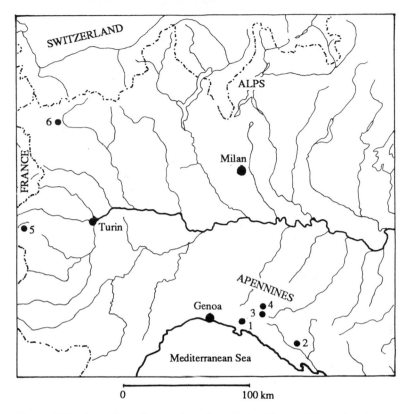

Figure 17.1   Location of map of northern Italy, Alps and Apennine sites. 1: Uscio; 2: Suvero and Zignano; 3: Prato Mollo; 4: Lago Nero; 5: Balm'Chanto; 6: Vislario

features mainly flint artifacts such as arrowheads, was transitory and confined to a small area. Also, although Late Bronze Age activity – including hut construction and terracing – spread upslope and increased in intensity, the artifactual evidence is interpreted as suggesting only part-time (seasonal?) habitation. In contrast, the Iron Age was marked by probable single-phase reoccupation of the Late Bronze Age site and levelling of an area for a substantial structure which featured two well-formed hearths.

17.3 Location and strategy

The Castellaro di Uscio is situated at the top (728 m) of Monte Borgo in an area of sharply dissected, (relative relief, i.e. the difference between ridge tops and valley bottoms, is *c.* 200 and 450 m locally), impure Cretaceous limestones (Maggi *et al.*, in press). The mountain-top site comprises a steeply sloping (13°– 20°) *c.* 50 metre long area bounded by mainly extremely steep and precipitous (40°–60° – sheer) slopes. The vegetation and soils are governed by aspect, as follows. Neutral soils and post-Second World War regenerated woodlands are present on the north-facing side, whereas soils on the south face are moderately alkaline and support a mainly herbaceous flora – a pattern of vegetation probably operating since major clearance of the area.

Profiles from non-archaeological contexts of the mountain-top and nearby small low-slope area of the wooded north face (local soil; profile/section 1) were described with reference to four sections (2–5) examined from the *c.* 30-m long trench cut through the site (Figure 17.2). The undisturbed samples taken for micromorphology are located in the profile and section descriptions.

Through micromorphology it was hoped to identify:

(a)   Differences both between archaeological levels (for example, in section 2 there is the 'pre-occupation soil', Chalcolithic, two different Late Bronze Age and Iron Age layers) and

(b)   The contemporary land use across the site, including the clearance history across the whole slope, the Late Bronze Age terracing upslope and occupation at the footslope, the Iron Age domestic occupation, house construction and re-use of the terraced areas.

The aim was then to comprehend these variations and relate them to the archaeological interpretation of the different periods of occupation, asking the following questions: What was the nature of the pre-Chalcolithic environment and was it already affected by man? Was Chalcolithic activity merely transitory? Was Late Bronze Age occupation seasonal? What were the terraces for and why do the two major Late Bronze Age layers differ? What was the nature of the Iron Age re-use of the terraces and was there only one phase of levelling, construction and occupation? Lastly, what was the post-occupation environment like and how did it affect the archaeological layers?

Reference thin sections were made of Iron Age burned daub and floor, and complementary samples were taken for the bulk analyses of C, N, Fe, grain size and magnetic susceptibility enhancement (MS).

17.4 Local contemporary soil profile (1)

This profile occurs at 695 OD, under post-Second World War regenerated woodland (mainly *Corylus avellana* and *Ostrya carpinifolia*) within approximately 150m of the site of Monte Borgo.

For brevity, only the micromorphology of the subsoil (sampled at 51–58 cm depth) is presented here.

17.4.1 *Micromorphological description*
Profile 1 (local soil) Btg horizon (Figure 17.3a)
Structure is coarse prismatic with fine subangular blocky with low total porosity (10%), mainly expressed as fine to medium vughs.

The coarse fraction (C/F: 3/7) is dominantly stone-sized rock fragments of ferruginous siltstones and mudstones with common silt-sized quartz and a little mica set in a heterogeneous silty clay fine fraction of dominant fine fabric (a) – dark yellowish-brown, low birefringent material, which is orange in reflected

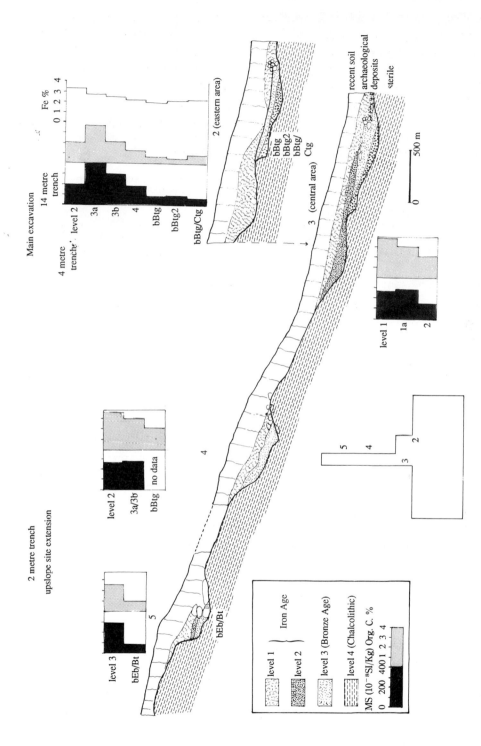

Figure 17.2 Schematic *catena* giving archaeology, magnetic susceptibility (MS), organic carbon content (Org. C) and iron content.

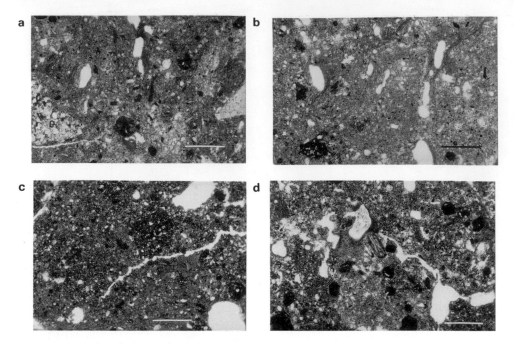

Figure 17.3   (a) Profile 1, local soil (deforested in the Second World War), Btg horizon; clear areas of juxtaposed fine fabric (a) dark yellowish brown (Bt) material and fine fabric (b) pale brown (A2) and rather more sandy soil; with very dusty clay or coarse soil infilling between these ped fragments. PPL. (Bar = 550 μm)

(b) Section 2, bBtg horizon (way up is to left); the subtle mixture of A2 and Bt soil (which are still visible) has produced this generally brown type (c) fine fabric which now also includes rounded (transported) nodules and charcoal; subsequent cracking (e.g. upper right) of the soil has encouraged infilling by fine and coarse soil, whereas the later superimposed porosity (centre left and bottom) feature coatings containing fine organic matter. PPL. (Bar = 550 μm)

(c) Section 2. Layer 4 (Chalcolithic); typical mixture of various anthropic fabrics – the moderately charcoal-rich type (d) and the less frequent very charcoal-rich, very dark reddish-brown type (e); very dusty clay pore coatings are also present (left margin); these result from the trampling-in of charcoal and *in situ* slaking of floors. PPL. (Bar = 550μm)

(d) Section 2. Layer 3b (Late Bronze Age); a dump of clean soil, comprising A2 and Bt horizon material, including nodules and rock fragments, is present here (resting on charcoal-rich layer 4); it was laid as a floor and trampling and slaking have produced a typical vesicular porosity coated by very dusty clay. PPL. (Bar = 550μm)

Table 17.1. *Analytical data (Profile 1)*

Horizon	pH	% Loss on ignition	% Org. carbon	Clay	Silt				Sand				(MS)	Thin section
					F	M	C	total	F	M	C	total		
A	5.4	8.3	3.5	40	26	27	3	56	2	1	1	4	113	
A2(Eb)	5.8	2.3	0.7	40	23	25	7	55	1	2	2	5	47	
Btg	6.3	2.3	1.1	47	26	16	5	47	2	2	2	6	78	A

Note:
(MS): Magnetic susceptibility enhancement (SI units 10^{-8} SI/Kg)

light (OIL), and juxtaposed (Figure 17.3a) to common fine fabric (b) pale brown, low birefringent, pale orange (OIL). Rare coarse roots and occasional fine organic matter is present.

Pedofeatures comprise many compound very dusty clay and impure clay infills and coatings in the coarse fissures between soil fragments (a) and (b), whereas occasional microlaminated fine dusty to moderately limpid clay coatings occur in the fine pores of aggregates of type (a) material. The latter textural features are often not in line with the vertical orientation of the thin section. Depletion – pale fabric (b) is noticeably lower in iron than fabric (a). Fabric differences comprise the juxtaposition of contrasting aggregates of type (a) and (b) material.

17.4.2 Interpretation

The soil can be divided into three main components (Figure 17.3a): the coarse inter-aggregate infills, the dark brown soil (a) and the pale brown soil (b). Hierarchically, the coarse infills post-date the mixing of the two fabric types. In contrast to the coarse infills, the intra-ped clay coatings in (a) are mainly unrelated to the present way up, which again indicates the earlier formation of soil type (a). Similarly, the apparently depleted fabric (b) anomalously shows no clear relationship to any ferruginous illuvial features. Thus, the interpretative questions are: Where do the sharply contrasting aggregates of (a) and (b) come from, and how do they relate to the coarse infills? What does the overall micromorphological picture mean?

Firstly, the two fabric types most reasonably represent the differing horizons produced by the pedological process of clay translocation or lessivage occurring under a forest cover. Type (a) represents a slightly ferruginous illuvial argillic (Bt) horizon of alfisol (luvisol/*sol lessivé*), whereas type (b) originates from an A2(Eb) horizon depleted of clay, and some iron. In alfisols these horizons are not normally found mixed as aggregates but as two vertically stratified horizons. Thus, major physical disruption has to be envisaged to mix these two normally discrete horizons. The occurrence of very coarse and microlaminated dusty clay infillings betweed peds is also atypical.

Material from the A2 and Bt horizons became juxtaposed and the original porosity coatings within the Bt horizon became unorientated to the vertical as soil aggregates were rotated. However, any mechanism that disturbed the natural horizonation of the alfisol would damage the soil aggregates, allowing broken soil to be easily slaked by rainfall. As a consequence unsorted soil must have been rapidly washed down into fissures created during the profile disturbance, to produce the coarse infills. Local information suggests that mature forest soils at Uscio were disturbed by Second World War deforestation.

17.4.3 *Summary of events in contemporary profile*

Event	
Pedological	Anthropogenic
1 Weathering and decalcification of impure limestones containing siltstones and mudstones	
2 Acidification and depletion of upper soil (A2) under a deciduous cover, and translocation of (probable iron and) clay into an argillic Bt subsoil	
	3a Deforestation, soil disruption by uprooting
3b Mixing of Eb and Bt horizons, slaking of 'broken' soil into large pores as coarsely laminated infills	

17.5 **The archaeological** *catena* (see Figure 17.2)

Excavation of the Castellaro had concentrated on the low-slope part of the mountain-top site, where the full sequence of Chalcolithic (layer 4), two Late Bronze Age (3b and 3a) and Iron Age (2 and 1) deposits occur, although a trench extending 30 m upslope to near the summit found two Late Bronze Age terraces. In the lower part of the site, the locations of a Chalcolithic hut, several Late Bronze Age huts and a substantial cut and fill Iron Age house platform that featured two well-formed hearths, were established.

17.5.1 *Section 2*

17.5.1.1 Field description

> Altitude 728 m. Slope: 13 west
> Microrelief: in low slope hollow
> Site: occupation of Iron Age, two Late Bronze Age phases, and Chalcolithic
> Soil type: colluvial soil over alfisol (argillic brown earth)
>
> Locally buried by 17 cm of recent colluvium with bracken cover
> **Layer 2 (Iron Age) 0–12 cm** (thin section B):

Dark brown (7.5YR4/2) moderately weak clay to silty clay (see Table 17.2); well-developed medium subangular blocky; low porosity; pottery but mainly stone free; moderately humose; common fine and medium roots; little earthworm activity; charcoal; possible fine coatings; pH 5.2; abrupt, smooth boundary.

Layer 3a (Late Bronze Age) 12–25 cm (thin section C):
Very dark grey (5YR3/1) moderately firm silty clay; well-developed fine prisms; moderately low porosity; pottery but mainly stone-free; very humose; few fine and medium roots; little earthworm activity; very much charcoal; possible fine coatings; pH 5.2; abrupt, smooth boundary.

Layer 3b (Late Bronze Age) 25–33 cm (thin section D):
Dark brown (7.5YR3/2) moderately weak silty clay; well-developed medium prisms; low porosity; pottery but mainly stone-free; moderately humose; few fine roots; little earthworm activity; charcoal; possible fine coatings; pH 5.2; clear, wavy boundary.

Layer 4 (Chalcolithic) 33–43 cm (thin section E)
Dark brown (7.5YR3/2) moderately weak silty clay; with many medium faint mottles; well-developed medium prisms; moderately high porosity; few fine roots; little earthworm activity; charcoal present; fine coatings present; pH 5.4; clear, wavy boundary.

Layer 6 (bBtg horizon) 43–54 (thin section F)
Reddish-brown (5YR4/3) moderately weak silty clay with few faint and distinct medium mottles; well-developed coarse prisms; moderately high porosity; common fine and medium-shale fragments; little humus; rare fine roots; relic earthworm channels; well-developed in ped pore and ped face coatings; pH 5.5; gradual, irregular boundary.

bBtg2 54–109 cm:
Brown to strong brown (7.5YR4/4–4/6) moderately weak silty clay with common faint medium mottles; well-developed coarse prisms; common medium and coarse shale fragments; rare fine roots; relic earthworm channels; well-developed in ped pore and ped face coatings; pH 5.9; gradual, irregular boundary.

bB(t)g/C(t)g 109–159 + :
Yellowish-brown (10YR5/4) and brown (7.5YR4/4) moderately weak silty clay with common faint medium mottles; weakly developed coarse prisms; abundant fine, medium and coarse silty and sandy shale fragments; rare fine roots; few coatings; pH 5.9.

17.5.1.2 Micromorphology of Section 2

As the deposits in this profile have developed primarily from natural soil materials, the micromorphology of Section 2 is described from the base (Layer 6) upwards.

Thin section F; Layer 6 (bBtg horizon, pre-occupation soil) (Figure 17.3b):
Structure is coarse prismatic with channel porosity (10–15%).

The coarse fraction contains very dominant silt-sized quartz, frequent fine sand-sized rounded sharp-edged ferruginous nodules (parent material fragments), and few sand to stone size siltstone, sandstone and mudstone fragments and few micas.

Fine fabric (type c) is generally brown (PPL), low birefringent, and palish orange (OIL) and speckled because of much organic matter and occasional charcoal, and has an overall subtle heterogeneous character. Occasional coarse root fragments and charcoal occur.

Table 17.2. *Analytical data (Section 2)*

Horizon/ layer	pH	% Loss on ignition	% Org. carbon	Clay	Silt	Sand	(MS)	%N	C/N	%Fe	Thin section
2	5.2	4.6	2.0	43	45	11	208			3.29	B
3a	5.2	8.1	3.8	39	53	7	387	.23	17	2.67	C
3b	5.2	4.4	2.7	41	53	6	292	.14	15	2.38	D
4	5.4	3.8	1.3	43	52	8	185	.11	12	2.20	E
6 (bBtg)	5.5	2.0	0.6	38	46	17	83	.06	10	1.91	F
bBtg2	5.9	2.3	0.5	39	52	11	86	.07	7	2.01	
bBtg3	5.9	2.2	0.8	41	48	10	60	.08	11	2.24	

Pedofeatures: textural features are hierarchically grouped as (i) rare relic finely dusty pale brown clay coatings in the form of papules, (ii) occasional brown dusty clay and silty clay coatings and infills within porosity but mainly distributed around poorly defined structural aggregates; they are sometimes affected by subsequent soil cracking, as in the case of the fractured coarse charcoal, (iii) occasional pale brownish finely dusty clay, with later dark brown coarse to very dusty poorly birefringent clay coatings and infills. Included rounded humic soil fragments occur in porosity, later infilled with dusty clay.

Fabric features include the subtle fine fabric heterogeneity, silty areas that may relate to reworked intercalations, and humic soil fragments.

Thin section E; Layer 4 (Chalcolithic) (Figure 17.3c):

Similar structure, porosity and coarse mineral as F, but contains three main fabric types:

(d) dominant very speckled reddish-brown, low birefringent, very dark brown (OIL),

(e) frequently highly speckled very dark reddish-brown, very low birefringent, very dark brown (OIL);

and (f) few dark yellowish-brown, moderate birefringent, bright orange (OIL) areas, all having sharp boundaries with each other as they occur as abutting soil fragments.

Coarse organic matter includes occasional roots and much charcoal whereas fine organic matter, predominantly of charred material, varies from extremely abundant in (e), abundant in (d), but only 'many' = 5–10% (Bullock *et al.*, 1985) in (f).

Textural features of fine clay coatings in (f) are not oriented to present way up; similarly, rare dusty clay coatings within (d) again occur often unrelated to way up and fabric (d) also includes papules or fragments of relic clay coatings. Only within the coarse porosity of (e) do occasional very coarse (matrix), thick (200 μm) clay coatings occur, often associated with intercalations.

Thin section D; Layer 3b (Late Bronze Age):

Structure and coarse mineral as in E, but general porosity of common vughs and channels has increased to 30%.

In the lower half of the slide many stones occur alongside juxtaposed dark yellowish-brown and pale brown fine fabrics, resembling types (a) and (b) of the local unburied soil. Moreover, this level gives an impression of microlayering, in the form of lines of vesicles in places, the latter featuring thick, very dusty clay coatings.

Further up the slide fine fabric type (d) as defined in layer E becomes dominant, this part containing increasing amounts of fine charred organic matter.

Generally, textural pedofeatures occur as rare, finely dusty papules and occasional dusty clay coatings (nearly always succeeded by many extremely dusty clay coatings) and infills, the latter associated with intercalations. Rounded soil fragments and charcoal also occur (Figure 17.3d).

Thin section C; Layer 3a (Late Bronze Age):
Very similar to the upper part of D, but here fine fabric (e) is very dominant, relating to the very abundant fine charred organic matter (Figure 17.4a). Fabric mix and textural pedofeatures as in the upper part of D.

Thin section B; Layer 2 (Iron Age):
Structure becoming subangular blocky, and porosity (35%) and biological activity increasing. Stones occur in a fine fabric dominated by type (d), containing less organic matter than thin section C; with common type (c). Few (f) occur, birefringence being low, but OIL colours are bright. Also within (c) and (d) iron nodules and intra-ped coatings (as noticed in many of the thin sections) may display slightly reddish OIL colours. Again rare papules are present and many dusty and very dusty void coatings are found in coarse porosity post-dating the fabric mixture. Horizontally layered vesicular areas occur and feature abundant very coarse coatings, whereas clay coatings within fine fabric areas are poorly oriented to way-up. Different fabric types do not always have sharp boundaries.

17.5.2 *Section 3*
17.5.2.1 Field description

Altitude as Section 2; Slope: 16 west; Microrelief: site on moderately to steeply sloping (5 9) ground above Section 2; Deposits developed on moderately (4) sloping artificial platform. (Soil as Section 2.)

Locally buried by 33 cm of 'recent' colluvium with mainly bracken cover.

Layer 1 (Roman ?) 0–4 cm:
Very dark grey (10YR3/1) moderately firm silty clay; moderately well-developed medium subangular blocky with minor medium granules; common fine fissures; low porosity; rare pottery; few stones; moderately humose; common fine and medium roots; abrupt, smooth boundary.

Layer 1a (Iron Age) 4–18 cm (thin section G):
Very dark grey (5YR3/3) with dark brown (10YR3/3) firm silty clay; well-developed medium blocky to fine prisms; very low porosity; few fissures; little pottery and few stones; moderately humose; few fine roots; rare earthworms; common charcoal; few dark coatings; abrupt, smooth boundary.

Layer 2b (Iron Age) 18–31 cm (thin section H):
Dark brown (7.5YR3/2–10YR3/3) moderately firm silty clay; well-developed medium prisms; very low porosity; few pottery and stones; low to moderately humose; few fine roots; common charcoal; common coatings; abrupt, smooth boundary.

Layer 6 (Iron Age platform) 31+ cm:
Brown (7/5YR4/4) to yellowish-brown (10YR5/8) firm silty clay; well-developed medium prisms; low porosity; few fissures; rare stones; rootless; few charcoal.

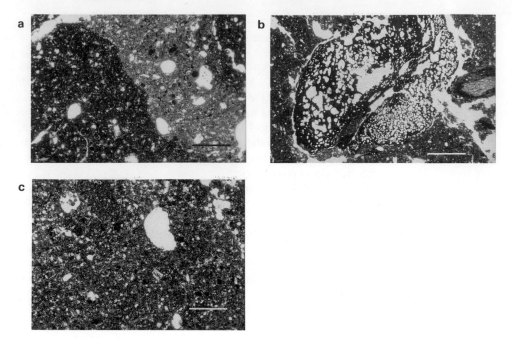

Figure 17.4   (a) Section 2. Layer 3a (Late Bronze Age); the uniformly charcoal-rich soil is the result of trampling-in of charred organic matter (from fires and burned waste from food processing) into a floor originally composed of discrete soil types, as in Figure 17.3b; *in situ* coatings relate to 'contemporary' slaking, whereas papules occur from the disruption of earlier mud floors or daub fabrics now broken up; very high organic carbon and loss on ignition, and very strongly enhanced magnetic susceptibility substantiate this evidence for intensive occupation. PPL. (Bar = 550μm)

(b) Section 3. Layer 2 (Iron Age); perfect section through a charred *Triticum* (wheat) cereal grain (elsewhere extracted by wet, sieving for archaeobotanical studies) resulting from food processing; note clay mobilised by occupation activities has preferentially infilled the porosity within the grain because of the absorption properties of charcoal. PPL. (Bar = 860μm)

(c) Section 5. bA2/Bt horizon; dominant type (c) fabric made up of A2 and Bt horizon components mixed by soil disturbance caused by forest clearance; fragments of charcoal-rich dark brown type (d) fabric are present, derived from a phase of occupation after clearance; obvious dusty clay coatings may relate to cultivation of this overlying soil which is now missing. PPL. (Bar = 550μm)

17.5.2.2 Micromorphology (described from the base upwards)

Thin section H; Layer 2b (Iron Age)
Structure: prisms with vughy and channel (15–20% porosity) microstructure.

Coarse mineral as B. Fine fabric comprises very dominant dark brown (d), moderately low birefringent, pale orange (OIL) material, with a little dark yellowish brown (c), moderately low birefringent, pale yellow brown (OIL) material. The many coarse charcoal fragments include a perfect section through a charred grain of

Table 17.3. *Analytical data (Section 3)*

Layer	pH	% Org. carbon	(MS)	Thin section
1	5.6	3.9	274	
1a	5.6	3.1	278	H
2b	5.6	2.2	172	G

wheat (*Triticum*), (Figure 17.4b); abundant fine organic matter occurs in (e), whereas in (c) only much organic matter is present, mostly uncharred.

Textural pedofeatures include rare rounded papules, occasional dusty clay coatings unoriented to way-up in almost all fabric types, and occasional *in situ* dusty and impure clay coatings and infills. Many features similar to B, although fabric boundaries may be more diffuse.

Thin section G; Layer 1b (Iron Age)

As H, but with occasional dark reddish-brown fine fabric (e), highly speckled with abundant fine charcoal.

17.5.3 *Section 4: Late Bronze Age terrace*
17.5.3.1 Field description

Slope: 14–18 west; Microrelief: colluvial sequence Layer 3b (10), Layer 3a (12), Layer 2 (14), upslope of section 4, against stone-wall tumble, acting as positive lynchet.

Locally buried by 31 cm of 'recent' colluvium.

Layer 2 (Iron Age) 0–27 cm:

Dark to very dark grey (7.5YR4/1–3/1) moderately weak silty clay; common fine granular to medium subangular blocky; common fine fissures; low porosity; little pottery; few stones, increasing shaly fragments at base of horizon; humose; few fine roots; earthworms; charcoal present; rare coatings; abrupt, smooth boundary.

Layers 3a and 3b (Late Bronze Age) 27–38 cm (thin section I):

Dark brown to brown (7.5YR3/2–4/2) moderately firm silty clay; well-developed medium prisms; moderate porosity; pottery common; few stones; moderately humose; few fine roots; abrupt, irregular boundary.

Layer 6 (bBtg horizon) 38–44+ cm

Yellowish-red to strong brown (5YR4/6–7.5YR4/6) firm clay; well-developed coarse prisms; high porosity; few fissures; few stones but large boulders of weathering limestone; rare charcoal.

17.5.3.2 Micromorphology

Thin section I; Layer 3a/3b (Late Bronze Age)

Subangular blocky structure, with medium channel porosity (15–20%). Mineral as D. Strongly heterogeneous; dominant fine fabrics of type (d) and (e), with common (c) and few (f). Few textural pedofeatures – inherited, rotated and *in situ*, as in H.

Table 17.4. *Analytical data (Section 4)*

Horizon/ layer	pH	% Org. carbon	Clay	Silt	Sand	(MS)	Thin section
2	5.7	2.2	41	52	7	242	
3a/3b	5.9	2.4	39	47	13	248	I
bBtg	5.8	1.2	41	53	6		

17.5.4 *Section 5: Late Bronze Age terrace (near top of catena)*
17.5.4.1 Field description

Slope: 6 west near crest of mountain top, 30 west above section; Microrelief – colluvial (positive lynchet) sequence above wall tumble, upslope of section; limestone bedrock exposed just upslope; common ants.

Locally 28 cm of 'recent' colluvium.

Dump (post Late Bronze Age) 0–41 cm:
Pinkish grey to brown (7.5YR7/2–4/4) homogeneous dump of weathered shales forming a subhorizontal surface; abrupt, irregular boundary.

Layer 3 (Late Bronze Age) 41–67 cm:
Black (7.5YR2/0) moderately weak silty clay; well-developed fine to medium granular; common fine fissures; very humose; few fine roots; clear, irregular boundary.

Layer 6 (bA2/Bt horizon) 66–77+ cm (thin section K):
Brown (10YR4/3) moderately firm silty clay; coarse blocky to fine prisms; moderate porosity; few stones; limestone boulders present; rare roots; charcoal present at upper junction; old earthworm channels; few coatings.

17.5.4.2 Micromorphology (described from the base up)

Thin section K; Layer 6 (buried soil)
Structure is coarse prisms with channel and vughy porosity (10–15%), (Figure 17.4c).
C/F: 2/8. Mineral material ratio similar to thin section F. Fine material is made up of dominant (c) brown, moderately low birefringent, pale orange (OIL), with more pale (type b?) silt-rich zones; and common dark brown (d). Organic matter occurs as occasional coarse charcoal in (d); very little fine organic material in (c), but abundant charred material in (d).
Textural pedofeatures include rare primary limpid clay coatings (in c) that are somewhat rotated; many dusty clay coatings throughout total porosity, e.g. around (c); and few very dusty and coarse (silt and charcoal) clay coatings and infills in major pores – also associated with (c).

Thin section J; Layer 3 (Late Bronze Age)
Structure is crumb and welded crumb, with high porosity (25–30%) of channels and well-accommodated planes.
Mineral (C/F: 15/85), fine is dominant, very dark reddish-brown (e), frequent (d) and few (c), as in K. Organic matter, in addition to many roots there are occasional

Table 17.5. *Analytical data (Section 5)*

Horizon/ layer	pH	% Org. carbon	Clay	Silt	Sand	(MS)	Thin section
3	6.8	3.7	31	47	22	288	J
6 (bA$_2$/Bt)	6.7	1.1	38	54	8	81	K

finely fragmented charcoal, whereas fine charred organic matter is extremely abundant in fine fabric (e).

Pedofeatures relate mainly to its being a strongly biologically homogenised fabric with only rare textural pedofeatures.

17.5.5 *Reference material*

The fabrics described from the archaeological catena appeared to include both natural soil and 'anthropic soil' materials and the only definitive way to differentiate these, other than just theoretically, was to examine known anthropic soil materials. Iron Age floor and daub, which retained coarse wattle impressions, were selected. Both had been moderately baked by burning. Natural soil fabrics have already been described from profile 1.

17.5.5.1 Micromorphology

Thin section L; burned daub (Iron Age):

The hand specimen is a very dark brown, firm clay loam with deep wattle impressions. Medium-smooth wall vughs relating to pseudomorph plant porosity – plant tempering lost by oxidation. Mineral material C/F: 2/8, very dominant quartz silt; fine material is reddish brown (PPL), non-birefringent (except for finest silt), bright orange with red ferruginous inclusions (OIL). No obvious organic matter.

Pedofeatures of dusty microlaminated clay coatings suggest slaking was part of daub-making process; reddening of these coatings and of the matrix of the daub were caused by burning.

Thin section M; burned floor (Iron Age):

The hand specimen is again a very dark brown, firm clay loam and is darker on the upper side. Porosity mainly composed of vughs with some vesicles. Fine mineral varies from a pale brown (PPL), moderately birefringent interior to a reddish-brown (PPL) low birefringent surface. Under OIL, surface is somewhat reddened, especially ferruginous nodules; abundant charred organic matter present.

Pedofeatures include many textural types at the surface, both fine and extremely dusty void coatings, some related to intercalations; also present are unoriented coatings and papules: rounded soil fragments occur in this heterogenous mix of both charcoal-rich and 'cleaner', 'natural' soil material. Development of floor here included the mixing of different soil materials and transported soil, some of 'natural' soil, others where trampling has intimately mixed in fine charcoal. Trampling has also pre-conditioned the soil for slaking that produced such well-developed textural pedofeatures.

17.6 **Interpretation**

17.6.1 *Chalcolithic and earlier*

The sequence at Section 2 commences with Layer 6 (F), regarded as the 'natural' subsoil by the archaeologists. The inclusion of organic matter and charcoal, rounded soil relics and nodules, including papules of translocated clay and rather subtle but differing brown soil materials (fine fabric c), however, indicate a colluvial origin for this layer. Its anthropogenic origin probably relates to the erosion of Bt (fine fabric a) and A2 (fine fabric b) horizon material from an argillic forest soil (fabric c is a probable resultant of the incomplete homogenisation of these two fabrics). Once in position, the mixed soil (Table 17.2, Layer 6 Btg horizons) continued to develop as an argillic soil profile, but clay translocation appears to have occurred under a vegetation cover that continued to be disturbed, as indicated by the abundance of much coarse material in the coatings. Later a phase of soil cracking, relating to wetting and drying effects enhanced by the sub-Mediterranean climate, caused new soil structures to form which post-date the earlier clay translocation. At the same time 'coarse soil' was washed in, including rounded fragments of humic soil. These features may suggest that a disturbance phase caused erosion, which exposed the profile to subsoil drying-out and cracking, a phenomenon not repeated once the soil was buried. Disturbance also led to topsoil movement, some soil being washed into the eroded and cracked subsoil at this receiving downslope site at Section 2. This erosional phase and coarse soil translocation is tentatively dated to the major Chalcolithic (*c.* 1800 BC) impact of clearance, occupation and possible cultivation at this site, although Mesolithic and Early, Middle and Late Neolithic finds (e.g. arrowheads) demonstrate continued earlier human activity here. Coarse soil translocation is succeeded by translocation of dusty clay and finely dusty clay, which is interpreted as evidence of continued human disturbance of the area but, as the anthropogenic layers thicken, mobilised soil material becomes rather better sorted (and finer) with increased depth. This leads us to Layer 4, which is clearly dated to the Chalcolithic.

Layer 4 (E) is a strongly heterogeneous deposit and the three major types of soil fabric identified (Figure 17.3c) clearly differ from the buried 'soil' of F, firstly because the very dark (e) and dark (d) reddish-brown fabrics contain amounts of charred organic matter varying from extremely abundant to abundant (Table 17.2). The type of organic matter includes both wood and, because of its flaky character, grass charcoal. The third fabric (f) is less obviously anthropogenic because it contains little charcoal. It contrasts strongly with the natural soil by being bright orange under reflected light, indicating that it has been burned, and in fact compares well with reference burned floor and daub (Iron Age) which have been examined (thin sections L and M). Its rather pure character suggests that it came from a 'virgin' or clean soil source (see lack of fine charred organic matter in F). In contrast, the dark soil fabrics relate to the intimate physical mixing of 'natural' soil with large quantities of charred organic matter, such mixing in the presence of water giving rise to slaking and the development of clay coating which, when disrupted by human activity, produces the papules also present in this layer. There are probably two main mechanisms responsible for this mixing: mud-daub manufacture and churning of the hut floor by trampling. It is possible that the very dark reddish fabric relates more to floors – this soil material appears to be *in situ* – while the dark reddish fabric, which occurs as non-*in situ* fragments, may relate to the inclusion of mud wall daub into the floor. Chalcolithic activity is restricted to a rather small area in the lower part of the site and the archaeological assemblage indicates that it was just 'frequented'. The micromorphology, however, suggests that there was actually rather intense occupation, and possible hut renewal to account for this 10 cm thick layer of mixed anthropic soil fabrics.

Summary of events (early Holocene to Chalcolithic)

Event	
Pedological	Anthropogenic
1 Weathering and decalcification of impure limestone – development of A2 and Bt horizons of argillic 'forest' soil	(Forest cover)
2 Soil disturbance and colluviation	2 Mesolithic; Early, Middle and Late Neolithic hunting and forest disturbance
3 Argillic (forest) soil development in downslope colluvium	3 Mesolithic; Early, Middle and Late Neolithic hunting and forest disturbances
4 Erosion, drying out of exposed subsoil, cracking and 'anthropogenic' soil inwash; formation of charcoal-rich deposits from hut floor, hut wall and burned 'daub' fabrics	4 Chalcolithic forest clearance; possible cultivation; probable intensive occupation, domestic fires in a restricted area

17.6.2 *Late Bronze Age*

Late Bronze Age deposits are the most extensive at Uscio, not only occurring in Sections 2 and 3 but upslope at the two terraced areas of 4 and 5 (Figure 17.2). At Section 5 (beneath the terrace wall and Late Bronze Age [Layer 3] deposits), the buried soil (Layer 6:K) resembles the argillic profile in Section 2. In contrast, however, it appears to be an *in situ* soil, with a character comparable to thin section A of the local present-day soil and appears to be similarly disturbed (Figure 17.4b). Firstly, fragments of iron- and clay-depleted (probable A2 horizon) and clay-rich (probably argillic Bt horizon) material have become juxtaposed, and secondly coarse soil has washed into the intervening voids as infills and coatings (see Figure 17.3a). In this way it is closely comparable to the Btg horizon (thin section A) of the local, recently deforested soil, and thus is itself interpreted as a deforested soil. Of course this buried paleosol has been influenced by the overlying occupation and by 3,000 years of weathering. The latter effects have led to contamination of the post-clearance soil by anthropogenic soil materials, whereas continued subsoil weathering has made the differences between the two horizon types of the original forest soil (A2 and Bt) less stark.

As the microfabric evidence of soil disturbance here is clearer than at Section 2, it may indicate that a possible phase of woodland clearance and the resulting soil disturbance at Section 5 is related to expansion of Late Bonze Age activity upslope. As stated above, Layer 6 here has also been contaminated by minor mixing of presumed Late Bronze Age dark brown soil and dark impure clay coatings containing charcoal. Notably, this dark brown anthropogenic soil (fabric d) included in Layer 6 contains far less charred organic matter than the overlying very dark reddish-brown Layer 3 (J;fabric e). In fact, this type of dark brown soil is next apparent downslope in Section 4 in Layer 3a/3b (I), which also includes transported fragments of dark yellowish-brown material (fabric c) of 'natural' soil origin. This leads to the conclusion that a probable early layer of dark brown anthropogenic soil, which occurred at Section 5 in the Late Bronze Age before terrace wall construction, was eroded, or dug out to aid terrace wall building – and resulting colluvium or soil became incorporated in downslope deposits at Section 4 (Figure 17.2). The low quantity of charcoal in the included dark brown soil in Layer 6 at Section 5, together with the dark and sometimes very coarse coatings here may indicate cultivation of this upslope area (including the terraced area at Section 4 at some time) during the early phase of Late Bronze Age activity, when the actual occupation, as identified at Section 2, commenced in the lower part of the site.

Here at Section 2, the primary Late Bronze Age deposits (Layer 3b) at the bottom of thin section D are in stark contrast to the underlying dark Chalcolithic deposits (E), because this layer (3b) is composed of surprisingly 'clean' brown A2 and Bt horizon material not mixed with fine charcoal (Figure 17.4b). Apparently the local natural argillic forest soil must have been dug up and purposely laid down to produce a surface, which, because it is characterised by typical horizontally layered vesicular porosity with dusty clay coatings, was apparently utilised as a hut floor – the latter features being a consequence of trampling and slaking. Further up the slide (i.e., later in the occupation) the deposits become more homogenised, with increasing inclusion of fine charcoal, as presumably mud-daub walls, made up of soil mixed with charred organic matter, collapsed. Papules and unorientated clay coatings perhaps relate to earlier phases of the daub-making process (some burned; see L) for hut construction, whereas intercalations and properly oriented textural features may result from the slaking of wall material as the deposit is re-used and accumulates *in situ*.

Layer 3a is mainly very dark reddish brown with very abundant fine charcoal throughout, testifying to the intensifying Late Bronze Age occupation (and extremely enhanced MS) and development of a deposit which continued to relate to the mixing of hut-wall and floor material. It is likely that floor deposits became darker from the continual trampling-in of burned organic matter, but it is difficult to differentiate clearly between fabric types because occupation and subaerial weathering, including localised colluviation after rainfall or even on-site tillage, which cannot be ruled out, have been so effective in homogenising the deposit (Figure 17.4a).

This layer 3a can be compared with the very dark reddish-brown fabrics of Layer 3(J) at Section 5 (formed upslope of the terrace wall) but significantly the magnetic susceptibility (Table 17.5) at the latter is much lower than at Section 2. This indicates that domestic occupation in the lower part of the site was more intense (more fires). In fact, archaeological excavation found only a few large Late Bronze Age sherds at Section 5, indicating a non-intensive domestic use of this part of the site, although very large quantities of charred organic matter became incorporated into the soil fabric. The artifact assemblage (only a few pots) for the Late Bronze Age occupation as a whole suggests to archaeologists that the site did not experience full-time occupation, although charred cereals (*Hordeum, Triticum*) and beans (*Vicia faba*) were present (Maggi *et al.*, 1982, in press). The micromorphology and other analytical data, however, all clearly suggest repeated, widespread and intense Late Bronze Age occupation of the Castellaro.

Summary of Late Bronze Age occupation at Sections 2, 4 and 5

Event	
Pedological	Anthropogenic
	1a Late Bronze Age clearance; domestic occupation – hut construction down-slope, possible cultivation of upslope areas
1b Upslope soil cover disturbed woodland clearance, downprofile translocation of dark coarse soil as the result of possible cultivation; downslope natural soils dug up and laid for hut floors	
	2a Construction of terraces and probable cultivation upslope; domestic occupation intensifies
2b Some erosion of upslope soils; development of very charcoal-rich soils	

17.6.3 *Iron Age*
The main archaeological feature relating to this period is the construction of an artificial house platform using a 'cut and fill' procedure (Figure 17.2, Section 3).

Two hearths and an *in situ* burned beam remain from a substantial, (probable) single-phase dwelling, which may have had a slate roof. Iron Age deposits (Layer 2) were mainly studied from Section 3 (the house) and Section 2 (adjacent to the house). The fabric of Layer 2 at these sections shows that a large amount of 'natural' soil was utilised; although it was mixed with organic matter, it never seems to have been so intensely reworked as the Layer 3a material and more closely resembles the early Late Bronze Age fabrics of Layer 3b. The Iron Age deposits can also contain clear fragments of vesicular floor-like fabrics, some brown, some rather darker because of higher amounts of included fine charred organic matter, and much brown soil with dusty clay coatings unoriented to present way-up, which are of probable daub origin (see L,M), like the rare papules that occur. Some of the material has been burned, enhancing the redness of nodules and the clay coatings. Post-depositional (right way-up) infills suggest some disturbance in this deposit, which also appears to have been affected by short-distance colluviation with general weathering effects tending to weakly homogenise an originally rather heterogeneous deposit (see Figure 17.4b).

Thus the dark brown field colours and only moderately charcoal-rich fabric, which are in contrast to the generally much darker Late Bronze Age deposits, support the archaeological theory of single-phase, non-intensive occupation. Other data (Tables 17.2 and 17.3) also substantiate this conjecture. Strongly burned fabrics such as floor material (M) could be related to the hearths, while the rather common occurrence of moderately pure, slightly burned daub (L) may possibly suggest that house destruction by fire, as put forward by the archaeologists to account for the demise of this substantial dwelling, can be considered as an interpretation. Certainly, collapse possibly led to coarse soil slaking and washing into the post-depositional deposit, which as stated above then underwent minor weathering.

Summary of Iron Age

Event	
Pedological	Anthropogenic
	1a Excavation and dumping for house platform; use of local soil for daub and floor materials; minor mixing; possible cultivation upslope on terraces; possible destruction by fire.
1b Mixing of natural soils with minor amounts of charcoal; development of several phases of textural features; reddening of some soil; moderate homogenisation of deposit.	

17.6.4 **Post-archaeological history**
Summary

Event	
Pedological	Anthropogenic 1a Abandonment; minor woodland regeneration; recent disturbance.
1b Some biological homogenisation and rooting of near-surface deposits, which retain charcoal but lose textural features; deep-rooting of plants keep deposits aerated; recent colluviation.	

17.7 **Conclusions**

The use of soil micromorphology enables the identification of the nature of the original soils and the impact of partial and full deforestation (the latter probably in the Chalcolithic) to be made and possibly also demonstrates contemporary cultivation and associated soil erosion. In addition, Chalcolithic occupation, which produced fabrics similar to the reference samples of known daub and floor, appeared to be more than transitory but rather intense, with probably more than one phase of hut construction and renewal. This may have connotations elsewhere, where only Chalcolithic arrowheads testify to man's presence.

In the Late Bronze Age the intensification of occupation after 'clean' natural soil had been employed, first to construct hut floors, indicates more than transitory use of the site, even if it were only seasonal. In addition, a second deforestation event and two phases of terrace use and construction were identified through thin-section analysis, although these were not obvious archaeologically.

In the Iron Age, levelling for a house platform and the subsequent collapse of the dwelling possibly after a fire and its abandonment after a single occupation phase were supported by micromorphology.

Interpretations made from the thin sections were complemented by the other analyses (Tables 17.1–17.5), which showed that intensive occupation led to enhanced C, and MS and anomalously high C/N ratios (Courty and Fedoroff, 1982; Allen and Macphail 1987).

Soil micromorphology was thus mainly successful in fulfilling the objectives of this study. Fabrics of deforested soils, colluvial soils and soils affected by cultivation were clearly distinguished from the anthropogenic occupation sediments, although the latter were shown to originate from local soils. The character of land use and the degree of and variations in occupation intensity in space and time were also identified, even though the mechanisms of daub manufacture and floor formation seemed universal. However, the effects of weathering, localised colluviation, any secondary human activity such as tillage and trampling and post-depositional biological activity, especially in layers near the surface, unfortunately only permitted the interpretations to go so far and some details of the site's history still remain obscure.

CHALCOLITHIC LAND USE IN
ITALIAN APENNINES AND ALPS

18.1 Introduction

The montane areas of Italy were classically thought to have been colonised during the late third and second millennium BC only for reasons of hunting and gathering and as a response to the demand for, and exploitation of, chalcopyrite ores; only subsequently did the peoples adapt to a mixed economy based on pastoral agriculture (Biagi *et al.*, 1984). However, as the following studies will demonstrate, Chalcolithic (Copper Age) activities had a marked effect on the environment, sometimes initiating vegetation and soil changes as the result of agricultural exploitation of the mountain areas, practices that extended from later prehistory to near-recent times.

The main examples (see Figure 17.1) are cited from Prato Mollo (Genoa) in the Ligurian Apennines, the Chisone Valley (Torino) and Vislario (Orco Valley, Torino) in the western Alps. At these sites, pedology and micromorphology form part of multi-disciplinary investigations with palaeobotany (e.g., pollen, charcoal, phytoliths), archaeozoology and archaeology to gain insights into past practices of large-scale land management.

18.1 Prato Mollo

18.1.1 *Location*

Prato Mollo with an average annual precipitation of 2,000 mm, is an Apennine plateau of open wet grassland and scattered beech trees typical of the oro-Mediterranean (montane) level (FAO/UNESCO, 1981). Here a shallow (*c.* 90 cm) peat at *c.* 1,400 m OD had developed in a low-slope shelf on serpentine rocks – an unusual occurrence in the mainly steeply sloping Apennines. The area was first associated with a Mesolithic site (Baffico *et al.*, 1983), although scatters of Chalcolithic flint artifacts are being found in increasing numbers (Maggi, personal communication) on this southern flank of Monte Aiona (1,692 m).

18.1.2 *Field characteristics and study problems*

The deposit comprises (Figure 18.1a):

> 13 cm of yellowish silty peat,
> 65 cm of brown silty peat, and
> 10 cm black peaty sands and gravels which contain two prominent charcoal bands.

305

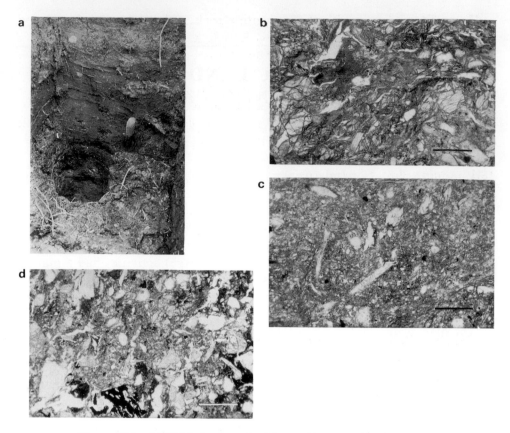

Figure 18.1   (a) Field photograph of the profile exposed at Prato Mollo showing the charcoal band at the bottom (see photomicrograph of the peat–charcoal band in Plate (Vd).

(b) Layer 5: weathered serpentinite mixed with crystals and neoformed clay from weathering and also local clay inwash. The ensuing decrease in permeability probably led to waterlogging and peat initiation. PPL. (Bar = 550μm)

(c) Prato Mollo Layer 2, coarse mineral band; coarse sand-sized mineral material (and gravel) occur with charcoal, set in a matrix of peat and silt. PPL. (Bar = 550μm)

(d) Lago Nero: dense silts occurring beneath peat; here waterlogging has been encouraged by a probable alluvial silt inwash sealing the serpentine substrate; later porosity relates to the rooting of aquatic plants. PPL. (Bar = 550μm)

The substrate is composed of greenish, weathered serpentine.

The two primary reasons for carrying out the micromorphological study were:

   to establish the cause of peat initiation in the area (a crucial question in these Apennine investigations) and

   to ascertain more accurately the nature of the charcoal bands (inwash or *in situ* burning) and mineral sedimentation at the base of the peat.

Hence the junction with the serpentine rock and the basal mineral and charcoal-rich bands was sampled. This was efficiently accomplished by one 13 cm long mammoth thin section. The investigation was in support of a palynological study, which, by using closely spaced sampling and two radiocarbon-dated levels, was concentrating on the earliest part of the peat sequence, where preliminary counting had shown major vegetation changes occurring. Micromorphology would thus act as a control for the interpretation of the contained pollen spectra and the radiocarbon assays.

18.1.3 *Pollen data (Cruise, 1987)*

> Pollen assemblage zone PM-1 (base of peat)
> 80–90 cm: *Abies – Pinus – Tilia – Corylus – Pteridium*
>
> PM-2 35–80 cm: *Fagus – Quercus – Abies – Alnus – Corylus* – Non-Arboreal Pollen (NAP)
>
> PM-3 1–35 cm: NAP – *Fagus – Quercus*

The basal pollen zone (^{14}C dates of 4300 ± 60 and 4130 ± 60 years BP – Berlin), which has the charcoal bands, is dominated by high *Abies* percentages that decrease continuously after reaching a peak in the middle of the zone. High percentages of *Pteridium* and charcoal, present in the pollen preparations, suggest a history of forest fires. Pollen zone 2 is characterised by a steady expansion of broad-leaved trees, stable *Abies* but rising herb pollen percentages, including at the beginning a number of possible indicators of anthropogenic activity, e.g., *Plantago lanceolata, Cruciferae*. In the most recent pollen zone (PM-3) *Abies* undergoes a final decline in favour of herbs and broad-leaved trees, including cultivated species.

Specifically, there did seem to be an association in the basal zone (PM-1) between declining fir (*Abies*), the rise in herb and beech (*Fagus*) pollen, and the occurrence of probable anthropogenic indicators suggesting human exploitation of the area. However, pollen concentrations are low, and poor pollen preservation and differential preservation of the various pollen types may have led to artificially high *Abies* percentages. Thus, complementary thin-section analysis of the basal 13 cm of the peat and serpentine substrate was crucial to the final interpretation of the pollen diagram.

18.1.4 *Micromorphology (Plate Vd; Figures 18.1b, 1c)*

Description:

Structure is massive with distinct layers; 30% porosity of predominantly compound packing pores, with few medium root channels – some within layers, other later ones penetrating right through the sediment.

C:F varies; coarse mineral is predominantly fragmented serpentinite, with weathering olivine and quartz. These occur as mainly silt in Layer 1 (C/F: 4/6), as gravel and stones in Layer 2 (C/F: 7/3), as sand and silt in Layer 3 (C/F: 7/3), as separate sand and silt lenses in Layer 4 (C/F: 4/6) and as stone-sized rock fragments in Layer 5

(C/F: 6/4). Fine mineral is mainly confined to yellow-brown, speckled (PPL), moderate birefringent, orange (OIL) clay in Layer 5. Organic matter is the dominant fine material in Layers 1–4. Coarse organic matter occurs as wood charcoal fragments, and as roots, some of which have reddened outer margins. Fine amorphous organic matter (peat) is especially important in Layers 2 and 4. Fine charcoal inclusions occur throughout. Patches of dark brownish-red and blackened peat are often present.

Pedofeatures include minor silt inwash in the coarse (root) channels; and in Layer 5, probable locally neoformed clay void infills.

Interpretation:

A diminution in porosity in the serpentine substrate probably encouraged waterlogging; slower organic decomposition and peat formation resulted. In this basal part of the deposit, the peat developed concurrently with phases of low-, medium- and high-energy mineral sedimentation. The rubification of the peat and contemporary roots in places indicates *in situ* burning, whereas the inclusion of wood charcoal suggest local forest fires.

18.1.5 *Discussion*

The study was first able to show that peat formation probably occurred through waterlogging, as the porosity within the weathering serpentine (Figure 18.1b) was infilled by neoformed clay. (This mechanism clearly differs from that at nearby Lago Nero, where peat formation began after an inwash of silts – Figure 18.1c). Secondly, at Prato Mollo, peat development occurred alongside various phases of mineral inwashing (Figure 18.1d) that were contemporary with the deposition of charcoal. The latter, because it has a porosity pattern of short pores thinning at both ends, appears to be mainly of coniferous wood origin (Clapham, personal communication). In addition to the charcoal inclusions, the peat itself had been burned, resulting in the dark reddish-brown and blackish colours (Plate Vd). Burning episodes were concentrated in the two 'charcoal' bands but there was evidence of minor charring throughout, including *in situ* roots, which had only their outside cells affected. It can only be assumed that both the local area (charcoal inwash source) and the peat itself were affected by at least two major fires and probably several minor fires during the development of the first 12 cm of peat. The coarse mineral inwash (Figure 18.1d), which is concentrated in these basal levels, may also indicate soil instability, perhaps associated with this burning.

When the archaeological, charcoal, pollen, radiocarbon and soil micromorphological data are combined, a composite picture of the environment of Prato Mollo can be interpreted. The absolute dating correlates with the Chalcolithic flint scatters in the area at a time when, as assumed from the pollen results, the fir (*Abies*) forest was undergoing changes that were to lead to its replacement by beech (*Fagus*) and herbs contemporary with both pollen indicators and micromorphological evidence of on-site peat and local coniferous forest burning. Moreover, these burning episodes were followed by possible pollen indicators of anthropic activity. All these factors lead to the suggestion

Table 18.1. *Micromorphology*

Deposit	Burning	Interpretation	Vegetation
1 Dominantly peaty with silt	Charred peat, charcoal inclusions	Low-energy inwash, peat formation, on-site and local burning	Decline in fir, increase in broad-leaved trees, herbs and grasses
2 Weakly peaty with gravel and stones	Charred peat, charcoal inclusions	As above, high-energy mineral inwash	Decline in fir, increase in broad-leaved trees, herbs and grasses
3 Weakly peaty with sand and silt	As above, *in situ* charred root	As above, medium-energy inwash	Decline in fir, increase in broad-leaved trees, herbs and grasses
4 Dominantly peaty with silts and separate sand lenses	Dominantly charred peat with charcoal inclusions	As above, low- and medium-energy inwash	Decline in fir, increase in broad-leaved trees, herbs and grasses
5 Weathered serpentine with void clay infills	Absent	Substrate becomes impermeable, causing waterlogging in this shallow basin	No data

that the fir forest was being opened up to produce grazing land for Chalcolithic pastoralism. Fire, as demonstrated in thin section, was the major mechanism used for clearance.

18.1.6 *Conclusions*

In this example, micromorphology clearly demonstrated:

> that peat was initiated by waterlogging, resulting from a diminution in permeability as the serpentine substrate weathered;
>
> that peat development occurred (a) alongside local burning, (b) whilst it was itself affected by various mineral inwashes and (c) at times when the peat itself was burned – helping to elucidate the differences in pollen preservation and concentrations.

18.2 **Chisone Valley**

18.2.1 *Location and environmental data*

The area of study is located some 40 km west of Turin up the Chisone Valley along the south-facing slope between Monte Cristalliera (2,801 m) to Villaretto

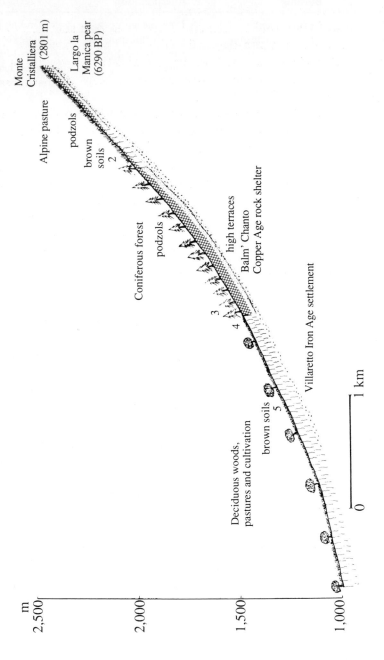

Figure 18.2   Chisone Valley: present-day soils and vegetation.

(1,000 m). This valley has served as an alpine routeway between France and Italy (over the Montegeneve Pass) at least since the second half of the third millennium BC (Biagi *et al.*, 1984). This study focused on the Chalcolithic (e.g., 4010 ± 60 BP; 2060 BC) rock shelter of Balm'Chanto at 1,390 m. The 270 cm of rocky and loose sediment infill contained for the most part sherds, stone and bone implements, which can be attributed to the late local Chalcolithic, with a short period of later use during the final Bronze and Iron Ages. Of note is a particular Chalcolithic greenstone (serpentine) technology, mainly of arrowheads (Biagi and Nisbet, 1987).

To understand the setting of this occupation, a multi-disciplinary team of palaeoenvironmentalists studied the palaeobotanical and faunal remains at the site, and the local area from the Iron Age settlement at Villaretto to Lago La Manica (2,365 m). The survey included the study of present-day soils and vegetation (Figure 18.2) and the investigation of pollen from the rock shelter sediments and from the 96 cm thick peat at Lago La Manica.

The geology is both basic and acid (Maurino, 1983) with gneiss, gabbro, micaschist and calcaschist and serpentine outcrops of Triassic and pre-Triassic age. The common cover of Pleistocene and Holocene superficial deposits (moraine and scree), however, has produced a complicated mosaic of parent materials.

The survey found moderately acid brown soils under a deciduous woodland and pasture cover below *c.* 1,600 m, many areas being terraced as high as 1,550 m. Beneath the present-day belt (*c.* 1,600–2,000 m) of coniferous larch forest (*Larix*), podzols occur, although it was noted that some post-war regenerated larch occurs over old pasture and that the underlying soils are complex. Above *c.* 2,000 m alpine pasture occurred over a mosaic of brown soils and podzols; the latter, as well as rankers, increase in frequency with higher altitudes as a scree vegetation became more dominant.

The soil, vegetation cover and land use of the *Larix* zone (Profile 1) and the subalpine terrace zone (Profile 2) is at the core of this particular case study. Both field descriptions are supported by physical and chemical data (Tables 18.2 and 18.3); micromorphological studies focused on the subalpine terraced area. Thin sections 1–3 examined a terraced soil sequence presently used for pasture, and these were compared with a pastoral terrace soil, known to have been cultivated (dug) until 1960 (4). In addition to fabrics developed by agricultural land use, occupation sediments were examined from an undated spot sample from a deep terrace section (5) and from an Iron Age context (6).

Table 18.2. *General analytical data*

No	Horizon/ depth cm	pH	% loss on ignition	% Org. carbon	Clay	Silt F	M	C	total	Sand F	M	C	total
Profile 1 (zone c, c. 1,680 m)													
7	Ah 0–3	5.7	9.3	4.6									
8	Ea/Al 3–27	5.9	6.7	1.9	16	6	12	8	28	25	18	20	62
9	Al/B 27–56	6.8	4.1	1.5	18	4	8	9	21	24	12	24	60
10	Bs 56–82	6.3	3.4	1.1	13	1	6	8	15	31	20	20	71
11	Bw/C 82–102	6.8	1.8	0.7	13	2	2	2	6	24	20	34	79

Table 18.3. *Chemistry and its interpretation (multi-phase profile)*

Horizon	Depth cm	Pyrophosphate extract C	Fe	Al	Dithionite extract Fe	Interpretation
Ah	0–3	1.5	0.3	0.02	0.3	Micropodzol under new *Larix* cover
Ea/Al	3–27	0.7	0.3	0.02	0.4	Biologically worked
Al/Bw	27–56	0.5	0.2	0.0	0.5	brown soil under pasture developed in old podzol
Bs	58–82	0.6	0.5	0.02	0.3	Base of podzol as
C	82–102	0.5	0.2	0.01	0.3	climax soil, formed original *Larix* cover

18.2.2 *Field description*

Profile 1:

Vegetation: *Larix* woodland (Quadrat 16); Zone: c; subalpine *Larix* over old pasture; Slope: 30 S; Relief: shedding convex slope above Malze; Altitude: *c.* 1,850 m.

Horizon, depth cm	
L 5–3	*Larix* needles, grass litter
F 3–0	*Larix* needles, grass litter and cones
Ah 0–3	Very dark grey (5YR3/1) loose fine loamy sand (Table 18.2); few very small stones; fine blocky; humose; abundant fine and very fine roots; ants; sharp, smooth boundary.
Ea/Al–Bw 3–27	Brown (7.5YR4/2) loose fine loamy sand; very common fine to medium stones; coarse blocky; relatively humose; common fine, few medium, few coarse *Larix* roots; relic earthworm channels; clear, smooth boundary.

Table 18.4. *General analytical data*

No	Horizon/ depth cm	pH	% loss on ignition	% Org. carbon	Clay	Silt F	Silt M	Silt C	Silt total	Sand F	Sand M	Sand C	Sand total
Profile 2 (zone d, c. *1,550 m)*													
12	Al 0–19 (thin section 1)	4.9	6.4	2.4	18	5	10	10	25	30	17	30	60
13	BW 19–50 (thin section 2)	4.7	4.7	1.9	16	6	11	9	26	32	14	13	59
14	Bw/Cw 50–80 (thin section 3)	6.2	1.8	0.7									
Seleiraut Terraces (zone d, c. *1,500 m)*													
15	garden 1–10	6.7	6.9	3.4									
16	garden until 1960, now pasture 0–10 (thin section 4)	6.8	6.1	2.3									
18	deep terrace subsoil B *c.* 1.20 (thin section 5)				14	11	20	8	39	19	10	17	46
Villaretto (zone e, c. *1,035 m)*													
22	occupation (thin section 6)	7.4	2.1	1.0									

Note:
(NB: grain size may contain inaccuracies because of the high mica content)

Bw 27–56	Brown (7.5YR4/4) moderately weak fine loamy sand; stones (as above); coarse blocky; roots (as above); low organic matter; relic earthworm channels; clear, wavy boundary.
Bs 56–82	Strong brown (7.5YR4/6) very weak fine loamy sand; stones (as above); coarse blocky; roots (as above); sesquioxidic coatings; relic (7.5YR4/2) earthworm channels; gradual wavy boundary.
Bw/C 82–102	Yellowish brown (10YR5/4) very weak; structureless; stones (as above), ochreous weathering; few fine roots.

Profile 2:

Vegetation: pasture (Quadrats 17-18); Zone: subalpine pasture and terrace with recent *Larix* incursions; Slope: 15–20; 20–30 SW; Relief: terrace soil, receiving from upslope (near Ors); Altitude: *c.* 1,550 m.

L 1.5–0	Root mat, leaf litter; turf
Al 1–19 (thin section 1)	Very dark greyish brown (10YR3/2) very weak fine sandy loam (Table 18.4); few small stones; granular to fine blocky; abundant fine; earthworms; gradual smooth boundary
Al/Bw 19–50	Very dark greyish brown (10YR3/2) very weak fine sandy loam; common small stones; poor fine prisms; many fine roots;

(thin section 2)   earthworms
local Bw/Cw   Brownish-yellow (10YR6/6–6/8) weak fine sandy loam; abun-
'50–70'   dant stones; angular blocky
(thin section 3)

18.2.3 *Micromorphological description*

Subalpine terraced pasture

1 **A1** Structure is intergrain microaggregate with a high (15–30%) vughy porosity. The coarse mineral fraction includes dominant fine to coarse quartz sand and common mica, frequent rock fragments and very few soil aggregates. Fine mineral is dark brown (PPL), low birefringent and pale brown (OIL). Frequent coarse roots and common fine organic matter are present, with little charcoal. Pedofeatures are dominated by abundant sub-rounded, very fine mineral excrements, and common passage features. The soil is weakly sesquioxidic with a minor colluvial element and highly biologically worked (Figure 18.3a).

2 **Bw** Structure is coarse blocky and less porous (15–20%) than 1. The fine fabric is dark yellowish brown and moderately birefringent, and although it contains less organic matter (Table 18.2), it includes more charcoal. Few rounded soil fragments occur. Pedofeatures include very few mineral excrements and frequent passage features. The soil is similar to 1, but is less biologically worked and contains a higher colluvial and charcoal content.

3 **Bw/Cw** Structure is blocky with high (25%) porosity of dominant channels, with frequent vughs and packing voids. Coarse mineral fraction comprises dominant sand-sized quartz, and mica and common rock fragments. Fine material is yellowish brown, medium birefringent and pale orange (OIL). Little organic matter. Pedofeatures include a few excrements and occasional dusty clay void coatings and infills. This moderately sesquioxidic subsoil displays the characteristics of an unweathered parent material that has been affected by biological activity and clay translocation.

4 **Old garden soil, now pasture** Structure is subangular fine blocky with a high (30%) vughy and channel porosity. Coarse mineral is dominantly quartz and mica sand. Fine material is darkish brown, similar to 1. Both coarse and fine organic matter are very abundant, whereas charcoal is very sparse. Pedofeatures include abundant organo-mineral and organic excrements and few passage features. This moderately sesquioxidic topsoil is highly biologically worked and displays no textural features of its prior cultivation, which ceased around 1960.

5 **Deep terrace (occupation dump) deposit** Structure is very coarse prisms with a moderate (20%) coarse vughy and channel porosity between very dense aggregates. Coarse mineral is composed of dominant soil fragments. It has a dark brown low birefringent fine fabric with little organic matter but much charcoal. Pedofeatures include many very dusty clay and matrix coatings and infills. Although this soil has the weathered character of a B horizon, it does appear only slightly perforated by biological activity.

6 **Iron Age occupation layer** Structure is massive with moderate (15–20%) vughy porosity. Coarse fraction is dominated by rock fragments, with common quartz and frequent mica. Two major fine fabrics occur: (a) very dominant, very dark brown (PPL), dark brown (OIL) and opaque, and (b) few darkish brown (PPL), pale brown (OIL) very low birefringent. In (a) fine, very abundant 'grassy' charcoal with

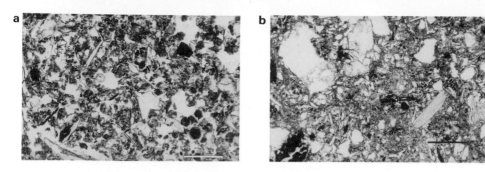

Figure 18.3   (a) Chisone Valley: subalpine terraced pasture, A1 horizon; fabric is dominated by fine organo-mineral excrements testifying to the high level of biological activity in this pasture soil (and lack of podzolic leaching); note also large micas from the schist parent material. PPL. (Bar = 550μm)

(b) Chisone Valley; Iron Age occupation at Villaretto; moderately dense soil with low vughy porosity, a variety of charcoal-rich fine fabrics, coarse charcoal and differing dusty clay void coatings all indicative of domestic occupation.PPL. (Bar = 550μm)

occasional organic matter, whereas in (b) only occasional fine charcoal occurs. Pedofeatures include many charcoal rich and ferruginous impure clay (silt-sized mica) coatings and infills, with rare finely dusty clay coatings. This heterogeneous soil shows mixing of charcoal-rich anthropogenic fabrics and the translocation of mainly coarse material followed by fine (Figure 18.3b).

18.2.4 *Discussion*
The data presented are interpreted here (Figure 18.4) in the light of the palaeoenvironmental and archaeological background to the area.

The high pastures
The peat at Lago la Manica (2,365 m) in the alpine high-pasture zone (where the base is dated to 6290 ± 60 BP [4340 BC] – Berlin) developed under a dominant pine, spruce and fir coniferous forest, the mid-Holocene tree-line being at least 170 m higher than at present (Scaife, 1987). Later (4430 ± 60 BP [2480 BC], 4360 ± 50 BP [2410 BC] – Berlin, on larch wood), there was a gradual decline in conifers, perhaps due to anthropogenic pressures bringing about a change in the open alpine herbaceous vegetation now developed over the podzol cover found at this altitude, which may have originally developed under a coniferous forest.

The larch zone
At Profile 1 within the lower part of the present-day coniferous belt, larch occurs over old pasture. Profile morphology and chemistry (Tables 18.2 and 18.3) clearly show a recent surface podzol (Ah/Ea) developed in brown soil horizons (A1, Bw), which in turn overlie a podzol subsoil (Bs). The soils of this

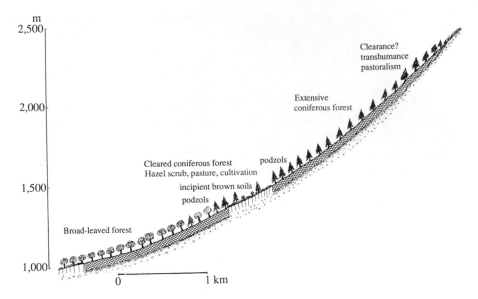

Figure 18.4   Chisone Valley: Chalcolithic soils and vegetation.

area have undergone dramatic changes: the alpine podzol first formed as the Holocene climax soil of the area was transformed into a brown soil (Cambisol). The earlier and very recent podzolic phases can be readily ascribed to the natural coniferous forest cover, whereas the brown soil phase is at the present anomalous at this altitude and can only be comprehended from the soil micromorphological study of the terrace zone.

The terrace zone
Nearer Balm'Chanto, old pasture (Nisbet and Biagi, 1987) is found on terraced brown soils, which, although acid, have a high level of biological activity with no evidence of podzolic leaching. Rather, the fabric has an overall sesquioxide aggregate character, any leached material being biologically homogenised with sesquioxidic illuvial soil. The micromorphological variation in the three horizons studied (1–3) suggests that the upper two horizons developed in part by colluvial accretion after terracing, the Bw(2) horizon including charcoal. The excremental character of the soil indicates a pastoral history, although it should be noted that the local faunally worked pastoral soil (4) was cultivated until the 1960s, displaying no textural features of ever having been tilled if such features ever existed, since high biological activity has rapidly destroyed this evidence.
   Brown soils now extend all the way down to Villaretto (Figures 18.2, 18.4).

Man's influence on the edaphic regime
The pattern of soil formation in the Chisone Valley seems generally unrelated to the variety of parent materials noted in the introduction. In general, it appears

that long Holocene weathering under vegetation has produced a uniform acidic soil cover, which apparently responds mainly to variations in land use and vegetation. The development of high alpine pastures from about 4000 BP has already been described. At the subalpine larch and terrace zone, soils may more clearly reflect human impact.

In his studies of modern alpine soils, Duchaufour (1958, 1982) has shown that the 'climax' iron podzol formed under *Larix* (larch) and other conifers could be ameliorated to a brown soil if the forest was replaced by pastures containing nitrogen-fixing *Leguminosae*, because biological activity was enhanced. The latter leads to the breakdown of raw humus and the intimate mixing of depleted and illuvial mineral material. A similar kind of evolution seems to be demonstrated by the faunal working of the relic Bs horizon (Profile 1; see also Figure 18.3a), converting mobile (pyrophosphate extractable) 'spodic' iron to immobile (dithionite extractable) 'cambic' iron in the Bw and Al horizons. Such faunal activity was noted in thin sections 1, 2 and 4 in contemporary pastoral soils. The origins of this change from alpine podzols to brown soils may be inferred from the evidence at Balm'Chanto. This Chalcolithic site was more than just a shelter for hunters and shepherds. In fact, geological, animal and plant materials were processed here and were combined with agricultural and pastoral activities and a hunting and gathering economy. The site occupied an ecotonal position, dominated by hazel woodland, at a boundary between a lower-altitude broad-leaved forest and higher-altitude coniferous forest (Biagi and Nisbet, 1987). The possibility that a herbaceous pastoral vegetation (Scaife, 1987) developed alongside cereal cultivation, both at the expense of the natural coniferous cover during the Chalcolithic occupation, may suggest that the amelioration of the local iron podzols (formed under conifers) to brown soils began at this time, possibly when transhumance pastoralism was also starting to create the high alpine pastures.

Terrace and occupation deposits were also examined in the area as a complementary part of the subalpine landscape (thin sections 5 and 6). The obvious dumped and disturbed sediments were created because of the scarcity of flat land and the needs of cultivation and building. Also, as noted earlier, pastures were improved by terrace construction, soil depths increasing by 'natural' colluviation. In contrast, others include high quantities of anthropogenic materials, and have the dense unworked fabrics typical of rapidly dumped sediments. At Villaretto, the deposits are dominated by anthropic charcoal-rich fabrics (Figure 18.3b) comparable to those from Uscio (see Chapter 17). Such material and its porosity coatings could also relate at Villaretto to Iron Age collapse and re-working of mud floors and walls (daub), slaking under the impact of trampling, and are more likely to relate to occupation at this site rather than be a result of dumping purely for terrace construction.

The use of micromorphology in the Chisone Valley project was very much supportive of other palaeoenvironmental and archaeological studies, particularly in that the mechanisms which produced the present-day brown soil/podzol pattern were isolated, thus allowing interpretation of the land use effects dating from the Chalcolithic onwards. A further example of alpine terrace construction is studied next.

18.3 **Vislario**

18.3.1 *Location and preliminary studies*

The site comprises a high (1,054 m) terrace on a mica schist and fine gneiss of the Sesia–Lanzo massif area in the Orco Valley at Canavese, some 60 km north of Turin, and is dated by pottery to the Late Bronze Age/Early Iron Age (eighth to fourth centuries BC) (Nisbet, 1983; Nisbet and Macphail, 1983). Eight metres of the two-metre thick terrace were excavated in conjunction with palaeo-botanical (charcoal and phytolith) studies (Figure 18.5). The latter gave some picture of the development and land use of the site but failed to establish the following points:

> whether the base of the terrace (Layer 2) was natural or a man-made deposit;
> exactly what kind of environment had existed during occupation;
> what the terrace deposits were composed of; how the terrace was used through its
> development.

Micromorphology was employed to answer these questions.

18.3.2 *Field description*

Terrace at Vislario

> Aspect: south; Slope: locally up to 30–40 to 550 m above the Soana valley: 5–7 on terrace; Vegetation: grass and herb meadow; Altitude: 1,054 m OD.
>
> 0–12 cm **Recent Ap:** Dark yellowish brown (10YR3/4) moderately fine silt loam; well-developed granular; many fine roots; moderately humose; earthworms; few small to medium stones; clear smooth boundary.
>
> 12–35(56) cm **Ap 2:** Dark brown (7.5YR4/2) moderately weak sandy silt loam; poorly developed large subangular blocky to prismatic; few coarse roots; moderately humose; earthworms; common small to large stones; fine charcoal; diffuse, irregular boundary.
>
> 35(56)–142 cm **Layer 4:** Dark reddish brown (5YR3/2) moderately weak loamy sand with dark lenses; poorly developed coarse prisms; few coarse roots; moderately humose; earthworms; common small to medium stones; common fine charcoal, charcoal bands; common large pottery sherds; diffuse, irregular boundary.
>
> 142–183 cm **Layer 3:** Yellowish red to strong brown (5YR5/8–7.5YR5/8) moderately weak loamy sand, with inclusion of Layer 4 material via earthworm channels; poorly developed coarse prisms; earthworms; few to common stones; rare charcoal fragments; few sherds; diffuse, irregular boundary.
>
> 183–240 cm **Layer 2:** Yellowish brown (10YR5/6) moderately weak loamy sand; poorly developed coarse prisms; abundant fine to medium stones; diffuse, irregular boundary.
>
> 240+ cm **C/D:** combination of colluvial/solifluction head; alternate fine and angular rock (mica schist and fine gneiss) debris sometimes on bedrock.

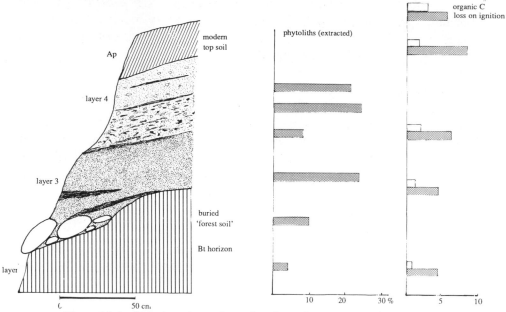

Figure 18.5   Vislario: schematic section through terrace and phytolith data.

18.3.3 *Micromorphology*

Layer 4:

Structure is subangular blocky with high (23%) mainly coarse channel porosity. Coarse mineral fraction (C:F 5:5) comprises dominant schist, quartzite and fine sandstone rock fragments, and soil fragments; with common fine quartz sand and silt-sized mica. Fine fabric is dark brown and speckled and almost non-birefringent whereas brown areas have low birefringence. It is dark orange in reflected light. Occasional organic matter and abundant charcoal are present. Pedofeatures include frequent intercalations of fine fabric with occasional low birefringent clay coatings, fabric heterogeneity of darker and lighter soil, and minor biological reworking; the end result is a generally dense fabric (Figure 18.6a).

Layer 3:

Structure is subangular blocky with moderate (15%) channel and vughy porosity. Coarse fraction (C:F 25:75) as above although the fine fraction differs by being more biologically worked and has a more speckled brownish, low birefringent character which is bright orange in OIL, indicating sesquioxidic staining. Pedofeatures are a mix of intercalated fine material with common dusty clay coatings strongly perforated by biological activity.

Layer 2:

Structure as above with low (6%) channel porosity. Coarse mineral (C:F 65:35) is dominated by rock fragments. Fine fabric is pale dusty brown, moderately birefringent and bright yellow in OIL. Organic matter and charcoal are very low. Pedofeatures include occasionally well-developed, fine, moderately birefringent clay coatings and infills, which appear unrelated to earlier (cryogenic ?) mixing and segregation (Figure 18.6b).

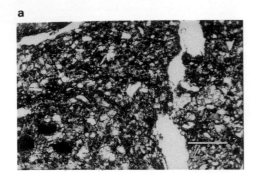

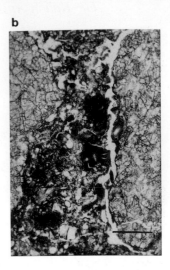

Figure 18.6   (a) Vislario. Layer 4; mainly dense charcoal-rich occupation soil with minor biological reworking; note dark bands of slaked soil (intercalations) and dusty clay coatings; these features mainly suggest an environment of rather rapid dumping. PPL. (Bar = 230μm)

(b) Vislario. Layer 2, Natural subsoil; void spaces between coarse rock fragments feature moderately fine clay coatings and infills relating to the soil's forest ancestry or possibly to through-flow of clay mobilised by cultivation higher up in the terrace. PPL. (Bar = 230μm)

18.3.4 *Interpretation*

In Layer 4 the low biological porosity and high charcoal content suggest the dumping of 'occupation soil' that has been little re-worked (Figure 18.6a); on the other hand, in Layer 3 features of homogenisation, slaking and biological activity indicate cultivation of this level in the terrace; in Layer 2 the fabric appears to represent the *situ* soil developed on the site, the fine clay coatings (Figure 18.6b) relating to a 'forest soil' ancestry or possibly to soil slaking as a result of cultivation in the overlying terrace deposits.

The soil micromorphological data when combined with the palaeobotanical and archaeological results allow the following interpretation of the site:

The low number of phytoliths in Layer 2 supports the conjecture that this cambisol subsoil did develop under a forest which, according to the charcoal, was of a mixed oak type. Clay coatings in the fabric are not inconsistent with this. In Layer 3, sharply increased numbers of phytoliths infer a more open environment, which from the micromorphology probably involved cultivation as well as pastoralism – cereals and grasses giving rise to enhanced phytoliths counts. As in Layer 3, cultural debris and charcoal were also dumped in Layer 4, and although the evidence indicates continuing open conditions, some of the phytoliths may derive from 'grass' included in occupation soils, i.e., daub and floors of a house, which produced varying fabric types noted in thin section.

The landscape setting of the site and the palaeoenvironmental studies (Nisbet, 1983) suggests that during occupation the ecotonal position was

Events	Evidence
(Layer 2) Relic freeze–thaw; Holocene development of brown soil (cambisol), possibly with minor clay translocation under a probable deciduous woodland.	Relic segregated fabric with weakly sesquioxidic cambic fabric; few clay coatings; very few phytoliths.
Clearance, erosion or truncation of soil	Narrow yellowish brown horizon over a head deposit
(Layer 3) Terrace wall building, dumping and accretion of local soil and occupation debris. Cultivation and possibly pastoral use of terrace.	Common cultural material and charcoal; very abundant phytoliths. Biologically worked slaked soil.
(Layer 4) Terrace wall heightening; rapid dumping of soil and dense occupation debris. Still open environment, minor pasture/cultivation.	Common cultural material and charcoal; dense heterogenous fine charcoal-rich fabrics; minor slaking and biological activity; very abundant phytoliths.

juxtaposed to mixed oak woodland resources at lower altitudes and to local beechwoods, and also permitted easy access to alpine high pastures for transhumance.

Soil micromorphology confirmed the presence and nature of the original soil cover prior to occupation, identified local soil and anthropic soil as the make-up of the terrace deposits, and supported the view that both cultivation and pastoralism were practised, although some phytoliths could have derived more directly from mud floor and daub materials.

18.4 Conclusions

These micromorphological studies indicated ways in which the subalpine and Apennine vegetation and landscape resources were taken into management (forests opened up, pastoralism and cultivation, terrace construction) in the Chalcolithic and later prehistoric periods. Specifically, at Prato Mollo soil micromorphology was directly correlated with the pollen spectra so that local forest fires, which affected the peat, and mineral inwashes could be related to the decline in the local fir forest, whereas at Vislario the combination of microfabric analysis with palaeobotanical studies showed the changeover from a deciduous forest environment to a terrace utilised for cultivation and pastoralism. On a much larger scale, the joining of soil survey, chemistry and key micromorphological investigations at the Chisone Valley contributed greatly to the understanding of Alpine land use as indicated by a suite of zoo-archaeological, palaeobotanical and archaeological data. In addition to this supportive role, soil micromorphology provided clear information on land use and the effects of land-use changes on the environment. The use of anthropogenic soils from occupation sites in formation of terrace deposits was also identified at both the Chisone Valley and at Vislario.

CONCLUSIONS

Soil micromorphology evolved principally from pedology, where thin sections are used to illustrate soils and some soil-forming processes, though a similar use of thin sections in sediments is called petrography. We have taken many of the ideas used in soil micromorphology and applied them to archaeologically related situations in an effort to reach two types of audiences who have distinctly different but clearly overlapping interests. The first group is made up of what we might term 'environmentalists' or persons with some scientific training in the sciences such as earth science, botany or zoology. Particularly for those with geological or pedological experience, where the technical aspects of the book should not pose a problem, we hope to have shown how the method can be used to glean information concerning the sequence of events in the history of landscape and soil development or to determine the nature or origin of materials found in archaeological sites. Thus for them the technique may not be something radically new in itself but its application to Quaternary, and geomorphological 'soft-rock' situations is. Though some earth scientists do concern themselves with studies of pottery temper, their numbers have been quite limited up to the present time.

The second group represents the archaeological community at large. We do not expect that many archaeologists will become experts in soil micromorphology for dealing with archaeological problems, especially since courses in micromorphology are virtually non-existent. We hope, however, that ideas are presented clearly enough to be understood by people with minimal background in the earth sciences and feel that we will have succeeded if they acquire a general awareness of the value of the technique, the principles behind it and the kinds of problems that can be solved. With this appreciation they will then know not only whether micromorphology is an appropriate tool to use in a research project and how it can be applied but also whether it is worthwhile to call in a specialist. It should also provide enough of the necessary background so that the archaeologist can communicate clearly with the specialist. It should also enable the archaeologist to remove some of the aura of hocus-pocus that is so common in specialists' reports.

More importantly, however, we would like to have demonstrated to archaeologists that micromorphology and the soils, sediments and objects that it can examine, form a fundamental and integral part of an archaeological investigation, and that the artifacts that are recovered must be viewed in the overall

323

'geological' context in which they are found. Micromorphology and micro-morphological samples should thus be treated like those used in palynological or faunal studies. This is most clearly illustrated in the field in instances where artifacts are seen to have been transported by runoff or mass movements. In other cases, however, smaller-scale and scarcely visible biological or pedological processes can modify both the distribution and occurrence of artifacts and the appearance of a stratigraphic section exposed at a site. Thus we feel that archaeologists should place the technique and what it can contribute on a par with the excavation itself.

Though micromorphology has developed from the more mature disciplines of soil science and, to a lesser extent, geology, its applications to archaeology are still in their incipient stages and development will continue, probably quite rapidly in the near future. Although we have tried to cover a variety of 'real life' instances in the case studies, the number and variety of situations is infinite. Throughout the text and particularly in the last part, we have attempted to identify specific features and interpret them and it is especially here that expansion would be appropriate. Many of our observations and interpretations – particularly for archaeological settings – are based upon what we deem to be analogous situations in geology and pedology. In the future we expect that, as the empirical data base broadens, both observations and interpretations will become more sophisticated, if not simply more correct.

We anticipate that this will come about for several reasons. The first is that we will have more experience that will permit greater facility in identifying and comparing observed features. Secondly and related to this, we presume that with greater effort devoted to micromorphological studies of archaeological sites and contexts – a subject virtually unknown until now – we shall see a marked expansion in the data base of catalogued features. Finally, we suspect that the avenue of research that will lead to the greatest advancements will originate from information collected by controlled experimentation, a sort of experimental ethno-micromorphological archaeology. Although experimental scenarios are endless and can be tailored for specific site settings, some reasonable generalised strategies could encompass:

> trampling experiments, whereby a given substrate is periodically sampled after continuous trampling and later checked for changes in size and shape of aggregates and voids;
> experimental burning and hearth formation, where different materials are burned and the residues and substrates are checked to monitor mineralogical and biological transformations. These products can also be experimented with by dumping, compacting or using in construction. With these types of experiments we shall have a greater ability to recognise accurately and interpret features from archaeological sites.

It is interesting to note that this experimental approach is only recently becoming more common in traditional soil micromorphological investigations, particularly in areas where compaction and illuviation are concerned. This is somewhat surprising considering that soil micromorphology is well beyond the infancy stage.

Finally, we wish to stress one additional point. This book cannot (or should not) be used as something like the Merck Manual, where it is possible to find the description, diagnosis, treatment and contra-indications of most archaeologically related diseases and maladies, a sort of cure-all of all site problems. Clearly this approach is precluded by the complexity and variability of geological and pedological systems, the unpredictability of human beings, and the youthfulness of the subject. It would be best, therefore, to approach the book with a flexible attitude.

REFERENCES

Agrawal, D.P., 1982. *The Archaeology of India. Scand. Inst. of Asian Studies* 46, 294pp.

Agrawal, D.P. and R.K. Sood, 1979. The ecological factors and the Harappan civilisation. In G.L. Possehl (ed.), *Harappan Civilization*, pp. 223–31. Oxford and I.B.H. Publishing.

Ahuja, R.L. and Mahendra Singh, 1983. *Soils of Hissar District and their Management.* Dept. of Soils, HAU, Hissar. 75pp.

Allchin B., A.S. Goudie and K.T.M. Hede, 1978. *The Prehistory and the Paleogeography of the Great Indian Desert.* Academic Press, London, 370pp.

Allen, M.J., 1987. Archaeological and environmental aspects of colluviation in south-east England. In: W. Groenman-van Waateringe and M. Robinson, (eds), *Man-Made Soils*, pp.67–92. B.A.R. Int. Series 410, Oxford.

Allen, M.J. and R.I. Macphail, 1987. Micromorphology and magnetic susceptibility studies: their combined role in interpreting archaeological soils and sediments. In: N. Fedoroff, L.M. Bresson and M.A. Courty (eds.), *Micromorphologie des Sols – Soil Micromorphology*, pp. 669–76. AFES, Plaisir.

Altschuler, Z.S., 1973. The weathering of phosphate deposits. Geochemical and environmental aspects. In: E.J. Griffith, A. Beeton, J.M. Spencer and D.T. Mitchel (eds.), *Environmental Phosphorous Handbook*, pp. 33–96. Wiley, N.Y.

Anderson, P.C., 1980. A testimony of prehistoric tasks: diagnostic residues on stone tool working edges. *World Archaeology*, 12: 181–94.

Anderson-Gerfaud, P., 1983. Consideration of the uses of certain backed and lustred stone tools from the Late Mesolithic and Natufian levels of Abu Hureyra and Mureybet. In: M.-Cl. Cauvin (ed.), *Traces d'utilisation sur les outils néolithiques du Proche-Orient. Trav. Maison Orient*, 5: 77–105.

Atkinson, R.J.C., 1957. Worms and weathering. *Antiquity*, 31: 219–33.

Avery, B.W., 1980. *Soil Classification for England and Wales.* Soil Survey Technical Monograph No. 14, Harpenden.

Avery, B.W., and C.L. Bascomb (eds.), 1974. *Soil Survey Laboratory Methods.* Soil Survey Technical Monograph No. 6, Harpenden.

Babel, U., 1975. Micromorphology of soil organic matter. In: J.E. Gieseking (ed.), *Soil Components.* Volume 1: *Organic Components*, pp. 369–473. Springer-Verlag, New York.

Baffico, O., P. Biagi and R. Maggi, 1983. Il Mesolitico. In: R. Maggi (ed.), *Preistoria nella Ligria Orientale*, pp. 33–44. Renato Siri Editore, Sestri Levante.

Bagnolo, R.A. and N.O. Baindorff-Nielsen, 1980. The pattern of natural size distributions. *Sedimentology*, 27: 199–207.

Bain, R.J., 1985. Petrography of Mayan mortar, Isla Mujeres, Quintana Roo, Mexico. Abstracts, Geological Society of America Annual Meeting, Orlando, Florida, 517.

de Bakker, H., 1979. *Major Soils and Soil Regions in the Netherlands.* Junk Pub., Pudoc, Wageningen, 203pp.

Bal, L., 1973. *Micromorphological Analysis of Soils.* Soil Survey Papers No. 6, Netherland Soil Survey Institute, Wageningen, 174pp.

    1975. Carbonate in soils: theoretical consideration on, and proposal for, its fabric analysis. 2. Crystal tubes, intercalary crystals, k-fabric. *Netherlands Jour. of Agr. Sci.*, 23: 163–76.

1982. *Zoological Ripening of Soils*. Agricultural Research Reports No. 850, Pudoc, Wageningen, 365pp.

Balaam, N.D. and H.M. Porter, 1982. The phosphate surveys. In: N.D. Balaam, K. Smith and G.J. Wainwright, The Shaugh Moor Project: fourth report. Environment, context and conclusions. *Proceedings Prehistoric Society*, 48: 203–78.

Balaam, N., M. Bell, A.E.U. David, M.A. Girling, B. Levitan, R.I. Macphail, M. Robinson and R. Scaife, in press. Prehistoric and Romano-British sites at Westward Ho!, Devon: archaeology and paleoenvironmental surveys 1983 and 1984. In N. Balaam, V.S. Straker and B. Levitan (eds.), *Studies in Palaeoeconomy and Environment in South West England*. B.A.R., Oxford.

Balout, L., 1955. *Préhistoire de l'Afrique du Nord*. Arts et Métiers Graphiques, Paris, 544pp.

Barrat, B.C., 1964. A classification of humus forms and microfabrics in temperate grasslands. *Journal Soil Science*, 15: 342–56.

1967. Differences in humus forms and their microfabrics induced by longterm topdressings in hayfields. *Geoderma*, 1: 197–227.

Bar-Yosef, O. 1985. 'A quoi servaient les murs de Jericho?'. *La Recherche*, 16 (no. 171); 1384–6.

Bar-Yosef, O. and B. Vandermeersch, 1972. The stratigraphical and cultural problems of the passage from Middle to Upper Palaeolithic in Palestinian caves. In: F. Bordes (ed.), *The Origin of* Homo sapiens, pp. 221–5. UNESCO, Paris.

Bar-Yosef, O., A. Gopher and A.N. Goring-Morris, 1980. Netiv Hagdud: 'Sultanian' mound in the Lower Jordan Valley. *Paléorient*, 6: 201–6.

Bar-Yosef, O., B. Vandermeersch, B. Arensburg, P. Goldberg, H. Laville, L. Meignen, Y. Rak, E. Tchernov and A–M. Tillier, 1986. New Data on the origin of modern man in the Levant. *Current Anthropology*, 27: 63–4.

Barzanji, A.F. and G.J. Stoops, 1974. Fabric and mineralogy of gypsum accumulations in some soils of Iraq. In: G.K. Rutherford (ed.), *Soil Microscopy*, pp. 271–7. Kingston, Ontario, Canada.

Baud, C.A. and D. Lacotte, 1984. Etude au microscope électronique à transmission de la colonisation bactérienne de l'os mort. *C.R. Acad. Sci., Paris*, 298 (2), no. 11: 507–10.

Begin, Z.B., A. Ehrlich and Y. Nathan, 1974. Lake Lisan, the Pleistocene precursor of the Dead Sea. *Geological Survey of Israel Bull.*, 63: 1–30.

Bell, M., 1981. Seaweed as a prehistoric resource. In: D. Brothwell and G. Dimbleby (eds.), *Environmental Aspects of Coasts and Islands*, pp. 117–26. B.A.R. Int. Series 94, Oxford.

1983. Valley sediments as evidence of prehistoric landuse on the South Downs. *Proceedings Prehistoric Society*, 49: 119–50.

Bertoldi de Pomar, H., 1975. Los silicofitolitos: sinopsis de su conocimiento. *De Darwinian*. 19: 173–206. Buenos Aires, Argentina.

1980. Analisis comparativo de silicobiolitos de diversos sedimentos continentales argentinos. *Ass. Geol. Argent. Revista*, 35: 547–57.

Bhan, S., 1975. Excavation at Mitathal (1968) and other explorations in the Sutlej–Yamuna divide. University Press, Kurukshetra, 132pp.

Biagi, P. and R. Nisbet, 1983. Prima campagna di scavo nel riparo sotto roccia di Balm'Chanto, Val Chisone (Torino). *Quaderni della Soprintendenza Archeologica del Piemonte*, 2: 21–42.

1987. *Balm'Chanto: a Copper Age Rock Shelter in the Cottian Alps*. Archeologia dell'Italia Settentronale, New Press, Como.

Biagi, P., R. Nisbet, R. Macphail and R. Scaife, 1984. Early farming communities and short range transhumance in the Cottian Alps (Chisone Valley, Turin) in the late third millennium BC. In: J. Lewthwaite and R.C. Kennard (eds.), *Early Settlement in the Western Mediterranean Islands and Peripheral Areas*, pp. 395–405. B.A.R. Int. Series 229, Oxford.

Bibby, J.S. and D. Mackney, 1969. *Landuse Capability Classification*. Soil Survey Technical Monograph No. 1, Harpenden.

Bisdom, E.B.A. (ed.), 1981. *Submicroscopy of Soils and Weathered Rocks*. Centre for Agricultural Publishing and Documentation, Wageningen, 320pp.

Bisdom, E.B.A. and J. Ducloux (eds.), 1983. Submicroscopic studies of soils. *Geoderma*, 30 (nos. 1–4): 1–356.

Bishnoi, O.P., 1975. Assessment of soil moisture storage from rainfall and its utility in Rabi crop planning in Haryana State. *Indian J. Met. Hydrol. Geophys.*, 26 (1): 97–100.

Boiffin, J. and L.M. Bresson, 1987. Dynamique de formation des croûtes superficielles: apport de l'analyse microscopique. In: N. Fedoroff, L.M. Bresson and M.A. Courty (eds.), *Micromorphologie des Sols – Soil Micromorphology*, pp. 393–9. Plaisir, AFES, France.

Bolt, A.J.J., H.J. Mücher, J. Sevink and J.M. Verstraten, 1980. A study on loess-derived colluvia in southern Limbourg (the Netherlands). *Netherlands Journal of Agricultural Science*, 28: 110–26.

Bonham, L.C. and J.H. Spotts, 1971. Measurement of grain orientation. In: R.E. Carver (ed.), *Procedures in Sedimentary Petrology*, pp. 285–312. John Wiley and Sons, New York.

Bonneau, M. and B. Souchier (eds.), 1982. *Constituents and Properties of Soils*. Academic Press, London, 496pp.

Bonucci, E. and G. Grazziani, 1975. Comparative thermogravimetric, X-ray diffraction and electron microscope investigations of burnt bones from recent, ancient and prehistoric age. *Accademia Nazionale dei Lincei*, Série VIII, vol. LIX, fasc. 5: 517–33.

Bordes, F., 1975. Sur la notion de sol d'habitat en préhistoire paléolithique. *Bulletin Societé Préhistorique Français*, 72: 139–44.

1984. Leçons sur le Paléolithique. *CNRS Cahiers du Quaternaire*, No. 7, Tome I. CNRS, Paris, 288pp.

Bresson, L.M., 1981. Ion micromilling applied to the ultra-microscopic study of soils. *Soil Science Society of America Journal*, 45: 568–73.

Brewer, R. 1964. *Fabric and Mineral Analysis of Soils*. Wiley and Sons, New York, 483pp.

Bridges, E.M., 1978a. *World Soils*, 2nd edition. Cambridge University Press, Cambridge, 89pp.

1978b. Interaction of soil and mankind in Britain. *Journal Soil Science*, 29: 125–39.

1982. Techniques of modern soil survey. In: E.M. Bridges and D.A. Davidson (eds.), *Principles and Applications of Soil Geography*, pp. 28–57. Longman, London.

Brooks, D.D., 1986. A review of the evidence for continuity in a British town in the 5th and 6th centuries. *Oxford Journal of Archaeology*, 5 (1): 77–102.

Bull, P.A., 1981. Environmental reconstruction by scanning electron microscopy. *Progress in Physical Geography*, 5: 368–97.

Bull, P.A. and P. Goldberg, 1985. Scanning electron microscope analysis of sediments from Tabun Cave, Mount Carmel, Israel. *Journal of Archaeological Science*, 12: 177–85.

Bullock, P. and C.P. Murphy, 1979. Evolution of a paleo-argillic brown earth (Paleudalf) from Oxfordshire, England. *Geoderma*, 22: 225–52.

Bullock, P., N. Fedoroff, A. Jongerius, G.J. Stoops and T. Tursina, 1985. *Handbook for Soil Thin Section Description*. Waine Research Publishers, Wolverhampton, 152pp.

Bunting, B.T. and L. Christensen, 1978. Micromorphology of calcareous crusts from the Canadian High Arctic. *Geologiska Foreningens i Stockholm Forhandlingar*, 100: 361–8.

Bunting, B.T. and N. Fedoroff, 1974. Micromorphological aspects of soil development in the Canadian High Arctic. In: G.K. Rutherford (ed.), *Soil Microscopy*, pp. 350–65. Limestone Press, Kingston (Ontario).

Buol, S.W., F.D. Hole and R.J. McCracken, 1973. *Soil Genesis and Classification*. Iowa State University Press, Ames, 320pp.

Butler, B.E., 1959. *Periodic Phenomena in Landscapes as a Basis for Soil Studies*. CSIRO, Australia, Soil Publication No. 14.

Butler, B.E. and H.M. Churchward, 1983. Aeolian processes. In: *Soils: an Australian Viewpoint*, pp. 91–9. Division of Soils, CSIRO. CSIRO, Melbourne/Academic Press, London.

Butzer, K.W., 1976. *Geomorphology from the Earth*. Harper and Row, New York, 463pp.
    1982. *Archaeology as Human Ecology*. Cambridge University Press, Cambridge, 364pp.
Cahen D., and J. Moeyersons, 1977. Subsurface movements of stone artifacts and their implications for the prehistory of Central Africa. *Nature*, 266: 812–15.
Carozzi, A. 1960. *Microscopic Sedimentary Petrography*. John Wiley and Sons, New York, 485pp.
Carver, R.E. (ed.), 1971. *Procedures in Sedimentary Petrology*. John Wiley and Sons, New York, 635pp.
Catt, J.A. and A.M. Weir, 1976. The study of archaeologically important sediments by petrographic techniques. In: D.A. Davidson and M.L. Shackley (eds.), *Geoarchaeology*, pp. 65–92. Duckworth, London.
Caudwell, C., 1987. Etude expérimentale de la formation de micrite et de sparite dans les stromatolites d'eau douce a Rivularia. *Bulletin de la Société Géologique de France*, 8e série, tome III, no. 2: 299–306.
Cent, J. and R. Brewer, 1971. *Preparation of Thin Sections of Soil Materials using Synthetic Resins*. CSIRO Division of Soils, Technical Paper No. 7, 18pp.
Chafetz, H.S. and R.L. Folk, 1984. Travertines: depositional morphology and the bacterially constructed constituents. *Journal of Sedimentary Petrology*, 54: 289–316.
Chorley, R.J., S.A. Schumm and D.E. Sugden, 1984. *Geomorphology*. Methuen, London, 605pp.
Clapham, A.J. and R.G. Scaife, 1988. A pollen and plant macrofossil investigation of Oakbank Crannog, Loch Tay, Scotland. In: P. Murphy and C. French (eds.), *The Exploitation of Wetlands*, pp. 293–325. B.A.R. Brit. Series, 186, Oxford.
Conacher, A.J. and J.B. Dalrymple, 1977. The nine unit landsurface model: an approach to pedomorphic research. *Geoderma*, 18: 1–154.
Conry, M.J., 1971. Irish plaggen soils, their distribution, origin and properties. *Journal Soil Science*, 22: 401–16.
Cook, S.F. and R.F. Heizer, 1965. *Studies on the Chemical Analysis of Archeological Sites*. University of California Press, Berkeley, 102pp.
Cornwall, I.W., 1953. Soil science and archaeology with illustrations from some British Bronze Age monuments. *Proceedings Prehistoric Society*, 2: 129–47.
    1958. *Soils for the Archaeologist*. Phoenix House, London, 230pp.
Courty, M.A., 1984. Formation et évolution des accumulations cendreuses: approche micromorphologique. *Actes du Colloque Interrégional sur le Néolithique*, Le Puy, 1981, pp. 341–53.
    1986. Quelques faciès d'altération des fragments carbonatées en grottes et abris sous roche préhistoriques. *Bull. Ass. Fr. Et. du Quat.*, 3/4: 281–9.
Courty, M.A. and N. Fedoroff, 1982. Micromorphology of a Holocene dwelling. *PACT*, 7: 257–77.
    1985. Micromorphology of recent and buried soils in a semi-arid region of North-West India. *Geoderma*, 35: 285–332.
Courty, M.A., R.P. Dhir and H. Raghavan, 1987. Microfabrics of calcium carbonate accumulations in arid soils of western India. In: N. Fedoroff, L.M. Bresson and M.A. Courty (eds.), *Micromorphologie des Sols – Soil Micromorphology*, pp. 227–34. AFES, Plaisir.
Cremaschi, M., 1985. Geoarchaeology: earth sciences in archaeological research. In: Homo: *Journey to the Origins of Man's History*, pp. 183–91. Cataloghi Marsilio, Venecia.
Cruise, G.M., in press. Palynological investigations in the Ligurian Apennines, northern Italy: preliminary results. *Archeologia in Liguria III*. Soprintendenza Archeologica della Liguria.
Curray, J.R., 1956. Dimensional grain orientation studies of Recent coastal sands. *Bulletin American Association Petroleum Geologists*, 40: 2440–56.
Dalrymple, J.B., 1958. The application of soil micromorphology to fossil soils and other deposits from archaeological sites. *Journal of Soil Science*, 9: 199–209.

1972. Experimental micropedological investigations of iron oxide–clay complexes and their interpretation with respect to the soil fabrics of paleosols. *Soil Micromorphology*, pp. 583–94. Warszawa, Pologne.

Dalrymple, J.B. and C.Y. Jim, 1984. Experimental study of soil microfabrics induced by isotropic stresses of wetting and drying. *Geoderma*, 34: 43–68.

Dalrymple, J.B. and S.R. Theocharopoulos, 1984. Intrapedal cutans – experimental production of depositional cutans (illuviation) channel argillans. *Geoderma*, 33: 237–43.

Dapples, E.C. and J.F. Rominger, 1945. Orientation analysis of fine grained clastic sediments: a report in progress. *Journal of Geology*, 53: 246–61.

Darmon, F. 1984. Analyses polliniques de deux sites de la Basse Vallée du Jourdain; Fazaël VIII et Salibya IX. *Paléorient*, 10: 106–10.

1986. La cadre écologique de sites épipaléolithiques et du Néolithique ancien dans la Basse Vallée du Jourdain: (analyses polliniques de la region de Fazaël–Salibiya). Paris: Université Panthéon–Sorbonne, Thèse de doctorat, 315pp.

1987. Analyses polliniques de trois sites natoufiens (ancient, recent, final) dans la région de Salibiya–Fazaël. *Paléorient*, 13: 121–9.

Davidson, D.A., 1973. Particle size and phosphate analysis – evidence for the evolution of a tell. *Archaeometry*, 15: 143–52.

1982. Soils and man in the past. In: E.M. Bridges and D.A. Davidson (eds.), *Principles and Applications of Soil Geography*, pp. 1–27. Longman, London.

Debénath, A., J.P. Raynal, J. Roche, J.P. Texier and D. Ferembach, 1986. Stratigraphie, habitat, typologie et devenir de l'Atérien marocain: données récentes.

DeConinck, F., 1980. Major mechanisms in formation of spodic horizons. *Geoderma*, 24: 101–28.

Delmas, A.B., J. Berrier and H. Chamayou, 1987. Les figures de corrosion de la calcite. Typologie et séquence évolutive. In: N. Fedoroff, L.M. Bresson and M.A. Courty (eds.), *Micromorphologie des Sols – Soil Micromorphology*, pp. 303–8. AFES, Plaisir.

Dewolf, Y., 1982. *Le contact Ile-de-France, Basse-Normandie. Evolution géodynamique*. Mém. et docts. de Géogr., Editions CNRS, Paris, 253pp.

Dimbleby, G.W., 1962. *The Development of British Heathlands and their Soils*. Clarendon Press, Oxford.

Dorioz, J.M. and M. Robert, 1987. Aspects microscopiques des relations entre les microorganismes ou végétaux et les argiles. Conséquence sur les microorganisations et la microstructuration des sols. In: N. Fedoroff, L.M. Bresson and M.A. Courty (eds.), *Micromorphologie des Sols – Soil Micromorphology*, pp. 353–61. AFES, Plaisir.

Drewett, P., 1985. The excavation of barrows, V–IX at West Heath, Harting, 1980. *Sussex Archaeological Collections*, 123: 355–60.

Duchaufour, P., 1958. Dynamics of forest soils under the Atlantic climate. Unpub. lectures in surveying and forest engineering, Institute Scientifique Franco-Canadien, Quebec.

1982. *Pedology*. Allen and Unwin, London, 448pp.

Eidt, R.C., 1984. *Advances in Abandoned Settlement Analysis: Application to Prehistoric Anthrosols in Colombia, South America*. The Center for Latin America, University of Wisconsin–Milwaukee, 159pp.

Embleton, C. and C.A.M. King, 1975. *Periglacial Geomorphology*. Edward Arnold, London, 203pp.

Evans, J.S., 1971. Habitat change on the calcareous soils of Britain: the impact of Neolithic man. In: D.D.A. Simpson (ed.), *Economy and Settlement in Neolithic and Early Bronze Age Britain and Europe*, pp. 27–74. University Press, Leicester.

1972. *Landsnails in Archaeology*. Seminar Press, London, 436pp.

Farrand, W.R., 1975. Sediment analysis of a prehistoric rock shelter: the Abri Pataud. *Quaternary Research*, 5: 1–26.

FAO-UNESCO, 1981. *Soil Map of the World*. Vol. V: *Europe*. UNESCO, Paris.

Faul, M.L. and R.T. Smith, 1980. Phosphate analysis and three possible Dark Age ecclesiastical sites in Yorkshire. *Landscape History*, 2: 21–38.

Fedoroff, N., 1966. Les cryosols. *Science du Sol*, 2: 77–110.

1979. Organisation du sol à l'échelle microscopique. In: M. Bonneau and B. Souchier (eds.), *Constituants et Propriétés du sol*, pp. 251–65. Masson, Paris.

Fedoroff, N. and P. Goldberg, 1982. Comparative micromorphology of two late Pleistocene palaeosols (in the Paris Basin). *CATENA*, 9: 227–51.

Feraud, G., D. York, C. Hall, N. Goren and H.P. Schwarcz, 1983. $^{40}/^{39}$Ar age limit for an Acheulean site in Israel (sample site: Berekhat Ram). *Nature*, 304: 263–5.

Finlayson, B.L., 1985. Soil creep: a formidable fossil misconception. In: H.S. Richards, R.R. Arnett and S. Ellis (eds.), *Geomorphology and Soils*, pp. 141–58. Allen and Unwin, London.

Fisher, P.F. and R.I. Macphail, 1985. Studies of archaeological soils and deposits by micromorphological techniques. In: N. Feiller, D.D. Gilbertson and N.G.A. Ralph (eds.), *Palaeoenvironmental Investigations: Research Design, Methods and Data Analysis*, pp. 93–112. B.A.R. Int. Series 258, Oxford.

Fisher, R.V. and H.-U. Schmincke, 1984. *Pyroclastic Rocks*. Springer-Verlag, Berlin, 472pp.

FitzPatrick, E.A., 1971. *Pedology*. Oliver and Boyd, Edinburgh, 306pp.

1984. *Micromorphology of soils*. Chapman and Hall, London, 433pp.

Flicoteaux, R. and J. Lucas, 1984. Weathering of phosphate minerals. In: J.O. Nriagu and P.B. Moore (eds.), *Phosphate Minerals*, pp. 292–317. Springer-Verlag, Berlin.

Folk, R.L., 1959. Practical petrographic classification of limestones. *Am. Assoc. Petrol. Geol. Bull.*, 43: 1–38.

Folk, R.L. and R. Assereto, 1976. Comparative fabrics of length-slow and length-fast calcite and calcitized aragonite in a Holocene speleothem, Carlsbad Caverns, New Mexico. *Journal of Sedimentary Petrology*, 46: 486–96.

Folk, R.L. and G.K. Hoops, 1982. An early Iron Age layer of glass made from plants at Tel Yin'am, Israel. *Journal of Field Archaeology*, 9: 455–66.

Fowler, P.J. and J.G. Evans, 1967. Plough-marks, lynchets and early fields. *Antiquity*, 41: 289–301.

Francfort H.P., 1985. *Prospections archéologiques au nord-ouest de l'Inde*. MAFI 1. Editions Recherches sur les Civilisations, mem. no. 62, 112pp.

Franzmeier, D.P. and E.P. Whiteside, 1963. A chronosequence of podzols in northern Michigan. I, II, III. *Michigan State University Agricultural Experimental Station Quarterly Bulletin*, 46: 2–20, 21–36, 37–57.

Friedman, G.M., 1958. Determination of sieve-size distribution from thin section data for sedimentary petrological studies. *Journal of Geology*, 66: 394–416.

Gasche, H. and O. Tunca, 1983. Guide to archaeostratigraphic classification and terminology: definitions and principles. *Journal of Field Archaeology*, 10: 325–35.

Geiss, J.W., 1973. Biogenic silica in selected species of deciduous angiosperms. *Soil Science*, 116: 113–19.

Gieseking, J.L. (ed.), 1975. *Soil Components*, Vol. 1: *Organic components*; Vol. 2: *Inorganic Components*. Springer-Verlag, Berlin, 534pp.

Gifford, J. and G.R. Rapp, (eds.), 1985. *Archaeological Geology*. Yale University Press, New Haven, 431pp.

Gladfelter, B. 1977. Geoarchaeology: the geomorphologist and archaeology. *American Antiquity*, 42: 519–38.

Goh, K.M. and B.P.J. Molloy, 1978. Radiocarbon dating of paleosols using soil organic matter components. *Journal Soil Science*, 29: 567–73.

Goldberg, P., 1978. Granulométrie des sédiments de la grotte de Taboun, Mont Carmel, Israel. *Géologie Méditerranéenne*, 5: 371–83.

1979a. Micromorphology of Pech de l'Azé II sediments. *Journal of Archaeological Science*. 6:17–47.

1979b. Geology of Late Bronze Age Mudbrick from Tel Lachish. *Tell-Aviv*, 6: 60–7.

1979c. Micromorphology of sediments from Hayonim Cave, Israel. *CATENA*, 6: 167–81.

1980. Micromorphology in archaeology and prehistory. *Paléorient*, 6: 159–64.

1983. Applications of micromorphology in archaeology. In: P. Bullock and C.P. Murphy (eds.), *Soil Micromorphology*, pp. 139–150. AB Academic Publishers, Berkhamsted.

1987. Soils, sediments and Acheulian artifacts at Berekhat Ram, Golan Heights. In: N. Fedoroff, L.M. Bresson and M.A. Courty (eds.), *Micromorphologie des Sols – Soil Micromorphology*, pp. 583–9. AFES, Plaisir.

Goldberg, P. and H. Laville, in press. Etude géologique des depôts de la grotte de Kebara (Mont Carmel): premiers résultats. B.A.R., Oxford.

Goldberg, P. and Y. Nathan, 1975. The phosphate mineralogy of et-Tabun Cave, Mount Carmel, Israel. *Mineralogical Magazine*, 40: 253–8.

Goren-Inbar, N., 1985. The lithic assemblage of the Berekhat Ram Acheulian site, Golan Heights. *Paléorient*, 11: 7–28.

Goudie, A.S., 1977. Sodium sulphate weathering and the disintegration of Mohenjo-Daro, Pakistan. *Earth Surface Processes*, 2: 75–86.

1981. *The Human Impact*. Basil Blackwell, Oxford, 326pp.

Goudie, A.S. and M.J. Day, 1980. Disintegration of fan sediments in Death Valley, California, by salt weathering. *Physical Geography*, 1–2: 126–37.

Grieve I.C., 1980. Some contrasts in soil development between grassland and deciduous woodland sites. *Journal Soil Science*, 31: 137–45.

Griffith, M.A., 1980. A pedological investigation of an archaeological site in Ontario, Canada – I. An examination of the soils in and adjacent to a former village. *Geoderma*, 24: 327–36.

1981. A pedological investigation of an archaeological site in Ontario, Canada – II. Use of chemical data to discriminate features of the Benson site. *Geoderma*, 25: 27–34.

 Grimes, W.F., 1968. *The Excavation of Roman and Medieval London*. Routledge-Kegal Paul, London.

Guilloré, P., 1983. Colour photograms of soil thin sections using the Ilford 'Cibachrome – A' print system. In: P. Bullock and C.P. Murphy (eds.), *Soil Micromorphology*, pp. 87–9. AB Academic Publishers, Berkhamsted.

1985. *Méthode de Fabrication Mécanique et en Série des Lames Minces*. Institut National Agronomique, Paris, Département des Sols, 22pp.

Halitim A., M. Robert and J. Berrier, 1983. A microscopic study of quartz evolution in arid areas. In: P. Bullock and C.P. Murphy (eds.), *Soil Micromorphology*, pp. 615–22. AB Academic Publishers, Berkhamsted.

Halitim, A. and M. Robert, 1987. Interactions du gypse avec les autres constituants du sol. Analyse microscopique de sols gypseux en zone aride (Algérie) et études expérimentales. In: N. Fedoroff, L.M. Bresson and M.A. Courty (eds.), *Micromorphologie des Sols – Soil Micromorphology*, pp. 179–86. AFES, Plaisir.

Hanna, F.S. and G.J. Stoops, 1976. Contribution to the micromorphology of some saline soils of the North Nile Delta in Egypt. *Pédologie*, 26: 55–73.

Hassan, F.A., 1977. Geoarchaeology: the geologist and archaeology. *American Antiquity*, 44: 267–70.

1978. Sediments in archaeology: methods and implications for palaeoenvironmental and cultural analysis. *Journal of Field Archaeology*, 5: 197–213.

Hayden, B. (ed.), 1986. *Report on the 1986 Excavations at Keatley Creek*. Submitted to SSHRC, Canada.

Hetier, J.M., F. Gutierrez Jerez and S. Bruckert, 1974. Morphoscopie et composition des complexes organo-minéraux des andosols. *C.R. Acad. Sci. Paris*, 278: 2735–7.

Hill, C.A., 1976. *Cave Minerals*. National Speleological Society, Huntsville, 137pp.

Hodgson, J.M., 1974. *Soil Survey Field Handbook*. Soil Survey Technical Monographs No. 5, Harpenden, 99pp.

Hole, F.D., 1961. A classification of pedoturbation and some other processes and factors of soil formation in relation to isotropism and anisotropism. *Soil Science*, 91: 375–7.

1981. Effects of animals on soil. *Geoderma*, 25: 75–112.

Houot, S. and J. Berthelin, 1987. Dynamique du fer et de la formation du colmatage ferrique des drains dans des sols hydromorphes à amphigley (Aquic Aplaquepts). In: N. Fedoroff, L.M. Bresson and M.A. Courty (eds.), *Micromorphologie des Sols – Soil Micromorphology*, pp. 345–52. AFES, Plaisir.

Hughes, P.J. and R.J. Lampert, 1977. Occupational disturbance and types of archaeological deposit. *Journal of Archaeological Science*, 4:135–40.

Hutchinson, G.E., 1950. *The Biogeochemistry of Vertebrate Excretion. American Museum of Natural History Bulletin*, 96: 554pp.

Hutton J.T., C.R. Twidale and A.R. Milnes, 1977. Characteristics and origin of some Australian silcretes. In: T. Langford Smith (ed.), *Silcretes in Australia*, pp. 19–40. Department of Geography, University of New England, Armidale.

Imeson, A.C. and P.D. Jungerius, 1974. Landscape stability in the Luxembourg Ardennes as exemplified by hydrological and (micro) pedological investigations of a catena in an experimental watershed. *CATENA* 1: 273–95.

1976. Aggregate stability and colluviation in the Luxembourg Ardennes: an experimental and micromorphological study. *Earth Surface Processes*, 1: 259–71.

Ismail, S.N.A., 1975. *Micromorphometric Soil-Porosity Characteristics by means of Electro-Optical Image Analysis (Quantimet 720)*. Soil Survey Papers, No. 9, Netherlands Soil Survey Institute, Wageningen.

Jackson, M.L., T.W.H. Levelt, J.K. Syers, R.W. Rex, R.N. Clayton, G.D. Sherman and G. Verhara, 1971. Geomorphological relationships of tropospherically derived quartz in the soils of Hawaiian Islands. *Soil Science Society of America Proceedings*, 35: 515–25.

Jacobsen, T. and R.M. Adams, 1958. Salt and silt in ancient Mesopotamian agriculture. *Science*, 128: 1251–7.

Jansen, M., 1985. Mohenjo-Daro, cité de l'Indus. *La Recherche*, 163 (16): 166–76.

Jenkinson, D.S. and J.H. Rayner, 1977. The turnover of soil organic matter in some of the Rothamsted classical experiments. *Soil Science*, 123: 298–305.

Jenny, H., 1941. *Factors of Soil Formation*. McGraw-Hill, New York, 281pp.

Jongerius, A., 1970. Some morphological aspects of regrouping phenomena in Dutch soils. *Geoderma*, 4: 311–31.

1973. Recent developments in soil micromorphometry. In: G.K. Rutherford (ed.), *Soil Microscopy*, pp. 67–83. Limestone Press, Kingston.

1975. Micromorphometric soil analysis by means of Quantimet 720. *Fortschritte der quantitativen Bildanalyse*, pp. 161–85. Vorträge Des imanco-Symposium.

1983. Micromorphology in agriculture. In: P. Bullock and C.P. Murphy (eds.), *Soil Micromorphology*. AB Academic Publishers, Berkhamsted.

Jongerius, A. and G. Heintzberger, 1963. *The Preparation of Mammoth-Sized Thin Sections*. Soil Survey Paper No. 1, Netherlands Soil Survey Institute, Wageningen, 48pp.

Jongerius, A. and G.K. Rutherford (eds.), 1979. *Glossary of Soil Micromorphology*. Centre for Agricultural Publishing and Documentation, Wageningen, 138pp.

Keef, P.A.M., J.J. Wymer and G.W. Dimbleby, 1965. A Mesolithic site on Iping Common, Sussex, England. *Proceedings Prehistoric Society*, 31: 85–92.

Keeley, H.C.M., 1982. Pedogenesis during the later prehistoric period in Britain. In: A.F. Harding (ed.), *Climatic Changes in Later Prehistory*, pp. 114–26. University Press, Edinburgh.

1984. *Environmental Archaeology: a Regional Review* (Vol. I) Department of the Environment, London, 181pp.

Keeley, H.C.M., 1987. *Environmental Archaeology: a Regional Review* (Vol. II). Historic Buildings and Monuments Commission for England, London. Occasional Paper No. II, 379pp.

Keeley, H.C.M., S.E. Hudson and J. Evans, 1977. Trace element contents of human bones in various states of preservation. 1: The soil silhouette. *Journal of Archaeological Science*, 4: 19–24.

Kemp, R.A., 1985. The Valley Farm soil in southern East Anglia. In: J. Boardman (ed.), *Soils and Quaternary Landscape Evolution*, pp. 179–96. John Wiley and Sons, London.

Kendall, A.C. and P.L. Broughton, 1978. Origin of fabrics in speleothems composed of columnar calcite crystals. *Journal of Sedimentary Petrology*, 48: 519–38.

Kerr, P.F., 1959. *Optical Mineralogy*. McGraw-Hill, New York, 442pp.

Kooistra, M.J., 1979. Two methods of preparing thin sections of wet soil from sediments in a marine intertidal zone on the Oosterschelde (The Netherlands). *Netherlands Journal of Agricultural Science*, 27: 235–40.

Krinsley, D.H. and J. Donahue, 1968. Environmental interpretation of sand-grain surface textures by electron microscopy. *Geological Society of America Bulletin*, 79: 743–8.

Krinsley, D.H. and J.C. Doornkamp, 1973. *Atlas of Quartz Sand Surface Textures*. Cambridge University Press, Cambridge, 91pp.

Kubiena, W.L. 1938. *Micropedology*. Collegiate Press, Ames, Iowa, 254pp.

1953. *The Soils of Europe*. Murby, London, 392pp.

Kukal, Z., 1971. *The Geology of Recent Sediments*. Science Press, Prague, 490pp.

Laville, H., 1976. Deposits in calcareous rock shelters: analytical methods and climatic interpretation. In: D.A. Davidson and M.L. Shackley (eds.), *Geoarchaeology*, pp. 137–55. Duckworth, London.

Le Ribault, L., 1977. *L'exoscopie des quartz*. Masson, Paris, 150pp.

Leshnik, L., 1973. Land use and ecological factors in prehistoric North-West India. In: R. Hammond (ed.), *South Asian Archaeology*, pp. 67–84. Duckworth, London.

Limbrey, S., 1975. *Soil Science and Archaeology*. Academic Press, London, 384pp.

Liversage, D., M.A.R. Munro, M.A. Courty and P. Nornberg, 1987. Studies of a buried early iron age field. *Acta Archaeologica*, 56: 1–84.

Loustau, D. and F. Toutain, 1987. Micromorphologie et fonctionnement de quelques humus des formes hydromull et anmoor de l'Est de la France. In: N. Fedoroff, L.M. Bresson and M.A. Courty (eds.), *Micromorphie des Sols – Soil Micromorphology*, pp. 385–9. AFES, Plaisir.

Lozet, J. and C. Mathieu, 1986. *Dictionnaire de Science du Sol*. Technique et Documentation, Lavoisier, Paris, 269pp.

Lutz, H.J. and F.S. Griswold, 1939. The influence of tree roots on soil morphology. *American Journal of Science*, 237: 389–400.

Macphail, R.I., 1981. Soil and botanical studies of the 'Dark Earth'. In: M. Jones and G. Dimbleby (eds.), *The Environment of Man: the Iron Age to the Anglo-Saxon Period*, pp. 309–31. B.A.R. Brit. Series 87, Oxford.

1983. The micromorphology of Dark Earth from Gloucester, London and Norwich: an analysis of urban anthropogenic deposits from the Late Roman to Early Medieval periods in England. In: P. Bullock and C.P. Murphy (eds.), *Soil Micromorphology*, pp. 245–52. AB Academic Publishers, Berkamsted.

1986. Paleosols in archaeology; their role in understanding Flandrian pedogenesis. In: V.P. Wright (ed.), *Paleosols*, pp. 263–90. Blackwell Scientific, Oxford.

1987. A review of soil science in archaeology in England. In: H.C.M. Keeley (ed.), *Environmental Archaeology of a Regional Review* Vol. II, pp. 332–79. Historic Buildings and Monuments Commission, London.

Macphail, R.I., in press. Soil report on Pianacchia di Suvero, near Rochetta, GE, Liguria. *Archeologia in Luguria III*. Soprintendenza Archeologica della Liguria.

Macphail, R.I. and M.A. Courty, 1984. Interpretation and significance of urban deposits. In: T. Edgren and H. Junger (eds.), *Proceedings 3rd Nordic Conference on the Application of*

Scientific Methods to Archaeology, pp. 71–84. ISKOS, Helsinki.

Macphail, R.I., J.C.C. Romans and L. Robertson, 1987. The application of micromorphology to the understanding of Holocene soil development in the British Isles, with special reference to early cultivation. In: N. Fedoroff, L.M. Bresson and M.A. Courty (eds.), *Micromorphologie des Sols – Soil Micromorphology*, pp. 647–56. AFES, Plaisir.

Maggi, R. (ed.), 1983. Il Neolitico and dell'eta' de Rame alla fine dell'eta' de Bronzo. *Preistoria nella Liguria Orientale*, pp. 45–78. Soprintendenza Archeologica della Liguria.

1984. Pianaccia di Suvero. *Archeologia in Liguria*, 2: 69–72. Soprintendenza Archeologica della Liguria.

Maggi, R., P. Melli and R. Nisbet, 1982. Uscio (Genova). Scavi 1981–1982. Rapporto preliminare. *Revista di Studi Luguri*, 48: 1–4. Bordighere.

Maggi, R., P. Melli, G.M. Macphail, R.I. Macphail, R. Nisbet, M. Del Soldato and L. Pintus, in press. Note preliminari sugli scavi del Castellaro di Uscio (GE), 1981–85. *Preistoria Alpina*, 21.

Mannoni, T. and M. Tizzoni, 1980. Lo scavo del Castellaro di Zignago (La Spezia). *Revist. di Scienze Preistoriche*, 35 (1–2): 249–79.

Marbut, C.F., 1935. Soils of the United States. In: *Atlas of American Agriculture*. US Department of Agriculture.

Martini, J. and I. Kavalieris, 1978. Mineralogy of the Transvaal caves. *Transactions of the Geological Society of South Africa*, 81: 47–54.

Matalucci, R.V., J.W. Shelton and M. Abdelhady, 1969. Grain orientation of Vicksburg Loess. *Journal of Sedimentary Petrology*, 39: 969–79.

Mathieu, C. and G. Stoops, 1972. Observations pétrographiques sur la paroi d'un four à chaux carolingien creusé en sol limoneux. *Extrait d'Archéologie médievale*, 2: 347–54.

Maurino, M., 1983. Geologia e geomorfologia della Val Chisone. In: R. Nisbet and D. Seglie (eds.), *Balm'Chanto. Quaderni di Antrologia e di Archaeologia*, pp. 18–22. Pinerolo.

Melli, P., 1983. L'Eta' del Ferro. *Preistoria nella Liguria Orientale*. Soprintendenza Archeologica della Liguria.

Merrifield, R. 1965. *The Roman City of London*. Ernst. Benn, London.

Mohen, J.-P. and A. Villes, 1984. *La reprise des fouilles au Fort-Harrouard à Sorel–Mousel (Eure-et-Loire)*. Bulletin de la Societé Amis d'Anet et Syndicat d'Initiative, Série Nouvelle, no. 8.

Moorhouse, W.W., 1959. *The Study of Rocks in Thin Section*. Harper and Row, New York, 514pp.

Mücher, H.J. and J. de Ploey, 1977. Experimental and micromorphological investigation of erosion and redeposition of loess by water. *Earth Surface Processes and Landforms*, 2: 117–24.

Mücher, H.J. and T.D. Morozova, 1983. The application of soil micromorphology in Quaternary geology and geomorphology. In: P. Bullock and C.P. Murphy (eds.), *Soil Micromorphology*, pp. 151–94. AB Academic Publishers, Berkhamsted.

Mücher, H.J. and W.J. Vreeken, 1981. (Re)Deposition of loess in southern Limbourg, the Netherlands. 2: Micromorphology of the lower silt loam complex and comparison with deposits produced under laboratory conditions. *Earth Surface Processes and Landforms*, 6: 355–63.

Murphy, C.P., 1986. *Thin Section Preparation of Soils and Sediments*. AB Academic Publishers, Berkhamsted.

Neev, D. and K.O. Emery, 1967. The Dead Sea: depositional processes and environments of evaporites. *Geological Survey of Israel Bull.*, 41: 1–47.

Nisbet, R., 1983. *Vislario, archeologia e paleoecologia di un terrazzamento alpino*. CORSAC/Cuorgne, Torino.

Nisbet, R. and P. Biagi, 1987. *Balm'Chanto: un Riparo sottoroccia dell'età del rame nelle Alpi Cozie*. New Press, Como, 154pp.

Nisbet, R. and R.I. Macphail, 1983. Organizzazione del territorio e terrazzamenti preistorici nell'Italia Settentrionale. *Quaderni della Soprintendenza Piemonte*, 2: 43–58.

Norman, P. and F.W. Reader, 1912. Further discoveries relating to Roman London, 1906–1912. *Archaeologia*, 63: 257–344.

Northcote, K.H., G.D. Hubble, R.F. Isbell, C.H. Thomson and E. Bettenay, 1975. *A Description of Australian Soils*. CSIRO, Australia.

Noy, T., J. Schuldenrein and E. Tchernov, 1980. Gilgal, a Pre-Pottery Neolithic A site in the Lower Jordan Valley. *Israel Exploration Journal*, 30: 63–82.

Nriagu, J., 1984. Phosphate minerals: their properties and general mode of occurrence. In: J. Nriagu and P.B. Moore (eds.), *Phosphate Minerals*, pp. 1–136. Springer-Verlag, Berlin.

Nriagu, J. and P.B. Moore (eds.), 1984. *Phosphate Minerals*. Springer-Verlag, Berlin, 442pp.

Orton, C., 1978. Sequence of Medieval and post-Medieval pottery. In: *Southwark Excavations, 1972–74*, pp. 140–6. Joint publication No. 1, Southwark and Lambeth Archaeological Excavation Committee, London and Middlesex Archaeological Society.

Osmond, D.A. and P. Bullock (eds.), 1970. *Micromorphological Techniques and Applications*, Agricultural Research Council, Soil Survey, Technical Monographs No. 2, Harpenden, 95pp.

Pal Y., S. Bladew, R.K. Sood and D.P. Agrawal, 1981. Remote sensing of the lost Sarasvati. *Proc. Indian Acad. of Science*, 89 (3): 317–22.

Peacock, D.P.S., 1967. The heavy mineral analysis of pottery: a preliminary report. *Archaeometry*, 10: 97–100.

1969. A petrological study of certain Iron Age pottery from western England. *Proceedings Prehistoric Society*, 34, 414–27.

1977. Bricks and tiles of the Classic Britannica: petrology and origin. *Britannia*, 8: 235–48.

Peacock, D.P.S. and D.F. Williams, 1986. *Amphorae and the Roman Economy: an Introductory Guide*. Longman, London, 239pp.

Pénaud, P., 1978. La Paragenèse Phosphatée de la Caune de l'Arago (Pyrénnées Orientales). Thèse 3ème Cycle, Université de Paris VII, 162pp.

Périnet, G., 1964. Détermination par diffraction X de la température de cuisson d'un ossement calciné. Application au matériel préhistorique. *C.R. Acad. des Sciences*, Tome 285, gpe 9: 4115–6.

Perlès, C., 1973. *Préhistoire du feu*. Masson, Paris, 180pp.

Perrin, R.M.S., H. Davies and M.D. Fysh, 1974. Distribution of Late Pleistocene aeolian deposits in eastern and southern England. *Nature*, London, 248: 320–3.

Pettijohn, F.J. 1975. *Sedimentary Rocks* (3rd edition). Harper and Row, New York.

Pettijohn, F.J., P.E. Potter and R. Siever. 1972. *Sand and Sandstone*. Springer, New York.

Philippe, J. 1936. Le Fort-Harrouard. *L'Anthropologie*, 46: 257–301; 541–612.

Le Fort-Harrouard. *L'Anthropologie*, 47: 253–308.

Pitty, A.F., 1978. *Geography and Soil Properties*. Methuen, London, 287pp.

Pobeguin, T., 1943. Les Oxalates de calcium chez quelques angiospermes. *Ann. Sci. Nat.*, 4: 1–95.

Postek, M.J., K.S. Howard, A.H. Johnson and K.K. McMichael, 1980. *Scanning Electron Microscopy – A Students Handbook*. Ladd Research Industries, Inc., 305pp.

Potter, P.E. and F.J. Pettijohn. 1977. *Paleocurrents and Basin Analysis* (2nd edition). Springer-Verlag, Berlin, 618pp.

Proudfoot, V.B., 1958. Problems of soil history. Podzol development at Goodland and Torr Townlands, Co. Antrim, Northern Ireland. *Journal Soil Science* 9: 186–98.

Raison, R.J., 1979. Modification of the soil environment by vegetation fires, with particular reference to nitrogen transformation: a review. *Plant and Soil*, 51: 73–108.

Rajaguru, S.N., 1983. Problems of Late Pleistocene aridity in India. *Man and Environment*, 7: 107–11.

Rapp, G.R., 1975. The archaeological field staff: the geologist. *Journal of Field Archaeology*, 2: 229–37.

Raynal, J.P., 1978. Taforalt. In: Mission préhistorique et paléontologique française au Maroc, rapport d'activité pour l'année 1978. *Bull. d'Archéol. Marocaine*, 12: 69–71.

Reece, R., 1980. Town and country: the end of Roman Britain. *World Archaeology*, 12: 77–92.

Reineck, H.-E. and I.B. Singh, 1975. *Depositional Sedimentary Environments*. Springer-Verlag, Berlin, 439pp.

Retallack, G.J., 1983. A paleopedological approach to the interpretation of terrestrial sedimentary rocks: the mix-Tertiary paleosols of Badlands National Park, South Dakota. *Bull. Geol. Soc. Am.*, 94: 823–40.

Rigaud, J.P., 1982. La Paléolithique en Périgord: les données du sud-ouest sarladais et leurs implications. Thèse de Doctorat ès Sciences, Univ. de Bordeaux I, France, 494pp.

   (ed.), in press. Grotte Vaufrey: paléoenvironments, chronologie et activités humaines. *Mém. de la Soc. Préhist. Française*.

Robert, M., J. Berrier and J. Evralde, 1983. Rôle des êtres vivants dans les premiers stades d'altération des minéraux. *Sci. Géol. Mém.*, 73: 95–103. Strasbourg.

Roche, J., 1963. *Le Paléolitique Marocain*. Livraria, Lisbon, 252pp.

   1976. Cadre chronologique de l'Epipaléolithique marocain. 9ème Congrès UISPP, Nice, Colloque 2: *Chronologie et synchronisme dans la préhistoire circum-méditerranéenne* pp. 153–67.

Romans, J.C.C. and L. Robertson, 1975a. Soils and archaeology in Scotland. In: J.G. Evans, S. Limbrey and H. Cleeve (eds.), *The Effect of Man on the Landscape: the Highland Zone*, pp. 37–9. CBA Research Report No. 11.

   1975b. Some genetic characteristics of the freely drained soils of the Ettrick Association in East Scotland. *Geoderma*, 14: 297–317.

   1983a. The general effects of early agriculture on the soil. In: G.S. Maxwell (ed.), *The Impact of Aerial Reconnaissance on Archaeology*, pp. 136–41. CBA Research Report No. 49.

   1983b. The environmnent of North Britain: soils. In: J.C. Chapman and H.C. Mytum (eds.), *Settlement in north Britain 1000 BC to AD 1000*, pp. 55–80. B.A.R. Brit. Series, 118, Oxford.

Roskams, S., 1981. GPO Newgate St., 1975–9: the Roman levels. *London Archaeologist*, 6: 403–7.

Roskams, S. and J. Schofield, 1978. The Mill Street excavations, part 2. *London Archaeologist*, 3: 227–34.

Rovner, I., 1971. Potential of opal phytoliths for use in palaeoecological reconstruction. *Quaternary Research*, 1: 343–59.

   1983. Plant opal phytolith analysis: major advances in archaeobotanical research. In: M.B. Schiffer (ed.), *Advances in Archaeological Method and Theory*, 6: 225–66.

Ruben, P. and J. Trichet, 1980. Méthode d'étude de l'origine de matériaux ayant servi à la confection de briques et de céramiques dans les sites de Suse et de Djaffarabad (Khusistan–Iran). *Paléorient*, 6: 129–59.

Ruellan, A., 1971. *Les sols à profil calcaire différencié de la basse Moulouya (Maroc Oriental)*. *Mémoire ORSTOM*, 54: 302pp.

Ruellan A., D. Nahon, H. Paquet and G. Millot, 1978. Figures d'épigénie par la calcite dans les encroûtements calcaires. In: M. Delgado (ed.), *Micromorfologia de Suelos*, pp. 1051–65. Granada, Spain.

Sandler, A., P. Goldberg and D. Gilbert, 1988. Sedimentology of the Nahal Heimar Cave deposits. *Atiqot*, 18; 64–7. Israel Department of Antiquities.

Scaife, R.S., 1987. Pollen analysis and the later prehistoric vegetational changes of the Val Chisone. In: R. Nisbet and P. Biagi (eds.), *Balm'Chanto: un Riparo Sottoroccia dell'eta del Rame nelle Alpi Cozie*, pp. 89–101. Archeologia dee'Italia Settentrionale 4, New Press, Como.

Scaife, R.S. and R.I. Macphail, 1983. The Post-Devensian development of heathland soils and vegetation. In: P. Burnham (ed.), *Soils of the Heathlands and Chalklands*, Vol. 1, pp. 70–99. South-East Soils Discussion Group.

Scarre, C., 1985. A survey of the French Neolithic. In: C. Scarre (ed.), *Ancient France, Neolithic Societies and their Landscapes, 6000–2000 BC.*, pp. 324–44. The University Press, Edinburgh.

Scharpenseel, H.W., 1971. Radiocarbon dating of soils – problems, troubles, hopes. In: D.H. Yaalon (ed.), *Palaeopedology*, pp. 77–88. International Society Soil Science, Israel Program Scientific Translations, Jerusalem.

Schick, T. and M. Stekelis, 1972. Mousterian assemblages in Kebara Cave, Mount Carmel. *Eretz Israel*, 13: 97*–149*.

Scholle, P., 1978. *A Color Illustrated Guide to Carbonate Rock Constituents, Textures, Cements and Porosities.* American Association of Petroleum Geologists, Mem. 27, 248pp.

1979. *A Color Illustrated Guide to Constituents, Textures, Cements, and Porosities of Sandstones and Associated Rocks.* American Association of Petroleum Geologists, Mem. 28, 201pp.

Schuldenrein, J. and P. Goldberg, 1981. Late Quaternary palaeoenvironments and prehistoric site distributions in the Lower Jordan Valley: a preliminary report. *Paléorient*, 7: 57–71.

Schwarcz, H.P. and K.C. Shane, 1969. Measurement of grain shape by Fourier analysis. *Sedimentology*, 13: 213–31.

Shackley, M.L., 1975. *Archaeological Sediments: a Survey of Analytical Methods.* Butterworths, London, 159pp.

Sheldon, H., 1978. *Southwark Excavation 1972–1974.* Joint publication no. 1, Southwark and Lambeth Archaeological Committee, London and Middlesex Archaeological Society.

Singer, A., 1983. The paleosols of Berekhat Ram, Golan Heights: morphology, chemistry, mineralogy, genesis. *Israel Journal of Earth-Science*, 32: 93–104.

Singh, G., 1971. The Indus Valley Culture (Paleobotanical study of climatic changes). *Puratattva. Bull. Indian Archaeol. Soc.*, 4: 68–76.

Slager, S. and H.T.J. Van der Wetering, 1977. Soil formation in archaeological pits and adjacent loess soils in Southern Germany. *Journal of Archaeological Science*, 4: 259–67.

Smithson, F., 1958. Grass opal in British soils. *Journal Soil Science*, 9: 148–54.

Sneed, E.D. and R.L. Folk, 1958. Pebbles in the lower Colorado River, Texas – a study in particle morphogenesis. *Journal of Geology*, 66: 114–50.

Soil Survey Staff, 1975. *Soil Taxonomy.* US Department of Agriculture, Agricultural Handbook 436, Washington DC.

Specklin, G., 1979. Application de la microscopie de reflexion et de fluorescence à l'étude micromorphologique des sols. Thèse, USTL, Montpellier, 144pp.

Stein, J.K., 1983. Earthworm activity: a source of potential disturbance of archaeological sediments. *American Antiquity*, 48: 277–89.

1985. Interpreting sediments in cultural settings. In: J.K. Stein and W.R. Farrand (eds.), *Archaeological Sediments in Context*, pp. 5–19. Center for the Study of Early Man, Orono.

Stoops, G.J., H. Eswaran and A. Abtahi, 1978. Scanning electron microscopy of authigenic sulphate minerals in soils. In: M. Delgado (ed.), *Micromorfologia de suelos*, pp. 1093–1113. Granada, Spain.

Stoops, G.J. and A. Jongerius, 1975. Proposal for a micromorphological classification in soil materials. I. A classification of the related distributions of coarse and fine particles. *Geoderma*, 13: 189–200.

Tessier, D., 1984. *Etude expérimentale de l'organisation des matériaux argileux. Hydratation, gonflement et structuration au cours de la dessication et de la réhumectation.* INRA, Paris, 361pp.

Theocharopoulos, S.P. and J.B. Dalrymple, 1987. Experimental construction of illuviation cutans (channel argillans) with differing morphological and optical properties. In: N. Fedoroff, L.M. Bresson and M.A. Courty (eds.), *Micromorphologie des sols – Soil Micromorphology*, pp. 245–50. AFES, Plaisir.

Thrailkill, J., 1976. Speleothems. In: M.R. Walter (ed.), *Stromatolites*, pp. 73–86. Developments in Sedimentology, Elsevier, Amsterdam.

Toutain, F., 1981. Les humus forestiers: structure et mode de fonctionnement. *Rev. Forest. Franc.*, 32: 449–77.

Toutain, F., J.J. Brun and Z. Rafidison, 1983. Rôle des organismes vivants dans les arrangements structuraux des sols. Biostructures et modes d'altération. *Sci. Géol. Mém., Strasbourg*, 73: 115–22.

Tucker, M.E., 1981. *Sedimentary Petrolology: an Introduction*. Blackwell Scientific Publications, Oxford, 252pp.

Turville-Petre, F., 1932. The excavations in the Mugharet el-Kebarah. *Jour. Royal Anthr. Inst. of Gt. Britain and Ireland*, 62: 271–6.

Twiss, P.C., E. Suess and R.M. Smith, 1969. Morphological classification of grass phytoliths. *Soil Sci. Soc. Am. Proc.*, 33: 109–14.

Valentine, K.W.G. and J.B. Dalrymple, 1975. The identification, lateral variation, and chronology of two buried paleocatenas at Woodhall Spa and West Runton, England. *Quaternary Research*, 5: 551–90.

1976. Quaternary buried paleosols: a critical review. *Quaternary Research*, 6: 209–22.

Vazart, M., 1983. Paléodynamiques weichséliennes des provinces normande et séquanienne. Analyse micrographique de 5 coupes de loess: Roumare, Mesnil–Esnard, Iville, Mantes-La-Ville, Chaudon. Thèse de doctorat de 3e cycle, Univ. Paris VII, 130pp.

Vergés, V., 1985. Dissolution and associated features of limestone fragments in a calcareous soil (lithic Calcixeroll) from Southern France. *Geoderma*, 36: 109–22.

Vita-Finzi, C., 1969. *The Mediterranean Valleys*. Cambridge University Press, Cambridge, 140pp.

van Vliet-Lanoë, B., 1980. Approche des conditions physico-chimiques favorisant l'autofluorescence des minéraux argileux. *Pédologie*, 30: 369–90.

1981. Micropédologie en autofluorescence. Colloques Internationaux du CNRS, n° 303: *Migrations organo-minérales dans les sols tempères*, pp. 491–3.

1985a. From frost to gelifluction: a new approach based on micromorphology. Its application to Arctic environments. *INTER-NORD*, 17: 15–20.

1985b. Frost effects in soils. In: J. Boardman (ed.), *Soils and Quaternary Landscape Evolution*, pp. 117–58. John Wiley and Sons, Chichester.

van Vliet-Lanoë, B., J.P. Coutard and A. Pissart, 1984. Structures caused by repeated freezing and thawing in various loamy sediments: a comparison of active, fossil and experimental data. *Earth Science Processes and Landforms*, 9: 553–65.

Vogt T., 1984. Problèmes de genèse des croûtes calcaires quaternaires. *Soc. Nat. Elf-Aquitaine*, 209–21.

1987. Quelques microstructures de croûtes calcaires quaternaires d'Afrique du Nord. In: N. Fedoroff, L.M. Bresson and M.A. Courty (eds.), *Micromorphologie des Sols – Soil Micromorphology*, pp. 563–8. AFES, Plaisir.

Wadell, H., 1935. Volume, shape, and roundness of rock particles. *Journal of Geology*, 43: 250–80.

Wahlstrom, E.E., 1979. *Optical Mineralogy* (5th edition). John Wiley and Sons, New York, 488pp.

Walker, P.H. and B.E. Butler, 1983. Fluvial processes. In: *Soils: an Australian Viewpoint*, pp. 83–90. Division of Soils, CSIRO. CSIRO, Melbourne/Academic Press, London.

Wattez, J. and M.A. Courty, 1987. Morphology of some plant materials. In: N. Fedoroff, L.M. Bresson and M.A. Courty (eds.), *Micromorphologie des Sols – Soil Micromorphology*, pp. 677–83. AFES, Plaisir.

Weir, A.H., J.A. Catt and P.A. Madgett, 1971. Postglacial soil formation in the loess of Pegwell Bay, Kent (England). *Geoderma*, 5: 131–49.

Wentworth, C.K., 1922. A scale of grade class terms for clastic sediments. *Journal of Geology*, 30: 377–92.

White, W.B., 1976. Cave minerals and speleothems. In: T.D. Ford and C.H.D. Cullingford (eds.), *The Science of Speleology*, pp. 267–327. Academic Press, London.

1982. Mineralogy of the Butler Cave–Sinking Creek System. *National Speleological Society Bulletin*, 44: 90–7.

Wood, W.R. and D.L. Johnson, 1978. A survey of disturbance processes in archaeological site formation. In: M.B. Schiffer (ed.), *Advances in Archaeological Method and Theory*, 1: 315–81.

Wooldridge, S.W. and D.L. Linton, 1933. The loam terrains of south-east England and their relation to its early history. *Antiquity*, 7: 297–310.

Wright, V.P. (ed.), 1986. *Paleosols: their Recognition and Interpretation*. Blackwell, Oxford, 315pp.

Yaalon, D.H. and D. Kalmar, 1972. Vertical movement in an undisturbed soil: continuous measurement of swelling and shrinkage with a sensitive apparatus. *Geoderma*, 8: 231–40.

Zingg, Th., 1935. Beitrage zur Schotteranalyse. *Min. Petrog. Mitt. Schweiz.*, 15: 39–140.

INDEX

Numbers in bold type refer to illustrations